A CRITICAL
AND CULTURAL
THEORY READER

A CRITICAL
AND CULTURAL
THEORY READER

edited by
Antony Easthope and
Kate McGowan

University of Toronto Press
Toronto and Buffalo

First published in North America in 1992 by
University of Toronto Press
Toronto and Buffalo

ISBN 0-8020-7416-2 (cloth)
ISBN 0-8020-2912-4 (paper)

Canadian Cataloguing in Publication Data

Main entry under title:

A critical and cultural theory reader

_ISBN 0-8020-7416-2 (bound)   ISBN 0-8020-2912-4 (pbk.)

1. Popular culture. 2. Criticism. 3. Culture.
4. Structuralism (Literary analysis). I. Easthope,
Antony. II. McGowan, Kate.

PN81.C75 1992   801′.95   C92-094197-4

Printed and bound in Great Britain

CONTENTS

ACKNOWLEDGEMENTS

In compiling this collection we have profited greatly from discussion with many people, from whom we have learned both through agreement and sometimes constructive disagreement: Margaret Beetham, Catherine Belsey, Erica Burman, Michael Green, Joanna Hodge, John Korner, Susan Purdie, Rick Rylance, John Storey, John Thompson, Peta Turvey, Peter Widdowson. We are also grateful to our readers at the Open University, Stuart Hall and Graham Martin, for their advice and criticisms, and to Ray Cunningham at the Open University Press who encouraged our project from the beginning.

The editor and publishers are grateful to the following for permission to reprint copyright material. All possible care has been taken to trace owner-ship of the selections included, and to make full acknowledgement of their use. Peter Owen Ltd for the extract from *Course in General Linguistics* by Ferdinand de Saussure, edited by Charles Bally and Albert Sechehaye, translated by Wade Baskin; Random Century Group and Hill and Wang (a division of Farrar, Straus and Giroux, Inc.) for an extract from *Mythologies* by Roland Barthes, translated by Annette Lavers, © 1972, reprinted by permission; Pierre Macherey and Routledge for an extract from *A Theory of Literary Production*, translated by Geoffrey Wall; the estate of Roland Barthes, Jonathan Cape and Hill and Wang (a division of Farrar, Straus and Giroux Inc.) for an extract from *S/Z* by Roland Barthes, translated by Richard Miller; Colin MacCabe, the editorial board of *Screen* and Manchester University Press for an extract from *Theoretical Essays*; Lawrence and Wishart Ltd for extracts from Karl Marx, *The Critique of political economy* and Marx and Frederick Engels, *The German Ideology* from the *Collected Works*; Verso for an extract from *Lenin and Philosophy* by Louis Althusser, translated by Ben Brewster; Edward Said and Random House for an extract from *Orientalism*; Routledge, Tavistock Publications and W. W. Norton and Company, Inc. for an extract from *Écrits*,

INTRODUCTION

The study of literary texts, taught in schools and colleges in the English-speaking world, is a relatively recent innovation which did not become properly established until the 1930s. It developed for a number of reasons. One was the decline of the Christian religion, which seemed to leave people without a proper sense of value – the study of great literature, it was hoped, would give a sense of value to human life which was otherwise becoming lost. Another reason was the explosion of the so-called mass media in the twentieth century, newspapers, cheap novels, radio, film, and, since 1945, television. If literature was getting ignored, then it would have to be kept alive by being seriously taught. But how? A number of assumptions, some of them ancient, some originating with the Romantic movement of the early nineteenth century, were put to work in teaching a selected 'canon' of poems, plays and novels, especially the idea that literary works were very special objects, shaped by the individual imagination, and so qualitatively different from the commercially motivated products of popular culture. Rapidly, and certainly by 1945, the establishment of the literary canon (and how to teach it) had become so instituted and habitual it seemed to be almost natural – just 'there' because it was there. In 1981 a professor of English at Cambridge saw it as his obvious duty 'to teach and uphold the canon of English literature' (Christopher Ricks, cited in the *Guardian*, 16 January 1981: 12).

However, in the past twenty years most of the assumptions about what makes literature valuable have been undermined. A main consequence of these 'theory wars' fought over literature in the 1970s and 1980s has been to show that literature cannot claim a special privilege and that the opposition between the canon and popular culture can no longer be upheld, not least because it would not be democratic to go on disparaging texts which the majority of people enjoy without having been specially taught to do so. Already, across the English-speaking world, a new form of study is quickly developing, a study of the traditional canon alongside and together with the texts of popular culture.

In 1983 another literary critic, Terry Eagleton, now a Professor of English at the University of Oxford, outlined how he saw the new study and what it might be called:

> My own view is that it is most useful to see 'literature' as a name which people give from time to time for different reasons to certain kinds of writing within a whole field of what Michel Foucault has called 'discursive practices', and that if anything is to be an object of study it is this whole field of practices rather than just those sometimes rather obscurely labelled 'literature'. I am countering the theories set out in this book not with a *literary* theory, but with a different kind of discourse – whether one calls it of 'culture', 'signifying practices' or whatever is not of first importance – which would include the objects ('literature') with which these other theories deal, but which would transform them by setting them in a wider context.
>
> (1983: 205)

The name 'cultural studies' may be the most suitable for the new discipline. This *Critical and Cultural Theory Reader* is meant to provide an accessible introduction to the analysis of the texts of high and popular culture together.

A central endeavour in poststructuralist and postmodern theory has been to affirm that for human beings nothing is simply 'there', natural, objective, self-evident, that there is no identity in class, race, gender or sexuality which can claim automatic privilege. However, the same principle means that there is no self-evident selection of texts for a *Critical and Cultural Theory Reader*. We are conscious that this book constructs a version of history, and one that can be contested (and of course should be). This is particularly an issue here because two tendencies are discernible in cultural studies, a textual wing and a sociological wing (as Stuart Hall described in his important essay, 'Cultural studies: two paradigms', 1980). One attraction of breaking with the supremacy of the canon – and the literary work as supposedly self-defining object – is that the text comes to be seen as *transitive*, an effect of the relation between text and reader. And we have included a range of work, influenced variously by semiology, psychoanalysis and theories of the subject, which explores how texts can become effects in and for their readers.

But further along this line, and signalled by the work of Raymond Williams, Richard Hoggart and Stuart Hall in the tradition of British cultural studies, there is a body of sociological analysis of reception, audiences, and the way groups and classes have reproduced and used cultural texts. To have done justice to this, and to the writings of Mikhail Bakhtin, Claude Lévi-Strauss, Jürgen Habermas, Pierre Bourdieu and Clifford Geertz (among others) would have required a second, companion volume. We have therefore decided to represent the textual wing of cultural studies, knowing that whatever analysis is made of particular uses made of cultural texts in determinate situations, the problem of textuality remains in any case – texts continue to be reproduced, re-used with a difference by other readers not accounted for in the analysis of a particular audience. No selection is natural, no anthology perfect.

The readings selected are grouped into seven sections. Five consist of 'Semiology', 'Ideology', 'Subjectivity', 'Difference' and 'Gender'. Another is used to indicate the crucial importance of understanding the present, a question acutely posed by the issue of postmodernism. And a final section reprints a number of 'Documents in Cultural Theory' which set out points in the debate over the opposition between high and popular culture. One special problem is posed by the fact that the medium of popular culture is frequently visual – film, television, advertising, journalistic photography. In response to this we include a number of essays which address the analysis of specifically visual material. Suggestions for further reading are contained in the section 'Biographies'.

Much of the work collected was written in France, particularly after the 'events' of May 1968, and has had to be translated into English. Some of it is difficult to follow, partly because it is written in general theoretical terms but often because it argues for views which are disturbingly unfamiliar. For this reason, as well as an 'Introduction' for each section, every text is given an outline summary at the end of the book. In writing these we have been guided by our experience in teaching students at Manchester Polytechnic, though these summaries represent only a version of each text, another voice in the discussion the texts should provoke.

Section one

SEMIOLOGY

Introduction

A sign is something that stands for something. In his foundational work, *Course in General Linguistics* (1916), Saussure (see 'Biographies') presciently anticipates a new kind of human science:

> *A science that studies the life of signs within society* is conceivable; it would be a part of social psychology and consequently of general psychology; I shall call it *semiology* (from the Greek *semeion*, 'sign'). Semiology would show what constitutes signs, what laws govern them.
>
> (1974: 16)

Semiology (or semiotics) would be based on the model of linguistics drawing on several of the distinctions Saussure introduced, 'signifier/signified', 'synchronic/diachronic', *'langue/parole'* (see Section 1.1).

Through the work of the Russian Formalists between 1915 and 1930 (see Bennett 1979) and the structuralism of the 1960s (see Hawkes 1977) semiology has developed as the study of signs, though it owes less to psychology (as Saussure thought) than to its association with theories of ideology and of subjectivity. Its basic principle is that where there is signification and a text, there must be a knowable underlying system giving rise to meaning. That methodological assumption rests on Saussure's distinction between *langue* and *parole*, between the synchronic system of a given language and anything anyone might actually say or write in that language. Obviously we are writing this and you are following it because both parties share in a familiarity with Modern English, its sound patterns and rules for making sentences. On this model texts can be analysed in terms of shared features in an attempt to describe the rules which would generate such texts as instances of these rules.

For example, in England inns or public houses have names, often with signs outside giving the name. Although knowing the name of a pub seems the most natural activity in the world, it can be asked whether there is in fact a sign system at work in pub names. If we knew the rules we could prove it by inventing some plausible names. Clearly one set of names is emblematic, often taking a title from a natural object, 'The Sun', 'The Moon', 'The White Horse'. Equally another set of names is heraldic, 'The King's Arms', 'The Royal Oak', or takes the name of a famous individual, 'The Duke of Wellington', 'The Nelson'. But another large group has doubled names, such as 'The Pig and Whistle', 'The Dog and Partridge', 'The Coach and Horses', 'The Lamb and Flag', 'The Rose and Crown', 'The Elephant and Castle'. Two systems seem to be at play here, one generating names by coupling a natural object with a human artifact ('Pig and Whistle', 'Lamb and Flag', 'Rose and Crown', 'Elephant and Castle'), another coupling two objects by causal association (dogs hunt partridges) though 'Coach and Horses' seems to embody both rules (horses pull coaches).

'Signs can only arise on inter-individual territory' and therefore the sign is always ideological, writes Voloshinov (1973: 12). Semiology remains merely formalist if it fails to recognize that the sign is not autonomous and self-sufficient but always determined within ideology and in relation to subjectivity. Each of the examples collected here applies semiology to different sign systems. Barthes in *Mythologies* summarizes a way to analyse the specific operation of the sign in popular culture, particularly with instances of visual signification (photography, advertising). Macherey argues that traditional notions of the literary text as unified must yield to awareness of the actual decentredness of any text. Leaning on the work of Macherey, Barthes, in another extract, aims for a would-be exhaustive discussion of a literary text and proposes five codes that can be seen in play across a text, even though no such systematic semiology can define all its possibilities. And in an account theorizing realism in both the novel and classic Hollywood cinema, Colin MacCabe explores the limits of semiology in an attempt to make it cohere with conceptions of ideology and of the position accorded to the reading subject by the realist text.

Working impartially on literary and popular texts these examples, taken together, imply the need to acknowledge:

1 that texts must be understood in terms of their specificity as forms of sign, and so their difference.
2 that signs are always ideological but that ideology is not just a matter of the signified meaning but also of the *operation* of the signifier.

1.1

Ferdinand de Saussure from *Course in General Linguistics* (1916)

1 Language as organized thought coupled with sound

To prove that language is only a system of pure values, it is enough to consider the two elements involved in its functioning: ideas and sounds.

Psychologically our thought – apart from its expression in words – is only a shapeless and indistinct mass. Philosophers and linguists have always agreed in recognizing that without the help of signs we would be unable to make a clear-cut, consistent distinction between two ideas. Without language, thought is a vague, uncharted nebula. There are no pre-existing ideas, and nothing is distinct before the appearance of language.

Against the floating realm of thought, would sounds by themselves yield predelimited entities? No more so than ideas. Phonic substance is neither more fixed nor more rigid than thought; it is not a mould into which thought must of necessity fit but a plastic substance divided in turn into distinct parts to furnish the signifiers needed by thought. The linguistic fact can therefore be pictured in its totality – i.e. language – as a series of contiguous subdivisions marked off on both the indefinite plane of jumbled ideas (*A*) and the equally vague plane of sounds (*B*). The following diagram gives a rough idea of it:

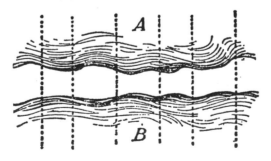

The characteristic role of language with respect to thought is not to create a material phonic means for expressing ideas but to serve as a link between thought and sound, under conditions that of necessity bring about the reciprocal delimitations of units. Thought, chaotic by nature, has to become ordered in the process of its decomposition. Neither are thoughts given material form nor are sounds transformed into mental entities; the somewhat mysterious fact is rather that 'thought-sound' implies division, and that language works out its units while taking shape between two shapeless masses. Visualize the air in contact with a sheet of water; if the atmospheric pressure changes, the surface of the water will be broken up into a series of divisions, waves; the waves resemble the union or coupling of thought with phonic substance.

Language might be called the domain of articulations, using the word as it was defined earlier. Each linguistic term is a member, an *articulus* in which an idea is fixed in a sound and a sound becomes the sign of an idea.

Language can also be compared with a sheet of paper: thought is the front and the sound the back; one cannot cut the front without cutting the back at the same time; likewise in language, one can neither divide sound from thought nor thought from sound; the division could be accomplished only abstractedly, and the result would be either pure psychology or pure phonology.

Linguistics then works in the borderland where the elements of sound and thought combine; *their combination produces a form, not a substance.*

These views give a better understanding of what was said before about the arbitrariness of signs. Not only are the two domains that are linked by the linguistic fact shapeless and confused, but the choice of a given slice of sound to name a given idea is completely arbitrary. If this were not true, the notion of value would be compromised, for it would include an externally imposed element. But actually values remain entirely relative, and that is why the bond between the sound and the idea is radically arbitrary.

The arbitrary nature of the sign explains in turn why the social fact alone can create a linguistic system. The community is necessary if values that owe their existence solely to usage and general acceptance are to be set up; by himself the individual is incapable of fixing a single value.

In addition, the idea of value, as defined, shows that to consider a term as simply the union of a certain sound with a certain concept is grossly misleading. To define it in this way would isolate the term from its system; it would mean assuming that one can start from the terms and construct the system by adding them together when, on the contrary, it is from the interdependent whole that one must start and through analysis obtain its elements.

To develop this thesis, we shall study value successively from the viewpoint of the signified or concept (Section 2), the signifier (Section 3), and the complete sign (Section 4).

Being unable to seize the concrete entities or units of language directly, we shall work with words. While the word does not conform exactly to the definition of the linguistic unit, it at least bears a rough resemblance to the unit and has the advantage of being concrete; consequently, we shall use words as specimens equivalent to real terms in a synchronic system, and the principles that we evolve with respect to words will be valid for entities in general.

2 Linguistic value from a conceptual viewpoint

When we speak of the value of a word, we generally think first of its property of standing for an idea, and this is in fact one side of linguistic value. But if this is true, how does *value* differ from *signification*? Might the two words be synonyms? I think not, although it is easy to confuse them, since the confusion results not so much from their similarity as from the subtlety of the distinction that they mark.

From a conceptual viewpoint, value is doubtless one element in signification, and it is difficult to see how signification can be dependent upon value and still be distinct from it. But we must clear up the issue or risk reducing language to a simple naming-process.

Let us first take signification as it is generally understood. As the arrows in the drawing show, it is only the counterpart of the sound-image. Everything that occurs concerns only the sound-image and the concept when we look upon the word as independent and self-contained.

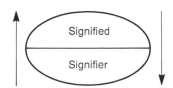

But here is the paradox: on the one hand the concept seems to be the counterpart of the sound-image, and on the other hand the sign itself is in turn the counterpart of the other signs of language.

Language is a system of interdependent terms in which the value of each term results solely from the simultaneous presence of the others, as in the diagram:

How, then, can value be confused with signification, i.e. the counterpart of the sound-image? It seems impossible to liken the relations represented here by horizontal arrows to those represented above by vertical arrows. Putting it another way – and again taking up the example of the sheet of paper that is cut in two (see p. 8) – it is clear that the observable relation between the different pieces A, B, C, D, etc. is distinct from the relation between the front and back of the same piece as in A/A', B/B', etc.

To resolve the issue, let us observe from the outset that even outside language all values are apparently governed by the same paradoxical principle. They are always composed:

(1) of a *dissimilar* thing that can be *exchanged* for the thing of which the value is to be determined; and

(2) of *similar* things that can be *compared* with the thing of which the value is to be determined.

Both factors are necessary for the existence of a value. To determine what a five-franc piece is worth one must therefore know: (1) that it can be exchanged for a fixed quantity of a different thing, e.g. bread; and (2) that it can be compared with a similar value of the same system, e.g. a one-franc piece, or with coins of another system (a dollar, etc.). In the same way a word can be exchanged for something dissimilar, an idea; besides, it can be compared with something of the same nature, another word. Its value is therefore not fixed so long as one simply states that it can be 'exchanged' for a given concept, i.e. that it has this or that signification: one must also compare it with similar values, with other words that stand in opposition to it. Its content is really fixed only by the concurrence of everything that exists outside it. Being part of a system, it is endowed not only with a signification but also and especially with a value, and this is something quite different.

A few examples will show clearly that this is true. Modern French *mouton* can have the same signification as English *sheep* but not the same value, and this for several reasons, particularly because in speaking of a piece of meat ready to be served on the table, English uses *mutton* and not *sheep*. The difference in value between *sheep* and *mouton* is due to the fact that *sheep* has beside it a second term while the French word does not.

Within the same language, all words used to express related ideas limit each other reciprocally; synonyms like French *redouter* 'dread', *craindre* 'fear,' and *avoir peur* 'be afraid' have value only through their opposition: if *redouter* did not exist, all its content would go to its competitors. Conversely, some words are enriched through contact with others: e.g. the new element introduced in *décrépit* (un vieillard *décrépit*) results from the co-existence of *décrépi* (un mur *décrépi*). The value of just any term is accordingly determined by its environment; it is impossible to fix even the value of the word signifying 'sun' without first considering its surroundings: in some languages it is not possible to say 'sit in the *sun.*'

Everything said about words applies to any term of language, e.g. to grammatical entities. The value of a French plural does not coincide with that of a Sanskrit plural even though their signification is usually identical; Sanskrit has three numbers instead of two (*my eyes, my ears, my arms, my legs,* etc. are dual),[1] it would be wrong to attribute the same value to the plural in Sanskrit and in French; its value clearly depends on what is outside and around it.

If words stood for pre-existing concepts, they would all have exact equivalents in meaning from one language to the next; but this is not true. French uses *louer* (*une maison*) 'let (a house)' indifferently to mean both 'pay for' and 'receive payment for,' whereas German uses two words, *mieten* and *vermieten*; there is obviously no exact correspondence of values. The German

verbs *schätzen* and *urteilen* share a number of significations, but that correspondence does not hold at several points.

Inflection offers some particularly striking examples. Distinctions of time,
which are so familiar to us, are unknown in certain languages. Hebrew does
not recognize even the fundamental distinctions between the past, present,
and future. Proto-Germanic has no special form for the future; to say that
the future is expressed by the present is wrong, for the value of the present
is not the same in Germanic as in languages that have a future along with
the present. The Slavic languages regularly single out two aspects of the
verb: the perfective represents action as a point, complete in its totality; the
imperfective represents it as taking place, and on the line of time. The
categories are difficult for a Frenchman to understand, for they are unknown
in French; if they were predetermined, this would not be true. Instead of
pre-existing ideas then, we find in all the foregoing examples *values* emanating
from the system. When they are said to correspond to concepts, it is
understood that the concepts are purely differential and defined not by their
positive content but negatively by their relations with the other terms of the
system. Their most precise characteristic is in being what the others are not.

Now the real interpretation of the diagram of the signal becomes apparent.
Thus

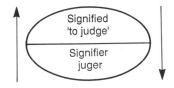

means that in French the concept 'to judge' is linked to the sound-image
juger; in short, it symbolizes signification. But it is quite clear that initially
the concept is nothing, that is only a value determined by its relations with
other similar values, and that without them the signification would not
exist. If I state simply that a word signifies something when I have in mind
the associating of a sound-image with a concept, I am making a statement
that may suggest what actually happens, but by no means am I expressing
the linguistic fact in its essence and fullness.

3 Linguistic value from a material viewpoint

The conceptual side of value is made up solely of relations and differences
with respect to the other terms of language, and the same can be said of its
material side. The important thing in the word is not the sound alone but
the phonic differences that make it possible to distinguish this word from all
others, for differences carry signification.

This may seem surprising, but how indeed could the reverse be possible?
Since one vocal image is no better suited than the next for what it is
commissioned to express, it is evident, even *a priori*, that a segment of
language can never in the final analysis be based on anything except its

noncoincidence with the rest. *Arbitrary* and *differential* are two correlative qualities.

The alteration of linguistic signs clearly illustrates this. It is precisely because the terms *a* and *b* as such are radically incapable of reaching the level of consciousness – one is always conscious of only the *a/b* difference – that each term is free to change according to laws that are unrelated to its signifying function. No positive sign characterizes the genitive plural in Czech *žen*; still the two forms *žena: žen* function as well as the earlier forms *žena: ženb; žen* has value only because it is different.

Here is another example that shows even more clearly the systematic role of phonic differences: in Greek, *éphēn* is an imperfect and *éstēn* an aorist although both words are formed in the same way; the first belongs to the system of the present indicative of *phēmí* 'I say,' whereas there is no present **stēmi*; now it is precisely the relation *phēmí: éphēn* that corresponds to the relation between the present and the imperfect (cf. *déiknūmi: edéiknūn*, etc.). Signs function, then, not through their intrinsic value but through their relative position.

In addition, it is impossible for sound alone, a material element, to belong to language. It is only a secondary thing, substance to be put to use. All our conventional values have the characteristic of not being confused with the tangible element which supports them. For instance, it is not the metal in a piece of money that fixes its value. A coin nominally worth five francs may contain less than half its worth of silver. Its value will vary according to the amount stamped upon it and according to its use inside or outside a political boundary. This is even more true of the linguistic signifier, which is not phonic but incorporeal – constituted not by its material substance but by the differences that separate its sound-image from all others.

The foregoing principle is so basic that it applies to all the material elements of language, including phonemes. Every language forms its words on the basis of a system of sonorous elements, each element being a clearly delimited unit and one of a fixed number of units. Phonemes are characterized not, as one might think, by their own positive quality but simply by the fact that they are distinct. Phonemes are above all else opposing, relative, and negative entities.

Proof of this is the latitude that speakers have between points of convergence in the pronunciation of distinct sounds. In French, for instance, general use of a dorsal *r* does not prevent many speakers from using a tongue-tip trill; language is not in the least disturbed by it; language requires only that the sound be different and not, as one might imagine, that it have an invariable quality. I can even pronounce the French *r* like German *ch* in *Bach*, *doch*, etc., but in German I could not use *r* instead of *ch*, for German gives recognition to both elements and must keep them apart.

4 The sign considered in its totality

Everything that has been said up to this point boils down to this: in language there are only differences. Even more important: a difference generally implies positive terms between which the difference is set up; but in language there are only differences *without positive terms*. Whether we take the signified or the signifier, language has neither ideas nor sounds that existed before the linguistic system, but only conceptual and phonic differences that have issued from the system. The idea or phonic substance that a sign contains is of less importance than the other signs that surround it. Proof of this is that the value of a term may be modified without either its meaning or its sound being affected, solely because a neighboring term has been modified (see p. 10).

But the statement that everything in language is negative is true only if the signified and the signifier are considered separately; when we consider the sign in its totality, we have something that is positive in its own class. A linguistic system is a series of differences of sound combined with a series of differences of ideas; but the pairing of a certain number of acoustical signs with as many cuts made from the mass of thought engenders a system of values; and this system serves as the effective link between the phonic and psychological elements within each sign. Although both the signified and the signifier are purely differential and negative when considered separately, their combination is a positive fact; it is even the sole type of facts that language has, for maintaining the parallelism between the two classes of differences is the distinctive function of the linguistic institution.

Note

1 The use of the comparative form for two and the superlative for more than two in English (e.g. *may the* better *boxer win*: *the* best *boxer in the world*) is probably a remnant of the old distinction between the dual and the plural number. (Tr.)

1.2

Roland Barthes
from *Mythologies* (1957)

Myth today

What is a myth, today? I shall give at the outset a first, very simple answer, which is perfectly consistent with etymology: *myth is a type of speech.*[1]

Myth is a type of speech

Of course, it is not *any* type: language needs special conditions in order to become myth: we shall see them in a minute. But what must be firmly established at the start is that myth is a system of communication, that it is a message. This allows one to perceive that myth cannot possibly be an object, a concept, or an idea; it is a mode of signification, a form. Later, we shall have to assign to this form historical limits, conditions of use, and reintroduce society into it: we must nevertheless first describe it as a form.

It can be seen that to purport to discriminate among mythical objects according to their substance would be entirely illusory: since myth is a type of speech, everything can be a myth provided it is conveyed by a discourse. Myth is not defined by the object of its message, but by the way in which it utters this message: there are formal limits to myth, there are no 'substantial' ones. Everything, then, can be a myth? Yes, I believe this, for the universe is infinitely fertile in suggestions. Every object in the world can pass from a closed, silent existence to an oral state, open to appropriation by society, for there is no law, whether natural or not, which forbids talking about things. A tree is a tree. Yes, of course. But a tree as expressed by Minou Drouet is no longer quite a tree, it is a tree which is decorated, adapted to a certain type of consumption, laden with literary self-indulgence, revolt, images, in short with a type of social *usage* which is added to pure matter.

Naturally, everything is not expressed at the same time: some objects become the prey of mythical speech for a while, then they disappear, others take their place and attain the status of myth. Are there objects which are *inevitably* a source of suggestiveness, as Baudelaire suggested about Woman? Certainly not: one can conceive of very ancient myths, but there are no eternal ones; for it is human history which converts reality into speech, and it alone rules the life and the death of mythical language. Ancient or not, mythology can only have an historical foundation, for myth is a type of speech chosen by history: it cannot possibly evolve from the 'nature' of things.

Speech of this kind is a message. It is therefore by no means confined to oral speech. It can consist of modes of writing or of representations; not only written discourse, but also photography, cinema, reporting, sport, shows, publicity, all these can serve as a support to mythical speech. Myth can be defined neither by its object nor by its material, for any material can arbitrarily be endowed with meaning: the arrow which is brought in order to signify a challenge is also a kind of speech. True, as far as perception is concerned, writing and pictures, for instance, do not call upon the same type of consciousness; and even with pictures, one can use many kinds of reading: a diagram lends itself to signification more than a drawing, a copy more than an original, and a caricature more than a portrait. But this is the point: we are no longer dealing here with a theoretical mode of representation: we are dealing with *this* particular image, which is given for *this* particular signification. Mythical speech is made of a material which has *already* been worked on so as to make it suitable for communication: it is because all the materials of myth (whether pictorial or written) presuppose a signifying consciousness, that one can reason about them while discounting their substance. This substance is not unimportant: pictures, to be sure, are more imperative than writing, they impose meaning at one stroke, without analysing or diluting it. But this is no longer a constitutive difference. Pictures become a kind of writing as soon as they are meaningful: like writing, they call for a *lexis*.

We shall therefore take *language, discourse, speech*, etc., to mean any significant unit or synthesis, whether verbal or visual: a photograph will be a kind of speech for us in the same way as a newspaper article; even objects will become speech, if they mean something. This generic way of conceiving language is in fact justified by the very history of writing: long before the invention of our alphabet, objects like the Inca *quipu*, or drawings, as in pictographs, have been accepted as speech. This does not mean that one must treat mythical speech like language; myth in fact belongs to the province of a general science, coextensive with linguistics, which is *semiology*.

Myth as a semiological system

For mythology, since it is the study of a type of speech, is but one fragment of this vast science of signs which Saussure postulated some forty years ago under the name of *semiology*. Semiology has not yet come into being. But since Saussure himself, and sometimes independently of him, a whole section of contemporary research has constantly been referred to the problem of meaning: psychoanalysis, structuralism, eidetic psychology, some new types of literary criticism of which Bachelard has given the first examples, are no longer concerned with facts except inasmuch as they are endowed with significance. Now to postulate a signification is to have recourse to semiology. I do not mean that semiology could account for all these aspects of research equally well: they have different contents. But they have a common status: they are all sciences dealing with values. They are not content with meeting the facts: they define and explore them as tokens for something else.

Semiology is a science of forms, since it studies significations apart from their content. I should like to say one word about the necessity and the limits of such a formal science. The necessity is that which applies in the case of any exact language. Zhdanov made fun of Alexandrov the philosopher, who spoke of *'the spherical structure of our planet.'* *'It was thought until now'*, Zhdanov said, *'that form alone could be spherical.'* Zhdanov was right: one cannot speak about structures in terms of forms, and vice versa. It may well be that on the plane of 'life', there is but a totality where structures and forms cannot be separated. But science has no use for the ineffable: it must speak about 'life' if it wants to transform it. Against a certain quixotism of synthesis, quite platonic incidentally, all criticism must consent to the *ascesis*, to the artifice of analysis; and in analysis, it must match method and language. Less terrorized by the spectre of 'formalism', historical criticism might have been less sterile; it would have understood that the specific study of forms does not in any way contradict the necessary principles of totality and History. On the contrary: the more a system is specifically defined in its forms, the more amenable it is to historical criticism. To parody a well-known saying, I shall say that a little formalism turns one away from History, but that a lot brings one back to it. Is there a better example of total criticism than the description of saintliness, at once formal and historical, semiological and ideological, in Sartre's *Saint-Genet*? The danger, on the contrary, is to consider forms as ambiguous objects, half-form and half-substance, to endow form with a substance of form, as was done, for instance, by Zhdanovian realism. Semiology, once its limits are settled, is not a metaphysical trap: it is a science among others, necessary but not sufficient. The important thing is to see that the unity of an explanation cannot be based on the amputation of one or other of its approaches, but, as Engels said, on the dialectical co-ordination of the particular sciences it makes use of. This is the case with mythology: it is a part both of semiology inasmuch as it is a formal science, and of ideology inasmuch as it is an historical science: it studies ideas-in-form.[2]

Let me therefore restate that any semiology postulates a relation between two terms, a signifier and a signified. This relation concerns objects which belong to different categories, and this is why it is not one of equality but one of equivalence. We must here be on our guard for despite common parlance which simply says that the signifier *expresses* the signified, we are dealing, in any semiological system, not with two, but with three different terms. For what we grasp is not at all one term after the other, but the correlation which unites them: there are, therefore, the signifier, the signified and the sign, which is the associative total of the first two terms. Take a bunch of roses: I use it to *signify* my passion. Do we have here, then, only a signifier and a signified, the roses and my passion? Not even that: to put it accurately, there are here only 'passionified' roses. But on the plane of analysis, we do have three terms; for these roses weighted with passion perfectly and correctly allow themselves to be decomposed into roses and passion: the former and the latter existed before uniting and forming this third object, which is the sign. It is as true to say that on the plane of experience I cannot dissociate the roses from the message they carry, as to say that on the plane of analysis I cannot confuse the roses as signifier and the roses as sign: the signifier is empty, the sign is full, it is a meaning. Or take a black pebble: I can make it signify in several ways, it is a mere signifier; but if I weigh it with a definite signified (a death sentence, for instance, in an anonymous vote), it will become a sign. Naturally, there are between the signifier, the signified and the sign, functional implications (such as that of the part to the whole) which are so close that to analyse them may seem futile; but we shall see in a moment that this distinction has a capital importance for the study of myth as semiological schema.

Naturally these three terms are purely formal, and different contents can be given to them. Here are a few examples: for Saussure, who worked on a particular but methodologically exemplary semiological system – the language or *langue* – the signified is the concept, the signifier is the acoustic image (which is mental) and the relation between concept and image is the sign (the word, for instance), which is a concrete entity.[3] For Freud, as is well known, the human psyche is a stratification of tokens or representatives. One term (I refrain from giving it any precedence) is constituted by the manifest meaning of behaviour, another, by its latent or real meaning (it is, for instance, the substratum of the dream); as for the third term, it is here also a correlation of the first two: it is the dream itself in its totality, the parapraxis (a mistake in speech or behaviour) or the neurosis, conceived as compromises, as economies effected thanks to the joining of a form (the first term) and an intentional function (the second term). We can see here how necessary it is to distinguish the sign from the signifier: a dream, to Freud, is no more its manifest datum than its latent content: it is the functional union of these two terms. In Sartrean criticism, finally (I shall keep to these three well-known examples), the signified is constituted by the original crisis in the subject (the separation from his mother for Baudelaire, the naming of the theft for Genet); Literature as discourse forms the signifier; and the relation between crisis and discourse defines the work, which is a signification. Of course, this tri-dimensional pattern, however constant in its form, is actualized in different ways: one cannot therefore say too often that semiology can have its unity only at the level of forms, not contents; its field is limited, it knows only one operation: reading, or deciphering.

In myth, we find again the tri-dimensional pattern which I have just described: the signifier, the signified and the sign. But myth is a peculiar system, in that it is constructed from a semiological chain which existed before it: it *is a second-order semiological system*. That which is a sign (namely the associative total of a concept and an image) in the first system, becomes a mere signifier in the second. We must here recall that the materials of mythical speech (the language itself, photography, painting, posters, rituals, objects, etc.), however different at the start, are reduced to a pure signifying function as soon as they are caught by myth. Myth sees in them only the same raw material; their unity is that they all come down to the status of a mere language. Whether it deals with alphabetical or pictorial writing, myth wants to see in them only a sum of signs, a global sign, the final term of a first semiological chain. And it is precisely this final term which will become the first term of the greater system which it builds and of which it is only a part. Everything happens as if myth shifted the formal system of the first significations sideways. As this lateral shift is essential for the analysis of myth, I shall represent it in the following way, it being understood, of course, that the spatialization of the pattern is here only a metaphor:

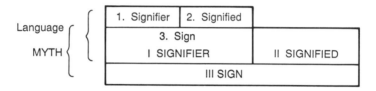

It can be seen that in myth there are two semiological systems, one of which is staggered in relation to the other: a linguistic system, the language (or the modes of representation which are assimilated to it), which I shall call the *language-object*, because it is the language which myth gets hold of in order to build its own system; and myth itself, which I shall call *metalanguage*, because it is a second language, *in which* one speaks about the first. When he reflects on a metalanguage, the semiologist no longer needs to ask himself questions about the composition of the language-object, he no longer has to take into account the details of the linguistic schema; he will only need to know its total term, or global sign, and only inasmuch as this term lends itself to myth. This is why the semiologist is entitled to treat in the same way writing and pictures: what he retains from them is the fact that they are both *signs*, that they both reach the threshold of myth endowed with the same signifying function, that they constitute, one just as much as the other, a language-object.

It is now time to give one or two examples of mythical speech. I shall borrow the first from an observation by Valéry.[4] I am a pupil in the second form in a French *lycée*. I open my Latin grammar, and I read a sentence, borrowed from Aesop or Phaedrus: *quia ego nominor leo*. I stop and think. There is something ambiguous about this statement: on the one hand, the words in it do have a simple meaning: *because my name is lion*. And on the other hand, the sentence is evidently there in order to signify something else to me. Inasmuch as it is addressed to me, a pupil in the second form, it tells me clearly: I am a grammatical example meant to illustrate the rule about the agreement of the predicate. I am even forced to realize that the sentence in no way *signifies* its meaning to me, that it tries very little to tell me something about the lion and what sort of name he has; its true and fundamental signification is to impose itself on me as the presence of a certain agreement of the predicate. I conclude that I am faced with a particular, greater, semiological system, since it is co-extensive with the language: there is, indeed, a signifier, but this signifier is itself formed by a sum of signs, it is in itself a first semiological system (*my name is lion*). Thereafter, the formal pattern is correctly unfolded: there is a signified (*I am a grammatical example*) and there is a global signification, which is none other than the correlation of the signifier and the signified; for neither the naming of the lion nor the grammatical example are given separately.

And here is now another example: I am at the barber's, and a copy of *Paris-Match* is offered to me. On the cover, a young Negro in a French uniform is saluting, with his eyes uplifted, probably fixed on a fold of the tricolour. All this is the *meaning* of the picture. But, whether naively or not, I see very well what it signifies to me: that France is a great Empire, that all her sons, without any colour discrimination, faithfully serve under her flag, and that there is no better answer to the detractors of an alleged colonialism than the zeal shown by this Negro in serving his so-called oppressors. I am therefore again faced with a greater semiological system: there is a signifier, itself already formed with a previous system (*a black soldier is giving the French salute*); there is a signified (it is here a purposeful mixture of Frenchness and militariness); finally, there is a presence of the signified through the signifier.

Before tackling the analysis of each term of the mythical system, one must agree on terminology. We now know that the signifier can be looked at, in myth, from two points of view: as the final term of the linguistic system, or as the first term of the mythical system. We therefore need two names. On the plane of language, that is, as the final term of the first system, I shall call the signifier: *meaning* (*my name is lion, a Negro is giving the French salute*); on the plane of myth, I shall call it: *form*. In the case of the signified, no ambiguity is possible: we shall retain the name *concept*. The third term is the correlation of the first two: in the linguistic system, it is the *sign*; but it is not possible to use this word again without ambiguity, since in myth (and this is the chief peculiarity of the latter), the signifier is already formed by the *signs* of the language. I shall call the third term of myth the *signification*. This word is here all the better justified since myth has in fact a double function: it points out and it notifies, it makes us understand something and it imposes it on us.

Notes

1 Innumerable other meanings of the word 'myth' can be cited against this. But I have tried to define things, not words.
2 The development of publicity, of a national press, of radio, of illustrated news, not to speak of the survival of a myriad rites of communication which rule social appearances, makes the development of a semiological science more urgent than ever. In a single day, how many really non-signifying fields do we cross? Very few,

sometimes none. Here I am, before the sea; it is true that it bears no message. But on the beach, what material for semiology! Flags, slogans, signals, sign-boards, clothes, suntan even, which are so many messages to me.

3 The notion of *word* is one of the most controversial in linguistics. I keep it here for the sake of simplicity.

4 *Tel Quel*, II, p. 191.

1.3

Pierre Macherey
from *A Theory of Literary Production* (1978)

Implicit and explicit

> In order to ascertain their real opinions, I ought to take cognisance of what
> they practised rather than of what they said, not only because, in the corrup-
> tion of our manners, there are few disposed to speak exactly as they believe,
> but also because very many are not aware of what it is that they really believe,
> for as the act of mind by which a thing is believed is different from that by
> which we know we believe it, the one act is often found without the other.
>
> (Descartes, *Discourse on Method*, III)

For there to be a critical discourse which is more than a superficial and futile
reprise of the work, the speech stored in the book must be incomplete;
because it has not said everything, there remains the possibility of saying
something else, *after another fashion*. The recognition of the area of shadow
in or around the work is the initial moment of criticism. But we must
examine the nature of this shadow: does it denote a true absence, or is it
the extension of a half-presence? This can be reformulated in terms of a
previous question: Will it be the pillar of an explanation or the pretext for
an interpretation?

Initially, we will be inclined to say that criticism, in relation to its object,
is its *explication*. What, then, is involved in making-explicit? Explicit is to
implicit as explication is to implication: these oppositions derive from the
distinction between the manifest and the latent, the discovered and the
concealed. That which is formally accounted for, expressed, and even
concluded, is explicit: the 'explicit' at the end of a book echoes the 'incipit'
at the beginning, and indicates that 'all is (has been) said'. To explicate
comes from *explicare*: to display and unfold. 'Spread eagle', a heraldic term:

one with wings outstretched. And thus the critic, opening the book – whether he intends to find buried treasure there, or whether he wants to see it flying with its own wings – means to give it a different status, or even a different appearance. It might be said that the aim of criticism is to *speak the truth*, a truth not unrelated to the book, but not as the content of its expression. In the book, then, not everything is said, and for everything to be said we must await the critical 'explicit', which may actually be interminable. Nevertheless, although the critical discourse is not spoken by the book, it is in some way the property of the book, constantly alluded to, though never announced openly. What is this silence – an accidental hesitation, or a statutory necessity? Whence the problem: are there books which say what they mean, without being critical books, that is to say, without *depending directly* on other books?

Here we recognise the classic problem of the interpretation of latent meaning. But, in this new instance, the problem tends to take a new form: in fact, the language of the book claims to be a language complete in itself, the source and measure of all 'diction'. The conclusion is inscribed even in its initial moments. Unwinding *within a closed circle*, this language reveals only . . . itself; it has only its *own* content and its *own* limits, and the 'explicit' is imprinted on each of these terms. Yet it is not perfect: under close scrutiny the speech inscribed by the book appears interminable; but it takes this absence of a conclusion as its ending. In the space in which the work unfolds, everything is to be said, and is therefore never said, but this does not suffer being altered by any other discourse, enclosed as it is within the definitive limits which constitute its imperfection. This seems to be the origin of criticism's inability to add anything to the discourse of the work: at most, it might extend the work – either in a reduction or in a pursuit of its discourse.

Yet it remains obvious that although the work is self-sufficient it does not contain or engender its own theory; it does not *know* itself. When the critic speaks he is not repeating, reproducing or remaking it; neither is he illuminating its dark corners, filling its margins with annotation, specifying that which was never specific. When the critical discourse begins from the hypothesis that the work speaks falteringly, it is not with the aim of *completing* it, reducing its deficiencies, as though the book were too small for the space it occupied. We have seen that a knowledge of the work is not elaborated within the work, but supposes a distance between knowledge and its object; to know what the writer is saying, it is not enough to *let him speak*, for his speech is hollow and can never be completed at its own level. Theoretical inquiry rejects the notion of the *space* or *site* of the work. Critical discourse does not attempt to complete the book, for theory begins from that incompleteness which is so radical that it cannot be located.

Thus, the silence of the book is not a lack to be remedied, an inadequacy to be made up for. It is not a temporary silence that could be finally abolished. We must distinguish the necessity of this silence. For example, it can be shown that it is the juxtaposition and conflict of several meanings which produces the radical otherness which shapes the work: this conflict it not resolved or absorbed, but simply *displayed*.

Thus the work cannot speak of the more or less complex opposition which structures it; though it is its expression and embodiment. In its every particle, the work *manifests*, uncovers, what it cannot say. This silence gives it life.

The spoken and the unspoken

The speech of the book comes from a certain silence, a matter which it endows with form, a ground on which it traces a figure. Thus, the book is not self-sufficient; it is necessarily accompanied by a *certain absence*, without which it would not exist. A knowledge of the book must include a consideration of this absence.

This is why it seems useful and legitimate to ask of every production what it tacitly implies, what it does not say. Either all around or in its wake the explicit requires the implicit: for in order to say anything, there are other things *which must not be said*. Freud relegated this *absence of certain words* to a new place which he was the first to explore, and which he paradoxically *named*: the unconscious. To reach utterance, all speech envelops itself in the unspoken. We must ask why it does not speak of this interdict: can it be identified before one might wish to acknowledge it? There is not even the slightest hint of the absence of what it does not, perhaps cannot, say: the disavowal (*dénégation*) extends even to the act that banished the forbidden term; its absence is unacknowledged.

This moment of absence founds the speech of the work. Silences shape all speech. Banality?

Can we say that this silence is hidden? What is it? A condition of existence – point of departure, methodical beginning – essential foundation – ideal culmination – absolute origin which lends meaning to the endeavour? Means or form of connection?

Can we make this silence speak? What is the unspoken saying? What does it mean? To what extent is dissimulation a way of speaking? Can something that has hidden *itself* be recalled to our presence? Silence as the source of expression. Is what I am really saying what I am not saying? Hence the main risk run by those who would say everything. After all, perhaps the work is not hiding what it does not say; this is simply *missing*.

Yet the unspoken has many other resources: it assigns speech to its exact position, designating its domain. By speech, silence becomes the centre and principle of expression, its vanishing point. Speech eventually has nothing more to tell us: we investigate the silence, for it is the silence that is doing the speaking.

Silence reveals speech – unless it is speech that reveals the silence.

These two methods of explanation by recourse to the latent or concealed are not equivalent: it is the second which allows least value to the latent, since there appears an absence of speech through the absent speech, that is to say, a certain presence which it is enough to extricate. There is agreement to relate speech to its contrary, figure and ground. But there is a reluctance to leave these terms in equilibrium, an urge to resolve them: figure or ground? Here, once again, we encounter all the ambiguities of the notions of origin and creation. The unacknowledged co-existence of the visible and the hidden: the visible is merely the hidden in a different guise. The problem is merely to *pass across* from the one to the other.

The first image is the more profound, in so far as it enables us to recuperate the form of the second without becoming trapped in a mechanical problematic of transition: in being a necessary medium of expression, this ground of silence does not lose its significance. It is not the sole meaning, but that which endows meaning with a meaning: it is this silence which tells us – not just anything, since it exists to say nothing – which informs us of the precise conditions for the appearance of an utterance, and thus its limits, giving its real significance, without, for all that, speaking in its place. The latent is an intermediate means: this does not amount to pushing it into the background; it simply means that the latent is not another meaning which ultimately and miraculously *dispels* the first (manifest) meaning. Thus, we can see that meaning is in the *relation* between the implicit and the explicit, not on one or the other side of that fence: for in the latter case, we should be obliged to choose, in other words, as ever, translation or commentary.

What is important in the work is what it does not say. This is not the same as the careless notation 'what it refuses to say', although that would in itself be interesting: a method might be built on it, with the task of *measuring silences*, whether acknowledged or unacknowledged. But rather than this, what the work *cannot say* is important, because there the elaboration of the utterance is acted out, in a sort of journey to silence.

The basic issue, then, is to know whether we can examine that absence of speech which is the prior condition of all speech.

> Insidious Questions: When we are confronted with any manifestation which someone has permitted us to see, we may ask: what is it meant to conceal? What is it meant to draw our attention from? What prejudice does it seek to raise? and again, how far does the subtlety of the dissimulation go? and in what respect is the man mistaken?
>
> (*The Dawn of Day*, section 523)

For Nietzsche, these are insidious questions, *Hinterfrage*, questions which come from behind, held in reserve, lying in wait, snares.

'It might be asked': thus Nietzsche inquires, and even before showing how to put questions, he points out the necessity of *asking* questions; for there are several. The object or target of these questions is 'all that a man allows to appear'. Everything: that is to say that the Nietzschean interrogation – which is the precise opposite of an examination, since, as we shall see, it reaches the point of calling itself into question – is of such theoretical generality that we may wonder if it is legitimate to apply it to the specific domain of literary production. What in fact 'becomes visible' is the work, all the works. We shall try to apply this general proposition to a specific domain.

'All that a man allows to appear': obviously the German words say more than the English. *Lassen*: this is both to do, to allow, and to oblige. This word, better than any other, designates the act of literary production. It reveals it – on condition that we do not search there for the shapes of some evocative magic: inspiration, visitation or creation. Production: to show and to reveal. The question 'What does he mean?' proves that it is not a matter of dispossession. Also 'to reveal' is an affirmation rather than a decision: the expression of an active force, which yet does not exclude a certain autonomous actualisation of the visible.

Interrogation penetrates certain actions: 'hiding', 'diverting attention', and, further on, 'cheating'. Obviously, linking all these, there is a single impulse: 'hiding' is to keep from sight; 'diverting attention' is to show without being seen, to prevent what is visible from being seen; which also expresses the image of 'dissimulation': to dissimulate requires action. Therefore everything happens as though the accent had been shifted: the work is revealed to itself and to others on two different levels: it makes visible, and it makes invisible. Not because something has to be hidden in order to show something else; but because attention is diverted from the very thing which is shown. This is the superposition of utterance and statement (*du parler et du dire*): if the author does not always say what he states, he does not necessarily state what he says.

In the text from Nietzsche, then, it is a question of a prejudice, a mystification, a deception. Not by virtue of this or that particular word, but because of speech itself, all speech. A prejudice is that which is not judged in language but before it, but which is nevertheless offered as a judgment. Prejudice, the pseudo-judgment, is the utterance which remains imperceptibly beyond language.

Yet this proposition has two meanings: speech evokes a prejudice as a judgment; but equally, by the *fact of evocation*, it holds it up as a prejudice. It creates an allegory of judgment. And speech exists because it wishes for this allegory whose appearance it prepares for. This is the portion of the visible and the invisible, the revealed and the concealed, of language and silence.

Then we arrive at the meaning of the last questions. '*And yet*': we move to a new level of the systematic order, in what is almost an inversion. It could be said that there is a question directed at the first questions. This question which completes the construction of the trap challenges the first question, setting off the structure of the work and the structure of the criticism of it.

$$\left.\begin{array}{l}\text{utterance}\\[4pt]\text{question 1}\end{array}\right\}\ \text{question 2}$$

We can then ask to what extent the first question was based on an error: because this dissimulation applies to everything it must not be thought that it is total and unlimited. Since it is a relative silence which depends on an even more silent margin, it is impossible to dissemble the truth of language.

Naturally it is incorrect to see in this equivocation of speech its division into the spoken and the unspoken; a division which is only possible because it makes speech depend on a fundamental veracity, a plenitude of expression, a reflection of the Hegelian dialectic – that dialectic which Nietzsche (like Marx, an enemy of idols) could only contemplate in its inverted form. If it is insisted that we find references to these questions in poetic form, we would do better to take them from the work of Spinoza. The transition from dissimulation to error, with the essential moment of 'and yet', is also the movement to the third kind of knowledge. In a famous book, Spinoza has posed Nietzsche's questions, posed them concerning Scripture, which could once have seemed to be the model of all books.

So the real trap of language is its tacit positiveness which makes it into a truly active insistence: the error belongs as much with the one who reveals it as it does with the one who asks the first questions, the critic.

The ordinary critic (the one who stops at the first question) and the author are equally remote from a true appreciation of the work: but there is another kind of critic who asks the second question.

The labyrinth of the two questions – a labyrinth in reverse, because it leads to a way out – endlessly proposes a choice between a false and a true subtlety: the one views the author from the critic's point of view, as a critic; the other only judges him when it has taken up position in the expressive veracity of language, and his language. Torn from the false limits of its empirical presence, the work then begins to acquire a significance.

The two questions

Thus the critical task is not simple: it necessarily implies the superposition of two questions. To know the work, we must move outside it. Then, in the second moment, we question the work in its alleged plenitude; not from a different point of view, a different side – by translating it into a different language, or by applying a different standard – but not entirely from within, from what it says and asserts that it says. Conjecturally, the work has its *margins*, an area of incompleteness from which we can observe its birth and its production.

The critical problem will be in the conjunction of the two questions; not in a choice between them, but in the point from which they appear to become differentiated. The complexity of the critical problem will be the articulation between the two questions. To grasp this *articulation* is to accept a discontinuity, to establish a discontinuity: the questions are not spontaneously given in their specificity. Initially, the questions must be asked – asked simultaneously, in a way that amounts to allowing them an equal status.

The recognition of this simultaneity, which precludes any notion of priority, is fundamental because it makes possible – from the beginning – an exorcism of the ghosts of aesthetic legality: by the fact that the question which is supposed to inhabit the mind of the writer is not simple, but divided by its reference to another question, the problem to be explicitly resolved will not be merely the realisation of a project according to the rules of validity (beauty) and conformity (fidelity). Even the question of the formal limits imposed on expression will no longer form part of the problem: it will be completely eliminated as a distinct element of the problematic. In so far as a conscious intention to realise a project of writing begins inevitably by taking the form of an ideological imperative – something *to say* (not the acceptance of rules), in other words something that must not be said – it will have to adopt the conditions of the possibility of such an undertaking: the implements, the actual means of this practice; and the rules will play their part in so far as they are *directly* useful.

The real problem is not that of being restricted by rules – or the absence of such a restriction – but the necessity of inventing forms of expression, or merely finding them: not ideal forms, or forms derived from a principle which transcends the enterprise itself, but forms which can be used immediately as the means of expression for a determinate content; likewise, the question of the value of these forms cannot reach beyond this immediate issue. However, these forms do not exist just in the mode of an immediate presence: they can survive beyond the moment of their usefulness, and it will be seen that this poses a very serious problem; they can be revived, in which case they will have undergone a slight but crucial change in value which must be determined. In fact, these forms do not appear instantaneously but at the end of a long history – a history of the elaboration of ideological themes. The history of forms – which will subsequently be designated as *themes*, in the strict sense of the word – corresponds to the history of ideological themes; indeed, they are exactly parallel, as can easily be demonstrated with the history of any idea: that of Robinson Crusoe, for example. The form takes shape or changes in response to new imperatives of the idea: but it is also capable of independent transformations, or of an inertia, which bends the path of ideological history. But, whatever the mode of its realisation, there is always a correspondence, which could thus be considered automatic: refuting the conception of these two histories as the expression of a superficial question – which is not self-sufficient, because it is based on a parallelism – the question of the work. The level of interpretation determined by this parallelism will only acquire meaning from the elucidation of another level, with which it will have a determining relationship: the question of this question.

The investigation into the conditions of the possibility of the work is accomplished in the answer to an explicit question, but it will not be able to seek the conditions of those conditions, nor will it be able to see that this answer constitutes a question. Nevertheless, the second question will necessarily be posed within the first question, or even through it. It is this second question which, for us, defines the space of history: it reveals the work in so far as it entertains a specific but undisguised (which does not mean innocent) relation with history. We must show, through the study of an effort of expression, how it is possible to render visible the conditions of this effort – conditions of which it has no awareness, though this does not mean that it does not apprehend them: the work encounters the question of questions as an obstacle; it is only aware of the conditions which it adopts or utilises. We could account for this latent knowledge (which necessarily exists, since without it the work would be accomplished no further than if the explicit conditions were not realised) by recourse to *the unconscious of the work* (not of the author). But this unconscious does not perform as an understudy – on the contrary, it arises in the interior of the labour itself: there it is at work – nor as an extension of the explicit purpose, since it derives from a completely different principle. Neither is it a question of another consciousness: the consciousness of another or others, or the other consciousness of the same thing. There is no understudy creative-unconscious to the creative pseudo-consciousness: if there is an unconscious it cannot be creative, in so far as it precedes all production as its condition. It is a question of something other than consciousness: what we are seeking is analogous to that relationship which Marx acknowledges when he insists on seeing material relations as being derived from the social infrastructure behind all ideological phenomena, not in order to explain these phenomena as emanations from the infrastructure, which would amount to saying that the ideological is the economic in another form: whence the possibility of reducing the ideological to the economic.

For Marx and Engels, the study of an ideological phenomenon – that is to say, a conflict at the level of ideology – cannot be isolated from the movement at the economic level: not because it is a different conflict, a different form of the conflict, but because it is the conflict of this conflict. The composition of *an* ideology implies the relation of the ideological to the economic.

The problem of the work, if it exists, is now squarely posed in and by the work, but it is something altogether different from the awareness of a problem. This is why an authentic explanation must attend to several levels at once, though never failing to consider them separately, in their specificity:

1 The first question, properly interior to the work, in the sense of an intimacy, remains diffuse: indeed, it is there and not there, divided between several determinations which give it the status of a quasi-presence. Materially scattered, it must be reconstituted, recalled, recognised. But it would be incorrect to present this task as a deciphering: the secret is not hidden, and in any case *does not conceal itself,* does not resist this census which is a simple classification, changing at most its form; it loses nothing of its nature, its vividness, its mystery.

This first procedure is a question, if you will, of structures. But we have gone far beyond that formulation: to conclude with structures is merely to gather the scattered limbs. It would not be correct to believe that one had thus established a system. What system? In what relation to other systems? In what relation to that which is not part of the system?

2 Once the question has emerged from its half-light, we must find its meaning and its importance. It might be suggested: inscribe it in ideological history, the history which generates the succession of questions and the thread of problematics. But this inscription is not calculated by the simple situation of the question in relation to other questions, or by the presence of history outside this particular work, in so far as it gives it both its domain and its place. This history is not in a simple external relation to the work: it is present in the work, in so far as the emergence of the work required this history, which is its only principle of reality and also supplies its means of expression. This history, which is not merely the history of works of the same nature, entirely determines the work: gives the work its reality, but also that which it is not, and this is the most important. To anticipate an example which will subsequently be analysed, if Jules Verne chose to be the spokesman of a certain ideological condition, he could not choose to be

what he in fact became. He chose to be the spokesman for a certain condition; he expressed that choice. These are two different operations, the conjuncture of which constitutes a specific enterprise: in this case, the production of a certain number of books. These are the two 'choices'; the gap between them measures the absence within the work, but they cannot be judged by the same standards, because they are not of the same nature.

It must then be possible to examine a work from an accurate description which respects the specificity of this work, but which is more than just a new exposition of its content, in the form of a systematisation, for example. For as we quickly come to realise, we can only describe, only remain within the work, if we also decide to go beyond it: to bring out, for example, what the work is *compelled* to say in order to say what it *wants* to say, because not only would the work have wanted not to say it (which is another question), but certainly the work did not want to say it. Thus, it is not a question of introducing a historical explanation which is stuck on to the work from the outside. On the contrary, we must show a sort of splitting within the work: this division is *its* unconscious, in so far as it possesses one – the unconscious which is history, the play of history beyond its edges, encroaching on those edges this is why it is possible to trace the path which leads from the haunted work to that which haunts it. Once again it is not a question of redoubling the work with an unconscious, but a question of revealing in the very gestures of expression that which it is not. Then, the reverse side of what is written will be history itself.

Moreover, we shall be looking within the work itself for reasons for moving beyond it: from the explicit question, and from the reply which it actually elicits – the form of the question being legible in this answer – we shall certainly be able to put the question of the question, and not the one apart from the other. This endeavour is full of surprises: we realise that in seeking the meaning of the work – not the meaning that it gives itself but the meaning that seizes hold of it – we have at our disposal, in turning to the work itself, material that is already prepared, already invested by the question which we are going to ask. The real resistances are elsewhere, in the reader we might say: but they do not hinder this unforeseen inquiry, for the work – it is absurd to repeat this – does not say what it does not say. This is precisely the opposite of an interpretation or a commentary: an interpretation seeks *pretexts*, but the explanation proposed here finds its object wholly prepared and is content to give a true idea of it.

To take a specific example which will later be studied in detail: the 'problem' of Jules Verne breaks down into *two questions*. The important thing is that this dissociation itself remains *within* the problem, that the coherence of the problem should survive: we shall not, for example, be trying to find two Jules Vernes, or to establish a preference for a particular Jules Verne at the expense of all the other possible Jules Vernes. This problem, because it concerns a literary object, is crystallised in what we can call a theme, which is, in its abstract form, the conquest of nature; in the ideological realisation which gives it the form of a *motif*: the voyage, or Robinson Crusoe (a veritable ideological obsession with Verne, and present in all his books, even if only as an allusion). This theme can be studied at two different levels:

1 The utilisation of the theme: initially the adventures of its form, which moreover contain (even though the collocation of the words is casual) the form of the adventure. This raises the question of the writer at work.
2 The meaning of the theme: not a meaning which exists independently of the work, but the meaning that the theme actually acquires within the work.

First question: the work originates in a secret to be *explained*.

Second question: the work is realised in the revelation of its secret. The simultaneity of the two questions defines a minute rupture, minutely distinct from a continuity. It is this rupture which must be studied.

1.4

Roland Barthes
from *S/Z* (1975)

X Sarrasine

The text I have chosen (Why? All I know is that for some time I have
wanted to make a complete analysis of a short text and that the Balzac story
was brought to my attention by an article by Jean Reboul,[1] who in turn is
supposed to have been inspired by Georges Bataille's reference; and thus I
was caught up in this 'series' whose scope I was to discover by means of the
text itself) is Balzac's *Sarrasine*.[2]

(1) *SARRASINE* * The title raises a question: *What is Sarrasine?* A noun? A name?
A thing? A man? A woman? This question will not be answered until much
later, by the biography of the sculptor named Sarrasine. Let us designate as
hermeneutic code (HER) all the units whose function it is to articulate in various
ways a question, its response, and the variety of chance events which can
either formulate the question or delay its answer; or even, constitute an
enigma and lead to its solution. Thus, the title *Sarrasine* initiates the first step
in a sequence which will not be completed until No. 153 (HER. Enigma 1 –
the story will contain others – : question). ** The word *Sarrasine* has an
additional connotation, that of femininity, which will be obvious to any
French-speaking person, since that language automatically takes the final 'e'
as a specifically feminine linguistic property, particularly in the case of a
proper name whose masculine form (*Sarrazin*) exists in French onomastics.
Femininity (connoted) is a signifier which will occur in several places in the
text; it is a shifting element which can combine with other similar elements
to create characters, ambiances, shapes, and symbols. Although every unit
we mention here will be a signifier, this one is of a very special type: it is
the signifier par excellence because of its connotation, in the usual meaning

of the term. We shall call this element a signifier (without going into further detail), or a *seme* (semantically, the seme is the unit of the signifier), and we shall indicate these units by the abbreviation SEM, designating each time by an approximate word the connotative signifier referred to in the lexia (SEM. Femininity).

(2) *I was deep in one of those daydreams* * There will be nothing wayward about the daydream introduced here: it will be solidly constructed along the most familiar rhetorical lines, in a series of antitheses: garden and salon, life and death, cold and heat, outside and interior. The lexia thus lays the groundwork, in introductory form, for a vast symbolic structure, since it can lend itself to many substitutions, variations, which will lead us from the garden to the castrato, from the salon to the girl with whom the narrator is in love, by way of the mysterious old man, the full-bosomed Mme de Lanty, or Vien's moonlit Adonis. Thus, on the symbolic level, an immense province appears, the province of the antithesis, of which this forms the first unit, linking at the start its two adversative terms (A/B) in the word *daydream*. (We shall mark all the units in this symbolic area with the letters SYM. Here – SYM. Antithesis: AB.) ** The state of absorption formulated here (*I was deep in . . .*) already implies (at least in 'readerly' discourse) some event which will bring it to an end (*. . . when I was roused by a conversation . . .* No. 14). Such sequences imply a logic in human behavior. In Aristotelian terms, in which *praxis* is linked to *proairesis*, or the ability rationally to determine the result of an action, we shall name this code of actions and behavior *proairetic* (in narrative, however, the discourse, rather than the characters, determines the action). This code of actions will be abbreviated ACT; furthermore, since these actions produce effects, each effect will have a generic name giving a kind of title to the sequence, and we shall number each of the terms which constitute it, as they appear (ACT. 'To be deep in': 1: to be absorbed).

(3) *which overtake even the shallowest of men, in the midst of the most tumultuous parties.* * The fact 'there is a party' (given here obliquely), soon to be followed by further data (a private house in the Faubourg Saint-Honoré), forms a pertinent signifier: the wealth of the Lanty family (SEM. Wealth). ** The phrase is a conversion of what might easily be a real proverb: '*Tumultuous parties: deep daydreams.*' The statement is made in a collective and anonymous voice originating in traditional human experience. Thus, the unit has been formed by a gnomic code, and this code is one of the numerous codes of knowledge or wisdom to which the text continually refers; we shall call them in a very general way *cultural codes* (even though, of course, all codes are cultural), or rather, since they afford the discourse a basis in scientific or moral authority, we shall call them reference codes (REF. Gnomic code).

XI The five codes

As chance would have it (but what is chance?), the first three lexias – the title and the first sentence of the story – have already provided us with the five major codes under which all the textual signifiers can be grouped: without straining a point, there will be no other codes throughout the story but these five, and each and every lexia will fall under one of these five codes. Let us sum them up in order of their appearance, without trying to put them in any order of importance. Under the hermeneutic code, we list the various (formal) terms by which an enigma can be distinguished, suggested, formulated, held in suspense, and finally disclosed (these terms will not always occur, they will often be repeated; they will not appear in any fixed order). As for the semes, we merely indicate them – without, in other words, trying either to link them to a character (or a place or an object) or to arrange them in some order so that they form a single thematic grouping; we allow them the instability, the dispersion, characteristic of motes of dust, flickers of meaning. Moreover, we shall refrain from structuring the symbolic grouping; this is the place for multivalence and for reversibility; the main task is always to demonstrate that this field can be entered from any number of points, thereby making depth and secrecy problematic. Actions (terms of the proairetic code) can fall into various sequences which should be indicated merely by listing them, since the proairetic sequence is never more than the result of an artifice of reading: whoever reads the text amasses certain data under some generic titles for actions (*stroll, murder, rendezvous*), and this title embodies the sequence; the sequence exists when and because it can be given a name, it unfolds as this process of naming takes place, as a title is sought or confirmed; its basis is therefore more empirical than rational, and it is useless to attempt to force it into a statutory order; its only logic is that of the 'already-done' or 'already-read' – whence the variety of sequences (some trivial, some melodramatic) and the variety of terms (numerous or few); here again, we shall not attempt to put them into any order. Indicating them (externally and internally) will suffice to demonstrate the plural meaning entangled in them. Lastly, the cultural codes are references to a science or a body of knowledge; in drawing attention to them, we merely indicate the type of knowledge (physical, physiological, medical, psychological, literary, historical, etc.) referred to, without going so far as to construct (or reconstruct) the culture they express.

XII The weaving of voices

The five codes create a kind of network, a *topos* through which the entire text passes (or rather, in passing, becomes text). Thus, if we make no effort to structure each code, or the five codes among themselves, we do so deliberately, in order to assume the multivalence of the text, its partial reversibility. We are, in fact, concerned not to manifest a structure but to produce a structuration. The blanks and looseness of the analysis will be like footprints marking the escape of the text; for if the text is subject to some form, this form is not unitary, architectonic, finite: it is the fragment, the shards, the broken or obliterated network – all the movements and inflections of a vast 'dissolve,' which permits both overlapping and loss of messages. Hence we use *Code* here not in the sense of a list, a paradigm that must be reconstituted. The code is a perspective of quotations, a mirage of structures; we know only its departures and returns; the units which have resulted from it (those we inventory) are themselves, always, ventures out of the text, the mark, the sign of a virtual digression toward the remainder of a catalogue (*The Kidnapping* refers to every kidnapping ever written); they are so many fragments of something that has always been *already* read, seen, done, experienced; the code is the wake of that *already*. Referring to what has been written, i.e., to the Book (of culture, of life, of life as culture), it makes the text into a prospectus of this Book. Or again: each code is one of the forces that can take over the text (of which the text is the network), one of the voices out of which the text is woven. Alongside each utterance,one might say that off-stage voices can be heard: they are the codes: in their interweaving, these voices (whose origin is 'lost' in the vast perspective of the *already-written*) de-originate the utterance: the convergence of the voices (of the codes) becomes *writing*, a stereographic space where the five codes, the five voices, intersect: the Voice of Empirics (the proairetisms), the Voice of the Person (the semes), the Voice of Science (the cultural codes), the Voice of Truth (the hermeneutisms), the Voice of Symbol.

Notes

1 Jean Reboul: 'Sarrasine ou la castration personnifiée', in *Cahiers pour l'analyse*, March–April, 1967.
2 *Scènes de la vie parisienne.*

1.5

Colin MacCabe
from 'Realism and the
Cinema' (1974)

The classic realist text

'Criticism, at least Marxist criticism, must proceed methodically and concretely
in each case, in short scientifically. Loose talk is of no help here, whatever its
vocabulary. In no circumstances can the necessary guide-lines for a practical
definition of realism be derived from literary works alone. (Be like Tolstoy –
but without his weaknesses! Be like Balzac – only up-to-date!) Realism is an
issue not only for literature: it is a major political, philosophical and practical
issue and must be handled and explained as such – as a matter of general
human interest.'[1]

One of the difficulties of any discussion about realism is the lack of any
really effective vocabulary with which to discuss the topic. Most discussions
turn on the problems of the production of discourse which will fully adequate
the real. This notion of adequacy is accepted both by the realists and indeed
by the anti-realists whose main argument is that no discourse can ever be
adequate to the multifarious nature of the real. This notion of the real is,
however, I wish to suggest, a notion which is tied to a particular type of
literary production – the nineteenth-century realist novel. The dominance
of this novel form is such that people still tend to confuse the general
question of realism with the particular forms of the nineteenth-century
realist novel. In order to make the discussion clearer I want therefore to
attempt to define the structure which typifies the nineteenth-century realist
novel and to show how that structure can also be used to describe a great
number of films. The detour through literature is necessary because, in
many ways, the structure is much more obvious there and also because of
the historical dominance of the classic realist novel over much film production.
What to a large extent will be lacking in this article is the specific nature of

the film form but this does not seem to me to invalidate the setting up of certain essential categories from which further discussion must progress. The structure I will attempt to disengage I shall call the classic realist text and I shall apply it to novels and films.

A classic realist text may be defined as one in which there is a hierarchy amongst the discourses which compose the text and this hierarchy is defined in terms of an empirical notion of truth. Perhaps the easiest way to understand this is through a reflection on the use of inverted commas within the classic realist novel. While those sections in the text which are contained in inverted commas may cause a certain difficulty for the reader – a certain confusion vis-à-vis what really is the case – this difficulty is abolished by the unspoken (or more accurately the unwritten) prose that surrounds them. In the classical realist novel the narrative prose functions as a metalanguage that can state all the truths in the object language – those words held in inverted commas – and can also explain the relation of this object language to the real. The metalanguage can thereby explain the relation of this object language to the world and the strange methods by which the object languages attempt to express truths which are straightforwardly conveyed in the metalanguage. What I have called an unwritten prose (or a metalanguage) is exactly that language, which while placing other languages between inverted commas and regarding them as certain material expressions which express certain meanings, regards those same meanings as finding transparent expression within the metalanguage itself. Transparent in the sense that the metalanguage is not regarded as material; it is dematerialised to achieve perfect representation – to let the identity of things shine through the window of words. For insofar as the metalanguage is treated itself as material – it, too, can be reinterpreted; new meanings can be found for it in a further metalanguage. The problem is the problem that has troubled western thought since the pre-Socratics recognised the separation between what was said and the act of saying. This separation must be thought both as time and space – as the space, which in the distance from page to eye or mouth to ear allows the possibility of misunderstanding – as the time taken to traverse the page or listen to an utterance which ensures the deferred interpretation of words which are always only defined by what follows. The problem is that in the moment that we say a sentence the meaning (what is said) seems fixed and evident but what is said does not exist solely for the moment and is open to further interpretations. Even in this formulation of the problem I have presupposed an original moment when there is strict contemporaneity between the saying and what is said, but the difficulty is more radical for there is no such original moment. The separation is always already there as we cannot locate the presence of what is said – distributed as it is through space – nor the present of what is said – distributed as it is through time.

This separation bears witness to the real as articulated. The thing represented does not appear in a moment of pure identity as it tears itself out of the world and presents itself, but rather is caught in an articulation in which each object is defined in a set of differences and oppositions.

It is this separation that the unwritten text attempts to *anneal*, to make whole, through denying its own status as writing – as marks of material difference distributed through time and space. Whereas other discourses within the text are considered as material which are open to re-interpretation, the narrative discourse simply allows reality to appear and denies its own status as articulation. This relationship between discourses can be clearly seen in the work of such a writer as George Eliot. In the scene in *Middlemarch* where Mr Brooke goes to visit the Dagley's farm we read two different languages. One is the educated, well-meaning, but not very intelligent discourse of Mr Brooke and the other is the uneducated, violent and very nearly unintelligible discourse of the drunken Dagley. But the whole dialogue is surrounded by a metalanguage, which being unspoken is also unwritten, and which places these discourses in inverted commas and can thus discuss these discourses' relation to truth – a truth which is illuminatingly revealed in the metalanguage. The metalanguage reduces the object languages into a simple division between form and content and extracts the meaningful content from the useless form. One can see this process at work in the following passage which ends the scene:

> He [Mr Brooke] had never been insulted on his own land before, and had been inclined to regard himself as a general favourite (we are all apt to do so, when we think of our own amiability more than what other people are likely to want of us). When he had quarrelled with Caleb Garth twelve years before he had thought that the tenants would be pleased at the landlord's taking everything into his own hands.
>
> Some who follow the narrative of this experience may wonder at the midnight darkness of Mr Dagley; but nothing was easier in those times than for a hereditary farmer of his grade to be ignorant, in spite somehow of having a rector in the twin parish who was a gentleman to the backbone, a curate nearer at hand who preached more learnedly than the rector, a landlord who had gone into everything, especially fine art and social improvement and all the lights of Middlemarch only three miles off.[2]

This passage provides the necessary interpretations for the discourses that we have read earlier in the chapter. Both the discourses of Dagley and Mr Brooke are revealed as springing from two types of ignorance which the metalanguage can expose and reveal. So we have Mr Brooke's attitude to what his tenants thought of him contrasted with the reality which is available through the narrative prose. No discourse is allowed to speak for itself but rather it must be placed in a context which will reduce it to a simple explicable content. And in the claim that the narrative prose has direct access to a final reality we can find the claim of the classic realist novel to present us with the truths of human nature. The ability to reveal the truth about Mr Brooke is the ability that guarantees the generalisations of human nature.

Thus then a first definition of the classic realist text – but does this definition carry over into films where it is certainly less evident where to locate the dominant discourse? It seems to me that it does and in the following fashion. The narrative prose achieves its position of dominance because it is in the position of knowledge and this function of knowledge is taken up in the cinema by the narration of events. Through the knowledge we gain from the narrative we can split the discourses of the various characters from their situation and compare what is said in these discourses with what has been revealed to us through narration. The camera shows us what happens – it tells the truth against which we can measure the discourses. A good example of this classical realist structure is to be found in Pakula's film *Klute*. This film is of particular interest because it was widely praised for its realism on its release. Perhaps even more significantly it tended to be praised for its realistic presentation of the leading woman, Bree (played by Jane Fonda).

In *Klute* the relationship of dominance between discourses is peculiarly accentuated by the fact that the film is interspersed with fragments of Bree talking to her psychiatrist. This subjective discourse can be exactly measured against the reality provided by the unfolding of the story. Thus all her talk of independence is portrayed as finally an illusion as we discover, to no great surprise but to our immense relief, what she really wants is to settle down in the mid-West with John Klute (the detective played by Donald Sutherland) and have a family. The final sequence of the film is particularly telling in this respect. While Klute and Bree pack their bags to leave, the soundtrack records Bree at her last meeting with her psychiatrist. Her own estimation of the situation is that it most probably won't work but the reality of the image ensures us that this is the way it will really be. Indeed Bree's monologue is even more interesting – for in relation to the reality of the image it marks a definite advance on her previous statements. She has gained insight through the plot development and like many good heroines of classic realist texts her discourse is more nearly adequate to the truth at the end of the film than at the beginning. But if a progression towards knowledge is what marks Bree, it is possession of knowledge which marks the narrative, the reader of the film and John Klute himself. For Klute is privileged by the narrative as the one character whose discourse is also a discourse of knowledge. Not only is Klute a detective and thus can solve the problem of his friend's disappearance – he is also a man, and a man who because he has not come into contact with the city has not had his virility undermined. And it is as a full-blooded man that he can know not only the truth of the mystery of the murders but also the truth of the woman Bree. Far from being a film which goes any way to portraying a woman liberated from male definition (a common critical response), *Klute* exactly guarantees that the real essence of woman can only be discovered and defined by a man.

The analysis sketched here is obviously very schematic but what, hopefully, it does show is that the structure of the classic realist text can be found in film as well. That narrative of events – the knowledge which the film provides of how things really are – is the metalanguage in which we can talk of the various characters in the film. What would still remain to be done in the elaboration of the structure of the classic realist text in cinema is a more detailed account of the actual mechanisms by which the narrative is privileged (and the way in which one or more of the characters within the narrative can be equally privileged) and also a history of the development of this dominant narrative. On the synchronic level it would be necessary to attempt an analysis of the relationship between the various types of shot and their combination into sequences – are there for example certain types of shot which are coded as subjective and therefore subordinate to others which are guaranteed as objective? In addition how does music work as the guarantee or otherwise of truth? On the diachronic level it would be necessary to study how this form was produced – what relationship obtains between the classic realist text and technical advances such as the development of the talkie? What ideological factors were at work in the production and dominance of the classic realist text?

To return, however, to the narrative discourse. It is necessary to attempt to understand the type of relations that this dominant discourse produces. The narrative discourse cannot be mistaken in its identifications because the narrative discourse is not present as discourse – as articulation. The unquestioned nature of the narrative discourse entails that the only problem that reality poses is to go and look and see what *Things* there *are*. The relationship between the reading subject and the real is placed as one of pure specularity. The real is not articulated – it is. These features imply two essential features of the classic realist text:

1 The classic realist text cannot deal with the real as contradictory.
2 In a reciprocal movement the classic realist text ensures the position of the subject in a relation of dominant specularity.

Notes

1 Bertholt Brecht, *Gesammelte Werke*, 20 vols. (Frankfurt: Suhrkamp Verlag, 1967), 19, p. 307.
2 George Eliot, *Middlemarch* (Harmondsworth, Middlesex: Penguin, 1965), pp. 432–3.

IDEOLOGY

Introduction

Every sign is ideological. Yet it is hard to give a relatively objective and impartial account of the concept of ideology, one that is not tendentious, because the question of ideology is so deeply bound up with politics, domination and issues of power. In introducing the topic for this collection a sense of our own position cannot be entirely withheld. There is a politics of ideology, one which in the West has taken the form of a particular history. When Marx and Engels were working on the foundational text, *The German Ideology*, in 1846 they were writing in a historical situation in which the control of ideas was relatively unimportant to the maintenance of the existing social order, and the exercise of force by the ruling class was relatively overt and unashamed. Since then, with the development of mass education, forms of parliamentary democracy and, in the twentieth century, the mass media, the social control of thought has become of major political importance, and with it, the question of ideology. Definitions of ideology have spread in widening circles, from a local concern with the ideologies of groups in a conjuncture, to those of a period, an epoch, and, especially since the success of the great post-war movements against European imperialism, a sense of ideology as perhaps characterizing the whole of Western culture since Ancient Greece. To give a preliminary map of this intellectual terrain it is useful to follow a rough but by no means comprehensive chronology, one that, significantly, begins with a sense of ideology as conscious and deliberate but develops increasingly to regard ideology as permeating lived experience, subjectivity and even the unconscious.

A base-line definition of ideology would contrast it with the notion of ideas. While the term ideas, in the general usage, envisages meanings as something individuals think up for themselves, ideology specifies meanings in so far as they are social and collective. 'It is not', writes Marx, 'the consciousness of people that determines their being, but, on the contrary, their social being that determines their consciousness' (below, p. 45). Of course, how to draw a line between ideas originating with the individual and ideology constituted socially is a matter of continuing debate. Terry Eagleton, in his fine book, *Ideology: An Introduction* (1991) suggests that a breakfast-time quarrel between husband and wife over who burned the toast need not be ideological but becomes so when, for example, 'it begins to engage questions of sexual power, beliefs about gender roles and so on' (p. 8) (though it is hard to imagine such a quarrel *not* engaging with those questions today).

Ideology as expression of class interests

Outside the academy, in journalism and on television, the word ideology is used with a precise meaning as the conscious political programme of a political party, for example in Britain with references to the ideology of the Labour party (promoting the welfare state) or the Conservative party (fostering entrepreneurship and 'private enterprise'). Originating in fact with Napoleon Bonaparte, this usage continues to be widely dominant. In *The German Ideology* and elsewhere (Sections 2.1 and 2.2) Marx and Engels developed an account of ideology in terms of 'economic base' and 'ideological superstructure'. If a person's class position is determined by his or her economic position in relation to the mode of production, then this individual will share an ideology representing the economic interests of the class they belong to.

In one of the clearest and most striking illustrations of ideology in this sense, Marx in *The Eighteenth Brumaire of Louis Napoleon*, writing of the events surrounding the failed revolution of 1848 in France, gives a sardonic and sweeping analysis of how ideology works. To win power for itself the re-volutionary class of capitalism, the bourgeoisie, had to overthrow the feudal order (as it did in France with the Revolution of 1789). Since, 'the tradition of all the dead generations weighs like a nightmare on the brain of the living' (1950, v. 1: 225), the bourgeoisie needed also to win a battle of ideas, and did so by performing two manoeuvres. One was to represent its own sectarian, class interests as universal and of democratic value, the other was to step aside from the religious ideology of the feudal epoch. Both these were achieved through neo-Classicism, reviving the discourses, styles, and outward institutions of the ancient Roman imperialism. At a stroke the bourgeoisie claimed a post-medieval originality for itself *and* aligned itself with a universal ideal comprehending ancient civilisation. In the 'resurrected Romanity' of the French Revolution the bourgeoisie found 'the self-deceptions that they needed' (p. 226). In this example two things come through strongly – that ideology consists of ideas in the service of class interests, that ideology is a gigantic masquerade.

This second issue, the falseness of ideology, has provided another topic for continuing debate. Is ideology simply 'false consciousness', an illusion, albeit one its proponents share in through self-deception, and so may be opposed to the true knowledge objectively obtained by science? If so, what does this 'false consciousness' consist of, since far from sounding like a material effect, it appears to be somehow not real at all? How does ideology gain credence, and what are the mechanisms by which it works?

Ideology as hegemony and subjectivity

In Britain in 1867 the Second Reform Bill was passed, vastly extending the franchise, and in 1870 an act introducing state education. A cynic might say that having got the vote the working class had to be taught who to vote for – in the 1890s Engels observed that many newly enfranchised members of the working class voted Tory, not even for the Liberals. In the twentieth century, with the extraordinary growth of the modern state and the development of parliamentary democracy, the question of whether ideology was 'false consciousness' became ever more crucial.

The Italian Marxist, Antonio Gramsci (see 'Biographies'), addressed these changed circumstances by exploring a concept he borrowed from Lenin, that of hegemony. Enormously impressed by the traditional power of the Catholic Church in Italy to hold allegiance in the hearts and minds of the people, Gramsci theorized that a ruling group, whether of the left or the right, must now govern through a balance of force and persuasion:

> The methodological criterion on which our own study must be based is the following: that the supremacy of a social group manifests itself in two ways, as 'domination' and as 'intellectual and moral leadership'. A social group dominates antagonistic groups, which it tends to 'liquidate', or to subjugate perhaps even by armed force; it leads kindred and allied groups. A social group can, and indeed must, already exercise 'leadership' before winning governmental power (this indeed is one of the principle [sic] conditions for the winning of such power); it subsequently becomes dominant when it exercises power, but even if it holds it firmly in its grasp, it must continue to 'lead' as well.
>
> (1971: 57–8)

Comprehending ideology, institutions and practices (such as education), the concept of hegemony (not represented elsewhere in this Reader) is at once suggestively flexible in detail and, at root, very simple. Essentially it repeats the Chartist aim summed up in the slogan, 'Peaceably if we can, forcibly if we must'. Hegemony specifies ideology as ways a ruling group, bloc or class must rule by winning consent *in conjunction with* the threat of force, the effectiveness of hegemony depending on how rarely force, always present, actually has to be used.

A problem with the notion of hegemony inheres in the question of how exactly one defines consent. For the question of consent is predicated on a conception of the subject: does the subject agree to be led through explicit, active and conscious choice or is a less premeditated and conscious acquiescence or non-resistance sufficient? Enormously influenced by Gramsci, Louis Althusser (see 'Biographies' and Section 2.3) analyses ideology as functioning across a range of state institutions to reproduce subjects who 'work by themselves' and live out their subordination unconsciously.

A false consciousness which reaches far into the subject, even hoping (with Althusser) to include the process of the unconscious, hardly qualifies any more as in any useful sense 'false' or 'conscious'. It also poses acutely the question of where exactly the analysts of ideology stand in relation to what they analyse. In Althusser in principle this is not a difficulty since 'ideological practice' is opposed to 'theoretical practice' (or science) in such a way that the application of theory can know ideology as it does not know itself. But in the writings of Michel Foucault that opposition is seen as untenable: ideology and science combine into a single conceptualization of discursive and social practices as the operation of 'power/knowledge' (see 'Biographies' and Sections 3.3 and 3.4). It would not be an excessive pre-judgement to say that Foucault's procedure has the advantage of making visible the work of ideology at intimately lived levels of human experience previously unnoticed and unchallenged (talking to your doctor about your backache, for instance); but it achieves this at a price, for there now appears to be no absolutely exterior point from which the prevailing and all-pervading operation of power can be made subject to critique so that it may be consciously and explicitly *resisted*.

Now extended to become so all-embracing, the concept of ideology risks vacuity and loss of substantial content. Three other problems compound that difficulty. One is that the concept of ideology, in having to work across so many different cultural discourses, tends to treat each of these as though they were merely transparent vehicles for ideology, tending therefore to ignore the signifier and what is specific in the operation of different signifying practices. Another is that, in the prevailing tradition, the concept of ideology can be accused of ignoring issues of gender or subsuming them in traditionally masculine concerns such as the economy and the outward institutions of political power. And a third, as briefly, is that ideology does not so obviously address the exercise of discursive power in the arenas of empire and race. Since the work of Edward Said on 'Orientalism' (see 'Biographies' and Section 2.4) is directed at a social critique of forms of ideology in just this last area, it has been included in the section on ideology. Overlapping definitions of ideology have come to exceed what is usefully discriminated as ideology, posing questions about the power of particular signifying practices in reproducing conceptions of gender, of race, and indeed of Western culture itself in its continuity from Athens. This is recognized in the present collection by marking out separate sections on subjectivity, on gender and on difference. In one respect, however, these are all concerned with ideology in its particularities and difference.

2.1

Karl Marx
from 'Preface' to
A Contribution to the
Critique of Political Economy
(1859)

The general result at which I arrived and which, once won, served as a guiding thread for my studies, can be briefly formulated as follows: In the social production of their life, men enter into definite relations that are indispensable and independent of their will, relations of production which correspond to a definite stage of development of their material productive forces. The sum total of these relations of production constitutes the economic structure of society, the real foundation, on which rises a legal and political superstructure and to which correspond definite forms of social consciousness. The mode of production of material life conditions the social, political and intellectual life process in general. It is not the consciousness of men that determines their being, but, on the contrary, their social being that determines their consciousness. At a certain stage of their development, the material productive forces of society come in conflict with the existing relations of production, or – what is but a legal expression for the same thing – with the property relations within which they have been at work hitherto. From forms of development of the productive forces these relations turn into their fetters. Then begins an epoch of social revolution. With the change of the economic foundation the entire immense superstructure is more or less rapidly transformed. In considering such transformations a distinction should always be made between the material transformation of the economic conditions of production, which can be determined with the precision of natural science, and the legal, political, religious, aesthetic or philosophic – in short, ideological forms in which men become conscious of this conflict and fight it out. Just as our opinion of an individual is not based on what he thinks of himself, so can we not judge of such a period of transformation by its own consciousness; on the contrary, this consciousness must be explained rather from the contradictions of material life, from the existing conflict between the social productive forces and the relations of production. No social order ever perishes before all the productive forces for which there is room in it have developed; and new, higher relations of production never appear before the material conditions of their existence have matured in the womb of the old society itself. Therefore mankind always sets itself only such tasks as it can solve; since, looking at the matter more closely, it will always be found that the task itself arises only when the material conditions for its solution already exist or are at least in the process of formation. In broad outlines Asiatic, ancient, feudal, and modern bourgeois modes of production can be designated as progressive epochs in the economic formation of society. The bourgeois relations of production are the last antagonistic form of the social process of production – antagonistic not in the sense of individual antagonism, but of one arising from the social conditions of life of the individuals; at the same time the productive forces developing in the womb of bourgeois society create the material conditions for the solution of that antagonism. This social formation brings, therefore, the prehistory of human society to a close.

2.2

Karl Marx and Frederick Engels from *The German Ideology* (1846)

The ruling class and the ruling ideas. How the Hegelian conception of the domination of the spirit in history arose

The ideas of the ruling class are in every epoch the ruling ideas: i.e., the class which is the ruling *material* force of society is at the same time its ruling *intellectual* force. The class which has the means of material production at its disposal, consequently also controls the means of mental production, so that the ideas of those who lack the means of mental production are on the whole subject to it. The ruling ideas are nothing more than the ideal expression of the dominant material relations, the dominant material relations grasped as ideas; hence of the relations which make the one class the ruling one, therefore, the ideas of its dominance. The individuals composing the ruling class possess among other things consciousness, and therefore think. Insofar, therefore, as they rule as a class and determine the extent and compass of an historical epoch, it is self-evident that they do this in its whole range, hence among other things rule also as thinkers, as producers of ideas, and regulate the production and distribution of the ideas of their age: thus their ideas are the ruling ideas of the epoch. For instance, in an age and in a country where royal power, aristocracy and bourgeoisie are contending for domination and where, therefore, domination is shared, the doctrine of the separation of powers proves to be the dominant idea and is expressed as an 'eternal law'.

The division of labour, which we already saw above as one of the chief forces of history up till now, manifests itself also in the ruling class as the division of mental and material labour, so that inside this class one part appears as the thinkers of the class (its active, conceptive ideologists, who make the formation of the illusions of the class about itself their chief source of livelihood), while the others' attitude to these ideas and illusions is more passive and receptive, because they are in reality the active members of this class and have less time to make up illusions and ideas about themselves. Within this class this cleavage can even develop into a certain opposition and hostility between the two parts, but whenever a practical collision occurs in which the class itself is endangered they automatically vanish, in which case there also vanishes the appearance of the ruling ideas being not the ideas of the ruling class and having a power distinct from the power of this class. The existence of revolutionary ideas in a particular period presupposes the existence of a revolutionary class; about the premises of the latter sufficient has already been said above.

If now in considering the course of history we detach the ideas of the ruling class from the ruling class itself and attribute to them an independent existence, if we confine ourselves to saying that these or those ideas were dominant at a given time, without bothering ourselves about the conditions of production and the producers of these ideas, if we thus ignore the individuals and world conditions which are the source of the ideas, then we can say, for instance, that during the time the aristocracy was dominant, the concepts honour, loyalty, etc., were dominant, during the dominance of the bourgeoisie the concepts freedom, equality, etc. The ruling class itself on the whole imagines this to be so. This conception of history, which is common to all historians, particularly since the eighteenth century, will necessarily come up against the phenomenon that ever more abstract ideas hold sway, i.e., ideas which increasingly take on the form of universality. For each new class which puts itself in the place of one ruling before it is compelled, merely in order to carry through its aim, to present its interest as the common interest of all the members of society, that is, expressed in ideal form: it has to give its ideas the form of universality, and present them as the only rational, universally valid ones. The class making a revolution comes forward from the very start, if only because it is opposed to a *class*, not as a class but as the representative of the whole of society, as the whole mass of society confronting the one ruling class.[1] It can do this because initially its interest really is as yet mostly connected with the common interest of all other non-ruling classes, because under the pressure of hitherto existing conditions its interest has not yet been able to develop as the particular interest of a particular class. Its victory, therefore, benefits also many individuals of other classes which are not winning a dominant position, but only insofar as it now enables these individuals to raise themselves into the ruling class. When the French bourgeoisie overthrew the rule of the aristocracy, it thereby made it possible for many proletarians to raise themselves above the proletariat, but only insofar as they became bourgeois. Every new class, therefore, achieves domination only on a broader basis than that of the class ruling previously; on the other hand the opposition of the non-ruling class to the new ruling class then develops all the more sharply and profoundly. Both these things determine the fact that the struggle to be waged against this new ruling class, in its turn, has as its aim a more decisive and more radical negation of the previous conditions of society than all previous classes which sought to rule could have.

This whole appearance, that the rule of a certain class is only the rule of certain ideas, comes to a natural end, of course, as soon as class rule in general ceases to be the form in which society is organised, that is to say, as soon as it is no longer necessary to represent a particular interest as general or the 'general interest' as ruling.

Note

1 Universality corresponds to: (1) the class versus the estate; (2) the competition, world intercourse etc.; (3) the great numerical strength of the ruling class; (4) the illusion of the *common* interests (in the beginning this illusion is true); (5) the delusion of the ideologists and the division of labour.

2.3

Louis Althusser from 'Ideology and Ideological State Apparatuses' (1970)

What are the ideological State apparatuses (ISAs)?

They must not be confused with the (repressive) State apparatus. Remember that in Marxist theory, the State Apparatus (SA) contains: the Government, the Administration, the Army, the Police, the Courts, the Prisons, etc., which constitute what I shall in future call the Repressive State Apparatus. Repressive suggests that the State Apparatus in question 'functions by violence' – at least ultimately (since repression, e.g. administrative repression, may take non-physical forms).

I shall call Ideological State Apparatuses a certain number of realities which present themselves to the immediate observer in the form of distinct and specialized institutions. I propose an empirical list of these which obviously have to be examined in detail, tested, corrected and reorganized. With all the reservations implied by this requirement, we can for the moment regard the following in situations as Ideological State Apparatuses (the order in which I have listed them has no particular significance):

- the religious ISA (the system of the different Churches),
- the educational ISA (the system of the different public and private 'Schools'),
- the family ISA,[1]
- the legal ISA,[2]
- the political ISA (the political system, including the different Parties),
- the trade-union ISA,
- the communications ISA (press, radio and television, etc.),
- the cultural ISA (Literature, the Arts, sports, etc.).

I have said that the ISAs must not be confused with the (Repressive) State Apparatus. What constitutes the difference?

As a first moment, it is clear that while there is *one* (Repressive) State Apparatus, there is a *plurality* of Ideological State Apparatuses. Even presupposing that it exists, the unity that constitutes this plurality of ISAs as a body is not immediately visible.

As a second moment, it is clear that whereas the – unified – (Repressive) State Apparatus belongs entirely to the *public* domain, much the larger part of the Ideological State Apparatuses (in their apparent dispersion) are part, on the contrary, of the *private* domain. Churches, Parties, Trade Unions, families, some schools, most newspapers, cultural ventures, etc., etc., are private.

We can ignore the first observation for the moment. But someone is bound to question the second, asking me by what right I regard as Ideological *State* Apparatuses, institutions which for the most part do not possess public status, but are quite simply *private* institutions. As a conscious Marxist, Gramsci already forestalled this objection in one sentence. The distinction between the public and the private is a distinction internal to bourgeois law, and valid in the (subordinate) domains in which bourgeois law exercises its 'authority'. The domain of the State escapes it because the latter is 'above the law': the State, which is the State of the ruling class is neither public nor private; on the contrary, it is the precondition for any distinction between public and private. The same thing can be said from the starting-point of our State Ideological Apparatuses. It is unimportant whether the institutions in which they are realized are 'public' or 'private'. What matters is how they function. Private institutions can perfectly well 'function' as Ideological State Apparatuses. A reasonably thorough analysis of any one of the ISAs proves it.

But now for what is essential. What distinguishes the ISAs from the (Repressive) State Apparatus is the following basic difference: the Repressive State Apparatus functions 'by violence', whereas the Ideological State Apparatuses *function 'by ideology'*.

I can clarify matters by correcting this distinction. I shall say rather that every State Apparatus, whether Repressive or Ideological, 'functions' both by violence and by ideology, but with one very important distinction which makes it imperative not to confuse the Ideological State Apparatuses with the (Repressive) State Apparatus.

This is the fact that the (Repressive) State Apparatus functions massively and predominantly *by repression* (including physical repression), while functioning secondarily by ideology. (There is no such thing as a purely repressive apparatus.) For example, the Army and the Police also function by ideology both to ensure their own cohesion and reproduction, and in the 'values' they propound externally.

In the same way, but inversely, it is essential to say that for their part the Ideological State Apparatuses function massively and predominantly *by ideology*, but they also function secondarily by repression, even if ultimately, but only ultimately, this is very attenuated and concealed, even symbolic. (There is no such thing as purely ideological apparatus.) Thus Schools and Churches use suitable methods of punishment, expulsion, selection, etc., to 'discipline' not only their shepherds, but also their flocks. The same is true of the Family . . . The same is true of the cultural IS Apparatus (censorship, among other things), etc.

Ideology is a 'representation' of the imaginary relationship of individuals to their real conditions of existence

In order to approach my central thesis on the structure and functioning of ideology, I shall first present two theses, one negative, the other positive. The first concerns the object which is 'represented' in the imaginary form of ideology, the second concerns the materiality of ideology.

THESIS I   Ideology represents the imaginary relationship of individuals to their real conditions of existence.

We commonly call religious ideology, ethical ideology, legal ideology, political ideology, etc., so many 'world outlooks'. Of course, assuming that we do not live one of these ideologies as the truth (e.g. 'believe' in God, Duty, Justice, etc. . . .), we admit that the ideology we are discussing from a critical point of view, examining it as the ethnologist examines the myths of a 'primitive society', that these 'world outlooks' are largely imaginary, i.e. do not 'correspond to reality'.

However, while admitting that they do not correspond to reality, i.e. that they constitute an illusion, we admit that they do make allusion to reality, and that they need only be 'interpreted' to discover the reality of the world behind their imaginary representation of that world (ideology = *illusion/allusion*).

Now I can return to a thesis which I have already advanced: it is not their real conditions of existence, their real world, that 'men' 'represent to themselves' in ideology, but above all it is their relation to those conditions of existence which is represented to them there. It is this relation which is at the centre of every ideological, i.e. imaginary, representation of the real world. It is this relation that contains the 'cause' which has to explain the imaginary distortion of the ideological representation of the real world. Or rather, to leave aside the language of causality it is necessary to advance the thesis that it is the *imaginary nature of this relation* which underlies all the imaginary distortion that we can observe (if we do not live in its truth) in all ideology.

To speak in a Marxist language, if it is true that the representation of the real conditions of existence of the individuals occupying the posts of agents of production, exploitation, repression, ideologization and scientific practice, does in the last analysis arise from the relations of production, and from relations deriving from the relations of production, we can say the following: all ideology represents in its necessarily imaginary distortion not the existing relations of production (and the other relations that derive from them), but above all the (imaginary) relationship of individuals to the relations of production and the relations that derive from them. What is represented in ideology is therefore not the system of the real relations which govern the existence of individuals, but the imaginary relation of those individuals to the real relations in which they live.

If this is the case, the question of the 'cause' of the imaginary distortion of the real relations in ideology disappears and must be replaced by a different question: why is the representation given to individuals of their (individual) relation to the social relations which govern their conditions of existence and their collective and individual life necessarily an imaginary relation? And what is the nature of this imaginariness? Posed in this way, the question explodes the solution by a 'clique',[3] by a group of individuals (Priests or Despots) who are the authors of the great ideological mystification, just as it explodes the solution by the alienated character of the real world. We shall see why later in my exposition. For the moment I shall go no further.

THESIS II: Ideology has a material existence.

I have already touched on this thesis by saying that the 'ideas' or 'representations', etc., which seem to make up ideology do not have an ideal (*idéale* or *idéelle*) or spiritual existence, but a material existence. I even suggested that the ideal (*idéale*, *idéelle*) and spiritual existence of 'ideas' arises exclusively in an ideology of the 'idea' and of ideology, and let me add, in an ideology of what seems to have 'founded' this conception since the emergence of the sciences, i.e. what the practicioners of the sciences represent to themselves in their spontaneous ideology as 'ideas', true or false. Of course, presented in affirmative form, this thesis is unproven. I simply ask that the reader be favourably disposed towards it, say, in the name of materialism. A long series of arguments would be necessary to prove it.

This hypothetical thesis of the not spiritual but material existence of 'ideas' or other 'representations' is indeed necessary if we are to advance in our analysis of the nature of ideology. Or rather, it is merely useful to us in order the better to reveal what every at all serious analysis of any ideology will immediately and empirically show to every observer, however critical.

While discussing the ideological State apparatuses and their practices, I said that each of them was the realization of an ideology (the unity of these different regional ideologies – religious, ethical, legal, political, aesthetic, etc. – being assured by their subjection to the ruling ideology). I now return to this thesis: an ideology always exists in an apparatus, and its practice, or practices. This existence is material.

Of course, the material existence of the ideology in an apparatus and its practices does not have the same modality as the material existence of a paving-stone or a rifle. But, at the risk of being taken for a Neo-Aristotelian (NB Marx had a very high regard for Aristotle), I shall say that 'matter is discussed in many senses', or rather that it exists in different modalities, all rooted in the last instance in 'physical' matter.

And I shall immediately set down two conjoint theses:

1 there is no practice except by and in an ideology;
2 there is no ideology except by the subject and for subjects.

I can now come to my central thesis.

Ideology interpellates individuals as subjects

This thesis is simply a matter of making my last proposition explicit: there is no ideology except by the subject and for subjects. Meaning, there is no ideology except for concrete subjects, and this destination for ideology is only made possible by the subject: meaning, *by the category of the subject* and its functioning.

By this I mean that, even if it only appears under this name (the subject) with the rise of bourgeois ideology, above all with the rise of legal ideology,[4] the category of the subject (which may function under other names: e.g., as the soul in Plato, as God, etc.) is the constitutive category of all ideology, whatever its determination (regional or class) and whatever its historical date – since ideology has no history.

I say: the category of the subject is constitutive of all ideology, but at the same time and immediately I add that *the category of the subject is only constitutive of all ideology insofar as all ideology has the function (which defines it) of 'constituting' concrete individuals as subjects.* In the interaction of this double constitution exists the functioning of all ideology, ideology being nothing but its functioning in the material forms of existence of that functioning.

In order to grasp what follows, it is essential to realize that both he who is writing these lines and the reader who reads them are themselves subjects, and therefore ideological subjects (a tautological proposition), i.e. that the author and the reader of these lines both live 'spontaneously' or 'naturally' in ideology in the sense in which I have said that 'man is an ideological animal by nature'.

That the author, insofar as he writes the lines of a discourse which claims to be scientific, is completely absent as a 'subject' from 'his' scientific discourse (for all scientific discourse is by definition a subject-less discourse, there is no 'Subject of science' except in an ideology of science) is a different question which I shall leave on one side for the moment.

As St Paul admirably put it, it is in the 'Logos', meaning in ideology, that we 'live, move and have our being'. It follows that, for you and for me, the category of the subject is a primary 'obviousness' (obviousnesses are always primary): it is clear that you and I are subjects (free, ethical, etc. . . . .). Like all obviousnesses, including those that make a word 'name a thing' or 'have a meaning' (therefore including the obviousness of the 'transparency' of language), the 'obviousness' that you and I are subjects – and that that does not cause any problems – is an ideological effect, the elementary ideological effect.[5] It is indeed a peculiarity of ideology that it imposes (without appearing to do so, since these are 'obviousnesses') obviousnesses as obviousnesses, which we cannot *fail to recognize* and before which we have the inevitable and natural reaction of crying out (aloud or in the 'still, small voice of conscience'): 'That's obvious! That's right! That's true!'

At work in this reaction is the ideological *recognition* function which is one of the two functions of ideology as such (its inverse being the function of *misrecognition* – *méconnaissance*).

To take a highly 'concrete' example, we all have friends who, when they knock on our door and we ask, through the door, the question 'Who's there?', answer (since 'it's obvious') 'It's me'. And we recognize that 'it is him', or 'her'. We open the door, and 'it's true, it really was she who was there'. To take another example, when we recognize somebody of our (previous) acquaintance ((*re*)-*connaissance*) in the street, we show him that we have recognized him (and have recognized that he has recognized us) by saying to him 'Hello, my friend', and shaking his hand (a material ritual practice of ideological recognition in everyday life – in France, at least; elsewhere, there are other rituals).

In this preliminary remark and these concrete illustrations, I only wish to point out that you and I are *always already* subjects, and as such constantly practice the rituals of ideological recognition, which guarantee for us that we are indeed concrete, individual, distinguishable and (naturally) irreplaceable subjects. The writing I am currently executing and the reading you are currently[6] performing are also in this respect rituals of ideological recognition, including the 'obviousness' with which the 'truth' or 'error' of my reflections may impose itself on you.

But to recognize that we are subjects and that we function in the practical rituals of the most elementary everyday life (the hand-shake, the fact of calling you by your name, the fact of knowing, even if I do not know what it is, that you 'have' a name of your own, which means that you are recognized as a unique subject, etc.) – this recognition only gives us the 'consciousness' of our incessant (eternal) practice of ideological recognition – its consciousness, i.e. its *recognition* – but in no sense does it give us the (scientific) *knowledge* of the mechanism of this recognition. Now it is this knowledge that we have to reach, if you will, while speaking in ideology, and from within ideology we have to outline a discourse which tries to break with ideology, in order to dare to be the beginning of a scientific (i.e. subjectless) discourse on ideology.

Thus in order to represent why the category of the 'subject' is constitutive of ideology, which only exists by constituting concrete subjects as subjects, I shall employ a special mode of exposition: 'concrete' enough to be recognized, but abstract enough to be thinkable and thought, giving rise to a knowledge.

As a first formulation I shall say: *all ideology hails or interpellates concrete individuals as concrete subjects*, by the functioning of the category of the subject.

This is a proposition which entails that we distinguish for the moment between concrete individuals on the one hand and concrete subjects on the other, although at this level concrete subjects only exist insofar as they are supported by a concrete individual.

I shall then suggest that ideology 'acts' or 'functions' in such a way that it 'recruits' subjects among the individuals (it recruits them all), or 'transforms' the individuals into subjects (it transforms them all) by that very precise operation which I have called *interpellation* or hailing, and which can be imagined along the lines of the most commonplace everyday police (or other) hailing: 'Hey, you there!'[7]

Assuming that the theoretical scene I have imagined takes place in the street, the hailed individual will turn round. By this mere one-hundred-and-eighty-degree physical conversion, he becomes a *subject*. Why? Because he has recognized that the hail was 'really' addressed to him, and that 'it was *really him* who was hailed' (and not someone else). Experience shows that the practical telecommunication of hailings is such that they hardly ever miss their man: verbal call or whistle, the one hailed always recognizes that it is really him who is being hailed. And yet it is a strange phenomenon, and one which cannot be explained solely by 'guilt feelings', despite the large numbers who 'have something on their consciences'.

Naturally for the convenience and clarity of my little theoretical theatre I have had to present things in the form of a sequence, with a before and an after, and thus in the form of a temporal succession. There are individuals walking along. Somewhere (usually behind them) the hail rings out: 'Hey, you there!' One individual (nine times out of ten it is the right one) turns round, believing/suspecting/ knowing that it is for him, i.e. recognizing that 'it really is he' who is meant by the hailing. But in reality these things happen without any succession. The existence of ideology and the hailing or interpellation of individuals as subjects are one and the same thing.

I might add: what thus seems to take place outside ideology (to be precise, in the street), in reality takes place in ideology. What really takes place in ideology seems therefore to take place outside it. That is why those who are in ideology believe themselves by definition outside ideology: one of the effects of ideology is the practical *denegation* of the ideological character of ideology by ideology: ideology never says, 'I am ideological'. It is necessary to be outside ideology, i.e. in scientific knowledge, to be able to say: I am in ideology (a quite exceptional case) or (the general case): I was in ideology. As is well known, the accusation of being in ideology only applies to others, never to oneself (unless one is really a Spinozist or a Marxist, which, in this matter, is to be exactly the same thing). Which amounts to saying that ideology *has no outside* (for itself), but at the same time *that it is nothing but outside* (for science and reality).

Let me summarize what we have discovered about ideology in general. The duplicate mirror-structure of ideology ensures simultaneously:

1 the interpellation of 'individuals' as subjects;
2 their subjection to the Subject;
3 the mutual recognition of subjects and Subject, the subjects' recognition of each other, and finally the subject's recognition of himself;[8]
4 the absolute guarantee that everything really is so, and that on condition that the subjects recognize what they are and behave accordingly, everything will be all right: Amen – 'So be it'.

Result: caught in this quadruple system of interpellation as subjects, of subjection to the Subject, of universal recognition and of absolute guarantee, the subjects 'work', they 'work by themselves' in the vast majority of cases, with the exception of the 'bad subjects' who on occasion provoke the intervention of one of the detachments of the (repressive) State apparatus. But the vast majority of (good) subjects work all right 'all by themselves', i.e. by ideology (whose concrete forms are realized in the Ideological State Apparatuses). They are inserted into practices governed by the rituals of the ISAs. They 'recognize' the existing state of affairs (*das Bestehende*), that 'it really is true that it is so and not otherwise', and that they must be obedient to God, to their conscience, to the priest, to de Gaulle, to the boss, to the engineer, that thou shalt 'love thy neighbour as thyself', etc. Their concrete, material behaviour is simply the inscription in life of the admirable words of the prayer: '*Amen – So be it*'.

Yes, the subjects 'work by themselves'. The whole mystery of this effect lies in the first two moments of the quadruple system I have just discussed, or, if you prefer, in the ambiguity of the term *subject*. In the ordinary use of the term, subject in fact means: (1) a free subjectivity, a centre of initiatives, author of and responsible for its actions; (2) a subjected being, who submits to a higher authority, and is therefore stripped of all freedom except that of freely accepting his submission. This last note gives us the meaning of this ambiguity, which is merely a reflection of the effect which produces it: the individual *is interpellated as a (free) subject in order that he shall submit freely to the commandments of the Subject, i.e. in order that he shall (freely) accept his subjection,* i.e. in order that he shall make the gestures and actions of his subjection 'all by himself'. *There are no subjects except by and for their subjection.* That is why they 'work all by themselves'.

'*So be it!* . . .' This phrase which registers the effect to be obtained proves that it is not 'naturally' so ('naturally': outside the prayer, i.e. outside the ideological intervention). This phrase proves that it *has* to be so if things are to be what they must be, and let us let the words slip: if the reproduction of the relations of production is to be assured, even in the processes of production and circulation, every day, in the 'consciousness', i.e. in the attitudes of the individual-subjects occupying the posts which the sociotechnical division of labour assigns to them in production, exploitation, repression, ideologization, scientific practice, etc. Indeed, what is really in question in this mechanism of the mirror recognition of the Subject and of the individuals interpellated as subjects, and of the guarantee given by the Subject to the subjects if they freely accept their subjection to the Subject's 'commandments'? The reality in question in this mechanism, the reality which is necessarily *ignored* (*méconnue*) in the very forms of recognition (ideology = misrecognition/ignorance) is indeed, in the last resort, the reproduction of the relations of production and of the relations deriving from them.

January–April 1969

Notes

1 The family obviously has other 'functions' than that of an ISA. It intervenes in the reproduction of labour power. In different modes of production it is the unit of production and/or the unit of consumption.
2 The 'Law' belongs both to the (Repressive) State Apparatuses and to the system of the ISAs.
3 I use this very modern term deliberately. For even in Communist circles, unfortunately, it is a commonplace to 'explain' some political deviation (left or right opportunism) by the action of a 'clique'.
4 Which borrowed the legal category of 'subject in law' to make an ideological notion: man is by nature a subject.
5 Linguists and those who appeal to linguistics for various purposes often run up against difficulties which arise because they ignore the action of the ideological effects in all discourses – including even scientific discourse.
6 NB This double 'currently' is one more proof of the fact that ideology is 'eternal',

since these two 'currentlys' are separated by an indefinite interval; I am writing these lines on April 1969, you may read them at any subsequent time.

7 Hailing as an everyday practice subject to a precise ritual takes a quite 'special' form in the policeman's practice of 'hailing' which concerns the hailing of 'suspects'.

8 Hegel is (unknowingly) an admirable 'theoretician' of ideology insofar as he is a 'theoretician' of Universal Recognition who unfortunately ends up in the ideology of Absolute Knowledge. Feurbach is an astonishing 'theoretician' of the mirror connection, who unfortunately ends up in the ideology of the Human Essence. To find the material with which to construct a theory of the guarantee, we must turn to Spinoza.

2.4

Edward Said
from *Orientalism* (1978)

My principal operating assumptions were – and continue to be – that fields of learning, as much as the works of even the most eccentric artist, are constrained and acted upon by society, by cultural traditions, by worldly circumstance, and by stabilizing influences like schools, libraries, and governments; moreover, that both learned and imaginative writing are never free, but are limited in their imagery, assumptions, and intentions; and finally, that the advances made by a 'science' like Orientalism in its academic form are less objectively true than we often like to think. In short, my study hitherto has tried to describe the *economy* that makes Orientalism a coherent subject matter, even while allowing that as an idea, concept, or image the word *Orient* has a considerable and interesting cultural resonance in the West.

I realize that such assumptions are not without their controversial side. Most of us assume in a general way that learning and scholarship move forward; they get better, we feel, as time passes and as more information is accumulated, methods are refined, and later generations of scholars improve upon earlier ones. In addition, we entertain a mythology of creation, in which it is believed that artistic genius, an original talent, or a powerful intellect can leap beyond the confines of its own time and place in order to put before the world a new work. It would be pointless to deny that such ideas as these carry some truth. Nevertheless the possibilities for work present in the culture to a great and original mind are never unlimited, just as it is also true that a great talent has a very healthy respect for what others have done before it and for what the field already contains. The work of predecessors, the institutional life of a scholarly field, the collective nature of any learned enterprise: these, to say nothing of economic and social circumstances, tend to diminish the effects of the individual scholar's production. A field like Orientalism has a cumulative and corporate identity, one that is particularly strong given its associations with traditional learning (the classics, the Bible, philology), public institutions (governments, trading companies, geographical societies, universities), and generically determined writing (travel books, books of exploration, fantasy, exotic description). The result for Orientalism has been a sort of consensus: certain things, certain types of statement, certain types of work have seemed for the Orientalist correct. He has built his work and research upon them, and they in turn have pressed hard upon new writers and scholars. Orientalism can thus be regarded as a manner of regularized (or Orientalized) writing, vision, and study, dominated by imperatives, perspectives, and ideological biases ostensibly suited to the Orient. The Orient is taught, researched, administered, and pronounced upon in certain discrete ways.

The Orient that appears in Orientalism, then, is a system of representations framed by a whole set of forces that brought the Orient into Western learning, Western consciousness, and later, Western empire. If this definition of Orientalism seems more political than not, that is simply because I think Orientalism was itself a product of certain political forces and activities. Orientalism is a school of interpretation whose material happens to be the Orient, its civilizations, peoples, and localities. Its objective discoveries – the work of innumerable devoted scholars who edited texts and translated them, codified grammars, wrote dictionaries, reconstructed dead epochs, produced positivistically verifiable learning – are and always have been conditioned by the fact that its truths, like any truths delivered by language, are embodied in language, and what is the truth of language, Nietzsche once said, but

> a mobile army of metaphors, metonyms, and anthropomorphisms – in short, a sum of human relations, which have been enhanced, transposed, and embellished poetically and rhetorically, and which after long use seem firm, canonical, and obligatory to a people: truths are illusions about which one has forgotten that this is what they are.[1]

Perhaps such a view as Nietzsche's will strike us as too nihilistic, but at least it will draw attention to the fact that so far as it existed in the West's awareness, the Orient was a word which later accrued to it a wide field of meanings, associations, and connotations, and that these did not necessarily refer to the real Orient but to the field surrounding the word.

Thus Orientalism is not only a positive doctrine about the Orient that exists at any one time in the West; it is also an influential academic tradition (when one refers to an academic specialist who is called an Orientalist), as well as an area of concern defined by travelers, commercial enterprises, governments, military expeditions, readers of novels and accounts of exotic adventure, natural historians, and pilgrims to whom the Orient is a specific kind of knowledge about specific places, peoples, and civilizations. For the Orient idioms became frequent, and these idioms took firm hold in European discourse. Beneath the idioms there was a layer of doctrine about the Orient; this doctrine was fashioned out of the experiences of many Europeans, all of them converging upon such essential aspects of the Orient as the Oriental character, Oriental despotism, Oriental sensuality, and the like. For any European during the nineteenth century – and I think one can say this almost without qualification – Orientalism was such a system of truths, truths in Nietzsche's sense of the word. It is therefore correct that every European, in what he could say about the Orient, was consequently a racist, an imperialist, and almost totally ethnocentric. Some of the immediate sting will be taken out of these labels if we recall additionally that human societies, at least the more advanced cultures, have rarely offered the individual anything but imperialism, racism, and ethnocentrism for dealing with 'other' cultures. So orientalism aided and was aided by general cultural pressures that tended to make more rigid the sense of difference between the European and Asiatic parts of the world. My contention is that Orientalism is fundamentally a political doctrine willed over the Orient because the Orient was weaker than the West, which elided the Orient's difference with its weakness.

Style, expertise, vision: Orientalism's worldliness

As he appears in several poems, in novels like *Kim*, and in too many catchphrases to be an ironic fiction, Kipling's White Man, as an idea, a persona, a style of being, seems to have served many Britishers while they were abroad. The actual color of their skin set them off dramatically and reassuringly from the sea of natives, but for the Britisher who circulated amongst Indians, Africans, or Arabs there was also the certain knowledge that he belonged to, and could draw upon the empirical and spiritual reserves of, a long tradition of executive responsibility towards the colored races. It was of this tradition, its glories and difficulties, that Kipling wrote when he celebrated the 'road' taken by White Men in the colonies:

> Now, this is the road that the White Men tread
> When they go to clean a land –
> Iron underfoot and the vine overhead
> And the deep on either hand.
> We have trod that road – and a wet and windy road –
> Our chosen star for guide.
> Oh, well for the world when the White Men tread
> Their highway side by side![2]

'Cleaning a land' is best done by White Men in delicate concert with each other, an allusion to the present dangers of European rivalry in the colonies; for failing in the attempt to coordinate policy, Kipling's White Men are quite prepared to go to war: 'Freedom for ourselves and freedom for our sons/ And, failing freedom, War.' Behind the White Man's mask of amiable leadership there is always the express willingness to use force, to kill and be killed. What dignifies his mission is some sense of intellectual dedication; he is a White Man, but not for mere profit, since his 'chosen star' presumably sits far above earthly gain. Certainly many White Men often wondered what it was they fought for on that 'wet and windy road,' and certainly a great number of them must have been puzzled as to how the color of their skins gave them superior ontological status plus great power over much of the inhabited world. Yet in the end, being a White Man, for Kipling and for those whose perceptions and rhetoric he influenced, was a self-confirming business. One became a White Man because one *was* a White Man; more important, 'drinking that cup,' living that unalterable destiny in 'the White Man's day,' left one little time for idle speculation on origins, causes, historical logic.

Being a White Man was therefore an idea and a reality. It involved a reasoned position towards both the white and the non-white worlds. It meant – in the colonies – speaking in a certain way, behaving according to a code of regulations, and even feeling certain things and not others. It meant specific judgments, evaluations, gestures. It was a form of authority before which nonwhites, and even whites themselves, were expected to bend. In the institutional forms it took (colonial governments, consular corps, commercial establishments) it was an agency for the expression, diffusion, and implementation of policy towards the world, and within this agency, although a certain personal latitude was allowed, the impersonal communal idea of being a White Man ruled. Being a White Man, in short, was a very concrete manner of being-in-the-world, a way of taking hold of reality, language, and thought. It made a specific style possible.

Kipling himself could not merely have happened; the same is true of his White Man. Such ideas and their authors emerge out of complex historical and cultural circumstances, at least two of which have much in common with the history of Orientalism in the nineteenth century. One of them is the culturally sanctioned habit of deploying large generalizations by which reality is divided into various collectives: languages, races, types, colors, mentalities, each category being not so much a neutral designation as an evaluative interpretation. Underlying these categories is the rigidly binomial opposition of 'ours' and 'theirs,' with the former always encroaching upon the latter (even to the point of making 'theirs' exclusively a function of 'ours'). This opposition was reinforced not only by anthropology, linguistics, and history but also, of course, by the Darwinian theses on survival and natural selection, and – no less decisive – by the rhetoric of high cultural humanism. What gave writers like Renan and Arnold the right to generalities about race was the official character of their formed cultural literacy. 'Our' values were (let us say) liberal, humane, correct; they were supported by the tradition of belles-lettres, informed scholarship, rational inquiry; as Europeans (and white men) 'we' shared in them every time their virtues were extolled. Nevertheless, the human partnerships formed by reiterated cultural values excluded as much as they included. For every idea about 'our' art spoken for by Arnold, Ruskin, Mill, Newman, Carlyle, Renan, Gobineau, or Comte, another link in the chain binding 'us' together was formed while another outsider was banished. Even if this is always the result of such rhetoric, wherever and whenever it occurs, we must remember that for nineteenth-century Europe an imposing edifice of learning and culture was built, so to speak, in the face of actual outsiders (the colonies, the poor, the delinquent), whose role in the culture was to give definition to what *they* were constitutionally unsuited for.[3]

The other circumstance common to the creation of the White Man and Orientalism is the 'field' commanded by each, as well as the sense that such a field entails peculiar modes, even rituals, of behavior, learning, and possession. Only an Occidental could speak of Orientals, for example, just as it was the White Man who could designate and name the coloreds, or nonwhites. Every statement made by Orientalists or White Men (who were usually interchangeable) conveyed a sense of the irreducible distance separating white from colored, or Occidental from Oriental; moreover, behind each statement there resonated the tradition of experience, learning, and education that kept the Oriental-colored to his position of *object studied by the Occidental-white*, instead of vice versa. Where one was in a position of power – as Cromer was, for example – the Oriental belonged to the system of rule whose principle was simply to make sure that no Oriental was ever allowed to be independent and rule himself. The premise there was that since the Orientals were ignorant of self-government, they had better be kept that way for their own good.

Since the White Man, like the Orientalist, lived very close to the line of tension keeping the coloreds at bay, he felt it incumbent on him readily to define and redefine the domain he surveyed. Passages of narrative description regularly alternate with passages of rearticulated definition and judgment that disrupt the narrative; this is a characteristic style of the writing produced by Oriental experts who operated using Kipling's White Man as a mask. Here is T. E. Lawrence, writing to V. W. Richards in 1918.

> ... the Arab appealed to my imagination. It is the old, old civilisation, which has refined itself clear of household gods, and half the trappings which ours hastens to assume. The gospel of bareness in materials is a good one, and it involves apparently a sort of moral bareness too. They think for the moment, and endeavour to slip through life without turning corners or climbing hills. In part it is a mental and moral fatigue, a race trained out, and to avoid difficulties they have to jettison so much that we think honorable and grave: and yet without in any way sharing their point of view, I think I can understand it enough to look at myself and other foreigners from their direction, and without condemning it. I know I am a stranger to them, and always will be; but I cannot believe them worse, any more than I could change to their ways.[4]

A similar perspective, however different the subject under discussion may seem to be, is found in these remarks by Gertrude Bell:

> How many thousand years this state of things has lasted [namely, that Arabs live in 'a state of war'], those who shall read the earliest records of the inner desert will tell us, for it goes back to the first of them, but in all the centuries the Arab has bought no wisdom from experience. He is never safe, and yet he behaves as though security were his daily bread.[5]

To which, as a gloss, we should add her further observation, this time about life in Damascus:

I begin to see dimly what the civilisation of a great Eastern city means, how they live, what they think; and I have got on to terms with them. I believe the fact of my being English is a great help . . . We have gone up in the world since five years ago. The difference is very marked. I think it is due to the success of our government in Egypt to a great extent . . . The defeat of Russia stands for a great deal, and my impression is that the vigorous policy of Lord Curzon in the Persian Gulf and on the India frontier stands for a great deal more. No one who does not know the East can realise how it all hangs together. It is scarcely an exaggeration to say that if the English mission had been turned back from the gates of Kabul, the English tourist would be frowned upon in the streets of Damascus.[6]

In such statements as these, we note immediately that 'the Arab' or 'Arabs' have an aura of apartness, definiteness, and collective self-consistency such as to wipe out any traces of individual Arabs with narratable life histories. What appealed to Lawrence's imagination was the clarity of the Arab, both as an image and as a supposed philosophy (or attitude) towards life: in both cases what Lawrence fastens on is the Arab as if seen from the cleansing perspective of one not an Arab, and one for whom such un-self-conscious primitive simplicity as the Arab possesses is something defined by the observer, in this case the White Man. Yet Arab refinement, which in its essentials corresponds to Yeats's visions of Byzantium where

> Flames that no faggot feeds, flint nor steel has lit,
> Nor storm disturbs, flames begotten of flame,
> Where blood-begotten spirits come
> And all complexities of fury leave[7]

is associated with Arab perdurability, as if the Arab had not been subject to the ordinary processes of history. Paradoxically, the Arab seems to Lawrence to have exhausted himself in his very temporal persistence. The enormous age of Arab civilization has thus served to refine the Arab down to his quintessential attributes, and to tire him out morally in the process. What we are left with is Bell's Arab: centuries of experience and no wisdom. As a collective entity, then, the Arab accumulates no existential or even semantical thickness. He remains the same, except for the exhausting refinements mentioned by Lawrence, from one end to the other of 'the records of the inner desert.' We are to assume that if *an* Arab feels joy, if he is sad at the death of his child or parent, if he has a sense of the injustices of political tyranny, then those experiences are necessarily subordinate to the sheer, unadorned, and persistent fact of being an Arab.

The primitiveness of such a state exists simultaneously on at least two levels: one, *in the definition*, which is reductive; and two (according to Lawrence and Bell), *in reality*. This absolute coincidence was itself no simple coincidence. For one, it could only have been made from the outside by virtue of a vocabulary and epistemological instruments designed both to get to the heart of things and to avoid the distractions of accident, circumstance, or experience. For another, the coincidence was a fact uniquely the result of method, tradition, and politics all working together. Each in a sense oblit-erated the distinctions between the type – *the* Oriental, *the* Semite, *the* Arab, *the* Orient – and ordinary human reality, Yeats's 'uncontrollable mystery on the bestial floor,' in which all human beings live. The scholarly investigator took a type marked 'Oriental' for the same thing as any individual Oriental he might encounter. Years of tradition had encrusted discourse about such matters as the Semitic or Oriental spirit with some legitimacy. And political good sense taught, in Bell's marvelous phrase, that in the East 'it all hangs together.' Primitiveness therefore inhered in the Orient, *was* the Orient, an idea to which anyone dealing with or writing about the Orient had to return, as if to a touchstone outlasting time or experience.

Notes

1 Friedrich Nietzsche, 'On Truth and lie in an extra-moral sense,' in *The Portable Nietzsche*, ed. and trans. Walter Kaufmann (New York: Viking Press, 1954), pp. 46–7.
2 Rudyard Kipling, *Verse* (Garden City, N.Y.: Doubleday and Co., 1954), p. 280.
3 The themes of exclusion and confinement in nineteenth-century culture have played an important role in Michel Foucault's work, most recently in his *Discipline and Punish: The Birth of the Prison* (New York: Pantheon Books, 1977), and *The History of Sexuality, Volume 1: An Introduction* (New York: Pantheon Books, 1978).
4 *The Letters of T.E. Lawrence*, ed. David Garnett (1938; reprint ed., London: Spring Books, 1964), p. 244.
5 Gertrude Bell, *The Desert and the Sown* (London: William Heinemann, 1907), p. 244.
6 Gertrude Bell, *From Her Personal Papers, 1889–1914*, ed. Elizabeth Burgoyne (London: Ernest Benn, 1958), p. 204.
7 William Butler Yeats, 'Byzantium', *The Collected Poems* (New York: Macmillan and Co., 1959), p. 244.

Section three

SUBJECTIVITY

Introduction

The sign is always in address to someone. When Descartes proclaimed 'I think, therefore I am', he was drawing upon the humanist notion that identity and being are mutually dependent factors of individual existence. Common sense tells us that human nature determines identity, that as human beings we are the authors of all that we think and speak, and that as such we shape the world around us and the knowledges which structure that world. Common sense, then, assumes that the nature of human 'being' is given in some way – that it exists *prior* to language simply to label the world of its own experience. Within this framework, the human individual is conceived as a unified centre of control from which meaning emanates.

Against this humanist notion, the concept of subjectivity decentres the individual by problematizing the simplistic relationship between language and the individual which common sense presumes. It replaces human nature with concepts of history, society and culture as determining factors in the *construction* of individual identity, and destabilizes the coherence of that identity by making it an *effect* rather than simply an origin of linguistic practice. Instead of being confirmed by recourse to a universalizing principle, 'humanity' (which then in turn confirms the world which surrounds it), the subject is seen as *made* and so open to transformation. In other words, the theory of the subject proposes a notion of identity as precariously constituted in the discourses of the social whereby it is both determined and regulated by the forces of power inherent in a given social formation, but capable also of undermining them.

The unstable I

Within the analysis which Jacques Lacan offers, for example, the subject is formed through a series of stages. In an initial stage the infant exists as an amorphous mass of uncoordinated limbs and sounds, and its experience of itself is continuous since it draws no distinction between self and other. In a second stage (the mirror stage – see Section 3.1) a distinction is introduced between the self and the other. As the infant sees its reflection in the mirror it becomes aware of a split between the 'I' which looks and the 'I' which is seen, though this split is immediately recuperated – for the reflected other *appears* to have the unity and control of itself which the perceiving 'I' lacks. Although such control is *imaginary*, the infant none the less desires and identifies with that which it does not have in the image of the other. With the entry into language (the final stage) comes the insertion of the subject into a position within the symbolic order in which it is both *produced* in language and *subjected* to the laws of the symbolic which pre-exist it. Produced from within language, identity depends upon both difference (between the self and the other realized at the mirror stage) and accession to the position of an 'I' within discourse, a position which (only provisionally) constructs meaning. [All of this is hard to explain because it must avoid the conventional humanist terms – 'I experience,' 'I know' – which suppose the 'I' is there *from the very start*. What's at issue is how the 'I' gets to be able to say 'I experience,' 'I know,' 'I think that . . .'.]

Though the subject may speak, it does so only within the terms which the laws of language allow. Just as Saussure had argued that language does not simply name a reality which pre-exists it, but rather *produces* the concept of reality through the system of differences which *is* language (see Section 1.1) so Lacan argues that the position of the 'I' within language does not simply represent the presence of a subject which pre-exists it, but rather produces the concept of the subject through a process of differentiation between the 'I' and 'not I' of discourse. This concept of difference, expanded by Jacques Derrida (see Section 4) is important since it removes the subject from the fixed position of presence and puts it into process dependent upon the exchange between presence and absence. Based upon difference, both subjectivity and the language which produces it constitute a process in which meaning is never fully present in any individual utterance (of the 'I') but is always deferred and always only ever provisional.

Lacan's analysis has provided a foundation upon which many subsequent theories of subjectivity are based, but it has also been critiqued for its privileging of the phallus (imaginary or not) as the governing signifier in the law of the symbolic organizing lack into an order of coherence. Julia Kristeva, for example, takes up the notion of language as the constituent of subjectivity, but focuses her analysis upon the transgressions of the law of the symbolic in the form of the semiotic which she argues is an integral and revolutionary part of symbolic language (see Section 3.2). Much of the work of French Feminist writers like Hélène Cixous (see Section 5.2) and Luce Irigaray (see Irigaray 1985a and b) also serves to challenge the authority of the phallus as the governing principle of gendered subjectivity, asserting instead various claims to the 'feminine' aspects of pre-Oedipal language, maintained by the polymorphous qualities of female sexuality, the bisexually charged body and the body of the mother.

Power/knowledge

While the work of these theorists focuses upon the constitution of subjectivity in terms of a kind of psycho-linguistics, there is yet another strand within contemporary theory which turns more towards history and the structures of society in order to understand the material circumstances and implications of subjective construction. The foundation of much of this work – on the *discursive* construction of subjectivity – has been provided by the work of Michel Foucault. This has suggested that many modern sciences, particularly social sciences, exercise power while claiming to be objective knowledge.

For Foucault the subject is constituted in discourse through the specific vocabulary of knowledges which circulate in society. In particular his work explores the *institutional* effects of discourse and the ways in which it operates to produce and govern individual subjects. *Discipline and Punish* (see Section 3.3), *The History of Sexuality* (Section 3.4) and *Madness and Civilisation* (1971) for example, provide detailed analyses of the ways in which power is exercised to produce and to police individual subjects through the production of detailed knowledges of 'the criminal', 'the pervert' and 'the lunatic' within the discourses of criminality, sexuality and psychiatry and the institutions (particularly state institutions) which guarantee them. That the individual is the site of this regime is crucial to the formulation of the social order, but the regime is also crucial to the formulation of the subject. It is not that the innocent and unsuspecting individual pre-exists the knowledges that are produced and is then somehow cruelly shaped into a subject by the power they wield, but rather that the individual is 'carefully fabricated' within them. Within the discourse of science, for example, 'the pervert' does not pre-exist a simple scientific labelling, but is *produced* (comes into existence) in and through discursive constructions of 'the pervert.'

Like the psycho-linguistic theories of subject construction, discursive theories also maintain that plurality and constant deferral of meaning are inherent in the structuring of the subject so that it remains precarious, open to change. Within any given social and historical moment a variety of discourses exist and compete for control of subjectivity. The subject thus becomes the site of a discursive battle for the meaning of their identity; their interpellation (see Section 2.3) as subjects within any single discourse can never be final. Though most forms of discourse deny their own partiality by laying claim to the 'truth' of individual existence, the contradictions brought about by the plurality of discursive fields ensures that the individual is constantly subjected to a range of possible meanings, and is therefore an unstable site of constructions and reconstructions which often overlap (see, for example, Foucault's, *Herculine Barbin* 1980 and *I, Pierre Rivière* 1978b).

In addition, while most discourses work to produce particular forms of subjectivity, their very organization also implies the possibility of other subject positions and with them the possibilities of resistance to meanings which may be dominant. Meanings also change over time, and although particular knowledges may initially serve the interests of specific forms of power, the relationship between them can never be guaranteed. Within the discourse of sexology in the late nineteenth and early twentieth centuries, for example, a whole medical language and knowledge of classifications emerged and a whole technology of power was exercised in the production of the 'homosexual' subject. While this initially served the interests of policing the norm of reproductive 'heterosexuality', the language which sexology provided has subsequently served the causes of gay liberation and a variety of resistances to the notion of the homosexual as either 'sick' or 'sorry.' In sum, then, through recent work represented in this section, the concept of ideology has been widened to include not just how we think but ways we are constituted as thinking, experiencing, gendered individuals in the first place.

3.1

Jacques Lacan
from 'The Mirror Stage'
(1949)

The conception of the mirror stage that I introduced at our last congress, thirteen years ago, has since become more or less established in the practice of the French group. However, I think it worthwhile to bring it again to your attention, especially today, for the light it sheds on the formation of the *I* as we experience it in psychoanalysis. It is an experience that leads us to oppose any philosophy directly issuing from the *Cogito*.

Some of you may recall that this conception originated in a feature of human behaviour illuminated by a fact of comparative psychology. The child, at an age when he is for a time, however short, outdone by the chimpanzee in instrumental intelligence, can nevertheless already recognize as such his own image in a mirror. This recognition is indicated in the illuminative mimicry of the *Aha-Erlebnis*, which Köhler sees as the expression of situational apperception, an essential stage of the act of intelligence.

This act, far from exhausting itself, as in the case of the monkey, once the image has been mastered and found empty, immediately rebounds in the case of the child in a series of gestures in which he experiences in play the relation between the movements assumed in the image and the reflected environment, and between this virtual complex and the reality it reduplicates – the child's own body, and the persons and things, around him.

This event can take place, as we have known since Baldwin, from the age of six months, and its repetition has often made me reflect upon the startling spectacle of the infant in front of the mirror. Unable as yet to walk, or even to stand up, and held tightly as he is by some support, human or artificial (what, in France, we call a *'trotte-bébé'*), he nevertheless overcomes, in a flutter of jubilant activity, the obstructions of his support and, fixing his attitude in a slightly leaning-forward position, in order to hold it in his gaze, brings back an instantaneous aspect of the image.

For me, this activity retains the meaning I have given it up to the age of eighteen months. This meaning discloses a libidinal dynamism, which has hitherto remained problematic, as well as an ontological structure of the human world that accords with my reflections on paranoiac knowledge.

We have only to understand the mirror stage as *an identification*, in the full sense that analysis gives to the term: namely, the transformation that takes place in the subject when he assumes an image – whose predestination to this phase-effect is sufficiently indicated by the use, in analytic theory, of the ancient term *imago*.

This jubilant assumption of his specular image by the child at the *infans* stage, still sunk in his motor incapacity and nursling dependence, would seem to exhibit in an exemplary situation the symbolic matrix in which the *I* is precipitated in a primordial form, before it is objectified in the dialectic of identification with the other, and before language restores to it, in the universal, its function as subject.

This form would have to be called the Ideal-I,[1] if we wished to incorporate it into our usual register, in the sense that it will also be the source of secondary identifications, under which term I would place the functions of libidinal normalization. But the important point is that this form situates the agency of the ego, before its social determination, in a fictional direction, which will always remain irreducible for the individual alone, or rather, which will only rejoin the coming-into-being (*le devenir*) of the subject asymptotically, whatever the success of the dialectical syntheses by which he must resolve as *I* his discordance with his own reality.

The fact is that the total form of the body by which the subject anticipates in a mirage the maturation of his power is given to him only as *Gestalt*, that is to say, in an exteriority in which this form is certainly more constituent than constituted, but in which it appears to him above all in a contrasting size (*un relief de stature*) that fixes it and in a symmetry that inverts it, in contrast with the turbulent movements that the subject feels are animating him. Thus, this *Gestalt* – whose pregnancy should be regarded as bound up with the species, though its motor style remains scarcely recognizable – by these two aspects of its appearance, symbolizes the mental permanence of the *I* at the same time as it prefigures its alienating destination; it is still pregnant with the correspondences that unite the *I* with the statue in which man projects himself, with the phantoms that dominate him, or with the automaton in which, in an ambiguous relation, the world of his own making tends to find completion.

Indeed, for the *imagos* – whose veiled faces it is our privilege to see in outline in our daily experience and in the penumbra of symbolic efficacity[2] – the mirror-image would seem to be the threshold of the visible world, if we go by the mirror disposition that the *imago of one's own body* presents in hallucinations or dreams, whether it concerns its individual features, or even its infirmities, or its object-projections; or if we observe the role of the mirror apparatus in the appearances of the *double*, in which psychical realities, however heterogeneous, are manifested.

That a *Gestalt* should be capable of formative effects in the organism is attested by a piece of biological experimentation that is itself so alien to the idea of psychical causality that it cannot bring itself to formulate its results in these terms. It nevertheless recognizes that it is a necessary condition for the maturation of the gonad of the female pigeon that it should see another member of its species, of either sex; so sufficient in itself is this condition that the desired effect may be obtained merely by placing the individual within reach of the field of reflection of a mirror. Similarly, in the case of the migratory locust, the transition within a generation from the solitary to the gregarious form can be obtained by exposing the individual, at a certain stage, to the exclusively visual action of a similar image, provided it is animated by movements of a style sufficiently close to that characteristic of the species. Such facts are inscribed in an order of homeomorphic identification that would itself fall within the larger question of the meaning of beauty as both formative and erogenic.

But the facts of mimicry are no less instructive when conceived as cases of heteromorphic identification, in as much as they raise the problem of the signification of space for the living organism – psychological concepts hardly seem less appropriate for shedding light on these matters than ridiculous attempts to reduce them to the supposedly supreme law of adaptation. We have only to recall how Roger Caillois (who was then very young, and still fresh from his breach with the sociological school in which he was trained) illuminated the subject by using the term *'legendary psychasthenia'* to classify morphological mimicry as an obsession with space in its derealizing effect.

I have myself shown in the social dialectic that structures human knowledge as paranoiac[3] why human knowledge has greater autonomy than animal knowledge in relation to the field of force of desire, but also why human knowledge is determined in that 'little reality' (*ce peu de réalité*), which the Surrealists, in their restless way, saw as its limitation. These reflections lead me to recognize in the spatial captation manifested in the mirror-stage, even before the social dialectic, the effect in man of an organic insufficiency in his natural reality – in so far as any meaning can be given to the word 'nature'.

I am led, therefore, to regard the function of the mirror-stage as a particular case of the function of the *imago*, which is to establish a relation between the organism and its reality – or, as they say, between the *Innenwelt* and the *Umwelt*.

In man, however, this relation to nature is altered by a certain dehiscence at the heart of the organism, a primordial Discord betrayed by the signs of uneasiness and motor unco-ordination of the neo-natal months. The objective notion of the anatomical incompleteness of the pyramidal system and likewise the presence of certain humoral residues of the maternal organism confirm the view I have formulated as the fact of a real *specific prematurity of birth* in man.

It is worth noting, incidentally, that this is a fact recognized as such by embryologists, by the term *foetalization*, which determines the prevalence of the so-called superior apparatus of the neurax, and especially of the cortex, which psycho-surgical operations lead us to regard as the intra-organic mirror.

This development is experienced as a temporal dialectic that decisively projects the formation of the individual into history. The *mirror stage* is a drama whose internal thrust is precipitated from insufficiency to anticipation – and

which manufactures for the subject, caught up in the lure of spatial identification, the succession of phantasies that extends from a fragmented body-
image to a form of its totality that I shall call orthopaedic – and, lastly, to
the assumption of the armour of an alienating identity, which will mark
with its rigid structure the subject's entire mental development. Thus, to
break out of the circle of the *Innenwelt* into the *Umwelt* generates the
inexhaustible quadrature of the ego's verifications.

This fragmented body – which term I have also introduced into our system
of theoretical references – usually manifests itself in dreams when the
movement of the analysis encounters a certain level of aggressive disinteg-
ration in the individual. It then appears in the form of disjointed limbs, or
of those organs represented in exoscopy, growing wings and taking up arms
for intestinal persecutions – the very same that the visionary Hieronymus
Bosch has fixed, for all time, in painting, in their ascent from the fifteenth
century to the imaginary zenith of modern man. But this form is even
tangibly revealed at the organic level, in the lines of 'fragilization' that
define the anatomy of phantasy, as exhibited in the schizoid and spasmodic
symptoms of hysteria.

Correlatively, the formation of the *I* is symbolized in dreams by a fortress,
or a stadium – its inner arena and enclosure, surrounded by marshes and
rubbish-tips, dividing it into two opposed fields of contest where the subject
flounders in quest of the lofty, remote inner castle whose form (sometimes
juxtaposed in the same scenario) symbolizes the id in a quite startling way.
Similarly, on the mental plane, we find realized the structures of fortified
works, the metaphor of which arises spontaneously, as if issuing from the
symptoms themselves, to designate the mechanisms of obsessional neurosis
– inversion, isolation, reduplication, cancellation and displacement.

But if we were to build on these subjective givens alone – however little
we free them from the condition of experience that makes us see them as
partaking of the nature of a linguistic technique – our theoretical attempts
would remain exposed to the charge of projecting themselves into the
unthinkable of an absolute subject. This is why I have sought in the present
hypothesis, grounded in a conjunction of objective data, the guiding grid for
a *method of symbolic reduction*.

It establishes in the *defences of the ego* a genetic order, in accordance with
the wish formulated by Miss Anna Freud, in the first part of her great work,
and situates (as against a frequently expressed prejudice) hysterical repression
and its returns at a more archaic stage than obsessional inversion and its
isolating processes, and the latter in turn as preliminary to paranoic alienation,
which dates from the deflection of the specular *I* into the social *I*.

This moment in which the mirror-stage comes to an end inaugurates,
by the identification with the *imago* of the counterpart and the drama of
primordial jealousy (so well brought out by the school of Charlotte Bühler
in the phenomenon of infantile *transitivism*), the dialectic that will henceforth
link the *I* to socially elaborated situations.

It is this moment that decisively tips the whole of human knowledge into
mediatization through the desire of the other, constitutes its objects in an
abstract equivalence by the co-operation of others, and turns the I into that

apparatus for which every instinctual thrust constitutes a danger, even though it should correspond to a natural maturation – the very normalization of this maturation being henceforth dependent, in man, on a cultural mediation as exemplified, in the case of the sexual object, by the Oedipus complex.

In the light of this conception, the term primary narcissism, by which analytic doctrine designates the libidinal investment characteristic of that moment, reveals in those who invented it the most profound awareness of semantic latencies. But it also throws light on the dynamic opposition between this libido and the sexual libido, which the first analysts tried to define when they invoked destructive and, indeed, death instincts, in order to explain the evident connection between the narcissistic libido and the alienating function of the *I*, the aggressivity it releases in any relation to the other, even in a relation involving the most Samaritan of aid.

In fact, they were encountering that existential negativity whose reality is so vigorously proclaimed by the contemporary philosophy of being and nothingness.

But unfortunately that philosophy grasps negativity only within the limits of a self-sufficiency of consciousness, which, as one of its premises, links to the *méconnaissances* that constitute the ego, the illusion of autonomy to which it entrusts itself. This flight of fancy, for all that it draws, to an unusual extent, on borrowings from psychoanalytic experience, culminates in the pretention of providing an existential psychoanalysis.

At the culmination of the historical effort of a society to refuse to recognize that it has any function other than the utilitarian one, and in the anxiety of the individual confronting the 'concentrational'[1] form of the social bond that seems to arise to crown this effort, existentialism must be judged by the explanations it gives of the subjective impasses that have indeed resulted from it; a freedom that is never more authentic than when it is within the walls of a prison; a demand for commitment, expressing the impotence of a pure consciousness to master any situation; a voyeuristic–sadistic idealization of the sexual relation; a personality that realizes itself only in suicide; a consciousness of the other that can be satisfied only by Hegelian murder.

These propositions are opposed by all our experience, in so far as it teaches us not to regard the ego as centred on the *perception–consciousness system*, or as organized by the 'reality principle' – a principle that is the expression of a scientific prejudice most hostile to the dialectic of knowledge. Our experience shows that we should start instead from the *function of méconnaissance* that characterizes the ego in all its structures, so markedly articulated by Miss Anna Freud. For, if the *Verneinung* represents the patent form of that function, its effects will, for the most part, remain latent, so long as they are not illuminated by some light reflected on to the level of fatality, which is where the id manifests itself.

We can thus understand the inertia characteristic of the formations of the *I*, and find there the most extensive definition of neurosis – just as the captation of the subject by the situation gives us the most general formula for madness, not only the madness that lies behind the walls of asylums, but also the madness that deafens the world with its sound and fury.

The sufferings of neurosis and psychosis are for us a schooling in the passions of the soul, just as the beam of the psychoanalytic scales, when we calculate the tilt of its threat to entire communities, provides us with an indication of the deadening of the passions in society.

At this junction of nature and culture, so persistently examined by modern anthropology, psychoanalysis alone recognizes this knot of imaginary servitude that love must always undo again, or sever.

For such a task, we place no trust in altruistic feeling, we who lay bare the aggressivity that underlies the activity of the philanthropist, the idealist, the pedagogue, and even the reformer.

In the recourse of subject to subject that we preserve, psychoanalysis may accompany the patient to the ecstatic limit of the *'Thou art that'*, in which is revealed to him the cipher of his mortal destiny, but it is not in our mere power as practitioners to bring him to that point where the real journey begins.

Notes

1 Throughout this article I leave in its peculiarity the translation I have adopted for Freud's *Ideal-Ich* (i.e., 'je-idéal'), without further comment, other than to say I have not maintained it since.
2 Cf. Claude Lévi-Strauss, *Structural Anthropology*, chapter X.
3 Cf. 'Aggressivity in psychoanalysis' (another paper collected in *Écrits*).
4 *'Concentrationnaire'*, an adjective coined after World War II (this article was written in 1949) to describe the life of the concentration-camp. In the hands of certain writers it became, by extension, applicable to many aspects of 'modern' life (Tr.).

3.2

Julia Kristeva from 'The System and the Speaking Subject' (1973)

In my view, a critique of this 'semiology of systems' and of its phenomenological foundations is possible only if it starts from a theory of meaning which must necessarily be a theory of the speaking subject. It is common knowledge that the linguistic revival which goes by the name of Generative Grammar – whatever its variants and mutations – is based on the rehabilitation of the Cartesian conception of language as an *act* carried out by a *subject*. On close inspection, as certain linguists (from Jakobson to Kuroda) have shown in recent years, this 'speaking subject' turns out in fact to be that *transcendental ego* which, in Husserl's view, underlies any and every predicative synthesis, if we 'put in brackets' logical or linguistic externality. Generative Grammar, based firmly on this subject, not only expresses the truth of language which structuralism describes as a system – namely that it is the act of an *ego* which has momentarily broken off its connection with that externality, which may be social, natural or unconscious – but creates for itself the opportunity of describing, better than its predecessors, the logic of this thetic act, starting out from an infinity of predication which each national language subjects to strict systems of rules. Yet this transcendental subject is not the essential concern of the semiological revival, and if it bases itself on the conception of language proper to Generative Grammar, semiology will not get beyond the reduction – still commonly characteristic of it – of signifying *practices* to their systematic aspect.

In respect of the subject and of signifying, it is the Freudian revolution which seems to me to have achieved the definitive displacement of the Western *épistémé* from its presumed centrality. But although the effects of that revolution have been superbly and authoritatively worked out in the writings of Jacques Lacan in France, or, in a rather different way, in the

English anti-psychiatry of R. D. Laing and David Cooper, it has by no means reached far enough yet to affect the semiotic conception of language and of practices. The theory of meaning now stands at a crossroad: either it will remain an attempt at formalizing meaning-systems by increasing sophistication of the logico-mathematical tools which enable it to formulate models on the basis of a conception (already rather dated) of meaning as the act of a *transcendental ego*, cut off from its body, its unconscious and also its history; or else it will attune itself to the theory of the speaking subject as a divided subject (conscious/unconscious) and go on to attempt to specify the types of operation characteristic of the two sides of this split, thereby exposing them to those forces extraneous to the logic of the systematic; exposing them, that is to say, on the one hand, to bio-physiological processes (themselves already inescapably part of signifying processes, what Freud labelled 'drives'); and, on the other hand, to social constraints (family structures, modes of production, etc.).

In following this latter path, semiology, or, as I have suggested calling it, *semanalysis*, conceives of meaning not as a sign-system but as a *signifying process*. Within this process one might see the release and subsequent articulation of the drives as constrained by the social code yet not reducible to the language system as a *genotext* and the signifying system as it presents itself to phenomenological intuition as a *phenotext*; describable in terms of structure, or of competence/performance, or according to other models. The presence of the *genotext* within the *phenotext* is indicated by what I have called a *semiotic disposition*. In the case, for example, of a signifying practice such as 'poetic language', the *semiotic disposition* will be the various deviations from the grammatical rules of the language: articulatory effects which shift the phonemative system back towards it articulatory, phonetic base and consequently towards the drive-governed bases of sound-production; the over-determination of a lexeme by multiple meanings which it does not carry in ordinary usage but which accrue to it as a result of its occurrence in other texts; syntactic irregularities such as ellipses, non-recoverable deletions, indefinite embeddings, etc.; the replacement of the relationship between the protagonists of any enunciation as they function in a locutory act – see here the work of J. L. Austin and John Searle – by a system of relations based on fantasy; and so forth.

These variations may be partly described by way of what are called the *primary* processes (displacement, condensation – or metonymy, metaphor), transversal to the logico-symbolic processes that function in the predicative synthesis towards establishing the language system. They had already been discovered by the structuralists, following Freud, at the 'lower', phonological, level of the linguistic synthesis. To them must be added the compulsion to repetition, but also 'operations' characteristic of topologies and capable of establishing *functions* between the signifying code and the fragmented body of the speaking subject as well as the bodies of his familial and social partners. All functions which suppose a *frontier* (in this case the fissure created by the act of naming and the logico-linguistic synthesis which it sets off) and the transgression of that frontier (the sudden appearance of new signifying chains) are relevant to any account of signifying *practice*, where practice is taken as meaning the acceptance of a symbolic law together with the transgression of that law for the purpose of renovating it.

The moment of transgression is the key moment in practice: we can speak of practice wherever there is a transgression of systematicity, i.e., a transgression of the unity proper to the *transcendental ego*. The subject of the practice cannot be the transcendental subject, who lacks the shift, the split in logical unity brought about by language which separates out, within the signifying body, the symbolic order from the workings of the libido (this last revealing itself by the *semiotic disposition*). Identifying the semiotic disposition means in fact identifying the shift in the speaking subject, his capacity for renewing the order in which he is inescapably caught up; and that capacity is, for the *subject*, the capacity for enjoyment.

It must, however, be remembered that although it can be described in terms of operations and concepts, this logic of shifts, splits and the infinitization of the symbolic limit leads us towards operations heterogeneous to meaning and its system. By that I mean that these 'operations' are *pre-meaning* and *pre-sign* (or *trans-meaning, trans-sign*), and that they bring us back to processes of division in the living matter of an organism subject to biological constraints as well as social norms. Here it seems indispensable that Melanie Klein's theory of drives should be refined and extended, together with the psycholinguistic study of the acquisition of language (provided that this study is conceived as something more than the mere reiteration of what is amply demonstrated in and by the linguistic system of the *transcendental ego*).

The point is not to replace the semiotics of signifying systems by considerations on the biological code appropriate to the nature of those employing them – a tautological exercise, after all, since the biological code has been modelled on the language system. It is rather to postulate the *heterogeneity* of biological operations in respect of signifying operations, and to study the dialectics of the former (that is, the fact that, though invariably subject to the signifying and/or social codes, they infringe the code in the direction of allowing the subject to get pleasure from it, renew it, even endanger it; where, that is, the processes are not blocked by him in repression or 'mental illness').

But since it is itself a metalanguage, semiotics can do no more than postulate this heterogeneity: as soon as it speaks about it, it homogenizes the phenomenon, links it with a system, loses hold of it. Its specificity can be preserved only in the signifying practices which set off the heterogeneity at issue: thus poetic language making free with the language code; music, dancing, painting, reordering the psychic drives which have not been harnessed by the dominant symbolization systems and thus renewing their own tradition; and (in a different mode) experiences with drugs – all seek out and make use of this heterogeneity and the ensuing fracture of a symbolic code which can no longer 'hold' its (speaking) subjects.

But if semiotics thus openly recognizes its inability to apprehend the heterogeneity of the signifying process other than by reducing it to a systematicity, does it thereby declare its own intellectual bankruptcy? Everything in current research that is solid and intellectually adequate impels those pursuing it to stress the limits of their own metalanguage in relation to the signifying process; their own metalanguage can apprehend only that part of the signifying process belonging to the domain of the general metalanguage to which their own efforts are tributary; the (vast) *remainder* has had, historically, to find a home in religion (notoriously, if more or less marginally, associated with semiotic reflection since the Stoics), moving up through medieval theories of the *modi significandi,* Leibniz's *Art of Combinations,* to phenomenology or positivism. It is only now, and only on the basis of a theory of the speaking subject as subject of a heterogeneous process, that semiotics can show that what lies outside its metalinguistic mode of operation – the 'remainder', the 'waste' – is what, in the process of the speaking subject, represents the moment in which it is set in action, put on trial, put to death: a heterogeneity with respect to system, operating within the practice and one which is liable, if not seen for what it is, to be reified into a transcendence.

3.3

Michel Foucault from *Discipline and Punish* (1977)

The following, according to an order published at the end of the seventeenth century, were the measures to be taken when the plague appeared in a town.[1]

First, a strict spatial partitioning: the closing of the town and its outlying districts, a prohibition to leave the town on pain of death, the killing of all stray animals; the division of the town into distinct quarters, each governed by an intendant. Each street is placed under the authority of a syndic, who keeps it under surveillance; if he leaves the street, he will be condemned to death. On the appointed day, everyone is ordered to stay indoors: it is forbidden to leave on pain of death. The syndic himself comes to lock the door of each house from the outside; he takes the key with him and hands it over to the intendant of the quarter; the intendant keeps it until the end of the quarantine. Each family will have made its own provisions; but, for bread and wine, small wooden canals are set up between the street and the interior of the houses, thus allowing each person to receive his ration without communicating with the suppliers and other residents; meat, fish and herbs will be hoisted up into the houses with pulleys and baskets. If it is absolutely necessary to leave the house, it will be done in turn, avoiding any meeting. Only the intendants, syndics and guards will move about the streets and also, between the infected houses, from one corpse to another, the 'crows', who can be left to die: these are 'people of little substance who carry the sick, bury the dead, clean and do many vile and abject offices'. It is a segmented, immobile, frozen space. Each individual is fixed in his place. And, if he moves, he does so at the risk of his life, contagion or punishment.

Inspection functions ceaselessly. The gaze is alert everywhere: 'A considerable body of militia, commanded by good officers and men of substance', guards at the gates, at the town hall and in every quarter to ensure the prompt obedience of the people and the most absolute authority of the magistrates, 'as also to observe all disorder, theft and extortion'. At each of the town gates there will be an observation post; at the end of each street sentinels. Every day, the intendant visits the quarter in his charge, inquires whether the syndics have carried out their tasks, whether the inhabitants have anything to complain of; they 'observe their actions'. Every day, too, the syndic goes into the street for which he is responsible; stops before each house: gets all the inhabitants to appear at the windows (those who live overlooking the courtyard will be allocated a window looking onto the street at which no one but they may show themselves); he calls each of them by name; informs himself as to the state of each and every one of them – 'in which respect the inhabitants will be compelled to speak the truth under pain of death'; if someone does not appear at the window, the syndic must ask why: 'In this way he will find out easily enough whether dead or sick are being concealed.' Everyone locked up in his cage, everyone at his window, answering to his name and showing himself when asked – it is the great review of the living and the dead.

This surveillance is based on a system of permanent registration: reports from the syndics to the intendants, from the intendants to the magistrates or mayor. At the beginning of the 'lock up', the role of each of the inhabitants present in the town is laid down, one by one; this document bears 'the name, age, sex of everyone, notwithstanding his condition': a copy is sent to the intendant of the quarter, another to the office of the town hall, another to enable the syndic to make his daily roll call. Everything that may be observed during the course of the visits – deaths, illnesses, complaints, irregularities – is noted down and transmitted to the intendants and magistrates. The magistrates have complete control over medical treatment; they have appointed a physician in charge; no other practitioner may treat, no apothecary prepare medicine, no confessor visit a sick person without having received from him a written note 'to prevent anyone from concealing and dealing with those sick of the contagion, unknown to the magistrates'. The registration of the pathological must be constantly centralized. The relation of each individual to his disease and to his death passes through the representatives of power, the registration they make of it, the decisions they take on it.

Five or six days after the beginning of the quarantine, the process of purifying the houses one by one is begun. All the inhabitants are made to leave; in each room 'the furniture and goods' are raised from the ground or suspended from the air; perfume is poured around the room; after carefully sealing the windows, doors and even the keyholes with wax, the perfume is set alight. Finally, the entire house is closed while the perfume is consumed; those who have carried out the work are searched, as they were on entry, 'in the presence of the residents of the house, to see that they did not have something on their persons as they left that they did not have on entering'. Four hours later, the residents are allowed to re-enter their homes.

This enclosed, segmented space, observed at every point, in which the individuals are inserted in a fixed place, in which the slightest movements are supervised, in which all events are recorded, in which an uninterrupted work of writing links the centre and periphery, in which power is exercised without division, according to a continuous hierarchical figure, in which each individual is constantly located, examined and distributed among the living beings, the sick and the dead – all this constitutes a compact model of the disciplinary mechanism. The plague is met by order; its function is to sort out every possible confusion: that of the disease, which is transmitted when bodies are mixed together; that of the evil, which is increased when fear and death overcome prohibitions. It lays down for each individual his place, his body, his disease and his death, his well-being, by means of an omnipresent and omniscient power that subdivides itself in a regular, uninterrupted way even to the ultimate determination of the individual, of what characterizes him, of what belongs to him, of what happens to him. Against the plague, which is a mixture, discipline brings into play its power, which is one of analysis. A whole literary fiction of the festival grew up around the plague: suspended laws, lifted prohibitions, the frenzy of passing time, bodies mingling together without respect, individuals unmasked, abandoning their statutory identity and the figure under which they had been recognized, allowing a quite different truth to appear. But there was also a political dream of the plague, which was exactly its reverse: not the collective festival, but strict divisions; not laws transgressed, but the penetration of regulation into even the smallest details of everyday life through the mediation of the complete hierarchy that assured the capillary functioning of power; not masks that were put on and taken off, but the assignment to each individual of his 'true' name, his 'true' place, his 'true' body, his 'true' disease. The plague as a form, at once real and imaginary, of disorder had as its medical and political correlative discipline. Behind the disciplinary mechanisms can be read the haunting memory of 'contagions', of the plague, of rebellions, crimes, vagabondage, desertions, people who appear and disappear, live and die in disorder.

If it is true that the leper gave rise to rituals of exclusion, which to a certain extent provided the model for and general form of the great Confinement, then the plague gave rise to disciplinary projects. Rather than the massive, binary division between one set of people and another, it called for multiple separations, individualizing distributions, an organization in depth of surveillance and control, an intensification and a ramification of power. The leper was caught up in a practice of rejection, of exile-enclosure; he was left to his doom in a mass among which it was useless to differentiate; those sick of the plague were caught up in a meticulous tactical partitioning in which individual differentiations were the constricting effects of a power that multiplied, articulated and subdivided itself; the great confinement on the one hand; the correct training on the other. The leper and his separation; the plague and its segmentations. The first is marked; the second analysed and distributed. The exile of the leper and the arrest of the plague do not bring with them the same political dream. The first is that of a pure community, the second that of a disciplined society. Two ways of exercising power over men, of controlling their relations, of separating out their dangerous mixtures. The plague-stricken town, traversed throughout with hierarchy, surveillance, observation, writing; the town immobilized by the functioning of an extensive power that bears in a distinct way over all individual bodies – this is the utopia of the perfectly governed city. The plague (envisaged as a possibility at least) is the trial in the course of which one may define ideally the exercise of disciplinary power. In order to make rights and laws function according to pure theory, the jurists place themselves in imagination in the state of nature; in order to see perfect disciplines functioning, rulers dreamt of the state of plague. Underlying disciplinary projects the image of the plague stands for all forms of confusion and disorder; just as the image of the leper, cut off from all human contact, underlies projects of exclusion.

They are different projects, then, but not incompatible ones. We see them coming slowly together, and it is the peculiarity of the nineteenth century that it applied to the space of exclusion of which the leper was the symbolic inhabitant (beggars, vagabonds, madmen and the disorderly formed the real population) the technique of power proper to disciplinary partitioning. Treat 'lepers' as 'plague victims', project the subtle segmentations of discipline onto the confused space of internment, combine it with the methods of analytical distribution proper to power, individualize the excluded, but use procedures of individualization to mark exclusion – this is what was operated regularly by disciplinary power from the beginning of the nineteenth century in the psychiatric asylum, the penitentiary, the reformatory, the approved school and, to some extent, the hospital. Generally speaking, all the authorities exercising individual control function according to a double mode; that of binary division and branding (mad/sane; dangerous/harmless; normal/abnormal); and that of coercive assignment, of differential distribution (who he is; where he must be; how he is to be characterized; how he is to be recognized; how a constant surveillance is to be exercised over him in an individual way, etc.). On the one hand, the lepers are treated as plague victims; the tactics of individualizing disciplines are imposed on the excluded; and, on the other hand, the universality of disciplinary controls makes it possible to brand the 'leper' and to bring into play against him the dualistic mechanisms of exclusion. The constant division between the normal and the abnormal, to which every individual is subjected, brings us back to our own time, by applying the binary branding and exile of the leper to quite different objects; the existence of a whole set of techniques and institutions for measuring, supervising and correcting the abnormal brings into play the disciplinary mechanisms to which the fear of the plague gave rise. All the mechanisms of power which, even today, are disposed around the abnormal individual, to brand him and to alter him, are composed of those two forms from which they distantly derive.

Bentham's *Panopticon* is the architectural figure of this composition. We know the principle on which it was based: at the periphery, an annular building; at the centre, a tower; this tower is pierced with wide windows that open onto the inner side of the ring; the peripheric building is divided into cells, each of which extends the whole width of the building; they have two windows, one on the inside, corresponding to the windows of the tower; the other, on the outside, allows the light to cross the cell from one end to the other. All that is needed, then, is to place a supervisor in a central tower and to shut up in each cell a madman, a patient, a condemned man, a worker or a schoolboy. By the effect of backlighting, one can observe from the tower, standing out precisely against the light, the small captive shadows in the cells of the periphery. They are like so many cages, so many small theatres, in which each actor is alone, perfectly individualized and constantly visible. The panoptic mechanism arranges spatial unities that make it possible to see constantly and to recognize immediately. In short, it reverses the principle of the dungeon; or rather of its three functions – to enclose, to deprive of light and to hide – it preserves only the first and eliminates the other two. Full lighting and the eye of a supervisor capture better than darkness, which ultimately protected. Visibility is a trap.

To begin with, this made it possible – as a negative effect – to avoid those compact, swarming, howling masses that were to be found in places of confinement, those painted by Goya or described by Howard. Each individual, in his place, is securely confined to a cell from which he is seen from the front by the supervisor; but the side walls prevent him from coming into contact with his companions. He is seen, but he does not see; he is the object of information, never a subject in communication. The arrangement of his room, opposite the central tower, imposes on him an axial visibility; but the divisions of the ring, those separated cells, imply a lateral invisibility. And this invisibility is a guarantee of order. If the inmates are convicts, there is no danger of a plot, an attempt at collective escape, the planning of new crimes for the future, bad reciprocal influences; if they are patients, there is no danger of contagion; if they are madmen there is no risk of their committing violence upon one another; if they are schoolchildren, there is no copying, no noise, no chatter, no waste of time; if they are workers, there are no disorders, no theft, no coalitions, none of those distractions that slow down the rate of work, make it less perfect or cause accidents. The crowd, a compact mass, a locus of multiple exchanges, individualities merging together, a collective effect, is abolished and replaced by a collection of separated individualities. From the point of view of the guardian, it is replaced by a multiplicity that can be numbered and supervised; from the point of view of the inmates, by a sequestered and observed solitude.

Hence the major effect of the Panopticon: to induce in the inmate a state of conscious and permanent visibility that assures the automatic functioning of power. So to arrange things that the surveillance is permanent in its effects, even if it is discontinuous in its action; that the perfection of power should tend to render its actual exercise unnecessary; that this architectural apparatus should be a machine for creating and sustaining a power relation independent of the person who exercises it; in short, that the inmates should be caught up in a power situation of which they are themselves the bearers. To achieve this, it is at once too much and too little that the prisoner should be constantly observed by an inspector: too little, for what matters is that he knows himself to be observed; too much, because he has no need in fact of being so. In view of this, Bentham laid down the principle that power should be visible and unverifiable. Visible: the inmate will constantly have before his eyes the tall outline of the central tower from which he is spied upon. Unverifiable: the inmate must never know whether he is being looked at at any one moment; but he must be sure that he may always be so. In order to make the presence or absence of the inspector unverifiable, so that the prisoners, in their cells, cannot even see a shadow, Bentham envisaged not only venetian blinds on the windows of the central observation hall, but, on the inside, partitions that intersected the hall at right angles and, in order to pass from one quarter to the other, not doors but zig-zag openings; for the slightest noise, a gleam of light, a brightness in a half-opened door would betray the presence of the guardian.[2] The Panopticon is a machine for dissociating the see/being seen dyad: in the peripheric ring, one is totally seen, without ever seeing; in the central tower, one sees everything without ever being seen.[3]

It is an important mechanism, for it automatizes and disindividualizes power. Power has its principle not so much in a person as in a certain concerted distribution of bodies, surfaces, lights, gazes; in an arrangement whose internal mechanisms produce the relation in which individuals are caught up. The ceremonies, the rituals, the marks by which the sovereign's surplus power was manifested are useless. There is a machinery that assures dissymmetry, disequilibrium, difference. Consequently, it does not matter who exercises power. Any individual, taken almost at random, can operate the machine: in the absence of the director, his family, his friends, his visitors, even his servants (Bentham, 45). Similarly, it does not matter what motive animates him: the curiosity of the indiscreet, the malice of a child, the thirst for knowledge of a philosopher who wishes to visit this museum of human nature, or the perversity of those who take pleasure in spying and punishing. The more numerous those anonymous and temporary observers are, the greater the risk for the inmate of being surprised and the greater his anxious awareness of being observed. The Panopticon is a marvellous machine which, whatever use one may wish to put it to, produces homogeneous effects of power.

A real subjection is born mechanically from a fictitious relation. So it is not necessary to use force to constrain the convict to good behaviour, the madman to calm, the worker to work, the schoolboy to application, the patient to the observation of the regulations. Bentham was surprised that panoptic institutions could be so light: there were no more bars, no more chains, no more heavy locks; all that was needed was that the separations should be clear and the openings well arranged. The heaviness of the old 'houses of security', with their fortress-like architecture, could be replaced by the simple, economic geometry of a 'house of certainty'. The efficiency of power, its constraining force have, in a sense, passed over to the other side – to the side of its surface of application. He who is subjected to a field of visibility, and who knows it, assumes responsibility for the constraints of power; he makes thcm play spontaneously upon himself; he inscribes in himself the power relation in which he simultaneously plays both roles; he becomes the principle of his own subjection. By this very fact, the external power may throw off its physical weight; it tends to the non-corporal; and, the more it approaches this limit, the more constant, profound and permanent are its effects: it is a perpetual victory that avoids any physical confrontation and which is always decided in advance.

• • •

The plague-stricken town, the panoptic establishment – the differences are important. They mark, at a distance of a century and a half, the trans- formations of the disciplinary programme. In the first case, there is an exceptional situation: against an extraordinary evil, power is mobilized; it makes itself everywhere present and visible; it invents new mechanisms; it separates, it immobilizes, it partitions; it constructs for a time what is both a counter-city and the perfect society; it imposes an ideal functioning, but one that is reduced, in the final analysis, like the evil that it combats, to a simple dualism of life and death: that which moves brings death, and one kills that which moves. The Panopticon, on the other hand, must be un- derstood as a generalizable model of functioning; a way of defining power relations in terms of the everyday life of men . . . But the Panopticon must not be understood as a dream building: it is the diagram of a mechanism of power reduced to its ideal form; its functioning, abstracted from any obstacle, resistance or friction, must be represented as a pure architectural and optical system: it is in fact a figure of political technology that may and must be detached from any specific use.

• • •

'Discipline' may be identified neither with an institution nor with an apparatus; it is a type of power, a modality for its exercise, comprising a whole set of instruments, techniques, procedures, levels of application, targets; it is a 'physics' or an 'anatomy' of power, a technology. And it may be taken over either by 'specialized' institutions (the penitentiaries or 'houses of correction' of the nineteenth century), or by institutions that use it as an essential instrument for a particular end (schools, hospitals), or by pre- existing authorities that find in it a means of reinforcing or reorganizing their internal mechanisms of power (one day we should show how intra- familial relations, essentially in the parents–children cell, have become 'disciplined', absorbing since the classical age external schemata, first educational and military, then medical, psychiatric, psychological, which have made the family the privileged locus of emergence for the disciplinary question of the normal and the abnormal); or by apparatuses that have made discipline their principle of internal functioning (the disciplinarization of the administrative apparatus from the Napoleonic period), or finally by state apparatuses whose major, if not exclusive, function is to assure that discipline reigns over society as a whole (the police).

On the whole, therefore, one can speak of the formation of a disciplinary society in this movement that stretches from the enclosed disciplines, a sort of social 'quarantine', to an indefinitely generalizable mechanism of 'panopticism'. Not because the disciplinary modality of power has replaced all the others; but because it has infiltrated the others, sometimes undermining them, but serving as an intermediary between them, linking them together, extending them and above all making it possible to bring the effects of power to the most minute and distant elements. It assures an infinitesimal distribution of the power relations.

A few years after Bentham, Julius gave this society its birth certificate. Speaking of the panoptic principle, he said that there was much more there than architectural ingenuity: it was an event in the 'history of the human mind'. In appearance, it is merely the solution of a technical problem; but, through it, a whole type of society emerges. Antiquity had been a civilization of spectacle. 'To render accessible to a multitude of men the inspection of a small number of objects': this was the problem to which the architecture of temples, theatres and circuses responded. With spectacle, there was a predominance of public life, the intensity of festivals, sensual proximity. In these rituals in which blood flowed, society found new vigour and formed for a moment a single great body. The modern age poses the opposite problem: 'To procure for a small number, or even for a single individual, the instantaneous view of a great multitude.' In a society in which the principal elements are no longer the community and public life, but, on the one hand, private individuals and, on the other, the state, relations can be regulated only in a form that is the exact reverse of the spectacle: 'It was to the modern age, to the ever-growing influence of the state, to its ever more profound intervention in all the details and all the relations of social life, that was reserved the task of increasing and perfecting its guarantees, by using and directing towards that great aim the building and distribution of buildings intended to observe a great multitude of men at the same time.'

Julius saw as a fulfilled historical process that which Bentham had described as a technical programme. Our society is one not of spectacle, but of surveillance; under the surface of images, one invests bodies in depth; behind the great abstraction of exchange, there continues the meticulous, concrete training of useful forces; the circuits of communication are the supports of an accumulation and a centralization of knowledge; the play of signs defines the anchorages of power; it is not that the beautiful totality of the individual is amputated, repressed, altered by our social order, it is rather that the individual is carefully fabricated in it, according to a whole technique of forces and bodies. We are much less Greeks than we believe. We are neither in the amphitheatre, nor on the stage, but in the panoptic machine, invested by its effects of power, which we bring to ourselves since we are part of its mechanism. The importance, in historical mythology, of the Napoleonic character probably derives from the fact that it is at the point of junction of the monarchical, ritual exercise of sovereignty and the hierarchical, permanent exercise of indefinite discipline. He is the individual who looms over everything with a single gaze which no detail, however minute, can escape: 'You may consider that no part of the Empire is without surveillance, no crime, no offence, no contravention that remains unpunished, and that the eye of the genius who can enlighten all embraces the whole of this vast machine, without, however, the slightest detail escaping his attention'.

Notes

1 Archives militaires de Vincennes, A 1,516 91 sc. Pièce. This regulation is broadly similar to a whole series of others that date from the same period and earlier.
2 In the *Postscript to the Panopticon*, 1791, Bentham adds dark inspection galleries painted in black around the inspector's lodge, each making it possible to observe two storeys of cells.
3 In his first version of the *Panopticon*, Bentham had also imagined an acoustic surveillance, operated by means of pipes leading from the cells to the central tower. In the *Postscript* he abandoned the idea, perhaps because he could not introduce into it the principle of dissymmetry and prevent the prisoners from hearing the inspector as well as the inspector's hearing them. Julius tried to develop a system of dissymmetrical listening Julius, N.H., *Leçons sur les prisons*, I, 1831 (Fr. trans.), p. 18.

3.4

Michel Foucault from *The History of Sexuality* (1978)

Those who believe that sex was more rigorously elided in the nineteenth century than ever before, through a formidable mechanism of blockage and a deficiency of discourse, can say what they please. There was no deficiency, but rather an excess, a redoubling, too much rather than not enough discourse, in any case an interference between two modes of production of truth: procedures of confession, and scientific discursivity.

And instead of adding up the errors, naïvetés, and moralisms that plagued the nineteenth-century discourse of truth concerning sex, we would do better to locate the procedures by which that will to knowledge regarding sex, which characterizes the modern Occident, caused the rituals of confession to function within the norms of scientific regularity: how did this immense and traditional extortion of the sexual confession come to be constituted in scientific terms?

1 *Through a clinical codification of the inducement to speak.* Combining confession with examination, the personal history with the deployment of a set of decipherable signs and symptoms; the interrogation, the exacting questionnaire, and hypnosis, with the recollection of memories and free association: all were ways of reinscribing the procedure of confession in a field of scientifically acceptable observations.

2 *Through the postulate of a general and diffuse causality.* Having to tell everything, being able to pose questions about everything, found their justification in the principle that endowed sex with an inexhaustible and polymorphous causal power. The most discrete event in one's sexual behavior – whether an accident or a deviation, a deficit or an excess – was deemed capable of entailing the most varied consequences throughout one's exist-

ence; there was scarcely a malady or physical disturbance to which the nineteenth century did not impute at least some degree of sexual etiology. From the bad habits of children to the phthises of adults, the apoplexies of old people, nervous maladies, and the degenerations of the race, the medicine of that era wove an entire network of sexual causality to explain them. This may well appear fantastic to us, but the principle of sex as a 'cause of any and everything' was the theoretical underside of a confession that had to be thorough, meticulous, and constant, and at the same time operate within a scientific type of practice. The limitless dangers that sex carried with it justified the exhaustive character of the inquisition to which it was subjected.

3 *Through the principle of a latency intrinsic to sexuality.* If it was necessary to extract the truth of sex through the technique of confession, this was not simply because it was difficult to tell, or stricken by the taboos of decency, but because the ways of sex were obscure; it was elusive by nature; its energy and its mechanisms escaped observation, and its causal power was partly clandestine. By integrating it into the beginnings of a scientific discourse, the nineteenth century altered the scope of the confession; it tended no longer to be concerned solely with what the subject wished to hide, but with what was hidden from himself, being incapable of coming to light except gradually and through the labor of a confession in which the questioner and the questioned each had a part to play. The principle of a latency essential to sexuality made it possible to link the forcing of a difficult confession to a scientific practice. It had to be exacted, by force, since it involved something that tried to stay hidden.

4 *Through the method of interpretation.* If one had to confess, this was not merely because the person to whom one confessed had the power to forgive, console, and direct, but because the work of producing the truth was obliged to pass through this relationship if it was to be scientifically validated. The truth did not reside solely in the subject who, by confessing, would reveal it wholly formed. It was constituted in two stages: present but incomplete, blind to itself, in the one who spoke, it could only reach completion in the one who assimilated and recorded it. It was the latter's function to verify this obscure truth: the revelation of confession had to be coupled with the decipherment of what it said. The one who listened was not simply the forgiving master, the judge who condemned or acquitted; he was the master of truth. His was a hermeneutic function. With regard to the confession, his power was not only to demand it before it was made, or decide what was to follow after it, but also to constitute a discourse of truth on the basis of its decipherment. By no longer making the confession a test, but rather a sign, and by making sexuality something to be interpreted, the nineteenth century gave itself the possibility of causing the procedures of confession to operate within the regular formation of a scientific discourse.

5 *Through the medicalization of the effects of confession.* The obtaining of the confession and its effects were recodified as therapeutic operations. Which meant first of all that the sexual domain was no longer accounted for simply by the notions of error or sin, excess or transgression, but was placed under

the rule of the normal and the pathological (which, for that matter, were the transposition of the former categories); a characteristic sexual morbidity was defined for the first time; sex appeared as an extremely unstable pathological field: a surface of repercussion for other ailments, but also the focus of a specific nosography, that of instincts, tendencies, images, pleasure, and conduct. This implied furthermore that sex would derive its meaning and its necessity from medical interventions: it would be required by the doctor, necessary for diagnosis, and effective by nature in the cure. Spoken in time, to the proper party, and by the person who was both the bearer of it and the one responsible for it, the truth healed.

Let us consider things in broad historical perspective: breaking with the traditions of the *ars erotica*, our society has equipped itself with a *scientia sexualis*. To be more precise, it has pursued the task of producing true discourses concerning sex, and this by adapting – not without difficulty – the ancient procedure of confession to the rules of scientific discourse. Paradoxically, the *scientia sexualis* that emerged in the nineteenth century kept as its nucleus the singular ritual of obligatory and exhaustive confession, which in the Christian West was the first technique for producing the truth of sex. Beginning in the sixteenth century, this rite gradually detached itself from the sacrament of penance, and via the guidance of souls and the direction of conscience – the *ars artium* – emigrated toward pedagogy, relationships between adults and children, family relations, medicine, and psychiatry. In any case, nearly one hundred and fifty years have gone into the making of a complex machinery for producing true discourses on sex: a deployment that spans a wide segment of history in that it connects the ancient injunction of confession to clinical listening methods. It is this deployment that enables something called 'sexuality' to embody the truth of sex and its pleasures.

'Sexuality': the correlative of that slowly developed discursive practice which constitutes the *scientia sexualis*. The essential features of this sexuality are not the expression of a representation that is more or less distorted by ideology, or of a misunderstanding caused by taboos; they correspond to the functional requirements of a discourse that must produce its truth. Situated at the point of intersection of a technique of confession and a scientific discursivity, where certain major mechanisms had to be found for adapting them to one another (the listening technique, the postulate of causality, the principle of latency, the rule of interpretation, the imperative of medicalization), sexuality was defined as being 'by nature': a domain susceptible to pathological processes, and hence one calling for therapeutic or normalizing interventions; a field of meanings to decipher; the site of processes concealed by specific mechanisms; a focus of indefinite causal relations; and an obscure speech (*parole*) that had to be ferreted out and listened to. The 'economy' of discourses – their intrinsic technology, the necessities of their operation, the tactics they employ, the effects of power which underlie them and which they transmit – this, and not a system of representations, is what determines the essential features of what they have to say. The history of sexuality – that is, the history of what functioned in the nineteenth century as a specific field of truth – must first be written from the viewpoint of a history of discourses.

Let us put forward a general working hypothesis. The society that emerged in the nineteenth century – bourgeois, capitalist, or industrial society, call it what you will – did not confront sex with a fundamental refusal of recognition. On the contrary, it put into operation an entire machinery for producing true discourses concerning it. Not only did it speak of sex and compel everyone to do so; it also set out to formulate the uniform truth of sex. As if it suspected sex of harboring a fundamental secret. As if it needed this production of truth. As if it was essential that sex be inscribed not only in an economy of pleasure but in an ordered system of knowledge. Thus sex gradually became an object of great suspicion; the general and disquieting meaning that pervades our conduct and our existence, in spite of ourselves; the point of weakness where evil portents reach through to us; the fragment of darkness that we each carry within us: a general signification, a universal secret, an omnipresent cause, a fear that never ends. And so, in this 'question' of sex (in both senses: as interrogation and problematization, and as the need for confession and integration into a field of rationality), two processes emerge, the one always conditioning the other: we demand that sex speak the truth (but, since it is the secret and is oblivious to its own nature, we reserve for ourselves the function of telling the truth of its truth, revealed and deciphered at last), and we demand that it tell us our truth, or rather, the deeply buried truth of that truth about ourselves which we think we possess in our immediate consciousness. We tell it its truth by deciphering what it tells us about that truth; it tells us our own by delivering up that part of it that escaped us. From this interplay there has evolved, over several centuries, a knowledge of the subject; a knowledge not so much of his form, but of that which divides him, determines him perhaps, but above all causes him to be ignorant of himself. As unlikely as this may seem, it should not surprise us when we think of the long history of the Christian and juridical confession, of the shifts and transformations this form of knowledge-power, so important in the West, has undergone: the project of a science of the subject has gravitated, in ever narrowing circles, around the question of sex. Causality in the subject, the unconscious of the subject, the truth of the subject in the other who knows, the knowledge he holds unbeknown to him, all this found an opportunity to deploy itself in the discourse of sex. Not, however, by reason of some natural property inherent in sex itself, but by virtue of the tactics of power immanent in this discourse.

Scientia sexualis versus *ars erotica*, no doubt. But it should be noted that the *ars erotica* did not disappear altogether from Western civilization; nor has it always been absent from the movement by which one sought to produce a science of sexuality. In the Christian confession, but especially in the direction and examination of conscience, in the search for spiritual union and the love of God, there was a whole series of methods that had much in common with an erotic art: guidance by the master along a path of initiation, the intensification of experiences extending down to their physical components, the optimization of effects by the discourse that accompanied them. The phenomena of possession and ecstasy, which were quite frequent in the Catholicism of the Counter Reformation, were undoubtedly effects that had got outside the control of the erotic technique immanent in this subtle science of the flesh. And we must ask whether, since the nineteenth century, the *scientia sexualis* – under the guise of its decent positivism – has not functioned, at least to a certain extent, as an *ars erotica*. Perhaps this production of truth, intimidated though it was by the scientific model, multiplied, intensified, and even created its own intrinsic pleasures. It is often said that we have been incapable of imagining any new pleasures. We have at least invented a different kind of pleasure: pleasure in the truth of pleasure, the pleasure of knowing that truth, of discovering and exposing it, the fascination of seeing it and telling it, of captivating and capturing others by it, of confiding it in secret, of luring it out in the open – the specific pleasure of the true discourse on pleasure.

The most important elements of an erotic art linked to our knowledge about sexuality are not to be sought in the ideal, promised to us by medicine, of a healthy sexuality, nor in the humanist dream of a complete and flourishing sexuality, and certainly not in the lyricism of orgasm and the good feelings of bio-energy (these are but aspects of its normalizing utilization), but in this multiplication and intensification of pleasures connected to the production of the truth about sex. The learned volumes, written and read; the consultations and examinations; the anguish of answering questions and the delights of having one's words interpreted; all the stories told to oneself and to others, so much curiosity, so many confidences offered in the face of scandal, sustained – but not without trembling a little – by the obligation of truth; the profusion of secret fantasies and the dearly paid right to whisper them to whoever is able to hear them; in short, the formidable 'pleasure of analysis' (in the widest sense of the latter term) which the West has cleverly been fostering for several centuries: all this constitutes something like the errant fragments of an erotic art that is secretly transmitted by confession and the science of sex. Must we conclude that our *scientia sexualis* is but an extraordinarily subtle form of *ars erotica*, and that it is the Western, sublimated version of that seemingly lost tradition? Or must we suppose that all these pleasures are only the by-products of a sexual science, a bonus that compensates for its many stresses and strains?

In any case, the hypothesis of a power of repression exerted by our society on sex for economic reasons appears to me quite inadequate if we are to explain this whole series of reinforcements and intensifications that our preliminary inquiry has discovered: a proliferation of discourses, carefully tailored to the requirements of power; the solidification of the sexual mosaic and the construction of devices capable not only of isolating it but of stimulating and provoking it, of forming it into focuses of attention, discourse, and pleasure; the mandatory production of confessions and the subsequent establishment of a system of legitimate knowledge and of an economy of manifold pleasures. We are dealing not nearly so much with a negative mechanism of exclusion as with the operation of a subtle network of discourses, special knowledges, pleasures, and powers. At issue is not a movement bent on pushing rude sex back into some obscure and inaccessible region, but on the contrary, a process that spreads it over the surface of things and bodies, arouses it, draws it out and bids it speak, implants it in reality and enjoins it to tell the truth: an entire glittering sexual array, reflected in a myriad of discourses, the obstination of powers, and the interplay of knowledge and pleasure.

All this is an illusion, it will be said, a hasty impression behind which a more discerning gaze will surely discover the same great machinery of repression. Beyond these few phosphorescences, are we not sure to find once more the somber law that always says no? The answer will have to come out of a historical inquiry. An inquiry concerning the manner in which a knowledge of sex has been forming over the last three centuries; the manner in which the discourses that take it as their object have multiplied, and the reasons for which we have come to attach a nearly fabulous price to the truth they claimed to produce. Perhaps these historical analyses will end by dissipating what this cursory survey seems to suggest. But the postulate I started out with, and would like to hold to as long as possible, is that these deployments of power and knowledge, of truth and pleasures, so unlike those of repression, are not necessarily secondary and derivative; and further, that repression is not in any case fundamental and overriding. We need to take these mechanisms seriously, therefore, and reverse the direction of our analysis: rather than assuming a generally acknowledged repression, and an ignorance measured against what we are supposed to know, we must begin with these positive mechanisms, insofar as they produce knowledge, multiply discourse, induce pleasure, and generate power; we must investigate the conditions of their emergence and operation, and try to discover how the related facts of interdiction or concealment are distributed with respect to them. In short, we must define the strategies of power that are immanent in this will to knowledge. As far as sexuality is concerned, we shall attempt to constitute the 'political economy' of a will to knowledge.

3.5

Roland Barthes
from *The Pleasure of the Text* (1973)

Is not the most erotic portion of a body *where the garment gapes*? In perversion (which is the realm of textual pleasure) there are no 'erogenous zones' (a foolish expression, besides); it is intermittence, as psychoanalysis has so rightly stated, which is erotic: the intermittence of skin flashing between two articles of clothing (trousers and sweater), between two edges (the open-necked shirt, the glove and the sleeve); it is this flash itself which seduces, or rather: the staging of an appearance-as-disappearance.

The pleasure of the text is not the pleasure of the corporeal striptease or of narrative suspense. In these cases, there is no tear, no edges: a gradual unveiling: the entire excitation takes refuge in the *hope* of seeing the sexual organ (schoolboy's dream) or in knowing the end of the story (novelistic satisfaction). Paradoxically (since it is mass-consumed), this is a far more intellectual pleasure than the other: an Oedipal pleasure (to denude, to know, to learn the origin and the end), if it is true that every narrative (every unveiling of the truth) is a staging of the (absent, hidden, or hypostatized) father – which would explain the solidarity of narrative forms, of family structures, and of prohibitions of nudity, all collected in our culture in the myth of Noah's sons covering his nakedness.

Yet the most classical narrative (a novel by Zola or Balzac or Dickens or Tolstoy) bears within it a sort of diluted tmesis: we do not read everything with the same intensity of reading; a rhythm is established, casual, unconcerned with the *integrity* of the text; our very avidity for knowledge impels us to skim or to skip certain passages (anticipated as 'boring') in order to get more quickly to the warmer parts of the anecdote (which are always its articulations: whatever furthers the solution of the riddle, the revelation of fate): we boldly skip (no one is watching) descriptions, explanations, analyses, conversations; doing so, we resemble a spectator in a nightclub who climbs onto the stage and speeds up the dancer's striptease, tearing off her clothing, *but in the same order*, that is: on the one hand respecting and on the other hastening the episodes of the ritual (like a priest *gulping down* his Mass). Tmesis, source or figure of pleasure, here confronts two prosaic edges with one another; it sets what is useful to a knowledge of the secret against what is useless to such knowledge; tmesis is a seam or flaw resulting from a simple principle of functionality; it does not occur at the level of the structure of languages but only at the moment of their consumption; the author cannot predict tmesis: he cannot choose to write *what will not be read*. And yet, it is the very rhythm of what is read and what is not read that creates the pleasure of the great narratives: has anyone ever read Proust, Balzac, *War and Peace*, word for word? (Proust's good fortune: from one reading to the next, we never skip the same passages.)

Thus, what I enjoy in a narrative is not directly its content or even its structure, but rather the abrasions I impose upon the fine surface: I read on, I skip, I look up, I dip in again. Which has nothing to do with the deep laceration the text of bliss inflicts upon language itself, and not upon the simple temporality of its reading.

Whence two systems of reading: one goes straight to the articulations of the anecdote, it considers the extent of the text, ignores the play of language (if I read Jules Verne, I go fast: I lose discourse, and yet my reading is not hampered by any verbal *loss* – in the speleological sense of that word); the other reading skips nothing; it weighs, it sticks to the text, it reads, so to speak, with application and transport, grasps at every point in the text the asyndeton which cuts the various languages – and not the anecdote: it is not (logical) extension that captivates it, the winnowing out of truths, but the layering of significance; as in the children's game of topping hands, the excitement comes not from a processive haste but from a kind of vertical din (the verticality of language and of its destruction); it is at the moment when each (different) hand skips over the next (and not one *after* the other) that the hole, the gap, is created and carries off the subject of the game – the subject of the text. Now paradoxically (so strong is the belief that one need merely *go fast* in order not to be bored), this second, *applied* reading (in the real sense of the word 'application') is the one suited to the modern text, the limit-text. Read slowly, read *all* of a novel by Zola, and the book will drop from your hands; read fast, in snatches, some modern text, and it becomes opaque, inaccessible to your pleasure: you want something to happen and nothing does, for *what happens to the language does not happen to the discourse:* what 'happens,' what 'goes away,' the seam of the two edges, the interstice of bliss, occurs in the volume of the languages, in the uttering, not in the sequence of utterances: not to devour, to gobble, but to graze, to browse scrupulously, to rediscover – in order to read today's writers – the leisure of bygone readings: to be *aristocratic* readers.

• • •

If I agree to judge a text according to pleasure, I cannot go on to say: this one is good, that bad. No awards, no 'critique,' for this always implies a tactical aim, a social usage, and frequently an extenuating image-reservoir. I cannot apportion, imagine that the text is perfectible, ready to enter into a play of normative predicates: it is too much *this*, not enough *that*; the text (the same is true of the singing voice) can wring from me only this judgment, in no way adjectival: *that's it!* And further still: *that's it for me!* This 'for me' is neither subjective nor existential, but Nietzschean ('. . . basically, it is always the same question: What is it *for me?* . . .').

The *brio* of the text (without which, after all, there is no text) is its *will to bliss:* just where it exceeds demand, transcends prattle, and whereby it attempts to overflow, to break through the constraint of adjectives – which are those doors of language through which the ideological and the imaginary come flowing in.

• • •

Text of pleasure: the text that contents, fills, grants euphoria; the text that comes from culture and does not break with it, is linked to a *comfortable* practice of reading. Text of bliss: the text that imposes a state of loss, the text that discomforts (perhaps to the point of a certain boredom), unsettles the reader's historical, cultural, psychological assumptions, the consistency of his tastes, values, memories, brings to a crisis his relation with language.

Now the subject who keeps the two texts in his field and in his hands the reins of pleasure and bliss is an anachronic subject, for he simultaneously and contradictorily participates in the profound hedonism of all culture (which permeates him quietly under cover of an *art de vivre* shared by the old books) and in the destruction of that culture: he enjoys the consistency of his selfhood (that is his pleasure) and seeks its loss (that is his bliss). He is a subject split twice over, doubly perverse.

• • •

Society of the Friends of the Text: its members would have nothing in common (for there is no necessary agreement on the texts of pleasure) but their enemies: fools of all kinds, who decree foreclosure of the text and of its pleasure, either by cultural conformism or by intransigent rationalism (suspecting a 'mystique' of literature) or by political moralism or by criticism of the signifier or by stupid pragmatism or by snide vacuity or by destruction of the discourse, loss of verbal desire. Such a society would have no site, could function only in total atopia; yet it would be a kind of phalanstery, for in it contradictions would be acknowledged (and the risks of ideological imposture thereby restricted), difference would be observed and conflict rendered insignificant (being unproductive of pleasure).

'Let difference surreptitiously replace conflict.' Difference is not what makes or sweetens conflict: it is achieved over and above conflict, it is *beyond and alongside* conflict. Conflict is nothing but the moral state of difference; whenever (and this is becoming frequent) conflict is not tactical (aimed at transforming a real situation), one can distinguish in it the failure-to-attain-bliss, the debacle of a perversion crushed by its own code and no longer able to invent itself: conflict is always coded, aggression is merely the most worn-out of languages. Forgoing violence, I forgo the code itself (in Sade's texts, outside all codes because they continually invent their own, appropriate only to themselves, there are no conflicts: only triumphs). I love the text because for me it is that rare locus of language from which any 'scene' (in the household, conjugal sense of the term), any logomachy is absent. The text is never a 'dialogue': no risk of feint, of aggression, of blackmail, no rivalry of ideolects; the text establishes a sort of islet within the human – the common – relation, manifests the asocial nature of pleasure (only leisure is social), grants a glimpse of the scandalous truth about bliss: that it may well be, once the image-reservoir of speech is abolished, *neuter*.

• • •

On the stage of the text, no footlights: there is not, behind the text, someone active (the writer) and out front someone passive (the reader); there is not a subject and an object. The text supersedes grammatical attitudes: it is the undifferentiated eye which an excessive author (Angelus Silesius) describes: 'The eye by which I see God is the same eye by which He sees me.'

Apparently Arab scholars, when speaking of the text, use this admirable expression: *the certain body*. What body? We have several of them; the body of anatomists and physiologists, the one science sees or discusses: this is the text of grammarians, critics, commentators, philologists (the pheno-text). But we also have a body of bliss consisting solely of erotic relations, utterly distinct from the first body: it is another contour, another nomination; thus with the text: it is no more than the open list of the fires of language (those living fires, intermittent lights, wandering features strewn in the text like seeds and which for us advantageously replace the *'semina aeternitatis,'* the *'zopyra,'* the common notions, the fundamental assumptions of ancient philosophy). Does the text have human form, is it a figure, an anagram of the body? Yes, but of our erotic body. The pleasure of the text is irreducible to physiological need.

The pleasure of the text is that moment when my body pursues its own ideas – for my body does not have the same ideas I do.

• • •

How can we take pleasure in a *reported* pleasure (boredom of all narratives of dreams, of parties)? How can we read criticism? Only one way: since I am here a second-degree reader, I must shift my position: instead of agreeing to be the confidant of this critical pleasure – a sure way to miss it – I can make myself its voyeur: I observe clandestinely the pleasure of others, I enter perversion; the commentary then becomes in my eyes a text, a fiction, a fissured envelope. The writer's perversity (his pleasure in writing is *without function*), the doubled, the trebled, the infinite perversity of the critic and of his reader.

Section four

DIFFERENCE

'What therefore is truth? A mobile army of metaphors, metonymies, anthropomorphisms . . . truths are illusions of which one has forgotten that they are illusions.'

> Nietzsche, cited in the 'Preface' by Gayatri Spivak to *Of Grammatology* (Derrida 1976), p. xxii.

Every sign is different

'What is difference? Difference is . . .' To us, situated as inheritors of a rational tradition stretching back to Plato and ancient Greek philosophy, it seems so obvious and natural that such questions should have clear and definite answers. Why bother with a writer such as Derrida who appears unable or unwilling to give a straight answer, to begin at the beginning, go on to the middle and end with the conclusion, explaining what he really means? Yet Derrida's work renders each of these terms problematic when applied to modes of writing: 'straight', 'beginning'/'middle'/'end', 'means', 'really', 'really means', even (especially) 'is'. His writing and his account of difference touch on so many of the texts gathered in this present collection that it becomes inescapable, represented here by the whole of the essay, 'Différance'. Again, because Derrida's writing, without fitting into any one category or discipline, breaches and runs across traditional boundaries (between culture and philosophy, linguistics and theories of the subject, between all of these and issues of gender) it requires its own separate section under 'Difference'.

The foregoing means that there can be no mastering 'introduction' to difference or concluding 'summary' of the essay of that title. An analogy and two matters for reflection may help to frame some of the issues over which the essay intervenes (intervening to promote the question of difference in February 1968, when the 'events' of that year were just starting to get under way on the streets of Paris).

There is a helpful analogy with the work of Jacques Lacan (see Section 3.1). It could be argued that Lacan, sharing with Derrida the philosophic inheritance of Heidegger's challenge to the tradition of Western metaphysics, turns Plato on his head. If Plato posited an ideal world of Forms in which Being was perfectly and timelessly present to itself and of which this mortal world is an unhappy copy, the effect of Lacan is to regard *manque à être* (lack in being) as originary and foundational; emerging from being into meaning, the human subject is constituted by its failed attempt to make good the lack it discovers as it enters language and the 'defiles' of the signifier. Within and on the grounds of the pre-existing intersubjective order of the Symbolic the I becomes present and substantial only in so far as it wins over from there an Imaginary identity for itself. There is, then, an analogy between Lacan's account of lack and identity, and Derrida's account of difference and presence. But it is an analogy only, for Derrida offers no comparable theory of the subject and has, moreover, differed fiercely with Lacan on the question of mastery and truth (see 'Le facteur de la vérité' in *The Post Card*, 1987; see also fn. 5, p. 130).

Speech/writing

One line of reflection on the writing of Derrida would take *Of Grammatology* (1976) as its point of departure. There Derrida cites a number of texts which show how often and unreflectingly the Western tradition takes a very partial and common-sense view of the nature of writing and particularly of the relation between speech and writing. Consistently writers who include Aquinas, Hegel, Rousseau and, more recently, Saussure and Lévi-Strauss (see 'Biographies'), have privileged speech over writing on the grounds that it is closer to inwardness and thought, and so treated writing as merely a technical derivation from speech, a writing down of what's already there. Speech has been placed as inside with writing outside in similar terms to the presumed relation of mind and body. For example, Derrida quotes Aristotle from *De Interpretatione* to the effect that 'spoken words (ta en tē phonē) are the symbols of mental experience (pathēmata tēs psychēs) and written words are the symbols of spoken words' (1976: 11). Writing is disparaged because it stands for something else of which it is a trace. There is a strong tendency, therefore, to equate being with mind and thought as though thought were fully present to itself, and writing had nothing to do with making meaning possible. This tendency or disposition Derrida names as *logocentrism* and regards as forming the very basis for metaphysics because it thus prioritizes presence. He hopes to see logocentrism yield to something else, a concern with 'archi-writing', that is, in the widest sense, the very *possibility* of writing; to give full weight to writing would be to recognize the dependence of presence on a trace.

Speech/writing stands as a binary opposition which Derrida offers to *deconstruct* when he argues (among other things) that thought, speech and writing all depend upon representation and the signifier. So it would be possible to begin at the other end, as it were, and propose that 'Writing precedes and follows speech, it comprehends it' (Derrida 1976: 238). But it is not so much writing itself Derrida is concerned with as the condition at work 'inside' writing, which makes it possible, the graphematic. (You might see a neon sign for SHELL with a faulty circuit for the s so that it reads HELL – though a similar chance occurrence might have made it read SHE or HE or S ELL; now, what produced those meanings, the reader or the material system on which the sign relied?)

The method of deconstruction is as important as its consequences. For to deconstruct (in this strict, Derridean sense) is to attend to a traditionally empowered binary hierarchy in which the first term is privileged over the second needed to define it and then to breach or unsettle that opposition in one way or another (*not* all binary oppositions but those whose hierarchy supports – and is supported by – power). Simply to invert the opposition by privileging the *second* term would retain the power relations exercised in the binary already in place. In *Dissemination* Derrida lists some oppositions that have sustained the metaphysics of presence in the Western tradition: 'speech/writing, life/death, father/son, master/servant, first/second, legitimate son/orphan-bastard, soul/body, inside/outside, seriousness/play' (1981: 85). And in the essay 'White mythology' (*Margins of Philosophy*) he adds the binary, literal/figurative (associated with philosophy/literature), though it would be easy to extend the list as they saturate the texts of contemporary culture, high and popular.

Is the most forceful and encompassing binary represented by the hierarchy masculine/feminine, linking all the others? Derrida has certainly encouraged this conclusion, identifying logocentrism with *phallogocentrism* and claiming that 'it is one and the same system: the erection of a paternal logos . . . and of the phallus as "privileged signifier"' (1973a: 311). If so, 'speech', 'life', 'master', 'first', 'soul', 'inside', 'seriousness' would make up a series which has been qualified as 'masculine', while 'writing', 'death', 'second', 'body', 'outside', 'play' would form another denoted as 'feminine' (a possibility whose implications have been explored by Cixous, see Section 5.2).

Different times

Speech/writing opens one approach to 'Différance'; the question of time broaches another and may help to focus a little what Derrida is writing against (though the very terms 'for' and 'against' suppose a fixed opposition between inside and outside that tempts deconstruction, and in any case it's hard to know how anyone nurtured in the Western tradition today could yet find themselves sufficiently apart from it to be genuinely *against* it). Nevertheless, there is a respect in which that post-Socratic tradition begins with a certain conception of time.

Until recently a watch was a large object carried on a chain slung across the waist, but since the 1920s almost every adult in the West carries time on their wrist, marking off seconds, minutes, hours, days, months in re-morseless accumulation. Such a conception of time as an absolute, even, continuous and homogeneous *linearity* has been dominant in the West since Ancient Greece. Implicit in commonplace metaphors of 'the stream of time' or 'the passage of time', this kind of time is thought of as spacelike, as though the now were either a stake driven into the bed of a river (the future flowing by the stake and into the past) or a train crossing the prairies (the lines in front leading to an invisible horizon in the future and those behind to one in the past). Aristotle in his foundational account (*Physics*, 217b–224a) envisages the now as a spatio-temporal succession of units, the now always the same but in a different position for it is the present. Intersected, absolute linear time makes it possible to make confident divisions into points of origin and points of completion in which a potential, already present in the beginning, is realized by the end, with only a middle to separate them: 'My beginning is my end' as Eliot says in *Four Quartets*.

But if, as Derrida argues (in *'Ousia* and *Gramme'* in *Margins of Philosophy*), time is thought of (as it should be) not as a kind of space but as time, then the now can no longer be considered as a *point* on a *line*. The now can be defined only by its difference from another now which this now is not. A conception of time as the present must give way to another sense of time as multidimensional, time not as a single line but something like an uneven bundle of swerves. And further, in that the apparently punctual and present now is a necessary condition for the I to appear to be present to itself as a pure self-consciousness, then this view of the subject must also be surrendered.

Différance

In French, as in English, *différence* and *différance* are both pronounced the same so that, looking almost like a Freudian slip (or lapse), the difference represents what is at issue between speech and writing. 'An interval must separate the present from what it is not in order for the present to be itself, but this interval that constitutes it as present must, by the same token, divide the present in and of itself, thereby also dividing, along with the present, everything that is thought on the basis of the present . . .' (p. 116 below). An interval separates two things in space as well as two in time – différance presides over such an interval, combining as it does both difference in space and deferral in time. It cannot be defined as 'a concept' because that would commit it in advance to a 'theology of being' ('ontotheology', p. 111), to a metaphysics of presence ('difference is . . .'). Of différance the essay provides three main instances.

The first is Saussurian linguistics, developed as it is from the notion of linguistic value. Whereas we may usually think of value as the property of a thing (and are always disappointed), the value of terms in linguistics, whether one takes signifier or signified, is purely relational, as Saussure explains in a passage Derrida quotes (and see pp. 12–13 above). Signification supposes both difference and deferral: that meaning is never present (fully formed) in individual signifiers but is produced through a series of differences; that meaning is always temporally deferred, sliding under a chain of signifiers which has no end. [With reference to Saussure, Derrida also recalls his criticism that even Saussure privileges speech over writing (see *Of Grammatology* 1976: 44–73).]

If Saussure tends to suggest that the presence of the subject in consciousness is, because of the nature of the differences within the sign, an effect, that view is confirmed by psychoanalysis. In the work of Freud (see Section 5.1) the subject can never be present to itself because drive is always deferred or deflected, for instance in the way that sexual drive becomes necessarily turned aside into human activities as divergent from a manifestly sexual aim as smoking cigarettes and editing anthologies of cultural criticism. It does so because 'the finding of an object is in fact a refinding of it', *SE*, vol. 7: 222): because (for example) through the demands of the Oedipus complex the mother has to be refound in another adult man or woman; because of the split between unconscious and conscious such that (in the same example) the incestuous drive towards the mother becomes repressed, even though it motivates adult love of which an individual will not be fully aware. Insisting on this detour of the pleasure principle, which seeks pleasure and avoids unpleasure, is the reality principle, which modifies the demands of the pleasure principle, postponing impossible satisfactions now in order to achieve more limited pleasures later. But finding/refinding, conscious/unconscious, reality/pleasure principle are not *opposites*, for each is defined dynamically in relation to the other, as are Eros and *Thanatos*, the life drives and the death drives in *Beyond the Pleasure Principle* (*SE*, vol. 18).

In Freud's concept of *Nachträglichkeit* or deferral the sense in which drives consist only of detours and differences appears particularly unsettling. Weaning and the loss of the breast happen at an earlier stage in the infant's physical development than the threat of castration – but once reached, Freud suggests, the earlier experience is reinterpreted retrospectively as an anticipation of the later experience. Deferral defines the way memories are reinterpreted in the light of subsequent experiences so that the subject is constantly and unendingly rearranging its past by re-transcribing it in the present. Such examples imply that for the unconscious there can be no absolute point of origin or conclusion, that each origin and conclusion exists only in relation to another and in the difference between them.

The 'ontico-ontological difference' is the distinction Heidegger in *Being and Time* (1962: 10) marks between entities or 'real things' (the 'ontic') and Being (or the 'ontological'). Being is the process, mode or condition of existence which makes entities possible. The first sentence of *Being and Time* says that the question of Being 'has today been forgotten' (p. 2), and the rest of the work seeks to rethink Being in contrast to the logocentric tradition which according to Heidegger, since the time of pre-Socratic philosophers such as Heraclitus and Parmenides, has disregarded the importance of Being. At the opening of *An Introduction to Metaphysics* Heidegger tries to reinstate a sense of Being by asking as a fundamental question (borrowed from Leibniz): 'Why are there essents rather than nothing?' (1959: 1; 'essents' = 'existents', 'things that are').

Logocentrism admits but seeks to recuperate the difference between Being and beings, for example, in the way that for Plato entities fallen away from the perfected Being of the world of Forms re-aspire to that state. For Heidegger

106 A CRITICAL AND CULTURAL THEORY READER

the distinction between Being and beings is like that between 'presencing' and what is present. Being appears as 'presencing' if the now is assumed to be a self-identical spot or point in which consciousness can be present to itself. But since time is not like that, human existence (*Dasein*, 'Being There') can never be present to itself and remains incomplete across a past continuous with a future: thrown by the past into a world it cannot master Being There projects itself from a present in which it is always contingent and dependent into a future which is only a possibility. Entities are to be defined not by their participation in Being but in their difference from it and from each other (*Differenz* is in fact a Heideggerian term, see 1962: 481, fn.). But since Being is not actually present, what can be said about it? If in *Being and Time* Heidegger seems to think he can address Being, in his later work he is clear that he can't, writing Being with a cross through it so that it appears only 'under erasure'.

Derrida's instances – from the order of the sign, the order of the subject, and the order of being – may not make his radical import as readily grasped as it might be if thought of in terms of traditional ideas of divinity. Logocentrism and the metaphysics of presence are certainly at work in the Platonism of the Hellenic tradition and in the idea of God in the Judaeo-Christian inheritance. After the visible natural signs (wind, earthquake, fire) and transcending these, God appears to Elijah as 'a still small voice' (1 Kgs. 19. 12). Or again there is the repeated claim that God is *alpha* and *omega*, absolute origin terminating in a correspondingly absolute end, another reason Derrida welcomes the insertion of an 'a' into *différance*, which is '"older" than Being itself' (p. 26). Derrida's task has been to suggest how a tran-scendental signified is at work, underground, in the post-Renaissance and Enlighten-ment tradition precisely because it felt so secure that it had purified itself of the idea of God.

A transcendental signified may appear not only in rationalist forms of philosophy but also in its negation. Thus Derrida is concerned to show he is not practising a negative theology (see fn. 5, p. 129). Cataphatic or positive theology describes what God is (inevitably in terms of human experience: God is love, etc.) while apophatic or negative theology says what God is not, and so in the mystical tradition terms such as *emptiness* and *void* have a positive force. For Derrida there is a dilemma here: if he defines *différance* positively (difference is . . .) he betrays its nature; if he says it is not presence and Being, he risks attributing to the absence of Being a comparable function to its presence. He is scrupulous, therefore, in working through the writings of Saussure, Freud and Heidegger, to resist the possibility of a nostalgia through which we might think of ourselves as lost or alienated from a sense of Being (which, negatively, would thus continue to be affirmed).

It's fair to ask what might be the consequences of taking on board something of Derrida's philosophically complex argument. What is at stake politically over *différance*?

> It governs nothing, reigns over nothing, and nowhere exercises any authority. It is not announced by any capital letter. Not only is there no kingdom of *différance*, but *différance* instigates the subversion of every

kingdom. Which makes it obviously threatening and infallibly dreaded by everything within us that desires a kingdom, the past or future presence of a kingdom (p. 123).

Wherever, within the cultural matrix, power claims privilege for itself in the name of Being, presence, authoritative speech, essential nature, absolute Truth, in sum as pure identity and sameness, then *différance* can be called on to instigate a relativization and subversion of that power. Three domains may particularly invite those strategies. One would be that of gender, whenever masculine and feminine are posed as opposites, self-identical and so the same all the way through. Another would be that of the social formation, particularly nationhood, if it is advanced as pure, not made up of differences. And a third is familiar already, for it is that by which Edward Said has shown Europe ascribes to itself a oneness and fixity in opposition to the differences of 'the Orient'. As someone born in Algeria and writing in Paris in 1968, Derrida is aware of the politics of *différance*.

4.1

Jacques Derrida
from 'Différance' (1968)

I will speak, therefore, of a letter.

Of the first letter, if the alphabet, and most of the speculations which have ventured into it, are to be believed.

I will speak, therefore, of the letter *a*, this initial letter which it apparently has been necessary to insinuate, here and there, into the writing of the word *difference*; and to do so in the course of a writing on writing, and also of a writing within writing whose different trajectories thereby find themselves, at certain very determined points, intersecting with a kind of gross spelling mistake, a lapse in the discipline and law which regulate writing and keep it seemly. One can always, de facto or de jure,[a] erase or reduce this lapse in spelling, and find it (according to situations to be analyzed each time, although amounting to the same), grave or unseemly, that is, to follow the most ingenuous hypothesis, amusing. Thus, even if one seeks to pass over such an infraction in silence, the interest that one takes in it can be recognized and situated in advance as prescribed by the mute irony, the inaudible misplacement, of this literal permutation. One can always act as if it made no difference. And I must state here and now that today's discourse will be less a justification of, and even less an apology for, this silent lapse in spelling, than a kind of insistent intensification of its play.

On the other hand, I will have to be excused if I refer, at least implicitly, to some of the texts I have ventured to publish. This is precisely because I would like to attempt, to a certain extent, and even though in principle and in the last analysis this is impossible, and impossible for essential reasons, to reassemble in a *sheaf* the different directions in which I have been able to utilize what I would call provisionally the word or concept of *différance*, or rather to let it impose itself upon me in its neographism, although as we shall see, *différance* is literally neither a word nor a concept. And I insist upon the word *sheaf* for two reasons. On the one hand, I will not be concerned, as I might have been, with describing a history and narrating its stages, text by text, context by context, demonstrating the economy that each time imposed this graphic disorder; rather, I will be concerned with the *general system of this economy*. On the other hand, the word *sheaf* seems to mark more appropriately that the assemblage to be proposed has the complex structure of a weaving, an interlacing which permits the different threads and different lines of meaning – or of force – to go off again in different directions, just as it is always ready to tie itself up with others.

Therefore, preliminarily, let me recall that this discreet graphic intervention, which neither primarily nor simply aims to shock the reader or the grammarian, came to be formulated in the course of a written investigation of a question about writing. Now it happens, I would say in effect, that this graphic difference (*a* instead of *e*), this marked difference between two apparently vocal notations, between two vowels, remains purely graphic: it is read, or it is written, but it cannot be heard. It cannot be apprehended in speech, and we will see why it also bypasses the order of apprehension in general. It is offered by a mute mark, by a tacit monument, I would even say by a pyramid, thinking not only of the form of the letter when it is printed as a capital, but also of the text in Hegel's *Encyclopedia*[b] in which the body of the sign is compared to the Egyptian Pyramid. The *a* of *différance*, thus, is not heard; it remains silent, secret and discreet as a tomb: *oikēsis*. And thereby let us anticipate the delineation of a site, the familial residence and tomb of the proper[1] in which is produced, by *différance*, the *economy of death*. This stone – provided that one knows how to decipher its inscription – is not far from announcing the death of the tyrant.[2]

And it is a tomb that cannot even be made to resonate. In effect, I cannot let you know through my discourse, through the speech being addressed at this moment to the French Society of Philosophy, what difference I am talking about when I talk about it. I can speak of this graphic difference only through a very indirect discourse on writing, and on the condition that I specify, each time, whether I am referring to difference with an *e* or *différance* with an *a*. Which will not simplify things today, and will give us all, you and me, a great deal of trouble, if, at least, we wish to understand each other. In any event, the oral specifications that I will provide – when I say 'with an *e*' or 'with an *a*' – will refer uncircumventably to a *written text* that keeps watch over my discourse, to a text that I am holding in front of me, that I will read, and toward which I necessarily will attempt to direct your hands and your eyes. We will be able neither to do without the passage through a written text, nor to avoid the order of the disorder produced within it – and this, first of all, is what counts for me.

The pyramidal silence of the graphic difference between the *e* and the *a* can function, of course, only within the system of phonetic writing, and within the language and grammar which is as historically linked to phonetic writing as it is to the entire culture inseparable from phonetic writing. But I would say that this in itself – the silence that functions within only a so-called phonetic writing – quite opportunely conveys or reminds us that, contrary to a very widespread prejudice, there is no phonetic writing. There is no purely and rigorously phonetic writing. So-called phonetic writing, by all rights and in principle, and not only due to an empirical or technical insufficiency, can function only by admitting into its system nonphonetic 'signs' (punctuation, spacing, etc.). And an examination of the structure and necessity of these nonphonetic signs quickly reveals that they can barely tolerate the concept of the sign itself. Better, the play of difference, which, as Saussure reminded us, is the condition for the possibility and functioning of every sign, is in itself a silent play. Inaudible is the difference between two phonemes which alone permits them to be and to operate as such. The inaudible opens up the apprehension of two present phonemes such as they present themselves. If there is no purely phonetic writing, it is that there is no purely phonetic *phōnē*.ᶜ The difference which establishes phonemes and lets them be heard remains in and of itself inaudible, in every sense of the word.

It will be objected, for the same reasons, that graphic difference itself vanishes into the night, can never be sensed as a full term, but rather extends an invisible relationship, the mark of an inapparent relationship between two spectacles. Doubtless. But, from this point of view, that the difference marked in the 'differ( )nce' between the *e* and the *a* eludes both vision and hearing perhaps happily suggests that here we must be permitted to refer to an order which no longer belongs to sensibility. But neither can it belong to intelligibility, to the ideality which is not fortuitously affiliated with the objectivity of *theōrein* or understanding.[3] Here, therefore, we must let ourselves refer to an order that resists the opposition, one of the founding oppositions of philosophy, between the sensible and the intelligible. The order which resists this opposition, and resists it because it transports it, is announced in a movement of *différance* (with an *a*) between two differences or two letters, a *différance* which belongs neither to the voice nor to writing in the usual sense, and which is located, as the strange space that will keep us together here for an hour, *between* speech and writing, and beyond the tranquil familiarity which links us to one and the other, occasionally reassuring us in our illusion that they are two.

What am I to do in order to speak of the *a* of *différance*? It goes without saying that it cannot be *exposed*. One can expose only that which at a certain moment can become *present*, manifest, that which can be shown, presented as something present, a being-present[4] in its truth, in the truth of a present or the presence of the present. Now if *différance* ᵢₛ (and I also cross out the 'is') what makes possible the presentation of the being-present, it is never presented as such. It is never offered to the present. Or to anyone. Reserving itself, not exposing itself, in regular fashion it exceeds the order of truth at a certain precise point, but without dissimulating itself as something, as a mysterious being, in the occult of a nonknowledge or in a hole with indeterminable borders (for example, in a topology of castration).[5] In every exposition it would be exposed to disappearing as disappearance. It would risk appearing: disappearing.

So much so that the detours, locutions, and syntax in which I will often have to take recourse will resemble those of negative theology, occasionally even to the point of being indistinguishable from negative theology. Already we have had to delineate *that différance is not*, does not exist, is not a present-being (*on*ᵈ) in any form; and we will be led to delineate also everything *that* it *is not*, that is, *everything*; and consequently that it has neither existence nor essence. It derives from no category of being, whether present or absent. And yet those aspects of *différance* which are thereby delineated are not theological, not even in the order of the most negative of negative theologies, which are always concerned with disengaging a superessentiality beyond the finite categories of essence and existence, that is, of presence, and always hastening to recall that God is refused the predicate of existence, only in order to acknowledge his superior, inconceivable, and ineffable mode of being. Such a development is not in question here, and this will be confirmed progressively. *Différance* is not only irreducible to any ontological or theological – ontotheological – reappropriation, but as the very opening of the space in which ontotheology – philosophy – produces its system and its history, it includes ontotheology, inscribing it and exceeding it without return.

For the same reason there is nowhere to *begin* to trace the sheaf or the graphics of *différance*. For what is put into question is precisely the quest for a rightful beginning, an absolute point of departure, a principal responsibility. The problematic of writing is opened by putting into question the value *arkhē*.⁶ What I will propose here will not be elaborated simply as a philosophical discourse, operating according to principles, postulates, axioms or definitions, and proceeding along the discursive lines of a linear order of reasons. In the delineation of *différance* everything is strategic and adventurous. Strategic because no transcendent truth present outside the field of writing can govern theologically the totality of the field. Adventurous because this strategy is not a simple strategy in the sense that strategy orients tactics according to a final goal, a *telos* or theme of domination, a mastery and ultimate reappropriation of the development of the field. Finally, a strategy without finality, what might be called blind tactics, or empirical wandering if the value of empiricism did not itself acquire its entire meaning in its opposition to philosophical responsibility. If there is a certain wandering in the tracing of *différance*, it no more follows the lines of philosophical-logical discourse than that of its symmetrical and integral inverse, empirical-logical discourse. The concept of *play* keeps itself beyond this opposition, announcing, on the eve of philosophy and beyond it, the unity of chance and necessity in calculations without end.

Also, by decision and as a rule of the game, if you will, turning these propositions back on themselves, we will be introduced to the thought of *différance* by the theme of strategy or the strategem. By means of this solely strategic justification, I wish to underline that the efficacity of the thematic of *différance* may very well, indeed must, one day be superseded, lending itself if not to its own replacement, at least to enmeshing itself in a chain that in truth it never will have governed. Whereby, once again, it is not theological.

I would say, first off, that *différance*, which is neither a word nor a concept, strategically seemed to me the most proper one to think, if not to master – thought, here, being that which is maintained in a certain necessary relationship with the structural limits of mastery – what is most irreducible about our 'era'. Therefore I am starting, strategically, from the place and the time in which 'we' are, even though in the last analysis my opening is not justifiable, since it is only on the basis of *différance* and its 'history' that we can allegedly know who and where 'we' are, and what the limits of an 'era' might be.

Even though *différance* is neither a word nor a concept, let us nevertheless attempt a simple and approximate semantic analysis that will take us to within sight of what is at stake.

We know that the verb *différer* (Latin verb *differre*) has two meanings which seem quite distinct;[7] for example in Littré[e] they are the object of two separate articles. In this sense the Latin *differre* is not simply a translation of the Greek *diapherein*, and this will not be without consequences for us, linking our discourse to a particular language, and to a language that passes as less philosophical, less originally philosophical than the other. For the distribution of meaning in the Greek *diapherein* does not comport one of the two motifs of the Latin *differre*, to wit, the action of putting off until later, of taking into account, of taking account of time and of the forces of an operation that implies an economical calculation, a detour, a delay, a relay, a reserve, a representation – concepts that I would summarize here in a word I have never used but that could be inscribed in this chain: *temporization*. *Différer* in this sense is to temporize, to take recourse, consciously or unconsciously, in the temporal and temporizing mediation of a detour that suspends the accomplishment or fulfillment of 'desire' or 'will', and equally effects this suspension in a mode that annuls or tempers its own effect. And we will see, later, how this temporization is also temporalization and spacing, the becoming-time of space and the becoming-space of time, the 'originary constitution' of time and space, as metaphysics or transcendental phenomenology would say, to use the language that here is criticized and displaced.

The other sense of *différer* is the more common and identifiable one: to be not identical, to be other, discernible, etc. When dealing with *differen(ts)(ds)*, a word that can be written with a final *ts* or a final *ds*, as you will, whether it is a question of dissimilar otherness or of allergic and polemical otherness, an interval, a distance, *spacing*, must be produced between the elements other, and be produced with a certain perseverence in repetition.[8]

Now the word *différénce* (with an *e*) can never refer either to *différer* as temporization or to *différends* as *polemos*.[9] Thus the word *différance* (with an *a*) is to compensate – economically – this loss of meaning, for *différance* can refer simultaneously to the entire configuration of its meanings. It is immediately and irreducibly polysemic, which will not be indifferent to the economy of my discourse here. In its polysemia this word, of course, like any meaning, must defer to the discourse in which it occurs, its interpretive context; but in a way it defers itself, or at least does so more readily than any other word, the *a* immediately deriving from the present participle (*différant*), thereby bringing us close to the very action of the verb *différer*, before it has even produced an effect constituted as something different or as *différence* (with an *e*).[10] In a conceptuality adhering to classical strictures '*différance*' would be said to designate a constitutive, productive, and originary causality, the process of scission and division which would produce or constitute different things or differences. But, because it brings us close to the infinitive and active kernel of *différer*, *différance* (with an *a*) neutralizes what the infinitive denotes as simply active, just as *mouvance* in our language does not simply mean the fact of moving, of moving oneself or of being moved. No more is resonance the act of resonating. We must consider that in the usage of our language the ending *-ance* remains undecided *between* the active and the passive. And we will see why that which lets itself be designated *différance* is neither simply active nor simply passive, announcing or rather recalling something like the middle voice, saying an operation that is not an operation, an operation that cannot be conceived either as passion or as the action of a subject on an object, or on the basis of the categories of agent or patient, neither on the basis of nor moving toward any of these *terms*. For the middle voice, a certain nontransitivity, may be what philosophy, at its outset, distributed into an active and a passive voice, thereby constituting itself by means of this repression.

Différance as temporization, *différance* as spacing. How are they to be joined?

Let us start, since we are already there, from the problematic of the sign and of writing. The sign is usually said to be put in the place of the thing itself, the present thing, 'thing' here standing equally for meaning or referent. The sign represents the present in its absence. It takes the place of the present. When we cannot grasp or show the thing, state the present, the being-present, when the present cannot be presented, we signify, we go through the detour of the sign. We take or give signs. We signal. The sign, in this sense, is deferred presence. Whether we are concerned with the verbal or the written sign, with the monetary sign, or with electoral delegation and political representation, the circulation of signs defers the moment in which we can encounter the thing itself, make it ours, consume or expend it, touch it, see it, intuit its presence. What I am describing here in order to define it is the classically determined structure of the sign in all the banality of its characteristics – signification as the *différance* of temporization. And this structure presupposes that the sign, which defers presence, is conceivable only on the *basis* of the presence that it defers and *moving toward* the deferred presence that it aims to reappropriate. According to this classical semiology, the substitution of the sign for the thing itself is both *secondary* and *provisional*: secondary due to an original and lost presence from which the sign thus derives; provisional as concerns this final and missing presence toward which the sign in this sense is a movement of mediation.

In attempting to put into question these traits of the provisional secondariness of the substitute, one would come to see something like an originary *différance*; but one could no longer call it originary or final in the extent to which the values of origin, archi-, *telos*, *eskhaton*, etc. have always denoted presence – *ousia*, *parousia*.[11] To put into question the secondary and provisional characteristics of the sign, to oppose to them an 'originary' *différance*, therefore would have two consequences.

1 One could no longer include *différance* in the concept of the sign, which always has meant the representation of a presence, and has been constituted in a system (thought or language) governed by and moving toward presence.

2 And thereby one puts into question the authority of presence, or of its simple symmetrical opposite, absence or lack. Thus one questions the limit which has always constrained us, which still constrains us – as inhabitants of a language and a system of thought – to formulate the meaning of Being in general as presence or absence, in the categories of being or beingness (*ousia*). Already it appears that the type of question to which we are redirected is, let us say, of the Heideggerian type, and that *différance seems* to lead back to the ontico-ontological difference. I will be permitted to hold off on this reference. I will note only that between difference as temporization-temporalization, which can no longer be conceived within the horizon of the present, and what Heidegger says in *Being and Time* about temporalization as the transcendental horizon of the question of Being, which must be liberated from its traditional, metaphysical domination by the present and the now, there is a strict communication, even though not an exhaustive and irreducibly necessary one.

But first let us remain within the semiological problematic in order to see *différance* as temporization and *différance* as spacing conjoined. Most of the semiological or linguistic researches that dominate the field of thought today, whether due to their own results or to the regulatory model that they find themselves acknowledging everywhere, refer genealogically to Saussure (correctly or incorrectly) as their common inaugurator. Now Saussure first of all is the thinker who put the *arbitrary character of the sign* and the *differential character* of the sign at the very foundation of general semiology, particularly linguistics. And, as we know, these two motifs – arbitrary and differential – are inseparable in his view. There can be arbitrariness only because the system of signs is constituted solely by the differences in terms, and not by their plenitude. The elements of signification function due not to the compact force of their nuclei but rather to the network of oppositions that distinguishes them, and then relates them one to another. 'Arbitrary and differential,' says Saussure, 'are two correlative characteristics'.

Now this principle of difference, as the condition for signification, affects the *totality* of the sign, that is the sign as both signified and signifier. The signified is the concept, the ideal meaning; and the signifier is what Saussure calls the 'image,' the 'psychical imprint' of a material, physical – for example, acoustical – phenomenon. We do not have to go into all the problems posed by these definitions here. Let us cite Saussure only at the point which interests us: 'The conceptual side of value is made up solely of relations and differences with respect to the other terms of language, and the same can be said of its material side . . . Everything that has been said up to this point boils down to this: in language there are only differences. Even more important: a difference generally implies positive terms between which the difference is set up; but in language there are only differences *without positive terms*. Whether we take the signified or the signifier, language has neither ideas nor sounds that existed before the linguistic system, but only conceptual and phonic differences that have issued from the system. The idea or phonic substance that a sign contains is of less importance than the other signs that surround it.'[12]

The first consequence to be drawn from this is that the signified concept is never present in and of itself, in a sufficient presence that would refer only to itself. Essentially and lawfully, every concept is inscribed in a chain or in a system within which it refers to the other, to other concepts, by means of the systematic play of differences. Such a play, *différance*, is thus no longer simply a concept, but rather the possibility of conceptuality, of a conceptual process and system in general. For the same reason, *différance*, which is not a concept, is not simply a word, that is, what is generally represented as the calm, present, and self-referential unity of concept and phonic material. Later we will look into the word in general.

The difference of which Saussure speaks is itself, therefore, neither a concept nor a word among others. The same can be said, a fortiori, of *différance*. And we are thereby led to explicate the relation of one to the other.

In a language, in the *system* of language, there are only differences. Therefore a taxonomical operation can undertake the systematic, statistical, and classificatory inventory of a language. But, on the one hand, these differences *play*: in language, in speech too, and in the exchange between language and speech. On the other hand, these differences are themselves *effects*. They have not fallen from the sky fully formed, and are no more inscribed in a *topos noētos*,[f] than they are prescribed in the gray matter of the brain. If the word 'history' did not in and of itself convey the motif of a final repression of difference, one could say that only differences can be 'historical' from the outset and in each of their aspects.

What is written as *différance*, then, will be the playing movement that 'produces' – by means of something that is not simply an activity – these differences, these effects of difference. This does not mean that the *différance* that produces differences is somehow before them, in a simple and unmodified – in-different – present. *Différance* is the non-full, non-simple, structured and differentiating origin of differences. Thus, the name 'origin' no longer suits it.

Since language, which Saussure says is a classification, has not fallen from the sky, its differences have been produced, are produced effects, but they are effects which do not find their cause in a subject or a substance, in a thing in general, a being that is somewhere present, thereby eluding the play of *différance*. If such a presence were implied in the concept of cause in general, in the most classical fashion, we then would have to speak of an effect without a cause, which very quickly would lead to speaking of no effect at all. I have attempted to indicate a way out of the closure of this framework via the 'trace,' which is no more an effect than it has a cause, but which in and of itself, outside its text, is not sufficient to operate the necessary transgression.

Since there is no presence before and outside semiological difference, what Saussure has written about language can be extended to the sign in general: 'Language is necessary in order for speech to be intelligible and to produce all of its effects; but the latter is necessary in order for language to be established; historically, the fact of speech always comes first.'[13]

Retaining at least the framework, if not the content, of this requirement formulated by Saussure, we will designate as *différance* the movement according to which language, or any code, any system of referral in general, is constituted 'historically' as a weave of differences. 'Is constituted', 'is produced', 'is created', 'movement,' 'historically', etc., necessarily being understood beyond the metaphysical language in which they are retained, along with all their implications. We ought to demonstrate why concepts like *production*, constitution, and history remain in complicity with what is at issue here. But this would take me too far today – toward the theory of the representation of the 'circle' in which we appear to be enclosed – and I utilize such concepts, like many others, only for their strategic convenience and in order to undertake their deconstruction at the currently most decisive point. In any event, it will be understood, by means of the circle in which we appear to be engaged, that as it is written here, *différance* is no more static than it is genetic, no more structural than historical. Or is no less so; and to object to this on the basis of the oldest of metaphysical oppositions (for example, by setting some generative point of view against a structural-taxonomical point of view, or vice versa) would be, above all, not to read what here is missing from orthographical ethics. Such oppositions have not the least pertinence to *différance*, which makes the thinking of it uneasy and uncomfortable.

Now if we consider the chain in which *différance* lends itself to a certain number of nonsynonymous substitutions, according to the necessity of the context, why have recourse to the 'reserve', to 'archi-writing', to the 'archi-trace', to 'spacing', that is, to the 'supplement', or to the *pharmakon*, and soon to the hymen, to the margin-mark-march, etc.[14]

Let us go on. It is because of *différance* that the movement of signification is possible only if each so-called 'present' element, each element appearing on the scene of presence, is related to something other than itself, thereby keeping within itself the mark of the past element, and already letting itself be vitiated by the mark of its relation to the future element, this trace being related no less to what is called the future than to what is called the past, and constituting what is called the present by means of this very relation to what it is not: what it absolutely is not, not even a past or a future as a modified present. An interval must separate the present from what it is not in order for the present to be itself, but this interval that constitutes it as present must, by the same token, divide the present in and of itself, thereby also dividing, along with the present, everything that is thought on the basis of the present, that is, in our metaphysical language, every being, and singularly substance or the subject. In constituting itself, in dividing itself dynamically, this interval is what might be called *spacing*, the becoming-space of time or the becoming-time of space (*temporization*). And it is this constitution of the present, as an 'originary' and irreducibly nonsimple (and therefore, *stricto sensu*[g] nonoriginary) synthesis of marks, or traces of retentions and protentions (to reproduce analogically and provisionally a phenomenological and transcendental language that soon will reveal itself to be inadequate), that I propose to call archi-writing, archi-trace, or *différance*. Which (is) (simultaneously) spacing (and) temporization.

Could not this (active) movement of (the production of) *différance* without origin be called simply, and without neographism, *differentiation*? Such a word, among other confusions, would have left open the possibility of an organic, original, and homogeneous unity that eventually would come to be divided, to receive difference as an event. And above all, since it is formed from the verb 'to differentiate', it would negate the economic signification of the detour, the temporizing delay, 'deferral.' Here, a remark in passing, which I owe to a recent reading of a text that Koyré (in 1934, in *Revue d'histoire et de philosophie réligieuse*, and reprinted in his *Études d'histoire de la pensée philosophique*) devoted to 'Hegel in Jena.' In this text Koyré gives long citations, in German, of the Jena *Logic*, and proposes their translation. On two occasions he encounters the expression *differente Beziehung* in Hegel's text. This word (*different*), with its Latin root, is rare in German and, I believe, in Hegel, who prefers *verschieden* or *ungleich*, calling difference *Unterschied* and qualitative variety *Verschiedenheit*. In the Jena *Logic* he uses the word *different* precisely where he treats of time and the present. Before getting to a valuable comment of Koyré's, let us look at some sentences from Hegel, such as Koyré translates them: 'The infinite, in this simplicity, is, as a moment opposed to the equal-to-itself, the negative, and in its moments, although it is (itself) presented to and in itself the totality, (it is) what excludes in general, the point or limit; but in its own (action of) negating, it is related immediately to the other and negates itself by itself. The limit or moment of the present (*der Gegen-wart*), the absolute "this" of time, or the now, is of an absolutely negative simplicity, which absolutely excludes from itself all multiplicity, and, by virtue of this, is absolutely determined; it is not whole or a *quantum* which would be extended in itself (and) which, in itself, also would have an undetermined moment, a diversity which, as indifferent (*gleichgultig*) or exterior in itself, would be related to an other (*auf ein anderes bezöge*), but in this is a relation absolutely different from the simple (*sondern es ist absolut differente Beziehung*).' And Koyré most remarkably specifies in a note: 'different Relation: *differente Beziehung*. One might say: "differentiating relation."' And on the next page, another text of Hegel's in which one can read this: '*Diese Beziehung ist Gegenwart, als eine differente Beziehung* (This relationship is [the] present as a different relationship).' Another note of Koyré's: 'The term *different* here is taken in an active sense.'[15]

Writing '*différant*'[16] or '*différance*' (with an *a*) would have had the advantage of making it possible to translate Hegel at that particular point – which is also an absolutely decisive point in his discourse – without further notes or specifications. And the translation would be, as it always must be, a transformation of one language by another. I contend, of course, that the word *différance* can also serve other purposes: first, because it marks not only the activity of 'originary' difference, but also the temporizing detour of deferral; and above all because *différance* thus written, although maintaining relations of profound affinity with Hegelian discourse (such as it must be read), is also, up to a certain point, unable to break with that discourse (which has no kind of meaning or chance); but it can operate a kind of infinitesimal and radical displacement of it, whose space I attempt to delineate elsewhere but of which it would be difficult to speak briefly here.

Differences, thus, are 'produced' – deferred – by *différance*. But *what* defers or *who* defers? In other words, *what is différance*? With this question we reach another level and another resource of our problematic.

What differs? Who differs? What is *différance*?

If we answered these questions before examining them as questions, before turning them back on themselves, and before suspecting their very form, including what seems most natural and necessary about them, we would immediately fall back into what we have just disengaged ourselves from. In effect, if we accepted the form of the question, in its meaning and its syntax ('what is?' 'who is?' 'who is it that?'), we would have to conclude that *différance* has been derived, has happened, is to be mastered and governed on the basis of the point of a present being, which itself could be something, a form, a state, a power in the world to which all kinds of names might be given, a *what*, or a present being as a *subject*, a *who*. And in this last case, notably, one would conclude implicitly that this present being, for example a being present to itself, as consciousness, eventually would come to defer or to differ: whether by delaying and turning away from the fulfillment of a 'need' or a 'desire,' or by differing from itself. But in neither of these cases would such a present being be 'constituted' by this *différance*.

Now if we refer, once again, to semiological difference, of what does Saussure, in particular, remind us? That 'language [which only consists of differences] is not a function of the speaking subject.' This implies that the subject (in its identity with itself, or eventually in its consciousness of its identity with itself, its self-consciousness) is inscribed in language, is a 'function' of language, becomes a *speaking* subject only by making its speech conform – even in so-called 'creation,' or in so-called 'transgression' – to the system of the rules of language as a system of differences, or at very least by conforming to the general law of *différance*, or by adhering to the principle of language which Saussure says is 'spoken language minus speech.' 'Language is necessary for the spoken word to be intelligible and so that it can produce all of its effects.'[17]

If, by hypothesis, we maintain that the opposition of speech to language is absolutely rigorous, then *différance* would be not only the play of differences within language but also the relation of speech to language, the detour through which I must pass in order to speak, the silent promise I must make; and this is equally valid for semiology in general, governing all the relations of usage to schemata, of message to code, etc. (Elsewhere I have attempted to suggest that this *différance* in language, and in the relation of speech and language, forbids the essential dissociation of speech and language that Saussure, at another level of his discourse, traditionally wished to delineate. The practice of a language or of a code supposing a play of forms without a determined and invariable substance, and also supposing in the practice of this play a retention and protention of differences, a spacing and a temporization, a play of traces – all this must be a kind of writing before the letter, an archi-writing without a present origin, without archi-. Whence the regular erasure of the archi-, and the transformation of general semiology into grammatology, this latter executing a critical labor on everything within semiology, including the central concept of the sign, that maintained metaphysical presuppositions incompatible with the motif of *différance*.)

One might be tempted by an objection: certainly the subject becomes a *speaking* subject only in its commerce with the system of linguistic differences;

or yet, the subject becomes a *signifying* (signifying in general, by means of speech or any other sign) subject only by inscribing itself in the system of differences. Certainly in this sense the speaking or signifying subject could not be present to itself, as speaking or signifying, without the play of linguistic or semiological *différance*. But can one not conceive of a presence, and of a presence to itself of the subject before speech or signs, a presence to itself of the subject in a silent and intuitive consciousness?

Such a question therefore supposes that, prior to the sign and outside it, excluding any trace and any *différance*, something like consciousness is possible. And that consciousness, before distributing its signs in space and in the world, can gather itself into its presence. But what is consciousness? What does 'consciousness' mean? Most often, in the very form of meaning, in all its modifications, consciousness offers itself to thought only as self-presence, as the perception of self in presence. And what holds for consciousness holds here for so-called subjective existence in general. Just as the category of the subject cannot be, and never has been, thought without the reference to presence as *hupokeimenon* or as *ousia*, etc., so the subject as consciousness has never manifested itself except as self-presence. The privilege granted to consciousness therefore signifies the privilege granted to the present; and even if one describes the transcendental temporality of consciousness, and at the depth at which Husserl[h] does so, one grants to the 'living present' the power of synthesizing traces, and of incessantly reassembling them.

This privilege is the ether of metaphysics, the element of our thought that is caught in the language of metaphysics. One can delimit such a closure today only by soliciting[18] the value of presence that Heidegger has shown to be the ontotheological determination of Being; and in thus soliciting the value of presence, by means of an interrogation whose status must be completely exceptional, we are also examining the absolute privilege of this form or epoch of presence in general that is consciousness as meaning[19] in self-presence.

Thus one comes to posit presence – and specifically consciousness, the being beside itself of consciousness – no longer as the absolutely central form of Being but as a 'determination' and as an 'effect.' A determination or an effect within a system which is no longer that of presence but of *différance*, a system that no longer tolerates the opposition of activity and passivity, nor that of cause and effect, or of indetermination and determination, etc., such that in designating consciousness as an effect or a determination, one continues – for strategic reasons that can be more or less lucidly deliberated and systematically calculated – to operate according to the lexicon of that which one is de-limiting.

Before being so radically and purposely the gesture of Heidegger, this gesture was also made by Nietzsche and Freud, both of whom, as is well known, and sometimes in very similar fashion, put consciousness into question in its assured certainty of itself. Now is it not remarkable that they both did so on the basis of the motif of *différance*?

Différance appears almost by name in their texts, and in those places where everything is at stake. I cannot expand upon this here; I will only recall that for Nietzsche 'the great principal activity is unconscious,' and that consciousness is the effect of forces whose essence, byways, and modalities are not proper to it. Force itself is never present; it is only a play of differences and quantities. There would be no force in general without the difference between forces; and here the difference of quantity counts more than the content of the quantity, more than absolute size itself. 'Quantity itself, therefore, is not separable from the difference of quantity. The difference of quantity is the essence of force, the relation of force to force. The dream of two equal forces, even if they are granted an opposition of meaning, is an approximate and crude dream, a statistical dream, plunged into by the living but dispelled by chemistry.'[20] Is not all of Nietzsche's thought a critique of philosophy as an active indifference to difference, as the system of adiaphoristic[i] reduction or repression? Which according to the same logic, according to logic itself, does not exclude that philosophy lives *in* and *on* *différance*, thereby blinding itself to the *same*, which is not the identical. The same, precisely, is *différance* (with an *a*) as the displaced and equivocal passage of one different thing to another, from one term of an opposition to the other. Thus one could reconsider all the pairs of opposites on which philosophy is constructed and on which our discourse lives, not in order to see opposition erase itself but to see what indicates that each of the terms must appear as the *différance* of the other, as the other different and deferred in the economy of the same (the intelligible as differing-deferring the sensible, as the sensible different and deferred; the concept as different and deferred, differing-deferring intuition; culture as nature different and deferred, differing-deferring; all the others of *physis* – *tekhnē, nomos, thesis*,[j] society, freedom, history, mind, etc. – as *physis* different and deferred, or as *physis* differing and deferring. *Physis* in *différance*. And in this we may see the site of a reinterpretation of *mimēsis* in its alleged opposition to *physis*). And on the basis of this unfolding of the same as *différance*, we see announced the sameness of *différance* and repetition in the eternal return. Themes in Nietzsche's work that are linked to the symptomatology that always diagnoses the detour or ruse of an agency disguised in its *différance*; or further, to the entire thematic of active interpretation, which substitutes incessant deciphering for the unveiling of truth as the presentation of the thing itself in its presence, etc. Figures without truth, or at least a system of figures not dominated by the value of truth, which then becomes only an included, inscribed, circumscribed function.

Thus, *différance* is the name we might give to the 'active,' moving discord of different forces, and of differences of forces, that Nietzsche sets up against the entire system of metaphysical grammar, wherever this system governs culture, philosophy, and science.

It is historically significant that this diaphoristics, which, as an energetics or economics of forces, commits itself to putting into question the primacy of presence as consciousness, is also the major motif of Freud's thought: another diaphoristics, which in its entirety is both a theory of the figure (or of the trace) and an energetics. The putting into question of the authority of consciousness is first and always differential.

The two apparently different values of *différance* are tied together in

Freudian theory: to differ as discernibility, distinction, separation, diastem, *spacing*; and to defer as detour, relay, reserve, *temporization*.

1 The concepts of trace (*Spur*), of breaching (*Bahnung*),²¹ and of the forces of breaching, from the *Project* on, are inseparable from the concept of difference. The origin of memory, and of the psyche as (conscious or unconscious) memory in general, can be described only by taking into account the difference between breaches. Freud says so overtly. There is no breach without difference and no difference without trace.

2 All the differences in the production of unconscious traces and in the processes of inscription (*Niederschrift*) can also be interpreted as moments of *différance*, in the sense of putting into reserve. According to a schema that never ceased to guide Freud's thought, the movement of the trace is described as an effort of life to protect itself by *deferring* the dangerous investment, by constituting a reserve (*Vorrat*). And all the oppositions that furrow Freudian thought relate each of his concepts one to another as moments of a detour in the economy of *différance*. One is but the other different and deferred, one differing and deferring the other. One is the other in *différance*, one is the *différance* of the other. This is why every apparently rigorous and irreducible *opposition* (for example the opposition of the secondary to the primary) comes to be qualified, at one moment or another, as a 'theoretical fiction.' Again, it is thereby, for example (but such an example governs, and communicates with, everything), that the difference between the pleasure principle and the reality principle is only *différance* as detour. In *Beyond the Pleasure Principle* Freud writes: 'Under the influence of the ego's instincts of self-preservation, the pleasure principle is replaced by the reality principle. This latter principle does not abandon the intention of ultimately obtaining pleasure, but it nevertheless demands and carries into effect the postponement of satisfaction, the abandonment of a number of possibilities of gaining satisfaction and the temporary toleration of unpleasure as a step on the long indirect road (*Aufschub*) to pleasure.'²²

Here we are touching upon the point of greatest obscurity, on the very enigma of *différance*, on precisely that which divides its very concept by means of a strange cleavage. We must not hasten to decide. How are we to think *simultaneously*, on the one hand, *différance* as the economic detour which, in the element of the same, always aims at coming back to the pleasure or the presence that have been deferred by (conscious or unconscious) calculation, and, on the other hand, *différance* as the relation to an impossible presence, as expenditure without reserve, as the irreparable loss of presence, the irreversible usage of energy, that is, as the death instinct, and as the entirely other relationship that apparently interrupts every economy? It is evident – and this is the evident itself – that the economical and the noneconomical, the same and the entirely other, etc., cannot be thought *together*. If *différance* is unthinkable in this way, perhaps we should not hasten to make it evident, in the philosophical element of evidentiality which would make short work of dissipating the mirage and illogicalness of *différance* and would do so with the infallibility of calculations that we are well acquainted with, having precisely recognized their place, necessity, and function in the structure of *différance*. Elsewhere, in a reading of Bataille, I have attempted to indicate what might come of a rigorous and, in a new sense, 'scientific' *relating* of the 'restricted economy' that takes no part in expenditure without reserve, death, opening itself to nonmeaning, etc., to a general economy that *takes into account* the nonreserve, that keeps in reserve the nonreserve, if it can be put thus. I am speaking of a relationship between a *différance* that can make a profit on its investment and a *différance* that misses its profit, the *investiture* of a presence that is pure and without loss here being confused with absolute loss, with death. Through such a relating of a restricted and a general economy the very project of philosophy, under the privileged heading of Hegelianism, is displaced and reinscribed. The *Aufhebung* – *la relève* – is constrained into writing itself otherwise. Or perhaps simply into writing itself. Or, better, into taking account of its consumption of writing.[23]

For the economic character of *différance* in no way implies that the deferred presence can always be found again, that we have here only an investment that provisionally and calculatedly delays the perception of its profit or the profit of its perception. Contrary to the metaphysical, dialectical, 'Hegelian' interpretation of the economic movement of *différance*, we must conceive of a play in which whoever loses wins, and in which one loses and wins on every turn. If the displaced presentation remains definitively and implacably postponed, it is not that a certain present remains absent or hidden. Rather, *différance* maintains our relationship with that which we necessarily misconstrue, and which exceeds the alternative of presence and absence. A certain alterity – to which Freud gives the metaphysical name of the unconscious – is definitively exempt from every process of presentation by means of which we would call upon it to show itself in person. In this context, and beneath this guise, the unconscious is not, as we know, a hidden, virtual, or potential self-presence. It differs from, and defers, itself; which doubtless means that it is woven of differences, and also that it sends out delegates, representatives, proxies; but without any chance that the giver of proxies might 'exist,' might be present, be 'itself' somewhere, and with even less chance that it might become conscious. In this sense, contrary to the terms of an old debate full of the metaphysical investments that it has always assumed, the 'unconscious' is no more a 'thing' than it is any other thing, is no more a thing than it is a virtual or masked consciousness. This radical alterity as concerns every possible mode of presence is marked by the irreducibility of the aftereffect, the delay. In order to describe traces, in order to read the traces of 'unconscious' traces (there are no 'conscious' traces), the language of presence and absence, the metaphysical discourse of phenomenology, is inadequate. (Although the phenomenologist is not the only one to speak this language.)

The structure of delay (*Nachträglichkeit*) in effect forbids that one make of temporalization (temporization) a simple dialectical complication of the living present as an originary and unceasing synthesis – a synthesis constantly directed back on itself, gathered in on itself and gathering – of retentional traces and protentional openings. The alterity of the 'unconscious' makes us concerned not with horizons of modified – past or future – presents, but with a 'past' that has never been present, and which never will be, whose future to come will never be a *production* or a reproduction in the form of presence. Therefore the concept of trace is incompatible with the concept of retention, of the becoming-past of what has been present. One cannot think the trace – and therefore, *différance* – on the basis of the present, or of the presence of the present.

A past that has never been present: this formula is the one that Emmanuel Levinas[k] uses, although certainly in a nonpsychoanalytic way, to qualify the trace and enigma of absolute alterity: the Other.[24] Within these limits, and from this point of view at least, the thought of *différance* implies the entire critique of classical ontology undertaken by Levinas. And the concept of the trace, like that of *différance* thereby organizes, along the lines of these different traces and differences of traces, in Nietzsche's sense, in Freud's sense, in Levinas's sense – these 'names of authors' here being only indices – the network which reassembles and traverses our 'era' as the delimitation of the ontology of presence.

Which is to say the ontology of beings and beingness. It is the domination of beings that *différance* everywhere comes to solicit, in the sense that *sollicitare*, in old Latin, means to shake as a whole, to make tremble in entirety. Therefore, it is the determination of Being as presence or as beingness that is interrogated by the thought of *différance*. Such a question could not emerge and be understood unless the difference between Being and beings were somewhere to be broached. First consequence: *différance* is not. It is not a present being, however excellent, unique, principal, or transcendent. It governs nothing, reigns over nothing, and nowhere exercises any authority. It is not announced by any capital letter. Not only is there no kingdom of *différance*, but *différance* instigates the subversion of every kingdom. Which makes it obviously threatening and infallibly dreaded by everything within us that desires a kingdom, the past or future presence of a kingdom. And it is always in the name of a kingdom that one may reproach *différance* with wishing to reign, believing that one sees it aggrandize itself with a capital letter.

Can *différance*, for these reasons, settle down into the division of the ontico-ontological difference, such as it is thought, such as its 'epoch' in particular is thought, 'through,' if it may still be expressed such, Heidegger's uncircum-ventable meditation?

There is no simple answer to such a question.

In a certain aspect of itself, *différance* is certainly but the historical and epochal *unfolding* of Being or of the ontological difference. The *a* of *différance* marks the *movement* of this unfolding.

And yet, are not the thought of the *meaning* or *truth* of Being, the deter-mination of *différance* as the ontico-ontological difference, difference thought within the horizon of the question of *Being*, still intrametaphysical effects of *différance*? The unfolding of *différance* is perhaps not solely the truth of Being, or of the epochality of Being. Perhaps we must attempt to think this unheard-of thought, this silent tracing: that the history of Being, whose thought engages the Greco-Western *logos* such as it is produced via the ontological difference, is but an epoch of the *diapherein*. Henceforth one could no longer even call this an 'epoch,' the concept of epochality belonging to what is within history as the history of Being. Since Being has never had a 'meaning,' has never been thought or said as such, except by dissimulating itself in beings, then *différance*, in a certain and very strange way, (is) 'older' than the ontological difference or than the truth of Being. When it has this age it can be called the play of the trace. The play of a trace which no longer belongs to the horizon of Being, but whose play transports and encloses the meaning of Being: the play of the trace, or the *différance*, which has no meaning and is not. Which does not belong. There is no maintaining, and no depth to, this bottomless chessboard on which Being is put into play.

Perhaps this is why the Heraclitean play of the *hen diapheron heautōi*, of the one differing from itself, the one in difference with itself, already is lost like a trace in the determination of the *diapherein* as ontological difference.

To think the ontological difference doubtless remains a difficult task, and any statement of it has remained almost inaudible. Further, to prepare, beyond our *logos*, for a *différance* so violent that it can be interpellated neither as the epochality of Being nor as ontological difference, is not in any way to dispense with the passage through the truth of Being, or to 'criticize,' 'contest,' or misconstrue its incessant necessity. On the contrary, we must stay within the difficulty of this passage, and repeat it in the rigorous reading of metaphysics, wherever metaphysics normalizes Western discourse, and not only in the texts of the 'history of philosophy.' As rigorously as possible we must permit to appear/disappear the trace of what exceeds the truth of Being. The trace (of that) which can never be presented, the trace which itself can never be presented: that is, appear and manifest itself, as such, in its phenomenon. The trace beyond that which profoundly links fundamental ontology and phenomenology. Always differing and deferring, the trace is never as it is in the presentation of itself. It erases itself in presenting itself, muffles itself in resonating, like the *a* writing itself, inscribing its pyramid in *différance*.

The annunciating and reserved trace of this movement can always be disclosed in metaphysical discourse, and especially in the contemporary discourse which states, through the attempts to which we just referred (Nietzsche, Freud, Levinas), the closure of ontology. And especially through the Heideggerean text.

This text prompts us to examine the essence of the present, the presence of the present.

What is the present? What is it to think the present in its presence?

Let us consider, for example, the 1946 text entitled *Der Spruch des Anaximander* ('The Anaximander Fragment').[25] In this text Heidegger recalls that the forgetting of Being forgets the difference between Being and beings: '. . . to be the Being *of* beings is the matter of Being (*die Sache des Seins*). The grammatical form of this enigmatic, ambiguous genitive indicates a genesis (*Genesis*), the emergence (*Herkunft*) of what is present from presencing (*des Anwesenden aus dem Anwesen*). Yet the essence (*Wesen*) of this emergence remains concealed (*verbogen*) along with the essence of these two words. Not only that, but even the very relation between presencing and what is present (*Anwesen und Anwesendem*) remains unthought. From early on it seems as though presencing and what is present were each something for itself. Presencing itself unnoticeably becomes something present . . . The essence of presencing (*Das Wesen des Anwesens*), and with it the distinction between presencing and what is present, remains forgotten. *The oblivion of Being is oblivion of the distinction between Being and beings'* (p. 50).

In recalling the difference between Being and beings (the ontological difference) as the difference between presence and the present, Heidegger advances a proposition, a body of propositions, that we are not going to use as a subject for criticism. This would be foolishly precipitate; rather, what we shall try to do is to return to this proposition its power to provoke.

Let us proceed slowly. What Heidegger wants to mark is this: the difference between Being and beings, the forgotten of metaphysics, has disappeared without leaving a trace. The very trace of difference has been submerged. If we maintain that *différance* (is) (itself) other than absence and presence, if it *traces*, then when it is a matter of the forgetting of the difference (between Being and beings), we would have to speak of a disappearance of the trace of the trace. Which is indeed what the following passage from 'The Anaximander Fragment' seems to imply: 'Oblivion of Being belongs to the self-veiling essence of Being. It belongs so essentially to the destiny of Being that the dawn of this destiny rises as the unveiling of what is present in its presencing. This means that the history of Being begins with the oblivion of Being, since Being – together with its essence, its distinction from beings – keeps to itself. The distinction collapses. It remains forgotten. Although the two parties to the distinction, what is present and presencing (*das Anwesende und das Anwesen*), reveal themselves, they do not do so as distinguished. Rather, even the early trace (*die frühe Spur*) of the distinction is obliterated when presencing appears as something present (*das Anwesen wie ein Anwesendes erscheint*) and finds itself in the position of being the highest being present (*in einem höchsten Anwesenden*)' (pp. 50–51).

Since the trace is not a presence but the simulacrum of a presence that dislocates itself, displaces itself, refers itself, it properly has no site – erasure belongs to its structure. And not only the erasure which must always be able to overtake it (without which it would not be a trace but an indestructible and monumental substance), but also the erasure which constitutes it from the outset as a trace, which situates it as the change of site, and makes it disappear in its appearance, makes it emerge from itself in its production. The erasure of the early trace (*die frühe Spur*) of difference is therefore the 'same' as its tracing in the text of metaphysics. This latter must have maintained the mark of what it has lost, reserved, put aside. The paradox of such a structure, in the language of metaphysics, is an inversion of metaphysical concepts, which produces the following effect: the present becomes the sign of the sign, the trace of the trace. It is no longer what every reference refers to in the last analysis. It becomes a function in a structure of generalized reference. It is a trace, and a trace of the erasure of the trace.

Thereby the text of metaphysics is *comprehended*. Still legible; and to be read. It is not surrounded but rather traversed by its limit, marked in its interior by the multiple furrow of its margin. Proposing *all at once* the monument and the mirage of the trace, the trace simultaneously traced and erased, simultaneously living and dead, and, as always, living in its simulation of life's preserved inscription. A pyramid. Not a stone fence to be jumped over but itself stonelike, on a wall, to be deciphered otherwise, a text without voice.

Thus one can think without contradiction, or at least without granting any pertinence to such a contradiction, what is perceptible and imperceptible in the trace. The 'early trace' of difference is lost in an invisibility without return, and yet its very loss is sheltered, retained, seen, delayed. In a text. In the form of presence. In the form of the proper. Which itself is only an effect of writing.

Having stated the erasure of the early trace, Heidegger can therefore, in a contradiction without contradiction, consign, countersign, the sealing of the trace. A bit further on: 'However, the distinction between Being and beings, as something forgotten, can invade our experience only if it has already unveiled itself with the presencing of what is present (*mit dem Anwesen des Anwesenden*); only if it has left a trace (*eine Spur geprägt hat*) which remains preserved (*gewahrt bleibt*) in the language to which Being comes' (p. 51).

Still further on, while meditating on Anaximander's *to khreon*, which he translates as *Brauch* (usage), Heidegger writes this: 'Enjoining order and reck (*Fug und Ruch verfügend*), usage delivers to each present being (*Anwesende*) the while into which it is released. But accompanying this process is the constant danger that lingering will petrify into mere persistence (*in das blosse Beharren verhärtet*). Thus usage essentially remains at the same time the distribution (*Aushändigung*: dis-maintenance) of presencing (*des Anwesens*) into disorder (*in den Un-fug*). Usage conjoins the dis[1] (*Der Brauch fügt das Un-*)' (p. 54).

And it is at the moment when Heidegger recognizes *usage* as *trace* that the question must be asked: can we, and to what extent, think this trace and the *dis* of *différance* as *Wesen des Seins*? Does not the *dis* of *différance* refer us beyond the history of Being, and also beyond our language, and everything that can be named in it? In the language of Being, does it not call for a necessarily violent transformation of this language by an entirely other language?

Let us make this question more specific. And to force the 'trace' out of it (and has anyone thought that we have been tracking something down, something other than tracks themselves to be tracked down?), let us read this passage: 'The translation of *to khreon* as "usage" has not resulted from a preoccupation with etymologies and dictionary meanings. The choice of the word stems from a prior crossing *over* (*Über-setzen*; trans-lation) of a thinking which tries to think the distinction in the essence of Being (*im Wesen des Seins*) in the fateful beginning of Being's oblivion. The word "usage" is dictated to thinking in the experience (*Erfahrung*) of Being's oblivion. What properly remains to be thought in the word "usage" has presumably left a trace (*Spur*) in *to khreon*. This trace quickly vanishes (*alsbald verschwindet*) in the destiny of Being which unfolds in world history as Western metaphysics' (p. 54).

How to conceive what is outside a text? That which is more or less than a text's *own, proper* margin? For example, what is other than the text of Western metaphysics? It is certain that the trace which 'quickly vanishes in the destiny of Being (and) which unfolds . . . as Western metaphysics' escapes every determination, every name it might receive in the metaphysical text. It is sheltered, and therefore dissimulated, in these names. It does not appear in them as the trace 'itself.' But this is because it could never appear itself, *as such*. Heidegger also says that difference cannot appear as such: 'Lichtung des Unterschiedes kann deshalb auch nicht bedeuten, dass der Unterschied als der Unterschied erscheint.' There is no essence of *différance*; it (is) that which not only could never be appropriated in the *as such* of its name or its appearing, but also that which threatens the authority of the *as such* in general, of the presence of the thing itself in its essence. That there is not a proper essence[26] of *différance* at this point, implies that there is neither a Being nor truth of the play of writing such as it engages *différance*.

For us, *différance* remains a metaphysical name, and all the names that it receives in our language are still, as names, metaphysical. And this is particularly the case when these names state the determination of *différance* as the difference between presence and the present (*Anwesen/Anwesend*), and above all, and is already the case when they state the determination of *différance* as the difference of Being and beings.

'Older' than Being itself, such a *différance* has no name in our language. But we 'already know' that if it is unnameable, it is not provisionally so, not because our language has not yet found or received this *name*, or because we would have to seek it in another language, outside the finite system of our own. It is rather because there is no *name* for it at all, not even the name of essence or of Being, not even that of '*différance*,' which is not a name, which is not a pure nominal unity, and unceasingly dislocates itself in a chain of differing and deferring substitutions.

'There is no name for it': a proposition to be read in its *platitude*. This unnameable is not an ineffable Being which no name could approach: God, for example. This unnameable is the play which makes possible nominal effects, the relatively unitary and atomic structures that are called names, the chains of substitutions of names in which, for example, the nominal effect *différance* is itself *enmeshed*, carried off, reinscribed, just as a false entry or a false exit is still part of the game, a function of the system.

What we know, or what we would know if it were simply a question here of something to know, is that there has never been, never will be, a unique word, a master-name. This is why the thought of the letter *a* in *différance* is not the primary prescription or the prophetic annunciation of an imminent and as yet unheard-of nomination. There is nothing kerygmatic[m] about this 'word,' provided that one perceives its decapita(liza)tion. And that one puts into question the name of the name.

There will be no unique name, even if it were the name of Being. And we must think this without *nostalgia*, that is, outside of the myth of a purely maternal or paternal language, a lost native country of thought. On the contrary, we must *affirm* this, in the sense in which Nietzsche puts affirmation into play, in a certain laughter and a certain step of the dance.

From the vantage of this laughter and this dance, from the vantage of this affirmation foreign to all dialectics, the other side of nostalgia, what I will call Heideggerian *hope*, comes into question. I am not unaware how shocking this word might seem here. Nevertheless I am venturing it, without exclud-ing any of its implications, and I relate it to what still seems to me to be the metaphysical part of 'The Anaximander Fragment': the quest for the proper word and the unique name. Speaking of the first word of Being (*das frühe Wort des Seins: to khreon*), Heidegger writes: 'The relation to what is present that rules in the essence of presencing itself is a unique one (*ist eine einzige*), altogether incomparable to any other relation. It belongs to the uniqueness of Being itself (*Sie gehört zur Einzigkeit des Seins selbst*). Therefore, in order to name the essential nature of Being (*das wesende Seins*), language would have to find a single word, the unique word (*ein einziges, das einzige Wort*). From this we can gather how daring every thoughtful word (*denkende Wort*) addressed to Being is (*das dem Sein zugesprochen wird*). Nevertheless such daring is not impossible, since Being speaks always and everywhere throughout language' (p. 52).

Such is the question: the alliance of speech and Being in the unique word, in the finally proper name. And such is the question inscribed in the simulated affirmation of *différance*. It bears (on) each member of this sentence: 'Being/speaks/always and everywhere/throughout/language.'

Notes [TN: translator's note]

1   TN. Throughout this book I will translate *le propre* as 'the proper.' Derrida most often intends all the senses of the word at once: that which is correct, as in *le sens propre* (proper, literal meaning), and that which is one's own, that which may be owned, that which is legally, correctly owned – all the links between proper, property, and propriety.

2   TN. The last three sentences refer elliptically and playfully to the following ideas. Derrida first plays on the 'silence' of the *a* in *différance* as being like a silent tomb, like a pyramid, like the pyramid to which Hegel compares the body of the sign. 'Tomb' in Greek is *oikēsis*, which is akin to the Greek *oikos* – house – from which the word 'economy' derives (*oikos* – house – and *nemein* – to manage). Thus Derrida speaks of the 'economy of death' as the 'familial residence and tomb of the proper.' Further, and more elliptically still, Derrida speaks of the tomb, which always bears an inscription in stone, announcing the death of the tyrant. This seems to refer to Hegel's treatment of the Antigone story in the *Phenomenology*. It will be recalled that Antigone defies the tyrant Creon by burying her brother Polynices. Creon retaliates by having Antigone entombed. There she cheats the slow death that awaits her by hanging herself. The tyrant Creon has a change of heart too late, and – after the suicides of his son and wife, his *family* – kills himself. Thus family, death, inscription, tomb, law, economy. In a later work, *Glas*, Derrida analyzes Hegel's treatment of the *Antigone*.

3   TN. ' . . . not fortuitously affiliated with the objectivity of *theōrein* or under-standing.' A play on words has been lost in translation here, a loss that makes this sentence difficult to understand. In the previous sentence Derrida says that the difference between the *e* and the *a* of *différence/différance* can neither be seen nor heard. It is not a sensible – that is, relating to the senses – difference. But, he goes on to explain, neither is this an intelligible difference, for the very names by which we conceive of objective intelligibility are already in complicity with sens-ibility. *Theōrein* – the Greek origin of 'theory' – literally means 'to look at,' to *see*;

and the word Derrida uses for 'understanding' here is *entendement*, the noun form of *entendre*, to *hear*.

4 TN. As in the past, *être* (*Sein*) will be translated as Being. *Etant* (*Seiendes*) will be either beings or being, depending on the context. Thus, here *étant-present* is 'being-present.' For a justification of this translation see Derrida, *Writing and Difference* (1978), Translator's Introduction, p. xvii.

5 TN. '. . . a hole with indeterminable borders (for example, in a topology of castration).' This phrase was added to 'La Différance' for its publication in the French edition of this volume and refers to the polemic Derrida had already engaged (in *Positions*; elaborated further in *le Facteur de la verité*) with Jacques Lacan. For Derrida, Lacan's 'topology of castration,' which assigns the 'hole' or lack to a place – 'a hole with determinable borders' – repeats the metaphysical gesture (albeit a negative one) of making absence, the lack, the hole, a transcendental principle that can be pinned down as such, and can thereby *govern* a theoretical discourse.

6 TN. The Greek *arkhē* combines the values of a founding principle and of government by a controlling principle (e.g. *arch*eology, mon*arch*y).

7 TN. In English the two distinct meanings of the Latin *differre* have become two separate words: to defer and to differ.

8 TN. The next few sentences will require some annotation, to be found in this note and the next two. In this sentence Derrida is pointing out that two words that sound exactly alike in French (*différents*, *différends*) refer to the sense of *differre* that implies spacing, otherness – difference in its usual English sense. *Les différents* are different things; *les différends* are differences of opinion, grounds for dispute – whence the references to *all*ergy (from the Greek *allos*, other) and polemics.

9 TN. However, to continue the last note, *différence* (in French) does not convey the sense of active putting off, of deferring (*différance* in what would be its usual sense in French, if it were a word in common usage), or the sense of active polemical difference, actively differing with someone or something. ('Active' here, though, is not really correct, for reasons that Derrida will explain below.) The point is that there is no noun-verb, no gerund for either sense in French.

10 TN. Such a gerund would normally be constructed from the present participle of the verb: *différant*. Curiously then, the noun *différance* suspends itself between the two senses of *différant* – deferring, differing. We might say that it defers differing, and differs from deferring, in and of itself.

11 TN. *Ousia* and *parousia* imply presence as both origin and end, the founding principle (*arkhe-*) as that toward which one moves (*telos*, *eskhaton*).

12 TN. Ferdinand de Saussure, *Course in General Linguistics*, trans. Wade Baskin (New York: Philosophical Library, 1959), pp. 117–18, 120 (see above, pp. 12–13).

13 TN. Ibid., p. 18.

14 TN. All these terms refer to writing and inscribe *différance* within themselves, as Derrida says, according to the context. The supplement (*supplément*) is Rousseau's word to describe writing (analyzed in *Of Grammatology*, 1976). It means *both* the missing piece and the extra piece. The *pharmakon* is Plato's word for writing (analyzed in 'Plato's Pharmacy' in *Dissemination*, 1981), meaning *both* remedy and poison; the hymen (*l'hymen*) comes from Derrida's analysis of Mallarme's writing and Mallarmé's reflections on writing ('The Double Session' in *Dissemination*) and refers *both* to virginity and to consummation; *marge-marque-marche* is the series *en différance* that Derrida applies to Sollers's *Nombres* ('Dissemination' in *Dissemination*).

15 TN. Alexandre Koyré, 'Hegel à Iena,' in *Etudes d'histoire de la pensée philosophique* (Paris: Armand Colin, 1961), pp. 153–4. In his translation of 'La différance' (in *Speech and Phenomena*, 1973), David Allison notes (p. 144) that the citation from

Hegel comes from 'Jensener Logik, Metaphysik, und Natur-philosophie' in *Sämtliche Werke* (Leipzig: F. Meiner, 1925), XVIII, 202. Allison himself translated Hegel's text, and I have modified his translation.

16 TN. The point here, which cannot be conveyed in English, is that Koyré's realization that Hegel is describing a 'differentiating relation,' or 'different' in an active sense, is precisely what the formation of *différance* from the participle *différant* describes, as explained in notes 9 and 10 above. And that it is the *present* that is described as differing from and deferring itself helps clarify Derrida's argument (at the end of the essay) that presence is to be rethought as the trace of the trace, as *différance* differed-and-deferred.

17 TN. Saussure, *Course in General Linguistics*, p. 37.

18 TN. The French *solliciter*, as the English *solicit*, derives from an Old Latin expression meaning to shake the whole, to make something tremble in its entirety. Derrida comments on this later, but is already using 'to solicit' in this sense here.

19 TN. 'Meaning' here is the weak translation of *vouloir-dire*, which has a strong sense of willing (*voluntas*) to say, putting the attempt to mean in conjunction with speech, a crucial conjunction for Derrida.

20 Gilles Deleuze, *Nietzsche et la philosophie* (Paris: Presses Universitaires de France, 1970), p. 49.

21 TN. Derrida is referring here to his essay 'Freud and the Scene of Writing' in *Writing and Difference*. 'Breaching' is the translation for *Bahnung* that I adopted there: it conveys more of the sense of breaking open (as in the German *Bahnung* and the French *frayage*) than the Standard Edition's 'facilitation.' The *Project* Derrida refers to here is the *Project for a Scientific Psychology* (1895), in which Freud attempted to cast his psychological thinking in a neurological framework.

22 TN. *The Standard Edition of the Complete Psychological Works* (1953) vol. 18, p. 10.

23 TN. Derrida is referring here to the reading of Hegel he proposed in 'From Restricted to General Economy: A Hegelianism Without Reserve,' in *Writing and Difference*. In that essay Derrida began his consideration of Hegel as the great philosophical *speculator*; thus all the economic metaphors of the previous sentences. For Derrida the deconstruction of metaphysics implies an endless confrontation with Hegelian concepts, and the move from a restricted, 'speculative' philosophical economy – in which there is nothing that cannot be made to make sense, in which there is nothing *other* than meaning – to a 'general' economy – which affirms that which exceeds meaning, the excess of meaning from which there can be no speculative profit – involves a reinterpretation of the central Hegelian concept: the *Aufhebung*. *Aufhebung* literally means 'lifting up'; but it also contains the double meaning of conservation and negation. For Hegel, dialectics is a process of *Aufhebung*: every concept is to be negated and lifted up to a higher sphere in which it is thereby conserved. In this way, there is nothing from which the *Aufhebung* cannot profit. However, as Derrida points out, there is always an effect of *différance* when the same word has two contradictory meanings. Indeed it is this effect of *différance* – the excess of the trace *Aufhebung* itself – that is precisely what the *Aufhebung* can never *aufheben*: lift up, conserve, and negate. This is why Derrida wishes to constrain the *Aufhebung* to write itself otherwise, or simply to write itself, to take into account its consumption of writing. Without writing, the trace, there could be no words with double, contradictory meanings.

As with *différance*, the translation of a word with a double meaning is particularly difficult, and touches upon the entire problematics of writing and *différance*. The best translators of Hegel usually cite Hegel's own delight that the most speculative of languages, German, should have provided this most speculative of words as the vehicle for his supreme speculative effort. Thus *Aufhebung* is usually best annotated and left untranslated. (Jean Hyppolite, in his French translations of Hegel, carefully annotates his rendering of *Aufheben* as both *supprimer* and *dépasser*. Baillies's rendering of *Aufhebung* as 'sublation' is misleading.) Derrida, however, in his attempt to make *Aufhebung* write itself otherwise, has proposed a new translation of it that *does* take into account the effect of *différance* in its double meaning. Derrida's translation is *la relève*. The word comes from the verb *relever*, which means to lift up, as does *Aufheben*. But *relever* also means to relay, to relieve, as when one soldier on duty relieves another. Thus the conserving-and-negating lift has become *la relève*, a 'lift' in which is inscribed an effect of substitution and difference, the effect of substitution and difference inscribed in the double meaning of *Aufhebung*. A. V. Miller's rendering of *Aufhebung* as 'supersession' in his recent translation of the *Phenomenology* comes close to *relever* in combining the senses of raising up and replacement, although without the elegance of Derrida's maintenance of the verb meaning 'to lift' (*heben*, *lever*) and change of prefix (*auf-*, *re-*). Thus we will leave *la relève* untranslated throughout, as with *différance*. For more on *la relève*, see below '*Ousia* and *Grammē*,' note 15;' The Pit and the Pyramid,' note 16; and 'The Ends of Man,' note 14.

24 TN. On Levinas, and on the translation of his term *autrui* by 'Other,' see 'Violence and Metaphysics,' note 6, in *Writing and Difference*.

25 TN. Martin Heidegger, *Holzwege* (Frankfurt: V. Klostermann, 1957). English translation ('The Anaximander Fragment') in *Early Greek Thinking*, trans. David Farrell Krell and Frank Capuzzi (New York: Harper and Row, 1975). All further references in the text.

26 *Différance* is not a 'species' of the genus *ontological difference*. If the 'gift of presence is the property of Appropriating (*Die Gabe von Anwesen ist Eigentum des Ereignens*)' ['Time and Being,' in *On Time and Being*, trans. Joan Stambaugh, New York: Harper and Row, 1972; p. 22], *différance* is not a process of propriation in any sense whatever. It is neither position (appropriation) nor negation (expropriation), but rather other. Hence it seems – but here, rather, we are marking the necessity of a future itinerary – that *différance* would be no more a species of the genus *Ereignis* than Being. Heidegger: '. . . then Being belongs into Appropriating (*Dann gehört das Sein in das Ereignen*). Giving and its gift receive their determination from Appropriating. In that case, Being would be a species of Appropriation (*Ereignis*), and not the other way around. To take refuge in such an inversion would be too cheap. Such thinking misses the matter at stake (*Sie denkt am Sachverhalt vorbei*). Appropriation (*Ereignis*) is not the encompassing general concept under which Being and time could be subsumed. Logical classifications mean nothing here. For as we think Being itself and follow what is its own (*seinem Eigenen folgen*), Being proves to be destiny's gift of presence (*gewahrte Gabe des Geschickes von Anwesenheit*), the gift granted by the giving (*Reichen*) of time. The gift of presence is the property of Appropriating (*Die Gabe von Anwesen ist Eigentum des Ereignens*).' (*On Time and Being*, pp. 21–22).

Without a displaced reinscription of this chain (Being, presence, -propriation, etc.) the relation between general or fundamental onto-logy and whatever ontology masters or makes subordinate under the rubric of a regional or particular science will never be transformed rigorously and irreversibly. Such regional sciences include not only political economy, psychoanalysis, semiolinguistics – in all of which, and perhaps more than elsewhere, the value of the *proper* plays an irreducible role – but equally all spiritualist or materialist metaphysics. The analyses articulated in this volume aim at such a preliminary articulation. It goes without saying that such a reinscription will never be contained in theoretical or philosophical discourse, or generally in any discourse or writing, but only on the scene of what I have called elsewhere the text in general (1972).

Additional notes

a *De facto/de jure*: 'in practice'/'in principle'.

b Hegel's *Encyclopedia of the Philosophical Sciences* was published at Heidelberg in 1817, a relatively short summary of his entire system and has three sections, on logic, nature and mind.

c *Phonē*: 'voice' in Greek.

d *On*: 'being' in Greek.

e Littré is the standard French dictionary.

f *Topos noētos*: an intellectual commonplace.

g *Stricto sensu*: 'in a strict sense' (Latin).

h Husserl (see 'Biographies').

i Adiaphoristic, 'not concerned with difference' (Greek); so also 'diaphoristics' (p. xxx), 'the study of difference', and *diapherein*, 'to differ' in Greek, p. 112.

j *Technē*, 'artifice'; *nomos*, 'law', 'convention'; *thesis*, 'arrangment'; *physis*, 'natural order', 'nature' (Greek).

k Levinas (see 'Biographies').

l Dis, 'twice, double' (Greek).

m Kerygmatic, or 'proclamatory'.

Section five

GENDER

Introduction

Every sign is gendered. Discussions of ideology, of language, difference and subjectivity – even the postmodern – inevitably involve questions of gender, and the question of gender itself pervades all areas of critical and cultural debate. However, given the extent and specificity of the many theoretical questions surrounding the issue of gender, its constructions and deconstructions, we have felt it necessary to devote a separate Section entirely to the concerns it raises.

Although the debate itself is vast – often including discussions of the interaction of gender with issues of race, class and sexuality – it none the less seems reasonable to suggest that there are three basic positions from which the debate has been engaged within the domain of critical and cultural theory. Gender can be understood in terms of social roles – of women and men; as determined by the body – female and male; or in terms of the attributes of feminine and masculine. It can be theorized in terms of its constitution of people on the grounds of *biology*; the *psyche*; and the cultural constitution of the *body*. The four extracts selected are intended to introduce some of the principles underlying those three perspectives; they do not represent *all* that there is to the debate as a whole.

Psychoanalysis and gender

A great deal of the work on gender through the twentieth century has emerged in the wake of the psychoanalytic work of Sigmund Freud. Indeed, the signifier 'Freud' itself has often provided a kind of litmus test against which positions within the debate about theories of gender are defined.

Briefly, there are those who embrace the founding principles of Freud's work and seek to develop analyses from them; there are those engaged in 'recuperative' re-readings of Freud in the interests of a politics of feminism and/or gay liberation; and there are those who define a position explicitly in resistance to the notions he advanced – usually, again, in the interests of a politics both of gender and of sexuality. Wherever we may situate ourselves within these ongoing debates, then, the importance of Freud's work remains.

For Freud, the psycho-sexual acquisition of gendered identity is fundamental to the entire question of identity itself, and in many ways the theories he produced represent a fairly radical departure from the biological determinism which preceded them. His notion of the polymorphously plural infant and the notion of the precariousness of repression (demanded by socially taboo desires) through the Oedipal and castration complexes (see, *SE*, vol. 7: 123–245), for example, make the acquisition of gender difference not only crucial to the production of the adult subject, but also problematic to it. Since it is the characteristic of the repressed to return (usually at moments when we least expect it), a great deal of Freud's work is based upon a notion of the gendered subject as fundamentally unstable and capable of change.

However, this theorization of gender difference as a provisional effect produced through the Oedipal and castration complexes is not altogether free from a certain determination in biology. Arguably, the psycho-sexual processes which Freud describes also rely upon the attribution of meaning to visible anatomical distinctions which centre around the presence or absence of the penis, and of drives which are related to bodily instincts (see, *SE*, vol. 19: 241–58). Because of these factors, the complexes which the child must go through are resolved differently (if they are resolved) for boys and for girls, and the resolution itself is based very firmly within the normalizing terrain of heterosexuality.

As with any established body of work which is widely disseminated, much within the canon of Freudian theory is contradictory and capable of varying interpretation from the cultural distance of the late twentieth century. It is perhaps this plurality of Freud's work which has led to the development of Freudian concepts within the work of contemporary theorists.

The work of Juliet Mitchell (1974) develops a theory of gendered identity which emphasizes the plurality and instabilities of the unconscious, and the repression of either the masculine or feminine capabilities of the individual subject through the social taboos and regulative norms of patriarchal society. While this work is still grounded within the domain of psychoanalysis, the work of Jacqueline Rose (1984; 1988) and Laura Mulvey (Section 5.3) takes the Freudian framework to the analysis of cultural texts. Within Laura Mulvey's work, the Freudian equation of the masculine and the feminine with activity and passivity (both of which are aspects of the single subject) forms the basis of an analysis of the reproduction of sexual imbalance through the specifically cultural economy of visual texts. Her primary concern is not with a description of patriarchal gender distinctions, or the psychic processes which give rise to them, but rather with an analysis of the cultural ramifications of the textual operation of gender identification which effaces the active desires of women. Within Mulvey's analysis psychic processes are more explicitly grounded in social and textual conditions.

Écriture féminine

This impulse to material grounding is also apparent in much of the work of French feminist theorists like Hélène Cixous (Section 5.2), Luce Irigaray (1985b) and Julia Kristeva (Section 3.2). Although much of this work is itself a product of psychoanalytic theory (dependent much more upon Lacan's re-reading of Freud – see Section 3.1), it also relies firmly on theories of language (Section 1.1) clearly focused upon resistance to the phallus as controlling signifier in the gendered metaphysics of Western thought. For these theorists the importance of gendered identity lies in its constitution and control in and through language – which itself is understood as the product of social and political operations of power and difference. Their model of analysis, then, is based upon language as a site of resistance to the production of gendered meanings, and to the perpetua-tion of heterosexually normative taboos. Cixous in particular privileges the potential bisexuality of human identity and argues (picking up on Julia Kristeva's notion of the semiotic chora of language) for a form of writing arising from the 'feminine' body. Such a move, Cixous affirms, is revolu-tionary precisely because it transgresses the norms of gender difference, but also because in transgressing those norms it opens the question of identity itself to the plurality and unpredictability of the free play of the signifier.

Social construction

Still further from the site of psychoanalysis, there is also a body of work concerned to theorize gender as an effect of social and cultural constructions. Much of the work of Michel Foucault (some of which we have included in Section Three – Subjectivity) provides a detailed analysis of ways in which gendered people are *discursively* constituted by forms of knowledge (of the body, sexuality, the family and so on) within specific social formations. While Foucault's analysis exposes the power relations inherent in social constructions of the subject – female and male – it also allows for the possibilities of resistance to the rigid binary categories of gendered subjectivity which may be privileged as the norm (see, for example, *The History of Sexuality*, 1978a, and *Herculine Barbin*, 1980).

Within the domain of critical and cultural theory and particularly in the field of social science, the notion of the subject as the site of discursive constructions and deconstructions of gendered identity has often been central. Celia Kitzinger's work on the social construction of lesbianism (1987) provides just one example; there has also been a proliferation of work (largely) by women focused upon the construction of gendered identity in relation to issues of race, class and sexuality (see, for example, Alvina Quintana (1990); and Rosaura Sánchez (1990)).

But what of the discursive construction of the female body and with it the placing of the collective feminist critic within the discourses of theory themselves? From her own position within deconstructivist theory, Gayatri Chakravorty Spivak investigates the implications of the potential undecidability of female identity as it has been theorized within the work of the French feminisms outlined above and exposes its appropriation as a model for the laws of textual operation within the works of male philosophers (primarily Hegel, Nietzsche and Derrida). It is Spivak's argument that within the irreducibly material dimensions of sexual difference male deconstructivists desire the displaced position of woman as their own, and that in taking that position for themselves they displace the figure of woman twice over. Her analysis warns of the implications of collapsing gender difference altogether within the domain of theory which itself is an inevitable part of the inequitable operations of power within a patriarchal society.

Theory itself is not immune to unacknowledged gender assumptions, nor is a critical and cultural theory reader, but perhaps nothing is.

5.1

Sigmund Freud 'On the Universal Tendency to Debasement in the Sphere of Love' (1912)

1

If the practising psychoanalyst asks himself on account of what disorder people most often come to him for help, he is bound to reply – disregarding the many forms of anxiety – that it is psychical impotence. This singular disturbance affects men of strongly libidinous[1] natures, and manifests itself in a refusal by the executive organs of sexuality to carry out the sexual act, although before and after they may show themselves to be intact and capable of performing the act, and although a strong psychical inclination to carry it out is present. The first clue to understanding his condition is obtained by the sufferer himself on making the discovery that a failure of this kind only arises when the attempt is made with certain individuals; whereas with others there is never any question of such a failure. He now becomes aware that it is some feature of the sexual object which gives rise to the inhibition of his male potency, and sometimes he reports that he has a feeling of an obstacle inside him, the sensation of a counter-will which successfully interferes with his conscious intention. However, he is unable to guess what this internal obstacle is and what feature of the sexual object brings it into operation. If he has had repeated experience of a failure of this kind, he is likely, by the familiar process of 'erroneous connection', to decide that the recollection of the first occasion evoked the disturbing anxiety-idea and so caused the failure to be repeated each time; while he derives the first occasion itself from some 'accidental' impression.

Pyschoanalytic studies of psychical impotence have already been carried out and published by several writers.[2] Every analyst can confirm the explanations provided by them from his own clinical experience. It is in fact a question of the inhibitory influence of certain psychical complexes which are withdrawn from the subject's knowledge. An incestuous fixation on mother or sister, which has never been surmounted, plays a prominent part in this pathogenic material and is its most universal content. In addition there is the influence to be considered of accidental distressing impressions connected with infantile sexual activity, and also those factors which in a general way reduce the libido that is to be directed on to the female sexual object.[3]

When striking cases of psychical impotence are exhaustively investigated by means of psychoanalysis, the following information is obtained about the psychosexual processes at work in them. Here again – as very probably in all neurotic disturbances – the foundation of the disorder is provided by an inhibition in the developmental history of the libido before it assumes the form which we take to be its normal termination. Two currents whose union is necessary to ensure a completely normal attitude in love have, in the cases we are considering, failed to combine. These two may be distinguished as the *affectionate* and the *sensual* current.

The affectionate current is the older of the two. It springs from the earliest years of childhood; it is formed on the basis of the interests of the self-preservative instinct and is directed to the members of the family and those who look after the child. From the very beginning it carries along with it contributions from the sexual instincts – components of erotic interest – which can already be seen more or less clearly even in childhood and in any event are uncovered in neurotics by psychoanalysis later on. It corresponds to *the child's primary object-choice*. We learn in this way that the sexual instincts find their first objects by attaching themselves to the valuations made by the ego-instincts, precisely in the way in which the first sexual satisfactions are experienced in attachment to the bodily functions necessary for the preservation of life.[4] The 'affection' shown by the child's parents and those who look after him, which seldom fails to betray its erotic nature ('the child is an erotic plaything'), does a very great deal to raise the contributions made by erotism to the cathexes of his ego-instincts, and to increase them to an amount which is bound to play a part in his later development, especially when certain other circumstances lend their support.

These affectionate fixations of the child persist throughout childhood, and continually carry along with them erotism, which is consequently diverted from its sexual aims. Then at the age of puberty they are joined by the powerful 'sensual' current which no longer mistakes its aims. It never fails, apparently, to follow the earlier paths and to cathect the objects of the primary infantile choice with quotas of libido that are now far stronger. Here, however, it runs up against the obstacles that have been erected in the meantime by the barrier against incest; consequently it will make efforts to pass on from these objects which are unsuitable in reality, and find a way as soon as possible to other, extraneous objects with which a real sexual life may be carried on. These new objects will still be chosen on the model (imago[5]) of the infantile ones, but in the course of time they will attract to themselves the affection that was tied to the earlier ones. A man shall leave his father and his mother – according to the biblical command – and shall cleave unto his wife; affection and sensuality are then united. The greatest intensity of sensual passion will bring with it the highest psychical valuation of the object – this being the normal overvaluation of the sexual object on the part of a man.

Two factors will decide whether this advance in the developmental path of the libido is to fail. First, there is the amount of *frustration in reality* which opposes the new object-choice and reduces its value for the person concerned. There is after all no point in embarking upon an object-choice if no choice is to be allowed at all or if there is no prospect of being able to choose anything suitable. Secondly, there is the amount of *attraction* which the infantile objects that have to be relinquished are able to exercise, and which is in proportion to the erotic cathexis attaching to them in childhood. If these two factors are sufficiently strong, the general mechanism by which the neuroses are formed comes into operation. The libido turns away from reality, is taken over by imaginative activity (the process of introversion), strengthens the images of the first sexual objects and becomes fixated to them. The obstacle raised against incest, however, compels the libido that has turned to these objects to remain in the unconscious. The masturbatory activity carried out by the sensual current, which is now part of the unconscious, makes its own contribution in strengthening this fixation. Nothing is altered in this state of affairs if the advance which has miscarried in reality is now completed in phantasy, and if in the phantasy-situations that lead to masturbatory satisfaction the original sexual objects are replaced by different ones. As a result of this substitution the phantasies become admissible to consciousness, but no progress is made in the allocation of the libido in reality. In this way it can happen that the whole of a young man's sensuality becomes tied to incestuous objects in the unconscious, or to put it another way, becomes fixated to unconscious incestuous phantasies. The result is then total impotence, which is perhaps further ensured by the simultaneous onset of an actual weakening of the organs that perform the sexual act.

Less severe conditions are required to bring about the state known specifically as psychical impotence. Here the fate of the sensual current must not be that its whole charge has to conceal itself behind the affectionate current; it must have remained sufficiently strong or uninhibited to secure a partial outlet into reality. The sexual activity of such people shows the clearest signs, however, that it has not the whole psychical driving force of the instinct behind it. It is capricious, easily disturbed, often not properly carried out, and not accompanied by much pleasure. But above all it is forced to avoid the affectionate current. A restriction has thus been placed on object-choice. The sensual current that has remained active seeks only objects which do not recall the incestuous figures forbidden to it; if someone makes an impression that might lead to a high psychical estimation of her, this impression does not find an issue in any sensual excitation but in affection which has no erotic effect. The whole sphere of love in such people remains divided in the two directions personified in art as sacred and profane (or animal) love. Where they love they do not desire and where they desire they cannot love. They seek objects which they do not need to love, in order to keep their sensuality away from the objects they love; and, in accordance with the laws of 'complexive sensitiveness'[6] and of the return of the repressed, the strange failure shown in psychical impotence makes its appearance whenever an object which has been chosen with the aim of avoiding incest recalls the prohibited object through some feature, often an inconspicuous one.

The main protective measure against such a disturbance which men have recourse to in this split in their love consists in a psychical *debasement* of the sexual object, the overvaluation that normally attaches to the sexual object being reserved for the incestuous object and its representatives. As soon as the condition of debasement is fulfilled, sensuality can be freely expressed, and important sexual capacities and a high degree of pleasure can develop. There is a further factor which contributes to this result. People in whom there has not been a proper confluence of the affectionate and the sensual currents do not usually show much refinement in their modes of behaviour in love; they have retained perverse sexual aims whose nonfulfilment is felt as a serious loss of pleasure, and whose fulfilment on the other hand seems possible only with a debased and despised sexual object.

We can now understand the motives behind the boy's phantasies mentioned in the first of these 'Contributions', which degrade the mother to the level of a prostitute. They are efforts to bridge the gulf between the two currents in love, at any rate in phantasy, and by debasing the mother to acquire her as an object of sensuality.

2

In the preceding section we have approached the study of psychical impotence from a medico-psychological angle of which the title of this paper gives no indication. It will however become clear that this introduction was required by us to provide an approach to our proper subject.

We have reduced psychical impotence to the failure of the affectionate and the sensual currents in love to combine, and this developmental inhibition has in turn been explained as being due to the influences of strong childhood fixations and of later frustration in reality through the intervention of the barrier against incest. There is one principal objection to the theory we advance; it does too much. It explains why certain people suffer from psychical impotence, but it leaves us with the apparent mystery of how others have been able to escape this disorder. Since we must recognize that all the relevant factors known to us – the strong childhood fixation, the incest-barrier and the frustration in the years of development after puberty – are to be found in practically all civilized human beings, we should be justified in expecting psychical impotence to be a universal affliction under civilization and not a disorder confined to some individuals.

It would be easy to escape from this conclusion by pointing to the quantitative factor in the causation of illness – to the greater or lesser extent of the contribution made by the various elements which determine whether a recognizable illness results or not. But although I accept this answer as correct, it is not my intention to make it a reason for rejecting the conclusion itself. On the contrary, I shall put forward the view that psychical impotence is much more widespread than is supposed, and that a certain amount of this behaviour does in fact characterize the love of civilized man.

If the concept of psychical impotence is broadened and is not restricted to failure to perform the act of coitus in circumstances where a desire to obtain pleasure is present and the genital apparatus is intact, we may in the first place add all those men who are described as psychanaesthetic: men who never fail in the act but who carry it out without getting any particular pleasure from it – a state of affairs that is more common than one would think. Psychoanalytic examination of such cases discloses the same aetiological factors as we found in psychical impotence in the narrower sense, without at first arriving at any explanation of the difference between their symptoms. An easily justifiable analogy takes one from these anaesthetic men to the immense number of frigid women; and there is no better way to describe or understand their behaviour in love than by comparing it with the more conspicuous disorder of psychical impotence in men.[7]

If however we turn our attention not to an extension of the concept of psychical impotence, but to the gradations in its symptomatology, we cannot escape the conclusion that the behaviour in love of men in the civilized world today bears the stamp altogether of psychical impotence. There are only a very few educated people in whom the two currents of affection and sensuality have become properly fused; the man almost always feels his respect for the woman acting as a restriction on his sexual activity, and only develops full potency when he is with a debased sexual object; and this in its turn is partly caused by the entrance of perverse components into his sexual aims, which he does not venture to satisfy with a woman he respects. He is assured of complete sexual pleasure only when he can devote himself unreservedly to obtaining satisfaction, which with his well-brought-up wife, for instance, he does not dare to do. This is the source of his need for a debased sexual object, a woman who is ethically inferior, to whom he need attribute no aesthetic scruples, who does not know him in his other social relations and cannot judge him in them. It is to such a woman that he prefers to devote his sexual potency, even when the whole of his affection belongs to a woman of a higher kind. It is possible, too, that the tendency so often observed in men of the highest classes of society to choose a woman of a lower class as a permanent mistress or even as a wife is nothing but a consequence of their need for a debased sexual object, to whom, psychologically, the possibility of complete satisfaction is linked.

I do not hestitate to make the two factors at work in psychical impotence in the strict sense – the factors of intense incestuous fixation in childhood and the frustration by reality in adolescence – responsible, too, for this extremely common characteristic of the love of civilized men. It sounds not only disagreeable but also paradoxical, yet it must nevertheless be said that anyone who is to be really free and happy in love must have surmounted his respect for women and have come to terms with the idea of incest with his mother or sister. Anyone who subjects himself to a serious self-examination on the subject of this requirement will be sure to find that he regards the sexual act basically as something degrading, which defiles and pollutes not only the body. The origin of this low opinion, which he will certainly not willingly acknowledge, must be looked for in the period of his youth in which the sensual current in him was already strongly developed but its satisfaction with an object outside the family was almost as completely prohibited as it was with an incestuous one.

In our civilized world women are under the influence of a similar after-effect of their upbringing, and, in addition, of their reaction to men's behaviour. It is naturally just as unfavourable for a woman if a man approaches her without his full potency as it is if his initial overvaluation of her when he is in love gives place to undervaluation after he has possessed her. In the case of women there is little sign of a need to debase their sexual object. This is no doubt connected with the absence in them as a rule of anything similar to the sexual overvaluation found in men. But their long holding back from sexuality and the lingering of their sensuality in phantasy has another important consequence for them. They are subsequently often unable to undo the connection between sensual activity and the prohibition, and prove to be psychically impotent, that is, frigid, when such activity is at last allowed them. This is the origin of the endeavour made by many women to keep even legitimate relations secret for a while; and of the capacity of other women for normal sensation as soon as the condition of prohibition is re-established by a secret love affair: unfaithful to their husband, they are able to keep a second order of faith with their lover.[8]

The condition of forbiddenness in the erotic life of women is, I think, comparable to the need on the part of men to debase their sexual object. Both are consequences of the long period of delay, which is demanded by education for cultural reasons, between sexual maturity and sexual activity. Both aim at abolishing the psychical impotence that results from the failure of affectionate and sensual impulses to coalesce. That the effect of the same causes should be so different in men and in women may perhaps be traced to another difference in the behaviour of the two sexes. Civilized women do not usually transgress the prohibition on sexual activity in the period during which they have to wait, and thus they acquire the intimate connection between prohibition and sexuality. Men usually break through this prohibition if they can satisfy the condition of debasing the object, and so they carry on this condition into their love in later life.

In view of the strenuous efforts being made in the civilized world today to reform sexual life, it will not be superfluous to give a reminder that psychoanalytic research is as remote from tendentiousness as any other kind of research. It has no other end in view than to throw light on things by tracing what is manifest back to what is hidden. It is quite satisfied if reforms make use of its findings to replace what is injurious by something more advantageous; but it cannot predict whether other institutions may not result in other, and perhaps graver, sacrifices.

3

The fact that the curb put upon love by civilization involves a universal tendency to debase sexual objects will perhaps lead us to turn our attention from the object to the instincts themselves. The damage caused by the initial frustration of sexual pleasure is seen in the fact that the freedom later given to that pleasure in marriage does not bring full satisfaction. But at the same time, if sexual freedom is unrestricted from the outset the result is no better. It can easily be shown that the psychical value of erotic needs is reduced as soon as their satisfaction becomes easy. An obstacle is required in order to heighten libido; and where natural resistances to satisfaction have not been sufficient men have at all times erected conventional ones so as to be able to enjoy love. This is true both of individuals and of nations. In times in which there were no difficulties standing in the way of sexual satisfaction, such as perhaps during the decline of the ancient civilizations, love became worthless and life empty, and strong reaction-formations were required to restore indispensable affective values. In this connection it may be claimed that the ascetic current in Christianity created psychical values for love which pagan antiquity was never able to confer on it. This current assumed its greatest importance with the ascetic monks, whose lives were almost entirely occupied with the struggle against libidinal temptation.

One's first inclination is no doubt to trace back the difficulties revealed here to universal characteristics of our organic instincts. It is no doubt also true in general that the psychical importance of an instinct rises in proportion to its frustration. Suppose a number of totally different human beings were all equally exposed to hunger. As their imperative need for food mounted, all the individual differences would disappear and in their place one would see the uniform manifestations of the one unappeased instinct. But is it also true that with the satisfaction of an instinct its psychical value always falls just as sharply? Consider, for example, the relation of a drinker to wine. Is it not true that wine always provides the drinker with the same toxic satisfaction, which in poetry has so often been compared to erotic satisfaction – a comparison acceptable from the scientific point of view as well? Has one ever heard of the drinker being obliged constantly to change his drink because he soon grows tired of keeping to the same one? On the contrary, habit constantly tightens the bond between a man and the kind of wine he drinks. Does one ever hear of a drinker who needs to go to a country where wine is dearer or drinking is prohibited, so that by introducing obstacles he can reinforce the dwindling satisfaction that he obtains? Not at all. If we listen to what our great alcoholics, such as Böcklin,[9] say about their relation to wine, it sounds like the most perfect harmony, a model of a happy marriage. Why is the relation of the lover to his sexual object so very different?

It is my belief that, however strange it may sound, we must reckon with the possibility that something in the nature of the sexual instinct itself is unfavourable to the realization of complete satisfaction. If we consider the long and difficult developmental history of the instinct, two factors immediately spring to mind which might be made responsible for this difficulty. Firstly, as a result of the diphasic onset of object-choice, and the interposition of the barrier against incest, the final object of the sexual instinct is never any longer the original object but only a surrogate for it. Psychoanalysis has shown us that when the original object of a wishful impulse has been lost as a result of repression, it is frequently represented by an endless series of substitutive objects none of which, however, brings full satisfaction. This may explain the inconstancy in object-choice, the 'craving for stimulation'[10] which is so often a feature of the love of adults.

Secondly, we know that the sexual instinct is originally divided into a great number of components – or rather, it develops out of them – some of which cannot be taken up into the instinct in its later form, but have at an earlier stage to be suppressed or put to other uses. These are above all the coprophilic instinctual components, which have proved incompatible with our aesthetic standards of culture, probably since, as a result of our adopting an erect gait, we raised our organ of smell from the ground.[11] The same is true of a large portion of the sadistic urges which are a part of erotic life. But all such developmental processes affect only the upper layers of the complex structure. The fundamental processes which produce erotic excitation remain unaltered. The excremental is all too intimately and inseparably bound up with the sexual; the position of the genitals – *inter urinas et faeces* – remains the decisive and unchangeable factor. One might say here, varying a well-known saying of the great Napoleon: 'Anatomy is destiny'.[12] The genitals themselves have not taken part in the development of the human body in the direction of beauty: they have remained animal, and thus love, too, has remained in essence just as animal as it ever was. The instincts of love are hard to educate; education of them achieves now too much, now too little. What civilization aims at making out of them seems unattainable except at the price of a sensible loss of pleasure; the persistence of the impulses that could not be made use of can be detected in sexual activity in the form of non-satisfaction.

Thus we may perhaps be forced to become reconciled to the idea that it is quite impossible to adjust the claims of the sexual instinct to the demands of civilization; that in consequence of its cultural development renunciation and suffering, as well as the danger of extinction in the remotest future, cannot be avoided by the human race. This gloomy prognosis rests, it is true, on the single conjecture that the non-satisfaction that goes with civilization is the necessary consequence of certain peculiarities which the sexual instinct has assumed under the pressure of culture. The very incapacity of the sexual instinct to yield complete satisfaction as soon as it submits to the first demands of civilization becomes the source, however, of the noblest cultural achievements which are brought into being by ever more extensive sublimation of its instinctual components. For what motive would men have for putting sexual instinctual forces to other uses if, by any distribution of those forces, they could obtain fully satisfying pleasure? They would never abandon that pleasure and they would never make any further progress. It seems, therefore, that the irreconcilable difference between the demands of the two instincts – the sexual and the egoistic – has made men capable of ever higher achievements, though subject, it is true, to a constant danger, to which, in the form of neurosis, the weaker are succumbing today.

It is not the aim of science either to frighten or to console. But I myself am quite ready to admit that such far-reaching conclusions as those I have drawn should be built on a broader foundation, and that perhaps developments in other directions may enable mankind to correct the results of the developments I have here been considering in isolation.

Notes

(Square brackets indicate editor's notes for *SE*.)

1 ['*Libidinös*'. Here 'libidinous', as contrasted with the technical 'libidinal'.]
2 Steiner (1907), Stekel (1908), Ferenczi (1908). [Freud had written a preface to Stekel's book (see *SE* v. 9, pp. 250–1).]
3 Stekel (1908, 191 ff.).
4 [The 'attachment' (or 'anaclitic') type of object-choice was discussed more fully in Freud's later paper on narcissism, *SE* v. 14.]
5 [This term was not often used by Freud, especially in his later writings. He attributed it to Jung ('Psycho-Analytic Notes', *SE* v. 12), in which passage Jung in turn says he partly chose the word from the title of a novel by the Swiss writer Carl Spitteler. The psychoanalytic journal *Imago* also owed its title to the same source, according to its co-founder, Hanns Sachs 1945, p. 63.]
6 [This term is borrowed from Jung's word-association experiments (Jung 1906).]
7 I am at the same time very willing to admit that frigidity in women is a complex subject which can also be approached from another angle. [The question is examined at length in 'The Taboo of Virginity', *SE* v. 11.]
8 [cf. 'The Taboo of Virginity'.]
9 Floerke (1902).
10 ['*Reizhunger*'. This term seems to have been introduced by Hoche and Bloch. See Freud's *Three Essays SE* v. 7.]
11 [cf. two long footnotes to Chapter IV of *Civilization and its Discontents* (*SE* v. 21), in which this idea is explored in greater detail.]
12 [This paraphrase appears again in 'The Dissolution of the Oedipus Complex' (*SE* v. 19.)]

See:

Ferenczi, S. (1908). 'Analytische Deutung und Behandlung der psychosexuellen Impotenz beim Mann', *Psychiat.-neurol. Wschr.*, 10, 298. [Trans.: 'The Analytic Interpretation and Treatment of Psycho-sexual Impotence', *First Contributions to Psycho-Analysis* (London, 1952), chapter 1].
Floerke, G. (1902). *Zehn Jahre mit Böcklin* (2nd ed) (Munich).
Jung, C. G. (1906). *Diagnostische Assoziationsstudien* 2 vols. (Leipzig) [Trans: *Studies in Word-Association* (London, 1918)].
Sachs, H. (1945). *Freud, Master and Friend* (Cambridge, Mass. and London).
Steiner, M. (1907). 'Die funktionelle Impotenz des Mannes und ihre Behandlung', *Wien. med. Pr..*, 48, 1535.
Stekel, W. (1908). *Nervöse Angstzustände und ihre Behandlung* (Berlin and Vienna).

5.2

Hélène Cixous
from 'Sorties' (1986)

Where is she?
Activity/Passivity
Sun/Moon
Culture/Nature
Day/Night

Father/Mother
Head/Heart
Intelligible/Palpable
Logos/Pathos.
Form, convex, step, advance, semen, progress.
Matter, concave, ground – where steps are taken, holding- and dumping-
  ground.
Man
———
Woman
  Always the same metaphor: we follow it, it carries us, beneath all its
figures, wherever discourse is organized. If we read or speak, the same
thread or double braid is leading us throughout literature, philosophy,
criticism, centuries of representation and reflection.
Thought has always worked through opposition,
Speaking/Writing
Parole/Écriture
High/Low
  Through dual, hierarchical oppositions. Superior/Inferior. Myths, legends,
books. Philosophical systems. Everywhere (where) ordering intervenes, where
a law organizes what is thinkable by oppositions (dual, irreconcilable; or

sublatable, dialectical). And all these pairs of oppositions are *couples*. Does that mean something? Is the fact that Logocentrism subjects thought – all concepts, codes and values – to a binary system, related to 'the' couple, man/woman?

Nature/History
Nature/Art
Nature/Mind
Passion/Action

Theory of culture, theory of society, symbolic systems in general – art, religion, family, language – it is all developed while bringing the same schemes to light. And the movement whereby each opposition is set up to make sense is the movement through which the couple is destroyed. A universal battlefield. Each time, a war is let loose. Death is always at work.
Father/son   Relations of authority, privilege, force.
The Word/Writing   Relations: opposition, conflict, sublation, return.
Master/slave   Violence. Repression.
We see that 'victory' always comes down to the same thing: things get hierarchical. Organization by hierarchy makes all conceptual organization subject to man. Male privilege, shown in the opposition between *activity* and *passivity*, which he uses to sustain himself. Traditionally, the question of sexual difference is treated by coupling it with the opposition: activity/passivity.

There are repercussions. Consulting the history of philosophy – since philosophical discourse both orders and reproduces all thought – one notices[1] that it is marked by an absolute *constant* which orders values and which is precisely this opposition, activity/passivity.

The masculine future

There are some exceptions. There have always been those uncertain, poetic persons who have not let themselves be reduced to dummies programmed by pitiless repression of the homosexual element. Men or women: beings who are complex, mobile, open. Accepting the other sex as a component makes them much richer, more various, stronger, and – to the extent that they are mobile – very fragile. It is only in this condition that we invent. Thinkers, artists, those who create new values, 'philosophers' in the mad Nietzschean manner, inventors and wreckers of concepts and forms, those who change life cannot help but be stirred by anomalies – complementary or contradictory. That doesn't mean that you have to be homosexual to create. But it does mean that there is no *invention* possible, whether it be philosophical or poetic, without there being in the inventing subject an abundance of the other, of variety: separate-people, thought-/people, whole populations issuing from the unconscious, and in each suddenly animated desert, the springing up of selves one didn't know – our women, our monsters, our jackals, our Arabs, our aliases, our frights. That there is no invention of any other I, no poetry, no fiction without a certain homosexuality (the I/ play of bisexuality) acting as a crystallization of my ultrasubjectivities.[2] I is this exuberant, gay, personal matter, masculine, feminine or other where I enchants, I agonizes me. And in the concert of personalizations called I, at the same time that a certain homosexuality is repressed, symbolically, substitutively, it comes through by various signs, conduct-character, behaviour-acts. And it is even more clearly seen in writing.

Thus, what is inscribed under Jean Genet's name, in the movement of a text that divides itself, pulls itself to pieces, dismembers itself, regroups, remembers itself, is a proliferating, maternal femininity. A phantasmic meld of men, males, gentlemen, monarchs, princes, orphans, flowers, mothers, breasts gravitates about a wonderful 'sun of energy' – love, – that bombards and disintegrates these ephemeral amorous anomalies so that they can be recomposed in other bodies for new passions.

She is bisexual:

What I propose here leads directly to a reconsideration of *bisexuality*. To reassert the value of bisexuality;[3] hence to snatch it from the fate classically reserved for it in which it is conceptualized as 'neuter' because, as such, it would aim at warding off castration. Therefore, I shall distinguish between two bisexualities, two opposite ways of imagining the possibility and practice of bisexuality.

1) Bisexuality as a fantasy of a complete being, which replaces the fear of castration and veils sexual difference insofar as this is perceived as the mark of a mythical separation – the trace, therefore, of a dangerous and painful ability to be cut. Ovid's Hermaphrodite, less bisexual than asexual, not made up of two genders but of two halves. Hence, a fantasy of unity. Two within one, and not even two wholes.

2) To this bisexuality that melts together and effaces, wishing to avert castration, I oppose the *other bisexuality*, the one with which every subject, who is not shut up inside the spurious Phallocentric Performing Theater, sets up his or her erotic universe. Bisexuality – that is to say the location within oneself of the presence of both sexes, evident and insistent in different ways according to the individual, the nonexclusion of difference or of a sex, and starting with this 'permission' one gives oneself, the multiplication of the effects of desire's inscription on every part of the body and the other body.

For historical reasons, at the present time it is woman who benefits from and opens up within this bisexuality beside itself, which does not annihilate differences but cheers them on, pursues them, adds more: in a certain way *woman is bisexual* – man having been trained to aim for glorious phallic monosexuality. By insisting on the primacy of the phallus and implementing it, phallocratic ideology has produced more than one victim. As a woman, I could be obsessed by the scepter's great shadow, and they told me: adore it, that thing you don't wield.

But at the same time, man has been given the grotesque and unenviable fate of being reduced to a single idol with clay balls. And terrified of homosexuality, as Freud and his followers remark. Why does man fear *being* a woman? Why this refusal (*Ablehnung*) of femininity? The question that stumps

Freud. The 'bare rock' of castration. For Freud, the repressed is not the other sex defeated by the dominant sex, as his friend Fliess (to whom Freud owes the theory of bisexuality) believed; what is repressed is leaning toward one's own sex.

Psychoanalysis is formed on the basis of woman and has repressed (not all that successfully) the femininity of masculine sexuality, and now the account it gives is hard to disprove.

We women, the derangers, know it only too well. But nothing compels us to deposit our lives in these lack-banks; to think that the subject is constituted as the last stage in a drama of bruising rehearsals; to endlessly bail out the father's religion. Because we don't desire it. We don't go round and round the supreme hole. We have no *woman's* reason to pay allegiance to the negative. What is feminine (the poets suspected it) affirms: . . . and yes I said yes I will Yes, says Molly (in her rapture), carrying *Ulysses* with her in the direction of a new writing; I said yes, I will Yes.

To say that woman is somehow bisexual is an apparently paradoxical way of displacing and reviving the question of difference. And therefore of writing as 'feminine' or 'masculine.'

I will say: today, writing is woman's. That is not a provocation, it means that woman admits there is an other. In her becoming-woman, she has not erased the bisexuality latent in the girl as in the boy. Femininity and bisexuality go together, in a combination that varies according to the individual, spreading the intensity of its force differently and (depending on the moments of their history) privileging one component or another. It is much harder for man to let the other come through him. Writing is the passageway, the entrance, the exit, the dwelling place of the other in me – the other that I am and am not, that I don't know how to be, but that I feel passing, that makes me live – that tears me apart, disturbs me, changes me, who? – a feminine one, a masculine one, some? – several, some unknown, which is indeed what gives me the desire to know and from which all life soars. This peopling gives neither rest nor security, always disturbs the relationship to 'reality,' produces an uncertainty that gets in the way of the subject's socialization. It is distressing, it wears you out; and for men this permeability, this nonexclusion is a threat, something intolerable.

In the past, when carried to a rather spectacular degree, it was called 'possession.' Being possessed is not desirable for a masculine Imaginary, which would interpret it as passivity – a dangerous feminine position. It is true that a certain receptivity is 'feminine.' One can, of course, as History has always done, exploit feminine reception through alienation. A woman, by her opening up, is open to being 'possessed,' which is to say, dispossessed of herself.

But I am speaking here of femininity as keeping alive the other that is confided to her, that visits her, that she can love as other. The loving to be other, another, without its necessarily going the rout of abasing what is same, herself.

As for passivity, in excess, it is partly bound up with death. But there is a nonclosure that is not submission but confidence and comprehension; that is not an opportunity for destruction but for wonderful expansion.

Through the same opening that is her danger, she comes out of herself to go to the other, a traveler in unexplored places; she does not refuse, she approaches, not to do away with the space between, but to see it, to experience what she is not, what she is, what she can be.

Writing is working; being worked; questioning (in) the between (letting oneself be questioned) of same *and of* other without which nothing lives; undoing death's work by willing the togetherness of one-another, infinitely charged with a ceaseless exchange of one with another – not knowing one another and beginning again only from what is most distant, from self, from other, from the other within. A course that multiplies transformations by the thousands.

And that is not done without danger, without pain, without loss – of moments of self, of consciousness, of persons one has been, goes beyond, leaves. It doesn't happen without expense – of sense, time, direction.

But is that specifically feminine? It is men who have inscribed, described, theorized the paradoxical logic of an economy without reserve. This is not contradictory; it brings us back to asking about their femininity. Rare are the men able to venture onto the brink where writing, freed from law, un-encumbered by moderation, exceeds phallic authority, and where the subjectivity inscribing its effects becomes feminine.

Where does difference come through in writing? If there is difference it is in the manner of spending, of valorizing the appropriated, of thinking what is not-the-same. In general, it is in the manner of thinking any 're-turn,' the relationship of capitalization, if this word 'return' (*rapport*) is understood in its sense of 'revenue.'

Today, still, the masculine return to the Selfsame is narrower and more restricted than femininity's. It all happens as if man were more directly threatened in his being by the nonselfsame than woman. Ordinarily, this is exactly the cultural product described by psychoanalysis: someone who still has something to lose. And in the development of desire, of exchange, he is the en-grossing party: loss and expense are stuck in the commercial deal that always turns the gift into a gift-that-takes. The gift brings in a return. Loss, at the end of a curved line, is turned into its opposite and comes back to him as profit.

But does woman escape this law of return? Can one speak of another spending? Really, there is no 'free' gift. You never give something for nothing. But all the difference lies in the why and how of the gift, in the values that the gesture of giving affirms, causes to circulate; in the type of profit the giver draws from the gift and the use to which he or she puts it. Why, how, is there this difference?

When one gives, what does one give oneself?

What does he want in return – the traditional man? And she? At first what *he* wants, whether on the level of cultural or of personal exchanges, whether it is a question of capital or of affectivity (or of love, of *jouissance*) – is that he gain more masculinity: plus-value of virility, authority, power, money, or pleasure, all of which reenforce his phallocentric narcissism at the same time. Moreover, that is what society is made for – how it is made; and men can hardly get out of it. An unenviable fate they've made for themselves. A man is always proving something; he has to 'show off,' show up the others. Masculine profit is almost always mixed up with a success that is socially defined.

How does she give? What are her dealings with saving or squandering, reserve, life, death? She too gives *for*. She too, with open hands, gives herself – pleasure, happiness, increased value, enhanced self-image. But she doesn't try to 'recover her expenses.' She is able not to return to herself, never setting down, pouring out, going everywhere to the other. She does not flee extremes; she is not the being-of-the-end (the goal), but she is how-far-being-reaches.

If there is a self proper to woman, paradoxically it is her capacity to de-propriate herself without self-interest: endless body, without 'end,' without principal 'parts'; if she is a whole, it is a whole made up of parts that are wholes, not simple, partial objects but varied entirety, moving and boundless change, a cosmos where eros never stops traveling, vast astral space. She doesn't revolve around a sun that is more star than the stars.

That doesn't mean that she is undifferentiated magma; it means that she doesn't create a monarchy of her body or her desire. Let masculine sexuality gravitate around the penis, engendering this centralized body (political anatomy) under the party dictatorship. Woman does not perform on herself this regionalization that profits the couple head-sex, that only inscribes it-self within frontiers. Her libido is cosmic, just as her unconscious is world-wide: her writing also can only go on and on, without ever inscribing or distinguishing contours, daring these dizzying passages in other, fleeting and passionate dwellings within him, within the hims and hers whom she inhabits just long enough to watch them, as close as possible to the un-conscious from the moment they arise; to love them, as close as possible to instinctual drives, and then, further, all filled with these brief identifying hugs and kisses, she goes and goes on infinitely. She alone dares and wants to know from within where she, the one excluded, has never ceased to hear what-comes-before-language reverberating. She lets the other tongue of a thousand tongues speak – the tongue, sound without barrier or death. She refuses life nothing. Her tongue doesn't hold back but holds forth, doesn't keep in but keeps on enabling. Where the wonder of being several and turmoil is expressed, she does not protect herself against these unknown feminines; she surprises herself at seeing, being, pleasuring in her gift of changeability. I am spacious singing Flesh: onto which is grafted no one knows which I – which masculine or feminine, more or less human but above all living, because changing I.

Writing femininity transformation:

And there is a link between the economy of femininity – the open, extravag-ant subjectivity, that relationship to the other in which the gift doesn't calculate its influence – and the possibility of love; and a link today between this 'libido of the other' and writing.

At the present time, *defining* a feminine practice of writing is impossible with an impossibility that will continue; for this practice will never be able to be *theorized*, enclosed, coded, which does not mean it does not exist. But it will always exceed the discourse governing the phallocentric system; it takes place and will take place somewhere other than in the territories subordinated to philosophical-theoretical domination. It will not let itself think except through subjects that break automatic functions, border runners never subjugated by any authority. But one can begin to speak. Begin to point out some effects, some elements of unconscious drives, some relations of the feminine Imaginary to the Real, to writing.

What I have to say about it is also only a beginning, because right from the start these features affect me powerfully.

First I sense femininity in writing by: a privilege of *voice: writing and voice* are entwined and interwoven and writing's continuity/voice's rhythm take each other's breath away through interchanging, make the text gasp or form it out of suspenses and silences, make it lose its voice or rend it with cries.

In a way, feminine writing never stops reverberating from the wrench that the acquisition of speech, speaking out loud, is for her – 'acquisition' that is experienced more as tearing away, dizzying flight and flinging oneself, diving. Listen to woman speak in a gathering (if she is not painfully out of breath): she doesn't 'speak,' she throws her trembling body into the air, she lets herself go, she flies, she goes completely into her voice, she vitally defends the 'logic' of her discourse with her body; her flesh speaks true. She exposes herself. Really she makes what she thinks materialize carnally, she conveys meaning with her body. She *inscribes* what she is saying because she does not deny unconscious drives the unmanageable part they play in speech.

Her discourse, even when 'theoretical' or political, is never simple or linear or 'objectivized,' universalized; she involves her story in history.

Every woman has known the torture of beginning to speak aloud, heart beating as if to break, occasionally falling into loss of language, ground and language slipping out from under her, because for woman speaking – even just opening her mouth – in public is something rash, a transgression.

A double anguish, for even if she transgresses, her word almost always falls on the deaf, masculine ear, which can only hear language that speaks in the masculine.

We are not culturally accustomed to speaking, throwing signs out toward a scene, employing the suitable rhetoric. Also, it is not where we find our pleasure: indeed, one pays a certain price for the use of a discourse. The logic of communication requires an economy both of signs – of signifiers – and of subjectivity. The orator is asked to unwind a thin thread, dry and taut. We like uneasiness, questioning. There is waste in what we say. We need that waste. To write is always to make allowances for superabundance and uselessness while slashing the exchange value that keeps the spoken word on its track. That is why writing is good, letting the tongue try itself out – as one attempts a caress, taking the time a phrase or a thought needs to make oneself loved, to make oneself reverberate.

It is in writing, from woman and toward woman, and in accepting the challenge of the discourse controlled by the phallus, that woman will affirm woman somewhere other than in silence, the place reserved for her in and through the Symbolic. May she get out of booby-trapped silence! And not have the margin or the harem foisted on her as her domain!

In feminine speech, as in writing, there never stops reverberating something that, having once passed through us, having imperceptibly and deeply touched us, still has the power to affect us – song, the first music of the voice of love, which every woman keeps alive.

The Voice sings from a time before law, before the Symbolic took one's breath away and reappropriated it into language under its authority of separation. The deepest, the oldest, the loveliest Visitation. Within each woman the first, nameless love is singing.

In woman there is always, more or less, something of 'the mother' repairing and feeding, resisting separation, a force that does not let itself be cut off but that runs codes ragged. The relationship to childhood (the child she was, she is, she acts and makes and starts anew, and unties at the place where, as a same she even others herself), is no more cut off than is the relationship to the 'mother,' *as it consists of* delights and violences. Text, my body: traversed by lilting flows; listen to me, it is not a captivating, clinging 'mother'; it is the equivoice that, touching you, affects you, pushes you away from your breast to come to language, that summons *your* strength; it is the rhyth-me that laughs you; the one intimately addressed who makes all metaphors, all body(?) – bodies(?) – possible and desirable, who is no more describable than god, soul, or the Other; the part of you that puts space between yourself and pushes you to inscribe your woman's style in language. Voice: milk that could go on forever. Found again. The lost mother/bitter-lost. Eternity: is voice mixed with milk.

Not the origin: she doesn't go back there. A boy's journey is the return to the native land, the *Heimweh* Freud speaks of, the nostalgia that makes man a being who tends to come back to the point of departure to appropriate it for himself and to die there. A girl's journey is farther – to the unknown, to invent.

How come this privileged relationship with voice? Because no woman piles up as many defenses against instinctual drives as a man does. You don't prop things up, you don't brick things up the way he does, you don't withdraw from pleasure so 'prudently.' Even if phallic mystification has contaminated good relations in general, woman is never far from the 'mother' (I do not mean the role but the 'mother' as no-name and as source of goods). There is always at least a little good mother milk left in her. She writes with white ink.

Voice! That, too, is launching forth and effusion without return. Exclamation, cry, breathlessness, yell, cough, vomit, music. Voice leaves. Voice loses. She leaves. She loses. And that is how she writes, as one throws a voice – forward, into the void. She goes away, she goes forward, doesn't turn back to look at her tracks. Pays no attention to herself. Running breakneck. Contrary to the self-absorbed, masculine narcissism, making sure of its image, of being seen, of seeing itself, of assembling its glories, of pocketing itself again. The reductive look, the always divided look returning, the mirror economy; he needs to love himself. But she launches forth; she seeks to love. Moreover, this is what Valéry sensed, marking his Young Fate in search of herself with ambiguity, masculine in her jealousy of herself: 'seeing herself see herself,' the motto of all phallocentric speculation/specularization, the motto of every Teste; and feminine in the frantic descent deeper deeper to where a voice that doesn't know itself is lost in the sea's churning.

Voice-cry. Agony – the spoken 'word' exploded, blown to bits by suffering and anger, demolishing discourse: this is how she has always been heard before, ever since the time when masculine society began to push her offstage, expulsing her, plundering her. Ever since Medea, ever since Electra.

Voice: unfastening, fracas. Fire! She shoots, she shoots away. Break. From their bodies where they have been buried, shut up and at the same time forbidden to take pleasure. Women have almost everything to write about femininity: about their sexuality, that is to say, about the infinite and mobile complexity of their becoming erotic, about the lightning ignitions of such a minuscule-vast region of their body, not about destiny but about the adventure of such an urge, the voyages, crossings, advances, sudden and slow awakenings, discoveries of a formerly timid region that is just now springing up. Woman's body with a thousand and one fiery hearths, when – shattering censorship and yokes – she lets it articulate the proliferation of meanings that runs through it in every direction. It is going to take much more than language for him to make the ancient maternal tongue sound in only one groove.

We have turned away from our bodies. Shamefully we have been taught to be unaware of them, to lash them with stupid modesty; we've been tricked into a fool's bargain: each one is to love the other sex. I'll give you your body and you will give me mine. But which men give women the body that they blindly hand over to him? Why so few texts? Because there are still so few women winning back their bodies. Woman must write her body, must make up the unimpeded tongue that bursts partitions, classes, and rhetorics, orders and codes, must inundate, run through, go beyond the discourse with its last reserves, including the one of laughing off the word 'silence' that has to be said, the one that, aiming for the impossible, stops dead before the word 'impossible' and writes it as 'end.'

In body/Still more: woman is body more than man is. Because he is invited to social success, to sublimation. More body hence more writing. For a long time, still, bodily, within her body she has answered the harassment, the familial conjugal venture of domestication, the repeated attempts to castrate her. Woman, who has run her tongue ten thousand times seven times around her mouth before not speaking, either dies of it or knows her tongue and her mouth better than anyone. Now, I-woman am going to blow up the Law: a possible and inescapable explosion from now on; let it happen, right now, in language.

When 'The Repressed' of their culture and their society come back, it is an explosive return, which is *absolutely* shattering, staggering, overturning, with a force never let loose before, on the scale of the most tremendous repressions: for at the end of the Age of the Phallus, women will have been either wiped out or heated to the highest, most violent, white-hot fire.

Throughout their deafening dumb history, they have lived in dreams, embodied but still deadly silent, in silences, in voiceless rebellions.

And with what force in their fragility: 'fragility,' a vulnerability to match their matchless intensity. Women have not sublimated. Fortunately. They have saved their skins and their energy. They haven't worked at planning the impass of futureless lives. They have furiously inhabited these sumptuous bodies. Those wonderful hysterics, who subjected Freud to so many voluptuous moments too shameful to mention, bombarding his mosaic statue/law of Moses with their carnal, passionate body-words, haunting him with their inaudible thundering denunciations, were more than just naked beneath their seven veils of modesty – they were dazzling. In a single word of the body they inscribed the endless vertigo of a history loosed like an arrow from all of men's history, from biblicocapitalist society. Following these yesterday's victims of torture, who anticipate the new women, no intersubjective relationship will ever be the same. It is you, Dora, you, who cannot be tamed, the poetic body, the true 'mistress' of the Signifier. Before tomorrow your effectiveness will be seen to work – when your words will no longer be retracted, pointed against your own breast, but will write themselves against the other and against men's grammar. Men must not have that place for their own any more than they have us for their own.

If woman has always functioned 'within' man's discourse, a signifier referring always to the opposing signifier that annihilates its particular energy, puts down or stifles its very different sounds, now it is time for her to displace this 'within,' explode it, overturn it, grab it, make it hers, take it in, take it into her women's mouth, bite its tongue with her women's teeth, make up her own tongue to get inside of it. And you will see how easily she will well up, from this 'within' where she was hidden and dormant, to the lips where her foams will overflow.

It is not a question of appropriating their instruments, their concepts, their places for oneself or of wishing oneself in their position of mastery. Our knowing that there is a danger of identification does not mean we should give in. Leave that to the worriers, to masculine anxiety and its obsessional relationship to workings they must control – knowing 'how it runs' in order to 'make it run.' Not taking possession to internalize or manipulate but to shoot through and smash the walls.

Feminine strength is such that while running away with syntax, breaking the famous line (just a tiny little thread, so they say) that serves men as a substitute cord, without which they can't have any fun (*jouir*), to make sure the old mother really is always behind them watching them play phallus, she goes to the impossible where she plays the other, for love, without dying of it.

De-propriation, depersonalization, because she, exasperating, immoderate, and contradictory, destroys laws, the 'natural' order. She lifts the bar separating the present from the future, breaking the rigid law of individuation. Nietzsche, in *The Birth of Tragedy*, said that this is the privilege of divinatory, magical forces. What happens to the subject, to the personal pronoun, to its possessives when, suddenly, gaily daring her metamorphoses (because from her within

– for a long time her world, she is in a pervasive relationship of desire with every being) she makes another way of knowing circulate? Another way of producing, of communicating, where each one is always far more than one, where her power of identification puts the same to rout. – And with the same traversing, dispersing gesture with which she becomes a feminine other, a masculine other, she breaks with explanation, interpretation, and all the authorities pinpointing localization. She forgets. She proceeds by lapse and bounds. She flies/steals.

To fly/steal is woman's gesture, to steal into language to make it fly. We have all learned flight/theft, the art with many techniques, for all the centuries we have only had access to having by stealing/flying; we have lived in a flight/theft, stealing/flying, finding the close, concealed ways-through of desire. It's not just luck if the word 'voler' volleys between the 'vol' of theft and the 'vol' of flight, pleasuring in each and routing the sense police. It is not just luck: woman partakes of bird and burglar, just as the burglar partakes of woman and bird: hesheits pass, hesheits fly by, hesheits pleasure in scrambling spatial order, disorienting it, moving furniture, things, and values around, breaking in, emptying structures, turning the selfsame, the proper upside down.

What woman has not stolen? Who has not dreamed, savored, or done the thing that jams sociality? Who has not dropped a few red herrings, mocked her way around the separating bar, inscribed what makes a difference with her body, punched holes in the system of couples and positions, and with a transgression screwed up whatever is successive, chain-linked, the fence of circumfusion?

A feminine text cannot not be more than subversive: if it writes itself it is in volcanic heaving of the old 'real' property crust. In ceaseless displacement. She must write herself because, when the time comes for her liberation, it is the invention of a *new, insurgent* writing that will allow her to put the breaks and indispensable changes into effect in her history. At first, individually, on two inseparable levels: – woman, writing herself, will go back to this body that has been worse than confiscated, a body replaced with a disturbing stranger, sick or dead, who so often is a bad influence, the cause and place of inhibitions. By censuring the body, breath and speech are censored at the same time.

To write – the act that will 'realize' the un-censored relationship of woman to her sexuality, to her woman-being giving her back access to her own forces; that will return her goods, her pleasures, her organs, her vast bodily territories kept under seal; that will tear her out of the superegoed, over-Mosesed structure where the same position of guilt is always reserved for her (guilty of everything, every time: of having desires, of not having any; of being frigid, of being 'too' hot; of not being both at once; of being too much of a mother and not enough; of nurturing and of not nurturing . . .). Write yourself: your body must make itself heard. Then the huge resources of the unconscious will burst out. Finally the inexhaustible feminine Imaginary is going to be deployed. Without gold or black dollars, our naphtha will spread values over the world, un-quoted values that will change the rules of the old game.

Notes

1 All Derrida's work traversing-detecting the history of philosophy is devoted to bringing this to light. In Plato, Hegel, and Nietzsche, the same process continues: repression, repudiation, distancing of woman; a murder that is mixed up with history as the manifestation and representation of masculine power.

2 *Prénoms de personne* [*Nobody's First Names*], Cixous, Editions du Seuil: 'Les Comtes de Hoffmann' ['Tales of Hoffmann'], pp. 112ff.

3 See *Nouvelle Revue de Psychoanalyse*, no. 7, *Bisexualité et différence des sexes* (Spring 1973).

5.3

Laura Mulvey
from 'Visual Pleasure and
Narrative Cinema' (1975)

I Introduction

(a) A political use of psychoanalysis

This paper intends to use psychoanalysis to discover where and how the fascination of film is reinforced by pre-existing patterns of fascination already at work within the individual subject and the social formations that have moulded him. It takes as its starting-point the way film reflects, reveals and even plays on the straight, socially established interpretation of sexual difference which controls images, erotic ways of looking and spectacle. It is helpful to understand what the cinema has been, how its magic has worked in the past, while attempting a theory and a practice which will challenge this cinema of the past. Psychoanalytic theory is thus appropriated here as a political weapon, demonstrating the way the unconscious of patriarchal society has structured film form.

The paradox of phallocentrism in all its manifestations is that it depends on the image of the castrated women to give order and meaning to its world. An idea of woman stands as linchpin to the system: it is her lack that produces the phallus as a symbolic presence, it is her desire to make good the lack that the phallus signifies. Recent writing in *Screen* about psychoanalysis and the cinema has not sufficiently brought out the importance of the representation of the female form in a symbolic order in which, in the last resort, it speaks castration and nothing else. To summarise briefly: the function of woman in forming the patriarchal unconscious is twofold: she firstly symbolises the castration threat by her real lack of a penis and secondly thereby raises her child into the symbolic. Once this has been achieved, her meaning in the process is at an end. It does not last into the world of law and language except as a memory, which oscillates between memory of maternal plenitude and memory of lack. Both are posited on nature (or on anatomy in Freud's famous phrase). Woman's desire is sub-jugated to her image as bearer of the bleeding wound; she can exist only in relation to castration and cannot transcend it. She turns her child into the signifier of her own desire to possess a penis (the condition, she imagines, of entry into the symbolic). Either she must gracefully give way to the word, the name of the father and the law, or else struggle to keep her child down with her in the half-light of the imaginary. Woman then stands in patriarchal culture as a signifier for the male other, bound by a symbolic order in which man can live out his fantasies and obsessions through linguistic command by imposing them on the silent image of woman still tied to her place as bearer, not maker, of meaning.

There is an obvious interest in this analysis for feminists, a beauty in its exact rendering of the frustration experienced under the phallocentric order. It gets us nearer to the roots of our oppression, it brings closer an articulation of the problem, it faces us with the ultimate challenge: how to fight the unconscious structured like a language (formed critically at the moment of arrival of language) while still caught within the language of the patriarchy? There is no way in which we can produce an alternative out of the blue, but we can begin to make a break by examining patriarchy with the tools it provides, of which psychoanalysis is not the only but an important one. We are still separated by a great gap from important issues for the female unconscious which are scarcely relevant to phallocentric theory: the sexing of the female infant and her relationship to the symbolic, the sexually mature woman as non-mother, maternity outside the signification of the phallus, the vagina. But, at this point, psychoanalytic theory as it now stands can at least advance our understanding of the *status quo*, of the patri-archal order in which we are caught.

(b) Destruction of pleasure as a radical weapon

As an advanced representation system, the cinema poses questions about the ways the unconscious (formed by the dominant order) structures ways of seeing and pleasure in looking. Cinema has changed over the last few decades. It is no longer the monolithic system based on large capital investment exemplified at its best by Hollywood in the 1930s, 1940s and 1950s. Technological advances (16mm and so on) have changed the economic conditions of cinematic production, which can now be artisanal as well as capitalist. Thus it has been possible for an alternative cinema to develop. However self-conscious and ironic Hollywood managed to be, it always restricted itself to a formal *mise en scène* reflecting the dominant ideological concept of the cinema. The alternative cinema provides a space for the birth of a cinema which is radical in both a political and an aesthetic sense and challenges the basic assumptions of the mainstream film. This is not to reject the latter moralistically, but to highlight the ways in which its formal preoccupations reflect the psychical obsessions of the society which produced it and, further, to stress that the alternative cinema must start specifically by reacting against these obsessions and assumptions. A politically and aesthetically avant-garde cinema is now possible, but it can still only exist as a counterpoint.

The magic of the Hollywood style at its best (and of all the cinema which fell within its sphere of influence) arose, not exclusively, but in one important aspect, from its skilled and satisfying manipulation of visual pleasure. Unchallenged, mainstream film coded the erotic into the language of the dominant patriarchal order. In the highly developed Hollywood cinema it was only through these codes that the alienated subject, torn in his imaginary memory by a sense of loss, by the terror of potential lack in fantasy, came near to finding a glimpse of satisfaction: through its formal beauty and its play on his own formative obsessions. This article will discuss the interweaving of that erotic pleasure in film, its meaning and, in particular, the central place of the image of woman. It is said that analysing pleasure, or beauty, destroys it. That is the intention of this article. The satisfaction and reinforcement of the ego that represent the high point of film history hitherto must be attacked. Not in favour of a reconstructed new pleasure, which cannot exist in the abstract, nor of intellectualised unpleasure, but to make way for a total negation of the ease and plenitude of the narrative fiction film. The alternative is the thrill that comes from leaving the past behind without simply rejecting it, transcending outworn or oppressive forms, and daring to break with normal pleasurable expectations in order to conceive a new language of desire.

II Pleasure in looking/fascination with the human form

A   The cinema offers a number of possible pleasures. One is scopophilia (pleasure in looking). There are circumstances in which looking itself is a source of pleasure, just as, in the reverse formation, there is pleasure in being looked at. Originally, in his *Three Essays on Sexuality*, Freud isolated scopophilia as one of the component instincts of sexuality which exist as drives quite independently of the erotogenic zones. At this point he associated scopophilia with taking other people as objects, subjecting them to a controlling and curious gaze. His particular examples centre on the voyeuristic activities of children, their desire to see and make sure of the private and forbidden (curiosity about other people's genital and bodily functions, about the presence or absence of the penis and, retrospectively, about the primal scene). In this analysis scopophilia is essentially active. (Later, in 'Instincts and Their Vicissitudes', Freud developed his theory of scopophilia further, attaching it initially to pre-genital auto-eroticism, after which, by analogy, the pleasure of the look is transferred to others. There is a close working here of the relationship between the active instinct and its further development in a narcissistic form.) Although the instinct is modified by other factors, in particular the constitution of the ego, it continues to exist as the erotic basis for pleasure in looking at another person as object. At the extreme, it can become fixated into a perversion, producing obsessive voyeurs and Peeping Toms whose only sexual satisfaction can come from watching, in an active controlling sense, an objectified other.

At first glance, the cinema would seem to be remote from the undercover world of the surreptitious observation of an unknowing and unwilling victim. What is seen on the screen is so manifestly shown. But the mass of mainstream film, and the conventions within which it has consciously evolved, portray a hermetically sealed world which unwinds magically, indifferent to the presence of the audience, producing for them a sense of separation and playing on their voyeuristic fantasy. Moreover the extreme contrast between the darkness in the auditorium (which also isolates the spectators from one another) and the brilliance of the shifting patterns of light and shade on the screen helps to promote the illusion of voyeuristic separation. Although the film is really being shown, is there to be seen, conditions of screening and narrative conventions give the spectator an illusion of looking in on a private world. Among other things, the position of the spectators in the cinema is blatantly one of repression of their exhibitionism and projection of the repressed desire onto the performer.

B The cinema satisfies a primordial wish for pleasurable looking, but it also goes further, developing scopophilia in its narcissistic aspect. The conventions of mainstream film focus attention on the human form. Scale, space, stories are all anthropomorphic. Here, curiosity and the wish to look intermingle with a fascination with likeness and recognition: the human face, the human body, the relationship between the human form and its surroundings, the visible presence of the person in the world. Jacques Lacan has described how the moment when a child recognises its own image in the mirror is crucial for the constitution of the ego. Several aspects of this analysis are relevant here. The mirror phase occurs at a time when children's physical ambitions outstrip their motor capacity, with the result that their recognition of themselves is joyous in that they imagine their mirror image to be more complete, more perfect than they experience in their own body. Recognition is thus overlaid with misrecognition: the image recognised is conceived as the reflected body of the self, but its misrecognition as superior projects this body outside itself as an ideal ego, the alienated subject which, reintrojected as an ego ideal, prepares the way for identification with others in the future. This mirror moment predates language for the child.

Important for this article is the fact that it is an image that constitutes the matrix of the imaginary, or recognition/misrecognition and identification, and hence of the first articulation of the I, of subjectivity. This is a moment when an older fascination with looking (at the mother's face, for an obvious example) collides with the initial inklings of self-awareness. Hence it is the birth of the long love affair/despair between image and self-image which has found such intensity of expression in film and such joyous recognition in the cinema audience. Quite apart from the extraneous similarities between screen and mirror (the framing of the human form in its surroundings, for instance), the cinema has structures of fascination strong enough to allow temporary loss of ego while simultaneously reinforcing it. The sense of forgetting the world as the ego has come to perceive it (I forgot who I am and where I was) is nostalgically reminiscent of that pre-subjective moment of image recognition. While at the same time, the cinema has distinguished itself in the production of ego ideals, through the star system for instance. Stars provide a focus or centre both to screen space and screen story where they act out a complex process of likeness and difference (the glamorous impersonates the ordinary).

C   Sections A and B have set out two contradictory aspects of the pleasurable structures of looking in the conventional cinematic situation. The first, scopophilic, arises from pleasure in using another person as an object of sexual stimulation through sight. The second, developed through narcissism and the constitution of the ego, comes from identification with the image seen. Thus, in film terms, one implies a separation of the erotic identity of the subject from the object on the screen (active scopophilia), the other demands identification of the ego with the object on the screen through the spectator's fascination with and recognition of his like. The first is a function of the sexual instincts, the second of ego libido. This dichotomy was crucial for Freud. Although he saw the two as interacting and overlaying each other, the tension between instinctual drives and self-preservation polarises in terms of pleasure. But both are formative structures, mechanisms without intrinsic meaning. In themselves they have no signification, unless attached to an idealisation. Both pursue aims in indifference to perceptual reality, and motivate eroticised phantasmagoria that affect the subject's perception of the world to make a mockery of empirical objectivity.

During its history, the cinema seems to have evolved a particular illusion of reality in which this contradiction between libido and ego has found a beautifully complementary fantasy world. In *reality* the fantasy world of the screen is subject to the law which produces it. Sexual instincts and identification processes have a meaning within the symbolic order which articulates desire. Desire, born with language, allows the possibility of transcending the instinctual and the imaginary, but its point of reference continually returns to the traumatic moment of its birth: the castration complex. Hence the look, pleasurable in form, can be threatening in content, and it is woman as representation/image that crystallises this paradox.

III Woman as image, man as bearer of the look

A   In a world ordered by sexual imbalance, pleasure in looking has been split between active/male and passive/female. The determining male gaze projects its fantasy onto the female figure, which is styled accordingly. In their traditional exhibitionist role women are simultaneously looked at and displayed, with their appearance coded for strong visual and erotic impact so that they can be said to connote *to-be-looked-at-ness*. Woman displayed as sexual object is the *leitmotif* of erotic spectacle: from pin-ups to strip-tease, from Ziegfeld to Busby Berkeley, she holds the look, and plays to and signifies male desire. Mainstream film neatly combines spectacle and narrative. (Note, however, how in the musical song-and-dance numbers interrupt the flow of the diegesis.) The presence of woman is an indispensable element of spectacle in normal narrative film, yet her visual presence tends to work against the development of a story-line, to freeze the flow of action in moments of erotic contemplation. This alien presence then has to be integrated into cohesion with the narrative. As Budd Boetticher has put it:

> What counts is what the heroine provokes, or rather what she represents. She is the one, or rather the love or fear she inspires in the hero, or else the concern he feels for her, who makes him act the way he does. In herself the woman has not the slightest importance.

(A recent tendency in narrative film has been to dispense with this problem altogether; hence the development of what Molly Haskell has called the 'buddy movie', in which the active homosexual eroticism of the central male figures can carry the story without distraction.) Traditionally, the woman displayed has functioned on two levels: as erotic object for the characters within the screen story, and as erotic object for the spectator within the auditorium, with a shifting tension between the looks on either side of the screen. For instance, the device of the show-girl allows the two looks to be unified technically without any apparent break in the diegesis. A woman performs within the narrative; the gaze of the spectator and that of the male characters in the film are neatly combined without breaking narrative verisimilitude. For a moment the sexual impact of the performing woman takes the film into a no man's land outside its own time and space. Thus Marilyn Monroe's first appearance in *The River of No Return* and Lauren Bacall's songs in *To Have and Have Not*. Similarly, conventional close-ups of legs (Dietrich, for instance) or a face (Garbo) integrate into the narrative a different mode of eroticism. One part of a fragmented body destroys the Renaissance space, the illusion of depth demanded by the narrative; it gives flatness, the quality of a cut-out or icon, rather than verisimilitude, to the screen.

B   An active/passive heterosexual division of labour has similarly controlled narrative structure. According to the principles of the ruling ideology and the psychical structures that back it up, the male figure cannot bear the burden of sexual objectification. Man is reluctant to gaze at his exhibitionist like. Hence the split between spectacle and narrative supports the man's role as the active one of advancing the story, making things happen. The man controls the film fantasy and also emerges as the representative of power in a further sense: as the bearer of the look of the spectator, transferring it behind the screen to neutralise the extra-diegetic tendencies represented by woman as spectacle. This is made possible through the processes set in motion by structuring the film around a main controlling figure with whom the spectator can identify. As the spectator identifies with the main male protagonist, he projects his look onto that of his like, his screen surrogate, so that the power of the male protagonist as he controls events coincides with the active power of the erotic look, both giving a satisfying sense of omnipotence. A male movie star's glamorous characteristics are thus not those of the erotic object of the gaze, but those of the more perfect, more complete, more powerful ideal ego conceived in the original moment of recognition in front of the mirror. The character in the story can make things happen and control events better than the subject/spectator, just as the image in the mirror was more in control of motor co-ordination.

In contrast to woman as icon, the active male figure (the ego ideal of the identification process) demands a three-dimensional space corresponding to that of the mirror recognition, in which the alienated subject internalised his own representation of his imaginary existence. He is a figure in a landscape. Here the function of film is to reproduce as accurately as possible the so-called natural conditions of human perception. Camera technology (as exemplified by deep focus in particular) and camera movements (determined by the action of the protagonist), combined with invisible editing (demanded by realism), all tend to blur the limits of screen space. The male protagonist is free to command the stage, a stage of spatial illusion in which he articulates the look and creates the action.[1]

C1 Sections III A and B have set out a tension between a mode of representation of woman in film and conventions surrounding the diegesis. Each is associated with a look: that of the spectator in direct scopophilic contact with the female form displayed for his enjoyment (connoting male fantasy) and that of the spectator fascinated with the image of his like set in an illusion of natural space, and through him gaining control and possession of the woman within the diegesis. (This tension and the shift from one pole to the other can structure a single text. Thus both in *Only Angels Have Wings* and in *To Have and Have Not*, the film opens with the woman as object of the combined gaze of spectator and all the male protagonists in the film. She is isolated, glamorous, on display, sexualised. But as the narrative progresses she falls in love with the main male protagonists and becomes his property, losing her outward glamorous characteristics, her generalised sexuality, her show-girl connotations; her eroticism is subjected to the male star alone. By means of identification with him, through participation in his power, the spectator can indirectly possess her too.)

But in psychoanalytic terms, the female figure poses a deeper problem. She also connotes something that the look continually circles around but disavows: her lack of a penis, implying a threat of castration and hence unpleasure. Ultimately, the meaning of woman is sexual difference, the visually ascertainable absence of the penis, the material evidence on which is based the castration complex essential for the organisation of entrance to the symbolic order and the law of the father. Thus the woman as icon, displayed for the gaze and enjoyment of men, the active controllers of the look, always threatens to evoke the anxiety it originally signified. The male unconscious has two avenues of escape from this castration anxiety: preoccupation with the re-enactment of the original trauma (investigating the woman, demystifying her mystery), counterbalanced by the devaluation, punishment or saving of the guilty object (an avenue typified by the concerns of the *film noir*); or else complete disavowal of castration by the substitution of a fetish object or turning the represented figure itself into a fetish so that it becomes reassuring rather than dangerous (hence overvaluation, the cult of the female star).

This second avenue, fetishistic scopophilia, builds up the physical beauty of the object, transforming it into something satisfying in itself. The first avenue, voyeurism, on the contrary, has associations with sadism: pleasure lies in ascertaining guilt (immediately associated with castration), asserting control and subjugating the guilty person through punishment or forgiveness. This sadistic side fits in well with narrative. Sadism demands a story, depends on making something happen, forcing a change in another person, a battle of will and strength, victory/defeat, all occurring in a linear time with a beginning and an end. Fetishistic scopophilia, on the other hand, can exist outside linear time as the erotic instinct is focused on the look alone.

IV Summary

The psychoanalytic background that has been discussed in this article is relevant to the pleasure and unpleasure offered by traditional narrative film. The scopophilic instinct (pleasure in looking at another person as an erotic object) and, in contradistinction, ego libido (forming identification processes) act as formations, mechanisms, which mould this cinema's formal attributes. The actual image of woman as (passive) raw material for the (active) gaze of man takes the argument a step further into the content and structure of representation, adding a further layer of ideological significance demanded by the patriarchal order in its favourite cinematic form – illusionistic narrative film. The argument must return again to the psychoanalytic background: women in representation can signify castration, and activate voyeuristic or fetishistic mechanisms to circumvent this threat. Although none of these interacting layers is intrinsic to film, it is only in the film form that they can reach a perfect and beautiful contradiction, thanks to the possibility in the cinema of shifting the emphasis of the look. The place of the look defines cinema, the possibility of varying it and exposing it. This is what makes cinema quite different in its voyeuristic potential from, say, striptease, theatre, shows and so on. Going far beyond highlighting a woman's to-be-looked-at-ness, cinema builds the way she is to be looked at into the spectacle itself. Playing on the tension between film as controlling the dimension of time (editing, narrative) and film as controlling the dimension of space (changes in distance, editing), cinematic codes create a gaze, a world and an object, thereby producing an illusion cut to the measure of desire. It is these cinematic codes and their relationship to formative external structures that must be broken down before mainstream film and the pleasure it provides can be challenged.

To begin with (as an ending), the voyeuristic–scopophilic look that is a crucial part of traditional filmic pleasure can itself be broken down. There are three different looks associated with cinema: that of the camera as it records the pro-filmic event, that of the audience as it watches the final product, and that of the characters at each other within the screen illusion. The conventions of narrative film deny the first two and subordinate them to the third, the conscious aim being always to eliminate intrusive camera presence and prevent a distancing awareness in the audience. Without these two absences (the material existence of the recording process, the critical reading of the spectator), fictional drama cannot achieve reality, obviousness and truth. Nevertheless, as this article has argued, the structure of looking in narrative fiction film contains a contradiction in its own premises: the female image as a castration threat constantly endangers the unity of the diegesis and bursts through the world of illusion as an intrusive, static, one-dimensional fetish. Thus the two looks materially present in time and space are obsessively subordinated to the neurotic needs of the male ego. The camera becomes the mechanism for producing an illusion of Renaissance space, flowing movements compatible with the human eye, an ideology of representation that revolves around the perception of the subject; the camera's look is disavowed in order to create a convincing world in which the spectator's surrogate can perform with verisimilitude. Simultaneously, the look of the audience is denied an intrinsic force: as soon as fetishistic representation of the female image threatens to break the spell of illusion, and the erotic image on the screen appears directly (without mediation) to the spectator, the fact of fetishisation, concealing as it does castration fear, freezes the look, fixates the spectator and prevents him from achieving any distance from the image in front of him.

This complex interaction of looks is specific to film. The first blow against the monolithic accumulation of traditional film conventions (already undertaken by radical film-makers) is to free the look of the camera into its materiality in time and space and the look of the audience into dialectics and passionate detachment. There is no doubt that this destroys the satisfaction, pleasure and privilege of the 'invisible guest', and highlights the way film has depended on voyeuristic active/passive mechanisms. Women, whose image has continually been stolen and used for this end, cannot view the decline of the traditional film form with anything much more than sentimental regret.[2]

Notes

1 There are films with a woman as main protagonist, of course. To analyse this phenomenon seriously here would take me too far afield. Pam Cook and Claire Johnston's study of *The Revolt of Mamie Stover* in Phil Hardy (ed.), *Raoul Walsh* (Edinburgh Film Festival, 1974), shows in a striking case how the strength of this female protagonist is more apparent than real.

2 This article is a reworked version of a paper given in the French Department of the University of Wisconsin, Madison, in the spring of 1973.

5.4

Gayatri Chakravorty Spivak from 'Displacement and the Discourse of Woman' (1983)

When in *The Philosophy of Right* Hegel writes of the distinction between thought and object, his example is Adam and Eve:

> Since it is in thought that I am first at home (*bei mir*), I do not penetrate (*durchbobren*) an object until I understand it; it then ceases to stand over against me and I have taken from it its ownness (*das Eigene*), that it had for itself against me. Just as Adam says to Eve: 'Thou art flesh of my flesh and bone of my bone,' so mind says: 'This is mind of my mind,' and the alienness (*Fremdheit* as opposed to *das Eigene*; alterity as opposed to ownness) disappears.[1]

It would be possible to assemble here a collection of 'great passages' from literature and philosophy to show how, unobtrusively but crucially, a certain metaphor of woman has produced (rather than merely illustrated) a discourse that we are obliged 'historically' to call the discourse of man.[2] Given the accepted charge of the notions of production and constitution, one might reformulate this: the discourse of man is in the metaphor of woman.

I

Jacques Derrida's critique of phallocentrism can be summarized as follows: the patronymic, in spite of all empirical details of the generation gap, keeps the transcendental ego of the dynasty identical in the eye of the law. By virtue of the father's name the son refers to the father. The irreducible importance of the name and the law in this situation makes it quite clear that the question is not merely one of psycho-socio-sexual behavior but of the production and consolidation of reference and meaning. The desire to make one's progeny represent his presence is akin to the desire to make one's words represent the full meaning of one's intention. Hermeneutic, legal, or patrilinear, it is the prerogative of the phallus to declare itself sovereign source.[3] Its causes are also its effects: a social structure – centered on due process and the law (logocentrism); a structure of argument centered on the sovereignty of the engendering self and the determinacy of meaning (phallogocentrism); a structure of the text centered on the phallus as the determining moment (phallocentrism) or signifier. Can Derrida's critique provide us a network of concept-metaphors that does not appropriate or displace the figure of woman? In order to sketch an answer, I will refer not only to Derrida, but to two of Derrida's acknowledged 'creditors' in the business of deconstruction, Nietzsche and Freud.[4] I will not refer to *La Carte postale*, my discussion of which is forthcoming.[5]

The deconstructive structure of how woman 'is' is contained in a well-known Nietzschean sentence: 'Finally – if one loved them . . . what comes of it inevitably? that they "give themselves," even when they – give themselves. The female is so artistic.'[6] Or: women impersonate themselves as having an orgasm even at the time of orgasm. Within the historical understanding of women as incapable of orgasm, Nietzsche is arguing that impersonation is woman's only sexual pleasure. At the time of the greatest self-possession-cum-ecstasy, the woman is self-possessed enough to organize a self-(re)presentation without an actual presence (of sexual pleasure) to re-present. This is an originary dis-placement. The virulence of Nietzsche's misogyny occludes an unacknowledged envy: a man cannot fake an orgasm. His pen must write or prove impotent.[7]

For the deconstructive philosopher, who suspects that all (phallogocentric) longing for a transcendent truth as the origin or end of semiotic gestures might be 'symptomatic,' woman's style becomes exemplary, for *his* style remains obliged to depend upon the stylus or stiletto of the phallus. Or, to quote Derrida reading Nietzsche:

> She writes (herself) [or (is) written – *Elle (s')écrit*]. Style amounts to [or returns to (*revient à*)] her. Rather: if style were (as for Freud the penis is 'the normal prototype of the fetish') the man, writing would be woman.[8]

A lot is going on here. Through his critique of Nietzsche, Derrida is questioning both the phallus-privileging of a certain Freud as well as the traditional view, so blindly phallocentric that it gives itself out as general, that 'the style is the man.' Throughout his work, Derrida asks us to notice that *all* human beings are irreducibly displaced although, in a discourse that privileges the center, women alone have been diagnosed as such; correspondingly, he attempts to displace all centrisms, binary oppositions, or centers. It is my suggestion, however, that the woman who is the 'model' for deconstructive discourse remains a woman generalized and defined in terms of the faked orgasm and other varieties of denial. To quote Derrida on Nietzsche again:

> She is twice model, in a contradictory fashion, at once lauded and condemned . . . (First), like writing . . . But, insofar as she does not believe, herself, in truth . . . she is again the model, this time the good

model, or rather the bad model as good model: she plays dissimulation, ornament, lying, art, the artistic philosophy. . .

(Ep, p. 66)

At this point the shadow area between Derrida on Nietzsche and Derrida on Derrida begins to waver. 'She is a power of affirmation,' Derrida continues. We are reminded of the opening of his essay:

> The circumspect title for this meeting would be
> *the question of style.*
> But woman will be my *subject.*
> It remains to wonder if that comes to the *same*
> (*revient au même*) – or to the *other.*
> The 'question of style,' as you no doubt have recognized, is a quotation. I wanted to indicate that I shall advance nothing here that does not belong to the space cleared in the last two years by readings that open a new phase in the process of deconstructive, *that is to say affirmative*, interpretation.

(Ep, pp. 34, 36; italics mine)

Quotation in Derrida is a mark of non-self-identity: the defining predication of a woman, whose very name is changeable.[9] '"Give themselves"' is thus distinguished from 'give themselves' in Nietzsche's description of woman. The reader will notice the carefully hedged articulation of the deconstructive philosopher's desire to usurp 'the place of displacement': between the reminder of an appropriate title and the invocation of the complicity of the same and the other (philosophical themes of great prestige), comes the sentence: 'Woman will be my subject.' We give the 'subject' its philosophical value of the capital I. In the place of the writer's 'I' will be woman. But, colloquially, 'my subject' means 'my object.' Thus, even if 'le style' (man?) 'revient à elle' (returns or amounts to her) is an affirmation of 'ce qui ne revient pas au père' (that which does not return or amount to the father), the author of *La question du style* – that displaced text that does not exist, yet does, of course, as *Éperons* – having stepped into the place of displacement, has displaced the woman-model doubly as shuttling between the author's subject and object. If, then, the 'deconstructive' is 'affirmative' by way of Nietzsche's woman, who is a 'power of affirmation,' we are already within the circuit of what I call double displacement: in order to secure the gesture of taking the woman as model, the figure of woman must be doubly displaced. For a type case of double displacement, I turn to 'Femininity,' a late text of Freud certainly as well known as the Nietzschean sentence.[10]

II

Freud's displacement of the subject should not be confused with Freud's notion of displacement (*Verschiebung*) in the dream-work, which is one of the techniques of the dream-work to transcribe the latent content of the dream to its manifest content. The displacement of the subject that is the theme of deconstruction relates rather to the dream-work in general; for the dream *as a whole* displaces the text of the latent content into the text of the manifest content. Freud calls this *Entstellung* (literally 'displacement'; more usually translated as 'distortion').[11]

Freud expanded the notion of the displacement of the dream-work in general into an account of the working of the psychic apparatus and thereby put the subject as such in question. One can produce a reading of the 'metapsychological' rather than the therapeutic Freud to show that this originarily displaced scene of writing is the scene of woman.[12] Let us consider Freud's description of woman's originary displacement.

'Psycho-analysis does not wish to describe *(nicht beschreiben will)* what the female *(das Weib)* is ... but investigates *(untersucht)* how she comes into being, how the female develops out of the bisexually disposed child' (*F* xxii, p. 116; *GW* xv, p. 125). The name of this primordial bisexuality is of course unisex. 'We are now obliged to recognize,' Freud writes, 'that the little girl is a little man' (*F* xxii, p. 118; *GW* xv, p. 126).

Here is the moment when woman is displaced out of this primordial masculinity. One of the crucial predications of the place of displacement – 'the second task with which a girl's development is burdened' – is that the girl-child must change the object of her love. For the boy it never changes. 'But in the Oedipus situation the girl's father has become *(ist geworden)* her love-object.' The unchanged object-situation and the fear of castration allow the boy to 'overcome *(überwinden)* the Oedipus complex':

> The girl is driven out of her attachment to her mother through the influence of her envy for the penis and she enters the Oedipus situation as though into a haven ... (She) dismantle(s) *[baut ab]* it late and, even so, imperfectly *[unvollkommen]*.
>
> (*F* xxiii, p. 129; *GW* xv, p. 138)

Through the subject-object topology of the I (ego) and the it (id), Freud displaces the structure of the psyche itself. The beginning of sexual difference is also given in the language of subject and object. The boy child is irreducibly and permanently displaced from the mother, the object of his desire. But the girl-child is doubly displaced. The boy is born as a subject that desires to copulate with the object. He has the wherewithal to make a 'proper' sentence, where the copula is intention or desire. The sentence can be

$$S \text{ (subject)} \xrightarrow{\text{desires}} O \text{ (object)}$$

The girl child is born an uncertain role-player – a little man playing a little girl or vice versa. The object she desires is 'wrong' – must be changed. Thus it is not only that her sentence must be revised. It is that she did not have the ingredients to put together a proper sentence in the first place. She is originarily written as

$$\text{(masquerading subject)} \xrightarrow{\text{desires (temporarily)}} \emptyset \text{ (wrong object)}$$

I have made this analysis simply to suggest that a deconstructive discourse, even as it criticizes phallocentrism or the sovereignty of consciousness (and thus seeks to displace or 'feminize' itself according to a certain logic), must displace the figure of the woman twice over. In Nietzsche and in Freud the critique of phallocentrism is not immediately evident, and the double displacement of woman seems all the clearer:

> There is no essence of woman because woman averts and averts herself from herself . . . For if woman *is* truth, *she* knows there is no truth, that truth has no place and that no one has the truth. She is woman insofar as she does not believe, herself, in truth, therefore in what she is, in what one believes she is, which therefore she is not.
>
> (*Ep*, pp. 50, 52)

Here Derrida interprets what I call double displacement into the sign of an abyss. But perhaps the point is that the deconstructive discourse of man (like the phallocentric one) can declare its own displacement (as the phallocentric its placing) by taking the woman as object or figure. When Derrida suggests that Western discourse is caught within the metaphysical or phallogocentric limit, his point is precisely that man can problematize but not fully disown his status as subject. I do, then, indeed find in deconstruction a 'feminization' of the practice of philosophy, and I do not regard it as just another example of the masculine use of woman as instrument of self-assertion. I learn from Derrida's critique of phallocentrism – but I must then go somewhere else with it. A male philosopher can deconstruct the discourse of the power of the phallus as 'his own mistake.' For him, the desire for the 'name of woman' comes with the questioning of the 'metaphysical familiarity which so naturally relates the *we* of the philosopher to "we-men," to the *we* in the horizon of humanity.'[13] This is an unusual and courageous enterprise, not shared by Derrida's male followers.[14]

Yet, 'we-women' have never been the heroes of philosophy. When it takes the male philosopher hundreds of pages (not to be able) to answer the question 'who, me?', we cannot dismiss our double displacement by saying to ourselves: 'In the discourse of affirmative deconstruction, "we" are a "female element," which does not signify "female person."' Women armed with deconstruction must beware of becoming Athenas, uncontaminated by the womb, sprung in armor from Father's forehead, ruling against Clytemnestra by privileging marriage, the Law that appropriates the woman's body over the claims of that body as Law. To the question: 'Where is there a spur so keen as to compel to murder of a mother?' the presumed answer is: 'Marriage appointed by fate 'twixt man and woman is mightier than an oath and Justice is its guardian.' The official view of reproduction is: 'the mother of what is called her child is not its parent, but only the nurse of the newly implanted germ.'[15] This role of Athena, 'the professional woman,' will come up again at the end of the next section.

III

Let us consider briefly the problem of double displacement in Derrida as he substitutes undecidable feminine figurations for the traditional masculine ones and rewrites the primal scene as the scene of writing.

My first example is the graphic of the hymen as it appears in *La double séance*, Derrida's essay on Mallarmé's occasional piece 'Mimique.'[16]

The hymen is the figure for undecidability and the 'general law of the textual effect' (*Dis*, p. 235) for at least two reasons. First, 'metaphorically' it is the ritual celebration of the breaking of the vaginal membrane, and 'literally' that membrane remains intact even as it opens up into two lips; second, the walls of the passage that houses the hymen are both inside and outside the body. It describes 'the more subtle and patient displacement which, with reference to a Platonic or Hegelian idealism, we here call "Mallarméan" by convention' (*Dis*, p. 235; I have arranged the word-order to fit my sentence). The indefinitely displaced undecidability of the effect of the text (as hymen) is not the transcendent or totalizable ideal of the patronymic chain. Yet, is there not an agenda unwittingly concealed in formulating *virginity* as the property of the sexually undisclosed challenger of the phallus as master of the dialectics of desire? The hymen is of course at once both itself and not-itself, always operated by a calculated dissymmetry rather than a mere contradiction or reconciliation. Yet if the one term of the dissymmetry is virginity, the other term is marriage, legal certification for appropriation in the interest of the passage of property. We cannot avoid remarking that marriage in *La double séance* remains an unquestioned figure of fulfilled indentification (*Dis*, pp. 237–38).

We must applaud Derrida's displacement of the old feminine metaphor of the truth as (of) unveiling: 'The hymen is therefore not the truth of unveiling. There is not *aletheia* (truth as unveiling), only a blink of the hymen.'[17] Yet desire here must be expressed as man's desire, if only because it is the only discourse handy. The language of a woman's desire does not enter this enclosure:

> the hymen as a protective screen (*écran*), jewel case (*écrin*; all re-
> minders of writing – *écriture* – and the written – *écrit*) of virginity, virginal
> wall, most subtle and invisible veil, which, in front of the hysteron,
> holds itself *between* the inside and the outside of the woman, *therefore
> between desire and accomplishment.*
>
> (*Dis*, p. 241; italics mine)

Even within this sympathetic scene, the familiar topoi appear. The opera-tion of the hymen is the 'outmanoeuvering (*déjouante* – literally "unplaying") economy of a seduction' (*Dis*, p. 255). We are reminded of Nietzsche as we notice that, in commenting upon the pantomime of a hilarious wife-murder (Pierrot kills Columbine by tickling the soles of her feet) that Mallarmé comments on in *Mimique*, Derrida writes as follows:

> The crime, the orgasm, is doubly mimed . . . Its author in fact disappears
> because Pierrot is (plays) also Columbine . . . The gestures represent
> nothing that had ever been or could ever become present: nothing
> before or after the mimodrama, and in the mimodrama, a crime-orgasm
> that was never committed . . .
>
> (*Dis*, pp. 228, 238–39)

The faked orgasm now takes center stage. The Pierrot of the pantomime 'acts' as the woman 'is' ('Pierrot is [plays] Columbine') by faking a faked orgasm which is also a faked crime.

Derrida's law of the textual operation – of reading, writing, philosophizing – makes it finally clear that, however denaturalized and non-empirical these sexual images might be, it is the phallus that learns the trick of coming close to faking the orgasm here, rather than the hymen coming into its own as the indefinitely displaced effect of the text. Thus the hymen is doubly displaced. Its 'presence' is appropriately deconstructed, and its curious property appropriated to deliver the signature of the philosopher. Hymen or writing 'gets ready to receive the seminal jet (*jet*; also throw) of a throw of dice' *(Dis,* p. 317; the last phrase – *un coup de dés* – is of course a reference to Mallarmé's famous poem; but, following Derrida's well-known signature-games, the passage can also read, 'the hymen gets ready to receive the seminal J. of a blow of a D'). In terms of the custodianship of meaning, the philosopher no longer wishes to engender sons but recognizes that, at the limit, the text's semes are scattered irretrievably abroad. But, by a double displacement of the vagina, dissemination remains on the ascendant and the hymen remains reactive. It is 'dissemination which *affirms* the always already divided generation of meaning' *(Dis,* p. 300). Textual operation is back to position one and fireworks on the lawn with a now 'feminized' phallus: 'Dissemination in the fold (*repli* – also withdrawal) of hymen' *(Dis,* p. 303).

One of the many projects of *Glas* is to learn the name of the mother.[18] There is an ideological phallocentrism in Freud that works to control some of his most radical breakthroughs. Derrida has traced this phallocentrism in Lacan, who has written in the name of the 'truth of Freud.'[19] Now in Lacan's gloss on the Oedipus complex, it is through the discovery of the 'name of the father' that the son passes the Oedipal scene and is inserted into the symbolic order or the circuit of the signifier. Upon that circuit, the transcendental signifier remains the phallus. Is it possible to undo this phallocentric scenario by staging the efforts of a critic who seeks to discover the name of the *mother*?

Within the argument from double displacement, this might still be a version of Freud's account of the right object-choice: the son's perennial longing for the mother. Whether interpreted this way or not, it remains the undertaking of the right-hand column of *Glas*, where Derrida writes on some writings of Genet. He needs an eccentric occasion to ask the oblique question of the name of the mother: Genet is an illegitimate homosexual son whose name is – if such an expression can be risked – a matronymic.

(This particular concern, the name or status of the mother, remains implicit in the left-hand column of *Glas* as well. Explicitly, Derrida learns to mourn for fathers: his natural father, Hegel, Nietzsche, Freud. Yet the subject-matter is the matter of the family, the place of mother, sister, wife in the Holy Family, in Greek tragedy, in the early writings of Hegel and Marx, in the story of Hegel's own life. Derrida comments repeatedly on the undisclosed homoeroticism of the official discourse of these phallogocentric philosophers – a discourse supported by the relegation of public homosexuals like Jean Genet to criminality.)

I will not attempt an exhaustive description of this search. Let us consider two sentences toward the end of the Genet column:

> I begin to be jealous of his mother who has been able to change her phallus to infinity without being cut up into pieces. Hypothesis Godcome father in himself (*en soi*; without gender differentiation in French) of not being there.

> (*G*, p. 290b)

The best way to deal with these lines would be to gloss them as mechanically as possible. Derrida has not been able to articulate the name of Genet's mother. The most he has been able to do is a great L made by the arrangement of the type – 'elle' being French for 'she' – cradling or being penetrated by a wedge of emptiness.[20] The lines I quote follow almost immediately.

Derrida is jealous because she can *displace* herself ad infinitum. She has stolen a march on the false price of the phallocentric Idea – which can merely repeat itself self-identically to infinity. She has taken phallus out of the circuit of castration, dismemberment, cutting up (*dé-tailler*). With her it is not a question of having or not having the phallus. She can change it, as if she had a collection of dildos or transvestite underwear. The Genet column of *Glas* has considered a phantasmagoria of such items, as evoked by Genet in his own texts.

Such a mother – the outcast male homosexual's vision of mother – is different from the phallic mother of fetishism. If Derrida is re-writing-the text of Freud here by suggesting that the male homosexual is *not* caught in the fear of castration by regarding the phallus itself as a representation of what is not there – a theme of self-castration carefully developed in *Glas* – he must also suggest that the 'feminization' of philosophizing for the male deconstructor might find its most adequate legend in male homosexuality defined as criminality, and that it cannot speak for the woman.

Such a recognition of the limits of deconstruction is in the admission that the shape of *Glas*, standing in here for the deconstructive project, might be a fetish, an object that the subject regards with superstitious awe. The book is divided into two columns – Hegel on the left, Genet on the right, and a slit in between. Derrida relates these two pillars with the fleece in the middle to Freud's reference 'to the circumstance that the inquisitive boy sought out (*gespäht*) the woman's genitals from below, from her legs up' (*F* xi, p. 155; *GW* xiv, p. 314). It is the classic case of fetishism, a uniquely shaped object (his bicolumnar book) that will allow the subject both to be and not to be a man – to have the phallus and yet accede to dissemination.

And indeed it is in terms of the concept-metaphor of fetishism that Derrida gives us a capsule history of the fate of dialectics. I can do no more here than mark a few moments of that 'history.' Hegel remarks on the fetishism of the African savage, who must eat the fetishized ancestor ceremonially. (*Glas* also is an act of mourning for fathers.) Hegel accuses Kant of a certain fetishism, since Kant sees the Divine Father merely as a jealous God, and must thus formulate a Categorical Imperative. (Derrida supplements the accusation by pointing out that, in French at least, the Categorical Imperative has the same initials as the fetishistic notion – saving the mother jealously from the father's phallus – of the Immaculate Conception: IC.)

The negation of the negation (*Aufhebung*, or sublation), at once denying a thing and preserving it on a higher level, Hegel's chief contribution to the morphology of the self-determination of the concept, was itself, Feuerbach suggested, the absolutely positive move. It may be called fetishistic because it allowed Hegel to keep both presence and its representation.

> Marx then exposes Feuerbach's critical movement . . . The speculative unity, the secular complicity of philosophy and religion – the former being the truth and essence of the latter, the latter the representation of the former . . . is the process of sublation.
>
> (*G*, p. 226a)

Marx also relates *Aufhebung* to supporting the Christian 'desire for maternity *as well as* virginity' (*G*, p. 228a).[21] The distance between deconstruction's project of displacement and the dialectic's project of sublation may be charted in terms of the son's longing for the mother. 'If *Aufhebung* were a Christian mother' (*G*, p. 225a) – at once marked and unmarked by the phallus – deconstruction looks for a mother who can change her phallus indefinitely and has an outcast homosexual son. Crudely put, a quarrel of sons is not the model for feminist practice.[22]

The project of philosophy, Derrida continues, as each philosopher presents a more correct picture of the way things are, is not merely to locate the fetish in the text of the precursor, but also to de-fetishize philosophy. 'If there were no thing – the thing itself par excellence – (in this case the truth of philosophy), the concept of the fetish would lose its invariant kernel. For the fetish is a substitute – of the thing itself' (*G*, p. 234a; I have modified the order of the sentences to make a summary). Rather than negating the thing itself – that would merely be another way of positing it – deconstruction gives it the undecidability of the fetish. The thing itself becomes its own substitute. Like the faked orgasm, the thing itself its own fake. Yet the fetish, to qualify as fetish, must carry within itself a trace of the thing itself that it replaces. Deconstruction cannot be pure undecidability. 'It constitutes an *economy* of the undecidable . . . It is not dialectical but plays with the dialectic' (*G*, p. 235a).

Thus *Glas* must end with an erection of the thing, not merely the oscillation of the phallus as fetish. The distance from the dialectic is measured simply by the fact that, 'the thing is oblique. It (*elle*) already makes an angle with the ground' (*G*, p. 292b). Its relationship with the ground (of things) has the obliqueness of an originary fetish. The graphic of that angle can be that large L on page 290b. In French, the 'it' of the second sentence above is 'elle.' Cradled in that angle between the fetish and the thing itself is the word *déjà* (already), separated out of the sentence by two commas. *Glas* makes clear that *déjà* is also a bilingual yes (*ja*) to the D (de) – the initial letter of Derrida's own patronymic – in reverse. It is the assent to the self that one must already have given (an assent at best reversed, never fully displaced). If the project of *La double séance* finally puts the phallus in the hymen, *Glas* is obliged to put the son with the patronymic in the arms of the phallic mother.

'Hypothesis Godcome father in himself of not being there' (*Hypothèse dieuvenue père en soi de n'être pas là*). This is the mother of whom, simply reversing Kant's position vis-à-vis the jealous father, Derrida begins to become jealous. As the possessor of the fetish, she carries a substitute of the thing itself – that father in himself; yet as the deconstructed fetish she also carries the trace of the thing itself; through not being there she *is* – one presumes, since the verb of being is strategically suppressed in the sentence – the father in himself. Here again that curious displacement – her separation from Athena or Mary. She allows the philosopher to question the concept of being by having no verb of being; she cannot be named. Yet she remains the miraculous hypothesis – 'the supposition, i.e., a fact *placed under* a number of facts as their common support and explanation; though in the majority of instances these hypotheses or suppositions better deserve the name of *hypopoiesis* or suffictions.'[23]

• • •

V

My attitude towards deconstruction can now be summarized: first, deconstruction is illuminating as a critique of phallocentrism; second, it is convincing as an argument against the founding of a hysterocentric to counter a phallocentric discourse; third, as a 'feminist' practice itself, it is caught on the other side of sexual difference.[24] At whatever remove of 'différance' (difference/deferment from/of any decidable statement of the concept of an identity or difference),[25] *sexual difference is thought,* sexual *differential* between 'man' and 'woman' remains irreducible. It is within the frame of these remarks that I hope the following parable will be read.

Within this frame, let us imagine a woman who is a (straight) deconstructivist of (traditional male) discourse. Let us assume that her position vis-à-vis the material she interprets is 'the same' as that of the male deconstructivist. Thinking of the irreducible sexual differential, she might say: in order to have used the discourse of the phallus as a sign of my power, I was obliged to displace myself from what has been defined as my originary displacement by that very discourse and thus (re)-present for myself a place. Should my gesture of deconstructive practice be a third-degree displacement so that, on the other side of the sexual differential, I can 'be myself'? Yet, the project of the critique of phallocentrism-logocentrism is an exposure of the ideology of self-possession – 'being myself' – in order to grasp the idea – 'the thing itself.' Should I not have an attitude parallel to the deconstructive philosopher's attitude to the discourse of the phallus towards any discourse of the womb that might get developed thanks to the sexual differential? What about the further problem of creating 'purposively' a discourse of the woman to match an official discourse of the man whose strength is that it is often arbitrary and unmotivated? Deconstruction puts into question the 'purposive' activities of a sovereign subject.

A certain historical 'differential' now begins to suggest itself. Even if all historical taxonomies are open to question, a minimal historical network must be assumed for interpretation, a network that suggests that the phallocentric discourse is the object of deconstruction because of its co-extensivity with the history of Western metaphysics, a history inseparable from political economy and from the property of man as holder of property. *Whatever their historical determination or conceptual allegiance*, the male users of the phallocentric discourse all trace the itinerary of the suppression of the trace. The differential political implications of putting oneself in the position of accomplice-critic with respect to an at best clandestinely determined hysterocentric subtext that is only today becoming 'authoritative' in bourgeois feminism, seems to ask for a different program. The collective project of our feminist critic must always be to rewrite the *social* text so that the historical and sexual differentials are operated together. Part of it is to notice that the argument based on the 'power' of the faked orgasm, of being-fetish, and hymen, is, all deconstructive cautions taken, 'determined' by that very political and social history that is inseparably co-extensive with phallocentric discourse and, in her case, either unrecorded in accessible ways, or recorded in terms of man.[26] Since she has, indeed, learned the lesson of deconstruction, this rewriting of the social text of motherhood cannot be an establishment of new meanings. It can only be to work away at concept-metaphors that deliberately establish and cast wide a different system of 'meanings.'

If she confines herself to asking the question of woman (what is woman?), she might merely be attempting to provide an answer to the honorable male question: what does woman want? She herself still remains the *object* of the question. To reverse the situation would be to ask the question of woman as a subject: what am I? That would bring back all the absolutely convincing deconstructive critiques of the sovereign subject.

The gesture that the 'historical moment' requires might be to ask the 'question of man' in that special way – what is man that the itinerary of his desire creates such a text? Not, in other words, simply, what is man? All the texts in the world are at our disposal, and the question cannot flounder into the delusions of a pure 'what am I?' Yet it restores to us the position of the questioning *subject* by virtue of the question-effect, a position that the sexual differential has never allowed women à propos of men in a licit way. This gesture must continue to supplement the collective and substantive work of 'restoring' woman's history and literature.[27] Otherwise the question 'what is man's desire?' asked by women from the peculiar *sub rosa* position of the doubly-displaced subject will continue to preserve masculinity's business as usual and produce answers that will describe themselves, with cruel if unselfconscious irony, as 'total womanhood'.

As a literary critic she might fabricate, strategic 'misreadings,' rather than perpetrating variations on 'received' or 'receivable' readings, especially upon a woman's text. She might, by the superimposition of a suitable allegory, draw a reading out of the text that relates it to the historico-social differential of the body. This move should, of course, be made scrupulously explicit. Since deconstruction successfully puts the ideology of 'correct readings' into question, our friend is content with this thought.[28] Even more content because, since she has never been considered a custodian of truth anyway (only its mysterious figure), this move seems to possess the virtue of turning that millennial accusation into a place of strength. To undo the *double* displacement, as it were, and to operate from displacement as such, if there can be such a thing. To produce useful and scrupulous fake readings in the place of the passively active fake orgasm.

Notes

1 Georg Wilhelm Friedrich Hegel, *Sämtliche Werke*, vii (Leipzig: F. Meiner, 1920–55), p. 47; Hegel, *Philosophy of Right*, trans. T. M. Knox (Oxford: Clarendon Press, 1942), p. 226. Throughout the essay I have modified all quotations from texts in translation when necessary.

2 I do not use the word 'patriarchy' – the rule of the father – because it is susceptible to biologistic, naturalistic, and/or positivist-historical interpretations, and most often provides us with no more (and no less) than a place of accusation. I am more interested in the workings of a certain 'discourse' – language in an operative and abyssal heterogeneity. I should add that the absence of Marxist issues in this paper signifies nothing that cannot be explained by the following conviction: as women claim legitimation as agents in a society, a congruent movement to re-distribute the forces of production and reproduction in that society must also be undertaken. Otherwise we are reduced to the prevailing philosophy of liberal feminism: 'a moralistically humanitarian and egalitarian philosophy of social improvement through the re-education of psychological attitudes' (Charnie Guettel, *Marxism and Feminism* [Toronto: Women's Press, 1974], p. 3). As a deconstructivist, my topic in the present essay is – can deconstruction help? That should not imply that I am blind to the larger issues outlined here.

3 For literary critics, the most recent articulation of this 'official philosophy' is in the concept of the hermeneutic circle. Digests can be found in Sarah N. Lawall, *Critics of Consciousness: The Existential Structures of Literature* (Cambridge: Harvard University Press, 1968); and Robert R. Magliola, *Phenomenology and Literature: An Introduction* (West Lafayette: Purdue University Press, 1977).

4 See Jacques Derrida, 'Speculations on "Freud,"' trans. Ian McLeod, *Oxford Literary Review* 3 (1978): 78–97.

5 Spivak, 'Love Me, Love My Ombre, Elle,' forthcoming in *Diacritics*.

6 Friedrich Wilhelm Nietzsche, *Werke; kritische Gesamtausgabe*, v, vol. 2, ed. Georgio Colli and Mazzino Montinari (Berlin: W. De Gruyter, 1970), p. 291, hereafter cited in the text as *CM*; Nietzsche, *The Gay Science*, trans. Walter J. Kaufmann (New York: Vintage Books, 1974), p. 317.

7 I do not believe Nietzsche's passage is necessarily read this way by everyone.

8 Jacques Derrida, *Éperons: Les Styles de Nietzsche; Spurs: Nietzsche's Styles*, trans. Barbara Harlow (Chicago: University of Chicago Press, 1979), p. 56, hereafter cited in the text as *Ep*. This is a bilingual edition of *Éperons*; I have used my own translations.

9 For a discussion of 'citationality', see Jacques Derrida, 'Limited Inc,' trans. Samuel Weber, *Glyph* 2 (1977): 162–254. For a discussion of citationality in Derrida, see Spivak, 'Revolutions That As Yet Have No Model: Derrida's *Limited Inc*,' *Diacritics* 10 (Winter 1980): 29–49.

10 Sigmund Freud, *Standard Edition of the Complete Psychological Works*, trans. James Strachey, xxii (London: Hogarth Press, 1964), hereafter cited in the text as *F*; *Gesammelte Werke*, xv (Frankfurt am Main: S. Fischer, 1940), hereafter cited in the text as *GW*. Citations indicate volume and page number.

11 For definitions of psychoanalytic terms, consult Jean Laplanche and J.-B. Pontalis, *Le Vocabulaire de la psychanalyse* (Paris: Presses Universitaires de France, 1967); *The Language of Psycho-Analysis*, trans. Donald Nicholson-Smith (New York: Norton, 1973). For a cautionary viewpoint against such a sourcebook, see Derrida, 'Moi-la psychanalyse,' introduction to Nicolas Abraham, *L'Écorce et le noyau* (Paris: Aubier-Montaigne, 1978); 'Me-Psychoanalysis: An Introduction to the Translation of *The Shell and the Kernel* by Nicolas Abraham,' trans. Richard Klein, *Diacritics* 9 (March 1979): 4–12.

12 Derrida produces such a reading, using *Beyond The Pleasure Principle* as his occasion, in 'Speculer-sur "Freud,"' in *La Carte postale* (Paris: Aubier-Flammarion, 1980), pp. 237–437. The full French text has not yet been translated.

13 Jacques Derrida, 'Les fins de l'homme,' *Marges de la philosophie* (Paris: Minuit, 1972), p. 137; 'Ends of Man,' trans. Edouard Morot-Sir et al., *Philosophy and Phenomenological Research* 30 (September 1969): 35.

14 Since I wrote this essay, Michael Ryan and Jonathan Culler have published studies of deconstruction that include chapters on feminism. See Ryan, *Marxism and Deconstruction: A Critical Articulation* (Baltimore: Johns Hopkins University Press, 1982), pp. 194–212; and Culler, *On Deconstruction: Theory and Criticism after Structuralism* (Ithaca: Cornell University Press, 1982).

15 *Aeschylus*, trans. Herbert W. Smyth, II (London: W. Heinemann, 1936), pp. 293, 311, 335.

16 Jacques Derrida, 'La double séance,' *La dissémination* (Paris: Seuil, 1972); *Dissemination*, trans. Barbara Johnson (Chicago: University of Chicago Press, 1981), hereafter cited in the text as *Dis*. Page references are to the French edition, and the translations are my own.

17 *Dis*, p. 293. The hymen is here also substituted for the imperious eye, whose blink measures the self-evident moment (in German *Augenblick*, literally the blink of an eye), in Husserlian philosophy as in the general Western tradition; see 'Le Signe et le clin d'oeil,' *La Voix et le phénomène* (Paris: Presses Universitaires de France, 1967); 'Signs and the Blink of an Eye,' *Speech and Phenomena*, trans. David Allison (Evanston: Northwestern University Press, 1973).

18 Jacques Derrida, *Glas* (Paris: Galilée, 1974), hereafter cited in the text as *G*.

19 Jacques Derrida, 'Le Facteur de la vérité,' *Poétique* 21 (1975): 96–147; 'The Purveyor of Truth,' trans. Willis Domingo et al., *Yale French Studies* 52 (1975): 31–114.

20 This particular reading of the capital L has been independently developed by Geoffrey Hartman in *Saving the Text* (Baltimore: Johns Hopkins University Press, 1981), p. 75.

21 In 'Freud and the Scene of Writing,' in *Writing and Difference*, and in *La double séance*, Derrida suggests that both in Freud and in Mallarmé the desire is to find a surface both marked and virgin. In *De la grammatologie* (Paris: Minuit, 1967); *Of Grammatology*, trans. Gayatri Spivak (Baltimore: Johns Hopkins University Press, 1976), he suggests that Rousseau wanted a category that was both transcendental (virgin) and supplementary (marked). An interpretation of Derrida's interpretation of the intellectual history of European men, in terms precisely of sons' longing for mothers, can perhaps be made.

22 I should make it clear that Derrida himself, like the Nietzsche of *Ecce Homo*, is, at least in theory, suspicious of discipleship. This particular 'feminist' charge would probably seem a mark of excellence to him.

23 Samuel Taylor Coleridge, *Biographia Literaria*, ed. J. Shawcross, I (London: Oxford University Press, 1907), p. 72.

24 From this point of view, it is worth noting that in Julia Kristeva's more mainstream or masculist celebration of motherhood, the child remains male ('Héréthique de l'amour,' *Tel Quel* 74 (Winter 1977): 30–49. 'Maternité selon Giovanni Bellini'

and 'Noms de lieu,' in *Polylogue* (Paris: Seuil, 1977); 'Motherhood According to Bellini' and 'Place Names,' in *Desire in Language: A Semiotic Approach to Literature and Art*, trans. Thomas Gorz et al. (New York: Columbia University Press, 1980).

25 Derrida, 'La Différance,' in *Marges*; 'Differance,' *Speech and Phenomena*.

26 I have tried to develop such a program since this essay was written. See especially Spivak, 'Feminism and the Critical Tradition,' forthcoming in a collection of essays edited by Paula Treichler, to be published by the University of Illinois Press.

27 Eleanor Fox-Genovese has written a pathbreaking essay on the subject that appeared after my own essay was completed. See her 'Placing Women's History in History,' *New Left Review* 133 (May–June 1982).

28 I have attempted to use this method of criticism in 'Unmaking and Making in *To the Lighthouse*,' in *Women and Language in Literature and Society*, ed. Sally McConnell-Ginet and Nelly Furman (New York: Praeger, 1980).

Section six

POSTMODERNISM

Introduction

Definitions of the term 'postmodernism' are notoriously difficult to pin down and, of course, are always produced from positions within culture and politics. While the term itself remains resolutely contradictory it has, none the less, provided a focus for much lively and often controversial debate about the nature of contemporary culture – gaining currency in discussions about architecture (see Jencks 1977), the visual arts and media (Burgin 1986; Debord 1983), literature (McHale 1987), dance (Trachtenberg 1985) and music (Morgan 1977), as well as providing a kind of catch-all term for the whole condition of late capitalist society itself.

As well as providing a focus for debate, the term 'postmodernism' also sets up a series of problematics for the study of culture as we may, traditionally, have known it. At a most basic level we might understand the mode of postmodernism as a heterogeneous interweaving of questions which escape any singular or unified answer. Or, as Linda Hutcheon has suggested in her illuminating study, *The Politics of Postmodernism*:

> In general terms it takes the form of self-conscious, self-contradictory, self-undermining statement. It is rather like saying something whilst at the same time putting inverted commas around what is being said. The effect is to highlight, or 'highlight,' and to subvert, or 'subvert,' and the mode is therefore a 'knowing' and ironic – or even 'ironic' – one. Postmodernism's distinctive character lies in this kind of wholesale 'nudging' commitment to doubleness or duplicity. In many ways it is an even-handed process because postmodernism ultimately manages to install and reinforce as much as undermine and subvert the con-ventions and presuppositions it appears to challenge.
>
> (1989: pp. 1–2)

In a sense this is the complex paradox of a mode of art, or of knowledge, which seeks to debate the present from a position within it. How do we conduct such a debate except through a continual questioning and undermining of the cultural processes of knowing, representing and debating the present? As Hutcheon's work also points out, the inevitably political dimensions of postmodernism render the debate intensely problematic but also crucially important. In the life of this *Reader*, we are aware that the debate about postmodernism might begin to look tired and familiar, yet it seems important to represent it here, since in a canon of critical and cultural theory which is ever ongoing the importance of addressing and re-addressing the present (and ways of knowing the present) must be central.

In the section which follows we have attempted to account for some of the underlying strands of the debate as it stands today. From the controversy and questioning inherent in that debate it would seem that two basic positions emerge: there are those who embrace the undermining and duplicitous mode which postmodernism suggests; and there are those who resist it.

For those who mourn the loss of the unifying or controlling narratives of the past, the problems with postmodernism are vast, and the objections which are raised are politically complex. At a basic level, however, those objections centre around what is perceived as the ahistorical nature of the postmodern condition. While the forms of pastiche, self-referential and explicitly intertextual 'style' of postmodernism owe something to the mode of modernism, they do, none the less, also break with the referent of the real (history, time, art and the artist) which modernism maintained. There is no recourse, within the terms of postmodernism, to a singular 'real' history (of class, or gender struggle, for example) or any singular 'real' style or art of the age. And no respect is maintained for the distinctions traditionally drawn between discrete disciplines of cultural investigation or the division within the cultural debate itself (see Section Seven) between forms of high and popular culture.

As has become apparent, the arguable 'depthlessness' which postmodernism envisages is a focus of concern across a wide political spectrum. For those of the neoconservative right it eclipses the supposedly unifying values which structure the social order; for the liberal centre it demolishes the autonomy of individual expression; and for the Marxist left it destroys the founding platform of unified struggle, giving rise to what Fredric Jameson has called the 'problem of micropolitics' (see p. 197 below). What seems to motivate all of these positions is the desire to return to a grand narrative of legitimation (as Lyotard describes it – see no. 1 below). Yet the objections to postmodernism are still more complex than that. While the disparate struggles of women, gays, blacks, colonials and postcolonials in and of themselves seem encouraged by the unmourned loss of a simplistic 'real', demanding a plural micropolitics of resistance, such activists have often resisted the incorporation of their work within the rubric of postmodernism on the grounds that its resolute undermining of the referent of the real diffuses their own very 'real' political agendas. The contradictions of postmodernism are seen to be both subversive and reconfirming of traditionally oppressive systems of thought and practice.

On the other hand, for those who would embrace the postmodern, its power lies precisely in its capacity to dissolve, or perhaps to de-naturalize, the relation between the sign and its referent. The modes of pastiche and self-reflexivity which foster the objections of depthlessness are, within these terms, understood to force the realization that *all* forms of cultural production and knowledge are grounded in ideology, and that no matter how 'worthy' their motivation they can never be free of the social and political frameworks which may precede and surround them, and which they may seek to undermine. The work of Jean-François Lyotard suggests that, although postmodernism may dissolve effective theories of the agency of the subject as the source of political *action* (an objection which the work of Jameson frequently raises), it does have the advantage of de-naturalizing the inevitable ideological grounding of the category of the subject as a whole, and of providing a continuing and relentless *critique* of the legitimacy of *any* form of social and ideological meaning. Against the very considerable power of western capitalism to normalize the relation between signs and their referents, postmodernism posits the notion that the referent is an *effect* of its sign, rather than its source. From this perspective, all forms of culture and knowledge are inextricably bound up with established systems of meaning production and the discourses which operate within culture, and it is always these links which postmodernism seeks to expose.

That this strategy of exposure and critique can itself be construed as important politically is perhaps best evidenced in the work of Jean Baudrillard on the political implications of the sustaining fictions of the 'real' within American culture (see Section 6.3) and politics (see the discussion of the Watergate affair, pp. 26–37, in *Simulations*, 1983). But it is apparent also in the phenomenon of postmodern architecture which surrounds us in the everyday. Indeed, discussions about postmodern architecture (see, for example, Jencks 1977) involve precisely those questions of history and of style around which the debate about postmodernism has been focused. The form of postmodern architecture is itself resolutely multiple and diverse, but it is also historical. It acknowledges uncritically the long heritage of its own 'built culture', but eclectically re-appropriates the forms of the past in order to address a culture and society from within it and from within the moment of the history of its present. While it explicitly avoids the assertion of an original and coherent form, it raises the inevitable questions about the drive to do so and acknowledges the implications of the heritage and expectations with which such a drive is necessarily stuck.

However we respond to the phenomenon of postmodern architecture and the questions about culture, style and meaning it highlights, whichever side of the debate we come down on, or even if we opt to maintain a kind of eclectic and strategic straddling of the boundaries which are now being drawn, the issues which the entire question of postmodernism raises will continue to reverberate in, and provide problems for, the discussions of culture upon which we embark.

6.1

Jean-François Lyotard from *The Postmodern Condition: A Report on Knowledge* (1984)

9 Narratives of the legitimation of knowledge

We shall examine two major versions of the narrative of legitimation. One is more political, the other more philosophical; both are of great importance in modern history, in particular in the history of knowledge and its institutions.

The subject of the first of these versions is humanity as the hero of liberty. All peoples have a right to science. If the social subject is not already the subject of scientific knowledge, it is because that has been forbidden by priests and tyrants. The right to science must be reconquered. It is understandable that this narrative would be directed more toward a politics of primary education, rather than of universities and high schools.[1] The educational policy of the French Third Republic powerfully illustrates these presuppositions.

It seems that this narrative finds it necessary to de-emphasize higher education. Accordingly, the measures adopted by Napoleon regarding higher education are generally considered to have been motivated by the desire to produce the administrative and professional skills necessary for the stability of the State.[2] This overlooks the fact that in the context of the narrative of freedom, the State receives its legitimacy not from itself but from the people. So even if imperial politics designated the institutions of higher education as a breeding ground for the officers of the State and secondarily, for the managers of civil society, it did so because the nation as a whole was supposed to win its freedom through the spread of new domains of knowledge to the population, a process to be effected through agencies and professions within which those cadres would fulfill their functions. The same reasoning is a fortiori valid for the foundation of properly scientific institutions. The State resorts to the narrative of freedom every time it assumes direct control over the training of the 'people,' under the name of the 'nation,' in order to point them down the path of progress.[3]

With the second narrative of legitimation, the relation between science, the nation, and the State develops quite differently. It first appears with the founding, between 1807 and 1810, of the University of Berlin,[4] whose influence on the organization of higher education in the young countries of the world was to be considerable in the nineteenth and twentieth centuries.

At the time of the University's creation, the Prussian ministry had before it a project conceived by Fichte and counterproposals by Schleiermacher. Wilhelm von Humboldt had to decide the matter and came down on the side of Schleiermacher's more 'liberal' option.

Reading Humboldt's report, one may be tempted to reduce his entire approach to the politics of the scientific institution to the famous dictum: 'Science for its own sake.' But this would be to misunderstand the ultimate aim of his policies, which is guided by the principle of legitimation we are discussing and is very close to the one Schleiermacher elucidates in a more thorough fashion.

Humboldt does indeed declare that science obeys its own rules, that the scientific institution 'lives and continually renews itself on its own, with no constraint or determined goal whatsoever.' But he adds that the University should orient its constituent element, science, to 'the spiritual and moral training of the nation.'[5] How can this *Bildung*-effect result from the disinterested pursuit of learning? Are not the State, the nation, the whole of humanity indifferent to knowledge for its own sake? What interests them, as Humboldt admits, is not learning, but 'character and action.'

The minister's adviser thus faces a major conflict, in some ways reminiscent of the split introduced by the Kantian critique between knowing and willing: it is a conflict between a language game made of denotations answerable only to the criterion of truth, and a language game governing ethical, social, and political practice that necessarily involves decisions and obligations, in other words, utterances expected to be just rather than true and which in the final analysis lie outside the realm of scientific knowledge.

However, the unification of these two sets of discourse is indispensable to the *Bildung* aimed for by Humboldt's project, which consists not only in the acquisition of learning by individuals, but also in the training of a fully legitimated subject of knowledge and society. Humboldt therefore invokes a Spirit (what Fichte calls Life), animated by three ambitions, or better, by a single, threefold aspiration: 'that of deriving everything from an original principle' (corresponding to scientific activity), 'that of relating everything to an ideal' (governing ethical and social practice), and 'that of unifying this principle and this ideal in a single Idea' (ensuring that the scientific search for true causes always coincides with the pursuit of just ends in moral and political life). This ultimate synthesis constitutes the legitimate subject.

Humboldt adds in passing that this triple aspiration naturally inheres in the 'intellectual character of the German nation.'[6] This is a concession, but a discreet one, to the other narrative, to the idea that the subject of knowledge is the people. But in truth this idea is quite distant from the narrative of the legitimation of knowledge advanced by German idealism. The suspicion that men like Schleiermacher, Humboldt, and even Hegel harbor towards the State is an indication of this. If Schleiermacher fears the narrow nationalism, protectionism, utilitarianism, and positivism that guide the public authorities in matters of science, it is because the principle of science does not reside in those authorities, even indirectly. The subject of knowledge is not the people, but the speculative spirit. It is not embodied, as in France after the Revolution, in a State, but in a System. The language game of legitimation is not state-political, but philosophical.

The great function to be fulfilled by the universities is to 'lay open the whole body of learning and expound both the principles and the foundations of all knowledge.' For 'there is no creative scientific capacity without the speculative spirit.'[7] 'Speculation' is here the name given the discourse on the legitimation of scientific discourse. Schools are functional; the University is speculative, that is to say, philosophical.[8] Philosophy must restore unity to learning, which has been scattered into separate sciences in laboratories and in pre-university education; it can only achieve this in a language game that links the sciences together as moments in the becoming of spirit, in other words, which links them in a rational narration, or rather metanarration. Hegel's *Encyclopedia* (1817–27) attempts to realize this project of totalization, which was already present in Fichte and Schelling in the form of the idea of the System.

It is here, in the mechanism of developing a Life that is simultaneously Subject, that we see a return of narrative knowledge. There is a universal 'history' of spirit, spirit is 'life,' and 'life' is its own self-presentation and formulation in the ordered knowledge of all of its forms contained in the empirical sciences. The encyclopedia of German idealism is the narration of the '(hi)story' of this life-subject. But what it produces is a metanarrative, for the story's narrator must not be a people mired in the particular positivity of its traditional knowledge, nor even scientists taken as a whole, since they are sequestered in professional frameworks corresponding to their respective specialities.

The narrator must be a metasubject in the process of formulating both the legitimacy of the discourses of the empirical sciences and that of the direct institutions of popular cultures. This metasubject, in giving voice to their common grounding, realizes their implicit goal. It inhabits the speculative University. Positive science and the people are only crude versions of it. The only valid way for the nation-state itself to bring the people to expression is through the mediation of speculative knowledge.

It has been necessary to elucidate the philosophy that legitimated the foundation of the University of Berlin and was meant to be the motor both of its development and the development of contemporary knowledge. As I have said, many countries in the nineteenth and twentieth centuries adopted this university organization as a model for the foundation or reform of their own system of higher education, beginning with the United States.[9] But above all, this philosophy – which is far from dead, especially in university circles[10]

– offers a particularly vivid representation of one solution to the problem of the legitimacy of knowledge.

Research and the spread of learning are not justified by invoking a principle of usefulness. The idea is not at all that science should serve the interests of the State and/or civil society. The humanist principle that humanity rises up in dignity and freedom through knowledge is left by the wayside. German idealism has recourse to a metaprinciple that simultaneously grounds the development of learning, of society, and of the State in the realization of the 'life' of a Subject, called 'divine Life' by Fichte and 'Life of the spirit' by Hegel. In this perspective, knowledge first finds legitimacy within itself, and it is knowledge that is entitled to say what the State and what Society are.[11] But it can only play this role by changing levels, by ceasing to be simply the positive knowledge of its referent (nature, society, the State, etc.), becoming in addition to that the knowledge of the knowledge of the referent – that is, by becoming speculative. In the names 'Life' and 'Spirit,' knowledge names itself.

A noteworthy result of the speculative apparatus is that all of the discourses of learning about every possible referent are taken up not from the point of view of their immediate truth-value, but in terms of the value they acquire by virtue of occupying a certain place in the itinerary of Spirit or Life – or, if preferred, a certain position in the Encyclopedia recounted by speculative discourse. That discourse cites them in the process of expounding for itself what it knows, that is, in the process of self-exposition. True knowledge, in this perspective, is always indirect knowledge; it is composed of reported statements that are incorporated into the metanarrative of a subject that guarantees their legitimacy.

The same thing applies for every variety of discourse, even if it is not a discourse of learning; examples are the discourse of law and that of the State. Contemporary hermeneutic discourse[12] is born of this presupposition, which guarantees that there is meaning to know and thus confers legitimacy upon history (and especially the history of learning). Statements are treated as their own autonyms[13] and set in motion in a way that is supposed to render them mutually engendering: these are the rules of speculative language. The University, as its name indicates, is its exclusive institution.

But, as I have said, the problem of legitimacy can be solved using the other procedures as well. The difference between them should be kept in mind: today, with the status of knowledge unbalanced and its speculative unity broken, the first version of legitimacy is gaining new vigor.

According to this version, knowledge finds its validity not within itself, not in a subject that develops by actualizing its learning possibilities, but in a practical subject – humanity. The principle of the movement animating the people is not the self-legitimation of knowledge, but the self-grounding of freedom or, if preferred, its self-management. The subject is concrete, or supposedly so, and its epic is the story of its emancipation from everything that prevents it from governing itself. It is assumed that the laws it makes for itself are just, not because they conform to some outside nature, but because the legislators are, constitutionally, the very citizens who are subject to the laws. As a result, the legislator's will – the desire that the laws be just – will always coincide with the will of the citizen, who desires the law and will therefore obey it.

Clearly, this mode of legitimation through the autonomy of the will[14] gives priority to a totally different language game, which Kant called imperative and is known today as prescriptive. The important thing is not, or not only, to legitimate denotative utterances pertaining to the truth, such as 'The earth revolves around the sun,' but rather to legitimate prescriptive utterances pertaining to justice, such as 'Carthage must be destroyed' or 'The minimum wage must be set at *x* dollars.' In this context, the only role positive knowledge can play is to inform the practical subject about the reality within which the execution of the prescription is to be inscribed. It allows the subject to circumscribe the executable, or what it is possible to do. But the executory, what should be done, is not within the purview of positive knowledge. It is one thing for an undertaking to be possible and another for it to be just. Knowledge is no longer the subject, but in the service of the subject: its only legitimacy (though it is formidable) is the fact that it allows morality to become reality.

This introduces a relation of knowledge to society and the State which is in principle a relation of the means to the end. But scientists must cooperate only if they judge that the politics of the State, in other words the sum of its prescriptions, is just. If they feel that the civil society of which they are members is badly represented by the State, they may reject its prescriptions. This type of legitimation grants them the authority, as practical human beings, to refuse their scholarly support to a political power they judge to be unjust, in other words, not grounded in a real autonomy. They can even go so far as to use their expertise to demonstrate that such autonomy is not in fact realized in society and the State. This reintroduces the critical function of knowledge. But the fact remains that knowledge has no final legitimacy outside of serving the goals envisioned by the practical subject, the autonomous collectivity.[15]

This distribution of roles in the enterprise of legitimation is interesting from our point of view because it assumes, as against the system-subject theory, that there is no possibility that language games can be unified or totalized in any metadiscourse. Quite to the contrary, here the priority accorded prescriptive statements – uttered by the practical subject – renders them independent in principle from the statements of science, whose only remaining function is to supply this subject with information.

Two remarks:

1 It would be easy to show that Marxism has wavered between the two models of narrative legitimation I have just described. The Party takes the place of the University, the proletariat that of the people or of humanity, dialectical materialism that of speculative idealism, etc. Stalinism may be the result, with its specific relationship with the sciences: in Stalinism, the sciences only figure as citations from the metanarrative of the march towards socialism, which is the equivalent of the life of the spirit. But on the other hand Marxism can, in conformity to the second version, develop into a form of critical knowledge by declaring that socialism is nothing other than the constitution of the autonomous subject and that the only justification for

the sciences is if they give the empirical subject (the proletariat) the means to emancipate itself from alienation and repression: this was, briefly, the position of the Frankfurt School.

2 The speech Heidegger gave on May 27, 1933, on becoming rector of the university of Freiburg-in-Breisgau,[16] can be read as an unfortunate episode in the history of legitimation. Here, speculative science has become the questioning of being. This questioning is the 'destiny' of the German people, dubbed an 'historico-spiritual people.' To this subject are owed the three services of labor, defense, and knowledge. The University guarantees a meta-knowledge of the three services, that is to say, science. Here, as in idealism, legitimation is achieved through a metadiscourse called science, with onto-logical pretensions. But here the metadiscourse is questioning, not totalizing. And the University, the home of this metadiscourse, owes its knowledge to a people whose 'historic mission' is to bring that metadiscourse to fruition by working, fighting, and knowing. The calling of this people-subject is not to emancipate humanity, but to realize its 'true world of the spirit,' which is 'the most profound power of conservation to be found within its forces of earth and blood.' This insertion of the narrative of race and work into that of the spirit as a way of legitimating knowledge and its institutions is doubly unfortunate: theoretically inconsistent, it was compelling enough to find disastrous echoes in the realm of politics.

10 Delegitimation

In contemporary society and culture – postindustrial society, postmodern culture[17] – the question of the legitimation of knowledge is formulated in different terms. The grand narrative has lost its credibility, regardless of what mode of unification it uses, regardless of whether it is a speculative narrative or a narrative of emancipation.

The decline of narrative can be seen as an effect of the blossoming of techniques and technologies since the Second World War, which has shifted emphasis from the ends of action to its means; it can also be seen as an effect of the redeployment of advanced liberal capitalism after its retreat under the protection of Keynesianism during the period 1930–60, a renewal that has eliminated the communist alternative and valorized the individual enjoyment of goods and services.

Anytime we go searching for causes in this way we are bound to be disappointed. Even if we adopted one or the other of these hypotheses, we would still have to detail the correlation between the tendencies mentioned and the decline of the unifying and legitimating power of the grand narratives of speculation and emancipation.

It is, of course, understandable that both capitalist renewal and prosperity and the disorienting upsurge of technology would have an impact on the status of knowledge. But in order to understand how contemporary science could have been susceptible to those effects long before they took place, we must first locate the seeds of 'delegitimation'[18] and nihilism that were inherent in the grand narratives of the nineteenth century.

First of all, the speculative apparatus maintains an ambiguous relation to knowledge. It shows that knowledge is only worthy of that name to the extent that it reduplicates itself ('lifts itself up,' *hebt sich auf*; is sublated) by citing its own statements in a second-level discourse (autonymy) that functions to legitimate them. This is as much as to say that, in its immediacy, denotative discourse bearing on a certain referent (a living organism, a chemical property, a physical phenomenon, etc.) does not really know what it thinks it knows. Positive science is not a form of knowledge. And speculation feeds on its suppression. The Hegelian speculative narrative thus harbors a certain skepticism toward positive learning, as Hegel himself admits.[19]

A science that has not legitimated itself is not a true science; if the discourse that was meant to legitimate it seems to belong to a prescientific form of knowledge, like a 'vulgar' narrative, it is demoted to the lowest rank, that of an ideology or instrument of power. And this always happens if the rules of the science game that discourse denounces as empirical are applied to science itself.

Take for example the speculative statement: 'A scientific statement is knowledge if and only if it can take its place in a universal process of engendering.' The question is: Is this statement knowledge as it itself defines it? Only if it can take its place in a universal process of engendering. Which it can. All it has to do is to presuppose that such a process exists (the Life of spirit) and that it is itself an expression of that process. This presupposition, in fact, is indispensable to the speculative language game. Without it, the language of legitimation would not be legitimate; it would accompany science in a nosedive into nonsense, at least if we take idealism's word for it.

But this presupposition can also be understood in a totally different sense, one which takes us in the direction of postmodern culture: we could say, in keeping with the perspective we adopted earlier, that this presupposition defines the set of rules one must accept in order to play the speculative game.[20] Such an appraisal assumes first that we accept that the 'positive' sciences represent the general mode of knowledge and second, that we understand this language to imply certain formal and axiomatic presuppositions that it must always make explicit. This is exactly what Nietzsche is doing, though with a different terminology, when he shows that 'European nihilism' resulted from the truth requirement of science being turned back against itself.[21]

There thus arises an idea of perspective that is not far removed, at least in this respect, from the idea of language games. What we have here is a process of delegitimation fueled by the demand for legitimation itself. The 'crisis' of scientific knowledge, signs of which have been accumulating since the end of the nineteenth century, is not born of a chance proliferation of sciences, itself an effect of progress in technology and the expansion of capitalism. It represents, rather, an internal erosion of the legitimacy principle of knowledge. There is erosion at work inside the speculative game, and by loosening the weave of the encyclopedic net in which each science was to find its place, it eventually sets them free.

The classical dividing lines between the various fields of science are thus called into question – disciplines disappear, overlappings occur at the borders between sciences, and from these new territories are born. The speculative hierarchy of learning gives way to an immanent and, as it were, 'flat' network of areas of inquiry, the respective frontiers of which are in constant flux. The old 'faculties' splinter into institutes and foundations of all kinds, and the universities lose their function of speculative legitimation. Stripped of the responsibility for research (which was stifled by the speculative narrative), they limit themselves to the transmission of what is judged to be established knowledge, and through didactics they guarantee the replication of teachers rather than the production of researchers. This is the state in which Nietzsche finds and condemns them.[22]

The potential for erosion intrinsic to the other legitimation procedure, the emancipation apparatus flowing from the *Aufklärung*, is no less extensive than the one at work within speculative discourse. But it touches a different aspect. Its distinguishing characteristic is that it grounds the legitimation of science and truth in the autonomy of interlocutors involved in ethical, social, and political praxis. As we have seen, there are immediate problems with this form of legitimation: the difference between a denotative statement with cognitive value and a prescriptive statement with practical value is one of relevance, therefore of competence. There is nothing to prove that if a statement describing a real situation is true, it follows that a prescriptive statement based upon it (the effect of which will necessarily be a modification of that reality) will be just.

Take, for example, a closed door. Between 'The door is closed' and 'Open the door' there is no relation of consequence as defined in propositional logic. The two statements belong to two autonomous sets of rules defining different kinds of relevance, and therefore of competence. Here, the effect of dividing reason into cognitive or theoretical reason on the one hand, and practical reason on the other, is to attack the legitimacy of the discourse of science. Not directly, but indirectly, by revealing that it is a language game with its own rules (of which the a priori conditions of knowledge in Kant provide a first glimpse) and that it has no special calling to supervise the game of praxis (nor the game of aesthetics, for that matter). The game of science is thus put on a par with the others.

If this 'delegitimation' is pursued in the slightest and if its scope is widened (as Wittgenstein does in his own way, and thinkers such as Martin Buber and Emmanuel Lévinas in theirs)[23] the road is then open for an important current of postmodernity: science plays its own game; it is incapable of legitimating the other language games. The game of prescription, for example, escapes it. But above all, it is incapable of legitimating itself, as speculation assumed it could.

The social subject itself seems to dissolve in this dissemination of language games. The social bond is linguistic, but is not woven with a single thread. It is a fabric formed by the intersection of at least two (and in reality an indeterminate number) of language games, obeying different rules. Wittgenstein writes: 'Our language can be seen as an ancient city: a maze of little streets and squares, of old and new houses, and of houses with additions from various periods; and this surrounded by a multitude of new boroughs with straight regular streets and uniform houses.'[24] And to drive home that the principle of unitotality – or synthesis under the authority of a metadiscourse of knowledge – is inapplicable, he subjects the 'town' of language to the old sorites paradox by asking: 'how many houses or streets does it take before a town begins to be a town?'[25]

New languages are added to the old ones, forming suburbs of the old town: 'the symbolism of chemistry and the notation of the infinitesimal calculus.'[26] Thirty-five years later we can add to the list: machine languages, the matrices of game theory, new systems of musical notation, systems of notation for nondenotative forms of logic (temporal logics, deontic logics, modal logics), the language of the genetic code, graphs of phonological structures, and so on.

We may form a pessimistic impression of this splintering: nobody speaks all of those languages, they have no universal metalanguage, the project of the system-subject is a failure, the goal of emancipation has nothing to do with science, we are all stuck in the positivism of this or that discipline of learning, the learned scholars have turned into scientists, the diminished tasks of research have become compartmentalized and no one can master them all.[27] Speculative or humanistic philosophy is forced to relinquish its legitimation duties,[28] which explains why philosophy is facing a crisis wherever it persists in arrogating such functions and is reduced to the study of systems of logic or the history of ideas where it has been realistic enough to surrender them.[29]

Turn-of-the-century Vienna was weaned on this pessimism: not just artists such as Musil, Kraus, Hofmannsthal, Loos, Schönberg, and Broch, but also the philosophers Mach and Wittgenstein.[30] They carried awareness of and theoretical and artistic responsibility for delegitimation as far as it could be taken. We can say today that the mourning process has been completed. There is no need to start all over again. Wittgenstein's strength is that he did not opt for the positivism that was being developed by the Vienna Circle,[31] but outlined in his investigation of language games a kind of legitimation not based on performativity. That is what the postmodern world is all about. Most people have lost the nostalgia for the lost narrative. It in no way follows that they are reduced to barbarity. What saves them from it is their knowledge that legitimation can only spring from their own linguistic practice and communicational interaction. Science 'smiling into its beard' at every other belief has taught them the harsh austerity of realism.[32]

Notes

1 A trace of this politics is to be found in the French institution of a philosophy class at the end of secondary studies, and in the proposal by the Groupe de recherches sur l'enseignement de la philosophie (GREPH) to teach 'some' philosophy starting at the beginning of secondary studies: see their *Qui a peur de la philosophie?* (Paris: Flammarion, 1977), sec. 2, 'La Philosophie déclassée.' This also seems to be the orientation of the curriculum of the CEGEP's in Quebec, especially of the philosophy courses (see for example the *Cahiers de l'enseignement collégial* (1975–76) for philosophy).

2 See H. Janne, 'L'Université et les besoins de la société contemporaine,' *Cahiers de*

l'Association internationale des Universités 10 (1970): 5; quoted by the Commission d'étude sur les universités, *Document de consultation* (Montréal, 1978).

3 A 'hard,' almost mystico-military expression of this can be found in Julio de Mesquita Filho, *Discorso de Paraninfo da primeiro turma de licenciados pela Faculdade de Filosofia, Ciêncas e Letras da Universidade de Saõ Paulo* (25 January 1937), and an expression of it adapted to the modern problems of Brazilian development in the *Relatorio do Grupo de Rabalho, Reforma Universitaria* (Brasilia: Ministries of Education and Culture, etc., 1968). These documents are part of a dossier on the university in Brazil, kindly sent to me by Helena C. Chamlian and Martha Ramos de Carvalho of the University of Saõ Paulo.

4 The documents are available in French thanks to Miguel Abensour and the Collège de philosophie: *Philosophes de l'Université: L'Idéalisme allemand et la question de l'université* (Paris: Payot, 1979). The collection includes texts by Schelling, Fichte, Schleiermacher, Humboldt, and Hegel.

5 'Über die innere und äussere Organisation der höheren wissenschaftlichen Anstalten in Berlin' (1810), in *Wilhelm von Humboldt* (Frankfurt, 1957), p. 126.

6 Ibid., p. 128.

7 Friedrich Schleiermacher, 'Gelegentliche Gedanken über Universitäten in deutschen Sinn, nebst einem Anhang über eine neu zu errichtende' (1808), in E. Spranger, ed., *Fichte, Schleiermacher, Steffens über das Wesen der Universität* (Leipzig, 1910), p. 126ff.

8 'The teaching of philosophy is generally recognized to be the basis of all university activity' (ibid., p. 128).

9 Alain Touraine has analyzed the contradictions involved in this transplantation in *Université et société aux Etats-Unis* (Paris: Seuil, 1972), pp. 32–40 [Eng. trans. *The Academic System in American Society* (New York: McGraw-Hill, 1974)].

10 It is present even in the conclusions of Robert Nisbet, *The Degradation of the Academic Dogma. The University in America, 1945–70* (London: Heinemann, 1971). The author is a professor at the University of California, Riverside.

11 See G. W. F. Hegel, *Philosophie des Rechts* (1821) [Eng. trans. T. M. Knox, *Hegel's Philosophy of Right* (Oxford: Oxford University Press, 1967)].

12 See Paul Ricoeur, *Le Conflit des interprétations. Essais d'herméneutique* (Paris: Seuil, 1969) [Eng. trans. Don Ihde, *The Conflict of Interpretations* (Evanston, Ill.: Northwestern University Press, 1974)]; Hans Georg Gadamer, *Wahrheit und Methode* 2d ed. (Tübingen: Mohr, 1965) [Eng. trans. Garrett Barden and John Cumming, *Truth and Method* (New York: Seabury Press, 1975)].

13 Take two statements: 1) 'The moon has risen'; 2) 'The statement/The moon has risen/is a denotative statement'. The syntagm /The moon has risen/ in statement 2 is said to be the autonym of statement 1. See Josette Rey-Debove, *Le Métalangage* (Paris: Le Robert, 1978), pt. 4.

14 Its principle is Kantian, at least in matters of transcendental ethics – see the *Critique of Practical Reason*. When it comes to politics and empirical ethics, Kant is prudent: since no one can identify himself with the transcendental normative subject, it is theoretically more exact to compromise with the existing authorities. See for example, 'Antwort an der Frage: "Was ist 'Aufklärung'?"' (1784) [Eng. trans. Lewis White Beck, in *Critique of Practical Reason and Other Writings in Moral Philosophy* (Chicago: Chicago University Press, 1949)].

15 See Kant, 'Antwort', Jürgen Habermas, *Strukturwandel der Öffentlichkeit* (Frankfurt: Luchterhand, 1962). The principle of *Öffentlichkeit* ('public' or 'publicity' in the sense of 'making public a private correspondence' or 'public debate') guided the action of many groups of scientists at the end of the 1960s, especially the group 'Survivre' (France), the group 'Scientists and Engineers for Social and Political Action' (USA), and the group 'British Society for Social Responsibility in Science.'

16 A French translation of this text by G. Granel can be found in *Phi,* supplement to the *Annales de l'université de Toulouse – Le Mirail* (Toulouse: January 1977).

17 See note 1. Certain scientific aspects of postmodernism are inventoried by Ihab Hassan in 'Culture, Indeterminacy, and Immanence: Margins of the (Postmodern) Age,' *Humanities in Society* 1 (1978): 51–85.

18 Claus Mueller uses the expression 'a process of delegitimation' in *The Politics of Communication* (New York: Oxford University Press, 1973), p. 164.

19 'Road of doubt . . . road of despair . . . skepticism,' writes Hegel in the preface to the *Phenomenology of Spirit* to describe the effect of the speculative drive on natural knowledge.

20 For fear of encumbering this account, I have postponed until a later study the exposition of this group of rules. [See 'Analyzing Speculative Discourse as Language-Game,' *The Oxford Literary Review* 4, no. 3 (1981): 59–67.]

21 Nietzsche, 'Der europäische Nihilismus' (MS. N VII 3); 'der Nihilism, ein normaler Zustand' (MS. W II 1); 'Kritik der Nihilism' (MS. W VII 3); 'Zum Plane' (MS. W II 1), in *Nietzshes Werke kritische Gesamtausgabe,* vol. 7, pts. 1 and 2 (1887–89) (Berlin: De Gruyter, 1970). These texts have been the object of a commentary by K. Ryjik, *Nietzsche, le manuscrit de Lenzer Heide* (typescript, Département de philosophie, Université de Paris VIII [Vincennes]).

22 'On the future of our educational institutions,' in *Complete Works* (note 35), vol. 3.

23 Martin Buber, *Ich und Du* (Berlin: Schocken Verlag, 1922) [Eng. trans. Ronald G. Smith, *I and Thou* (New York: Charles Scribner's Sons, 1937)], and *Dialogisches Leben* (Zürich: Müller, 1947); Emmanuel Lévinas, *Totalité et Infinité* (La Haye: Nijhoff, 1961) [Eng. trans. Alphonso Lingis, *Totality and Infinity: An Essay on Exteriority* (Pittsburgh: Duquesne University Press, 1969)], and 'Martin Buber und die Erkenntnis theorie' (1958), in *Philosophen des 20. Jahrhunderts* (Stuttgart: Kohlhammer, 1963) [Fr. trans. 'Martin Buber et la théorie de la connaissance,' in *Noms Propres* (Montpellier: Fata Morgana, 1976)].

24 *Philosophical Investigations, sec.* 18, p. 8.

25 Ibid.

26 Ibid.

27 See for example, 'La taylorisation de la recherche,' in (*Auto*) *critique de la science* (note 26), pp. 291–93. And especially D. J. de Solla Price, *Little Science, Big Science* (New York: Columbia University Press, 1963), who emphasizes the split between a small number of highly productive researchers (evaluated in terms of publication) and a large mass of researchers with low productivity. The number of the latter grows as the square of the former, so that the number of high productivity researchers only really increases every twenty years. Price concludes that science considered as a social entity is 'undemocratic' (p. 59) and that 'the eminent scientist' is a hundred years ahead of 'the minimal one' (p. 56).

28 See J. T. Desanti, 'Sur le rapport traditionnel des sciences et de la philosophie,' in *La Philosophie silencieuse, ou critique des philosophies de la science* (Paris: Seuil, 1975).

29 The reclassification of academic philosophy as one of the human sciences in this respect has a significance far beyond simply professional concerns. I do not think that philosophy as legitimation is condemned to disappear, but it is possible that it will not be able to carry out this work, or at least advance it, without revising its ties to the university institution. See on this matter the preamble to the *Projet d'un institut polytechnique de philosophie* (typescript, Département de philosophie, Université de Paris VIII [Vincennes], 1979).

30 See Allan Janik and Stephan Toulmin, *Wittgenstein's Vienna* (New York: Simon & Schuster, 1973), and J. Piel, ed., 'Vienne début d'un siècle,' *Critique,* 339–40 (1975).

31 See Jürgen Habermas, 'Dogmatismus, Vernunft unt Entscheidung – Zu Theorie

und Praxis in der verwissenschaftlichen Zivilisation' (1963), in *Theorie und Praxis* [*Theory and Practice*, abr. ed. of 4th German ed., trans. John Viertel (Boston: Beacon Press, 1971)].

32 'Science Smiling into its Beard' is the title of chap. 72, vol. 1 of Musil's *The Man Without Qualities*. Cited and discussed by J. Bouveresse, 'La Problématique du sujet' (note 54).

6.2

Fredric Jameson
from *Postmodernism or, The Cultural Logic of Late Capitalism* (1991)

II

The disappearance of the individual subject, along with its formal consequence, the increasing unavailability of the personal *style*, engender the well-nigh universal practice today of what may be called pastiche. This concept, which we owe to Thomas Mann (in *Doktor Faustus*), who owed it in turn to Adorno's great work on the two paths of advanced musical experimentation (Schoenberg's innovative planification, Stravinsky's irrational eclecticism), is to be sharply distinguished from the more readily received idea of parody.

This last found, to be sure, a fertile area in the idiosyncracies of the moderns and their 'inimitable' styles: the Faulknerian long sentence with its breathless gerundives, Lawrentian nature imagery punctuated by testy colloquialism, Wallace Stevens' inveterate hypostasis of nonsubstantive parts of speech ('the intricate evasions of as'), the fateful, but finally predictable, swoops in Mahler from high orchestral pathos into village accordeon sentiment, Heidegger's meditative-solemn practice of the false etymology as a mode of 'proof' . . . All these strike one as somehow 'characteristic', insofar as they ostentatiously deviate from a norm which then reasserts itself, in a not necessarily unfriendly way, by a systematic mimicry of their deliberate eccentricities.

Yet, in the dialectical leap from quantity to quality, the explosion of modern literature into a host of distinct private styles and mannerisms has been followed by a linguistic fragmentation of social life itself to the point where the norm itself is eclipsed: reduced to a neutral and reified media speech (far enough from the Utopian aspirations of the inventors of Esperanto or Basic English), which itself then becomes but one more idiolect among many. Modernist styles thereby become postmodernist codes: and that the stupendous proliferation of social codes today into professional and disciplinary jargons, but also into the badges of affirmation of ethnic, gender, race, religious, and class-fraction adhesion, is also a political phenomenon, the problem of micropolitics sufficiently demonstrates. If the ideas of a ruling class were once the dominant (or hegemonic) ideology of bourgeois society, the advanced capitalist countries today are now a field of stylistic and discursive heterogeneity without a norm. Faceless masters continue to inflect the economic strategies which constrain our existences, but no longer need to impose their speech (or are henceforth unable to); and the postliteracy of the late capitalist world reflects, not only the absence of any great collective project, but also the unavailability of the older national language itself.

In this situation, parody finds itself without a vocation; it has lived, and that strange new thing pastiche slowly comes to take its place. Pastiche is, like parody, the imitation of a peculiar mask, speech in a dead language: but it is a neutral practice of such mimicry, without any of parody's ulterior motives, amputated of the satiric impulse, devoid of laughter and of any conviction that alongside the abnormal tongue you have momentarily borrowed, some healthy linguistic normality still exists. Pastiche is thus blank parody, a statue with blind eyeballs: it is to parody what that other interesting and historically original modern thing, the practice of a kind of blank irony, is to what Wayne Booth calls the 'stable ironies' of the 18th century.

It would therefore begin to seem that Adorno's prophetic diagnosis has been realized, albeit in a negative way: not Schoenberg (the sterility of whose achieved system he already glimpsed) but Stravinsky is the true precursor of the postmodern cultural production. For with the collapse of the high-modernist ideology of style – what is as unique and unmistakable as your own fingerprints, as incomparable as your own body (the very source, for an early Roland Barthes, of stylistic invention and innovation) – the producers of culture have nowhere to turn but to the past: the imitation of dead styles, speech through all the masks and voices stored up in the imaginary museum of a now global culture.

This situation evidently determines what the architecture historians call 'historicism', namely the random cannibalization of all the styles of the past, the play of random stylistic allusion, and in general what Henri Lefebvre has called the increasing primacy of the 'neo'. This omnipresence of pastiche is, however, not incompatible with a certain humour (nor is it innocent of all passion) or at least with addiction – with a whole historically original consumers' appetite for a world transformed into sheer images of itself and for pseudo-events and 'spectacles' (the term of the Situationists). It is for such objects that we may reserve Plato's conception of the 'simulacrum' – the identical copy for which no original has ever existed. Appropriately enough, the culture of the simulacrum comes to *life* in a society where exchange-value has been generalized to the point at which the very memory of use-value is effaced, a society of which Guy Debord has observed, in an extraordinary phrase, that in it 'the image has become the final form of commodity reification' (*The Society of the Spectacle*).

The new spatial logic of the simulacrum can now be expected to have a momentous effect on what used to be historical time.

The past is thereby itself modified: what was once, in the historical novel as Lukács defines it, the organic genealogy of the bourgeois collective project – what is still, for the redemptive historiography of an E. P. Thompson or of American 'oral history', for the resurrection of the dead of anonymous and silenced generations, the retrospective dimension indispensable to any vital reorientation of our collective future – has meanwhile itself become a vast collection of images, a multitudinous photographic simulacrum. Guy Debord's powerful slogan is now even more apt for the 'prehistory' of a society bereft of all historicity, whose own putative past is little more than a set of dusty spectacles. In faithful conformity to poststructuralist linguistic theory, the past as 'referent' finds itself gradually bracketed, and then effaced altogether, leaving us with nothing but texts.

Yet it should not be thought that this process is accompanied by indifference: on the contrary, the remarkable current intensification of an addiction to the photographic image is itself a tangible symptom of an omnipresent, omnivorous and well-nigh libidinal historicism. The architects use this (exceedingly polysemous) word for the complacent eclecticism of postmodern architecture, which randomly and without principle but with gusto cannibalizes all the architectural styles of the past and combines them in overstimulating ensembles. Nostalgia does not strike one as an altogether satisfactory word for such fascination (particularly when one thinks of the pain of a properly modernist nostalgia with a past beyond all but aesthetic retrieval), yet it directs our attention to what is a culturally far more generalized manifestation of the process in commercial art and taste, namely the so-called 'nostalgia film' (or what the French call 'la mode rétro').

These restructure the whole issue of pastiche and project it onto a collective and social level, where the desperate attempt to appropriate a missing past is now refracted through the iron law of fashion change and the emergent ideology of the 'generation'. *American Graffiti* (1973) set out to recapture, as so many films have attempted since, the henceforth mesmerizing lost reality of the Eisenhower era: and one tends to feel that for Americans at least, the 1950s remain the privileged lost object of desire – not merely the stability and prosperity of a pax Americana, but also the first naive innocence of the countercultural impulses of early rock-and-roll and youth gangs (Coppola's *Rumble Fish* will then be the contemporary dirge that laments their passing, itself, however, still contradictorily filmed in genuine 'nostalgia film' style). With this initial breakthrough, other generational periods open up for aesthetic colonization: as witness the stylistic recuperation of the American and the Italian 1930s, in Polanski's *Chinatown* and Bertolluci's *Il Conformista* respectively. What is more interesting, and more problematical, are the ultimate attempts, through this new discourse, to lay siege either to our own present and immediate past, or to a more distant history that escapes individual existential memory.

Faced with these ultimate objects – our social, historical and existential present, and the past as 'referent' – the incompatibility of a postmodernist 'nostalgia' art language with genuine historicity becomes dramatically apparent. The contraction propels this model, however, into complex and interesting new formal inventiveness: it being understood that the nostalgia film was never a matter of some old-fashioned 'representation' of historical content, but approached the 'past' through stylistic connotation, conveying 'pastness' by the glossy qualities of the image, and '1930s-ness' or '1950s-ness' by the attributes of fashion (therein following the prescription of the Barthes of *Mythologies*, who saw connotation as the purveying of imaginary and stereotypical idealities, 'Sinité', for example, as some Disney-EPCOT 'concept' of China).

The insensible colonization of the present by the nostalgia mode can be observed in Lawrence Kazdan's elegant film, *Body Heat*, a distant 'affluent society' remake of James M. Cain's *The Postman Always Rings Twice*, set in a contemporary Florida small town not far from Miami. The word 'remake' is, however, anachronistic to the degree to which our awareness of the pre-existence of other versions, previous films of the novel as well as the novel itself, is now a constitutive and essential part of the film's structure: we are now, in other words, in 'intertextuality' as a deliberate, built-in feature of the aesthetic effect, and as the operator of a new connotation of 'pastness' and pseudo-historical depth, in which the history of aesthetic styles displaces 'real' history.

Yet from the outset a whole battery of aesthetic signs begin to distance the officially contemporary image from us in time: the art deco scripting of the credits, for example, serves at once to programme the spectator for the appropriate 'nostalgia' mode of reception (art deco quotation has much the same function in contemporary architecture, as in Toronto's remarkable Eaton Centre). Meanwhile, a somewhat different play of connotations is activated by complex (but purely formal) allusions to the institutions of the star system itself. The protagonist, William Hurt, is one of a new generation of film 'stars' whose status is markedly distinct from that of the preceding generation of male superstars, such as Steve McQueen or Jack Nicholson (or even, more distantly, Brando), let alone of earlier moments in the evolution of the institutions of the star. The immediately preceding generation projected its various roles through, and by way of, well-known 'off-screen' personalities, who often connoted rebellion and non-conformism. The latest generation of starring actors continues to assure the conventional functions of stardom (most notably, sexuality) but in the utter absence of 'personality' in the older sense, and with something of the anonymity of character acting (which in actors like Hurt reaches virtuoso proportions, yet of a very different kind from the virtuosity of the older Brando or Olivier). This 'death of the subject' in the institution of the star, however, opens up the possibility of a play of historical allusions to much older roles – in this case to those associated with Clark Gable – so that the very style of the acting can now also serve as a 'connotator' of the past.

Finally, the setting has been strategically framed, with great ingenuity, to eschew most of the signals that normally convey the contemporaneity of the United States in its multinational era: the small-town setting allows the camera to elude the high-rise landscape of the 1970s and 80s (even though a key episode in the narrative involves the fatal destruction of older buildings by land speculators); while the object world of the present-day – artifacts and appliances, even automobiles, whose styling would at once serve to date the image – is elaborately edited out. Everything in the film, therefore, conspires to blur its official contemporaneity and to make it possible for you to receive the narrative as though it were set in some eternal Thirties, beyond real historical time. The approach to the present by way of the art language of the simulacrum, or of the pastiche of the stereotypical past, endows present reality and the openness of present history with the spell and distance of a glossy mirage. But this mesmerizing new aesthetic mode itself emerged as an elaborated symptom of the waning of our historicity, of our lived possibility of experiencing history in some active way: it cannot therefore be said to produce this strange occultation of the present by its own formal power, but merely to demonstrate, through these inner contradictions, the enormity of a situation in which we seem increasingly incapable of fashioning representations of our own current experience.

As for 'real history' itself – the traditional object, however it may be defined, of what used to be the historical novel – it will be more revealing now to turn back to that older form and medium and to read its postmodern fate in the work of one of the few serious and innovative Left novelists at work in the United States today, whose books are nourished with history in the more traditional sense, and seem, so far, to stake out successive generational moments in the 'epic' of American history. E. L. Doctorow's *Ragtime* gives itself officially as a panorama of the first two decades of the century; his most recent novel, *Loon Lake*, addresses the Thirties and the Great Depression; while *The Book of Daniel* holds up before us, in painful juxtaposition, the two great moments of the Old Left and the New Left, of Thirties and Forties Communism and the radicalism of the 1960s (even his early Western may be said to fit into this scheme and to designate in a less articulated and formally self-conscious way the end of the frontier of the late nineteenth century).

The Book of Daniel is not the only one of these three major historical novels to establish an explicit narrative link between the reader's and the writer's present and the older historical reality which is the subject of the work; the astonishing last page of *Loon Lake*, which I will not disclose, also does this in a very different way; while it is a matter of some interest to note that the first sentence of the first version of *Ragtime* positions us explicitly in our own present, in the novelist's house in New Rochelle, New York, which will then at once become the scene of its own (imaginary) past in the 1900s. This detail has been suppressed from the published text, symbolically cutting its moorings and freeing the novel to float in some new world of past historical time whose relationship to us is problematical indeed. The authenticity of the gesture, however, may be measured by the evident existential fact of life that there no longer does seem to be any organic relationship between the American history we learn from the schoolbooks and the lived experience of the current multinational, high-rise, stagflated city of the newspapers and of our own daily life.

A crisis in historicity, however, inscribes itself symptomatically in several other curious formal features within this text. Its official subject is the transition from a pre-World-War I radical and working-class politics (the great strikes) to the technological invention and new commodity production of the 1920s (the rise of Hollywood and of the image as commodity): the interpolated version of Kleist's *Michael Kohlhaas*, the strange tragic episode of the Black protagonist's revolt, may be thought to be a moment related to this process. My point, however, is not some hypothesis as to the thematic coherence of this decentred narrative; but rather just the opposite, namely the way in which the kind of reading this novel imposes makes it virtually impossible for us to reach and to thematize those official 'subjects' which float above the text but cannot be integrated into our reading of the sentences. In that sense, not only does the novel resist interpretation, it is organized systematically and formally to short-circuit an older type of social and historical interpretation which it perpetually holds out and withdraws. When we remember that the theoretical critique and repudiation of interpretation as such is a fundamental component of poststructuralist theory, it is difficult not to conclude that Doctorow has somehow deliberately built this very tension, this very contradiction, into the flow of his sentences.

As is well known, the book is crowded with real historical figures – from Teddy Roosevelt to Emma Goldman, from Harry K. Thaw and Sandford White to J. Pierpont Morgan and Henry Ford, not to speak of the more central role of Houdini – who interact with a fictive family, simply designated as Father, Mother, Older Brother, and so forth. All historical novels, beginning with Scott himself, no doubt in one way or another involve a mobilization of previous historical knowledge, generally acquired through the schoolbook history manuals devised for whatever legitimizing purpose by this or that national tradition – thereafter instituting a narrative dialectic between what we already 'know' about The Pretender, say, and what he is then seen to be concretely in the pages of the novel. But Doctorow's procedure seems much more extreme than this; and I would argue that the designation of both types of characters – historical names or capitalized family roles – operates powerfully and systematically to reify all these characters and to make it impossible for us to receive their representation without the prior interception of already-acquired knowledge or doxa – something which lends the text an extraordinary sense of déjà-vu and a peculiar familiarity one is tempted to associate with Freud's 'return of the repressed' in 'The Uncanny', rather than with any solid historiographic formation on the reader's part.

Meanwhile, the sentences in which all this is happening have their own specificity, which will allow us a little more concretely to distinguish the moderns' elaboration of a personal style from this new kind of linguistic innovation, which is no longer personal at all but has its family kinship rather with what Barthes long ago called 'white writing'. In this particular novel, Doctorow has imposed upon himself a rigorous principle of selection in which only simple declarative sentences (predominantly mobilized by the verb 'to be') are received. The effect is, however, not really one of the condescending simplification and symbolic carefulness of children's literature, but rather something more disturbing, the sense of some profound sub-terranean violence done to American English which cannot, however, be detected empirically in any of the perfectly grammatical sentences with which this work is formed. Yet other more visible technical 'innovations' may supply a clue to what is happening in the language of *Ragtime*: it is for example well-known that the source of many of the characteristic effects of Camus' novel *Étranger* can be traced back to that author's wilful decision to substitute, throughout, the French tense of the 'passé composé' for the other past tenses more normally employed in narration in that language. I will suggest that it is *as if* something of that sort were at work here (without committing myself further to what is obviously an outrageous leap): it is, I say, *as though* Doctorow had set out systematically to produce the effect or the equivalent, in his language, of a verbal past tense we do not possess in English, namely the French preterite (or *passé simple*), whose 'perfective' movement, as Émile Benveniste taught us, serves to separate events from the present of enunciation and to transform the stream of time and action into so many finished, complete, and isolated punctual event-objects which find themselves sundered from any present situation (even that of the act of storytelling or enunciation).

E. L. Doctorow is the epic poet of the disappearance of the American radical past, of the suppression of older traditions and moments of the American radical tradition: no one with left sympathies can read these splendid novels without a poignant distress which is an authentic way of confronting our own current political dilemmas in the present. What is culturally interesting, however, is that he has had to convey this great theme formally (since the waning of the content is very precisely his subject), and, more than that, has had to elaborate his work by way of that very cultural logic of the postmodern which is itself the mark and symptom of his dilemma. *Loon Lake* much more obviously deploys the strategies of the pastiche (most notably in its reinvention of Dos Passos); but *Ragtime* remains the most peculiar and stunning monument to the aesthetic situation engendered by the disappearance of the historical referent. This historical novel can no longer set out to represent the historical past; it can only 'represent' our ideas and stereotypes about that past (which thereby at once becomes 'pop history'). Cultural production is thereby driven back inside a mental space which is no longer that of the old monadic subject, but rather that of some degraded collective 'objective spirit': it can no longer gaze directly on some putative real world, at some reconstruction of a past history which was once itself a present; rather, as in Plato's cave, it must trace our mental images of that past upon its confining walls. If there is any realism left here, therefore, it is a 'realism' which is meant to derive from the shock of grasping that confinement, and of slowly becoming aware of a new and original historical situation in which we are condemned to seek History by way of our own pop images and simulacra of that history, which itself remains forever out of reach.

6.3

Jean Baudrillard
from *Simulations* (1983)

The simulacrum is never that which conceals the truth – it is the truth which conceals that there is none.
The simulacrum is true.

Ecclesiastes

If we were able to take as the finest allegory of simulation the Borges tale where the cartographers of the Empire draw up a map so detailed that it ends up exactly covering the territory (but where the decline of the Empire sees this map become frayed and finally ruined, a few shreds still discernible in the deserts – the metaphysical beauty of this ruined abstraction, bearing witness to an Imperial pride and rotting like a carcass, returning to the substance of the soil, rather as an aging double ends up being confused with the real thing) – then this fable has come full circle for us, and now has nothing but the discrete charm of second-order simulacra.[1]

Abstraction today is no longer that of the map, the double, the mirror or the concept. Simulation is no longer that of a territory, a referential being or a substance. It is the generation by models of a real without origin or reality: a hyperreal. The territory no longer precedes the map, nor survives it. Henceforth, it is the map that precedes the territory – PRECESSION OF SIMULACRA – it is the map that engenders the territory and if we were to revive the fable today, it would be the territory whose shreds are slowly rotting across the map. It is the real, and not the map, whose vestiges subsist here and there, in the deserts which are no longer those of the Empire, but our own. *The desert of the real itself.*

In fact, even inverted, the fable is useless. Perhaps only the allegory of the Empire remains. For it is with the same Imperialism that present-day simulators try to make the real, all the real, coincide with their simulation models. But it is no longer a question of either maps or territory. Something has disappeared: the sovereign difference between them that was the abstraction's charm. For it is the difference which forms the poetry of the map and the charm of the territory, the magic of the concept and the charm of the real. This representational imaginary, which both culminates in and is engulfed by the cartographer's mad project of an ideal coextensivity between the map and the territory, disappears with simulation – whose operation is nuclear and genetic, and no longer specular and discursive. With it goes all of metaphysics. No more mirror of being and appearances, of the real and its concept. No more imaginary coextensivity: rather, genetic miniaturisation is the dimension of simulation. The real is produced from miniaturised units, from matrices, memory banks and command models – and with these it can be reproduced an indefinite number of times. It no longer has to be rational, since it is no longer measured against some ideal or negative instance. It is nothing more than operational. In fact, since it is no longer enveloped by an imaginary, it is no longer real at all. It is a hyperreal, the product of an irradiating synthesis of combinatory models in a hyperspace without atmosphere.

In this passage to a space whose curvature is no longer that of the real, nor of truth, the age of simulation thus begins with a liquidation of all referentials – worse: by their artificial resurrection in systems of signs, a more ductile material than meaning, in that it lends itself to all systems of equivalence, all binary oppositions and all combinatory algebra. It is no longer a question of imitation, nor of reduplication, nor even of parody. It is rather a question of substituting signs of the real for the real itself, that is, an operation to deter every real process by its operational double, a metastable, programmatic, perfect descriptive machine which provides all the signs of the real and short-circuits all its vicissitudes. Never again will the real have to be produced – this is the vital function of the model in a system of death, or rather of anticipated resurrection which no longer leaves any chance even in the event of death. A hyperreal henceforth sheltered from the imaginary, and from any distinction between the real and the imaginary, leaving room only for the orbital recurrence of models and the simulated generation of difference.

Hyperreal and imaginary

Disneyland is a perfect model of all the entangled orders of simulation. To begin with it is a play of illusions and phantasms: Pirates, the Frontier, Future World, etc. This imaginary world is supposed to be what makes the operation successful. But what draws the crowds is undoubtedly much more the social microcosm, the miniaturised and *religious* revelling in real America, in its delights and drawbacks. You park outside, queue up inside, and are totally abandoned at the exit. In this imaginary world the only phantasmagoria is in the inherent warmth and affection of the crowd, and in that sufficiently excessive number of gadgets used there to specifically maintain the multitudinous affect. The contrast with the absolute solitude of the parking lot – a veritable concentration camp – is total. Or rather: inside, a whole range of gadgets magnetise the crowd into direct flows – outside, solitude is directed onto a single gadget: the automobile. By an extraordinary coincidence (one that undoubtedly belongs to the peculiar enchantment of this universe), this deep-frozen infantile world happens to have been conceived and realised by a man who is himself now cryogenised: Walt Disney, who awaits his resurrection at minus 180 degrees centigrade.

The objective profile of America, then, may be traced throughout Disneyland, even down to the morphology of individuals and the crowd. All its values are exalted here, in miniature and comic strip form. Embalmed and pacified. Whence the possibility of an ideological analysis of Disneyland (L. Marin does it well in *Utopies, jeux d'espaces*): digest of the American way of life, panegyric to American values, idealised transposition of a contradictory reality. To be sure. But this conceals something else, and that 'ideological' blanket exactly serves to cover over a *third-order simulation*: Disneyland is there to conceal the fact that it is the 'real' country, all of 'real' America, which *is* Disneyland (just as prisons are there to conceal the fact that it is the social in its entirety, in its banal omnipresence, which is carceral). Disneyland is presented as imaginary in order to make us believe that the rest is real, when in fact all of Los Angeles and the America surrounding it are no longer real, but of the order of the hyperreal and of simulation. It is no longer a question of a false representation of reality (ideology), but of concealing the fact that the real is no longer real, and thus of saving the reality principle.

The Disneyland imaginary is neither true nor false; it is a deterrence machine set up in order to rejuvenate in reverse the fiction of the real. Whence the debility, the infantile degeneration of this imaginary. It is meant to be an infantile world, in order to make us believe that the adults are elsewhere, in the 'real' world, and to conceal the fact that real childishness is everywhere, particularly amongst those adults who go there to act the child in order to foster illusions as to their real childishness.

Moreover, Disneyland is not the only one. Enchanted Village, Magic Mountain, Marine World: Los Angeles is encircled by these 'imaginary stations' which feed reality, reality-energy, to a town whose mystery is precisely that it is nothing more than a network of endless, unreal circulation – a town of fabulous proportions, but without space or dimensions. As much as electrical and nuclear power stations, as much as film studios, this town, which is nothing more than an immense script and a perpetual motion picture, needs this old imaginary made up of childhood signals and faked phantasms for its sympathetic nervous system.

Note

1 Cf. J. Baudrillard, *L'échange symbolique et la mort* ('L'ordre des simulacres') (Paris: Gallimard, 1975).

Section seven

DOCUMENTS IN CULTURAL THEORY

Introduction

The debate about culture is ongoing and extensive, and the extracts collected together in this volume represent a particular kind of intervention within that debate. We have been concerned throughout to provide a range of introductions to the kinds of analyses of cultural texts which are available, and we consider useful, to the student of critical and cultural theory today. But these have also been carefully selected to reflect another concern: that the discipline of critical and cultural theory itself encompasses the analysis of the texts of high and popular culture together in an effort finally to deconstruct the divisions between them.

The high-culture/popular-culture split has fuelled an exhaustive debate amongst critics working in areas which include music, art and writing as well as social, historical and political studies, and has given rise to a number of documents concerning the nature of culture itself. We could not hope to represent them all. What we have selected here are just a few (five in all) of what may be the more interesting and influential of those documents in order to begin to introduce some of the positions taken up within the larger debate.

Amongst the extracts selected, four basic positions emerge. For F. R. Leavis, the primary concern is clearly to define and defend the terrain of high culture. Worried by the instabilities of British society after the First World War, his writing strongly invokes the calming reassurance of an élite canon of literary texts establishing timeless human values in the face of an unruly and threatening mass. Within Leavis's terms, high culture must be rigorously distinguished from popular culture and always from the position of the high cultural élite. Theodore Adorno maintains the split between high and popular culture, but develops his own analysis of popular music as a form of entertainment consumed by the labouring classes. Although he focuses upon the popular, he does so from his own position within the domain of high culture. Raymond Williams's primary concern, on the other hand, is to oppose the distinction drawn between the terms of high and popular culture. He reminds us of the élitism inherent within the terms 'culture' and 'popular', where culture has really come to mean the privileging of a high élite of art and literature, leaving the concept of working-class culture as virtually non-existent. And last there is Tristan Tzara's description of Dada performances in Paris in 1920. Although the shock of Dada reveals its dependence on the high culture it opposes, the account nevertheless invokes the power of cultural texts themselves as forms of action; they intervene against the reproduction of high art in an effort to expose and deconstruct the élitism it maintains. Though limited, it is a precedent many have warmed to since 1920.

7.1

F. R. Leavis
from *Mass Civilisation and Minority Culture* (1930)

In any period it is upon a very small minority that the discerning appreciation of art and literature depends: it is (apart from cases of the simple and familiar) only a few who are capable of unprompted, first-hand judgment. They are still a small minority, though a larger one, who are capable of endorsing such first-hand judgment by genuine personal response. The accepted valuations are a kind of paper currency based upon a very small proportion of gold. To the state of such a currency the possibilities of fine living at any time bear a close relation. There is no need to elaborate the metaphor: the nature of the relation is suggested well enough by this passage from Mr. I. A. Richards, which should by now be a *locus classicus*:

> But it is not true that criticism is a luxury trade. The rearguard of Society cannot be extricated until the vanguard has gone further. Goodwill and intelligence are still too little available. The critic, we have said, is as much concerned with the health of the mind as any doctor with the health of the body. To set up as a critic is to set up as a judge of values . . . For the arts are inevitably and quite apart from any intentions of the artist an appraisal of existence. Matthew Arnold, when he said that poetry is a criticism of life, was saying something so obvious that it is constantly overlooked. The artist is concerned with the record and perpetuation of the experiences which seem to him most worth having. For reasons which we shall consider . . . he is also the man who is most likely to have experiences of value to record. He is the point at which the growth of the mind shows itself.[1]

This last sentence gives the hint for another metaphor. The minority capable not only of appreciating Dante, Shakespeare, Donne, Baudelaire,

Hardy (to take major instances) but of recognising their latest successors constitute the consciousness of the race (or of a branch of it) at a given time. For such capacity does not belong merely to an isolated aesthetic realm: it implies responsiveness to theory as well as to art, to science and philosophy in so far as these may affect the sense of the human situation and of the nature of life. Upon this minority depends our power of profiting by the finest human experience of the past; they keep alive the subtlest and most perishable parts of tradition. Upon them depend the implicit standards that order the finer living of an age, the sense that this is worth more than that, this rather than that is the direction in which to go, that the centre is here rather than there. In their keeping, to use a metaphor that is metonymy also and will bear a good deal of pondering, is the language, the changing idiom, upon which fine living depends, and without which distinction of spirit is thwarted and incoherent. By 'culture' I mean the use of such a language. I do not suppose myself to have produced a tight definition, but the account, I think, will be recognised as adequate by anyone who is likely to read this pamphlet.

Note

1 I. A. Richards, *The Principles of Literary Criticism* (London: Routledge & Kegan Paul, 1924), pp. 60–1.

7.2

Theodore Adorno from 'On Popular Music' (1941)

The musical material

The two spheres of music

Popular music, which produces the stimuli we are here investigating, is usually characterized by its difference from serious music. This difference is generally taken for granted and is looked upon as a difference of levels considered so well defined that most people regard the values within them as totally independent of one another. We deem it necessary, however, first of all to translate these so-called levels into more precise terms, musical as well as social, which not only delimit them unequivocally but throw light upon the whole setting of the two musical spheres as well.

One possible method of achieving this clarification would be an historical analysis of the division as it occurred in music production and of the roots of the two main spheres. Since, however, the present study is concerned with the actual function of popular music in its present status, it is more advisable to follow the line of characterization of the phenomenon itself as it is given today than to trace it back to its origins. This is the more justified as the division into the two spheres of music took place in Europe long before American popular music arose. American music from its inception accepted the division as something pre-given, and therefore the historical background of the division applies to it only indirectly. Hence we seek, first of all, an insight into the fundamental characteristics of popular music in the broadest sense.

A clear judgment concerning the relation of serious music to popular music can be arrived at only by strict attention to the fundamental characteristic of popular music: standardization.[1] The whole structure of popular music is standardized, even where the attempt is made to circumvent standardization. Standardization extends from the most general features to the most specific ones. Best known is the rule that the chorus consists of thirty-two bars and that the range is limited to one octave and one note. The general types of hits are also standardized: not only the dance types, the rigidity of whose pattern is understood, but also the 'characters' such as mother songs, home songs, nonsense or 'novelty' songs, pseudo-nursery rhymes, laments for a lost girl. Most important of all, the harmonic cornerstones of each hit – the beginning and the end of each part – must beat out the standard scheme. This scheme emphasizes the most primitive harmonic facts no matter what has harmonically intervened. Complications have no consequences. This inexorable device guarantees that regardless of what aberrations occur, the hit will lead back to the same familiar experience, and nothing fundamentally novel will be introduced.

The details themselves are standardized no less than the form, and a whole terminology exists for them such as break, blue chords, dirty notes. Their standardization, however, is somewhat different from that of the framework. It is not overt like the latter but hidden behind a veneer of individual 'effects' whose prescriptions are handled as the experts' secret, however open this secret may be to musicians generally. This contrasting character of the standardization of the whole and part provides a rough, preliminary setting for the effect upon the listener.

The primary effect of this relation between the framework and the detail is that the listener becomes prone to evince stronger reactions to the part than to the whole. His grasp of the whole does not lie in the living experience of this one concrete piece of music he has followed. The whole is pre-given and pre-accepted, even before the actual experience of the music starts: therefore, it is not likely to influence, to any great extent, the reaction to the details, except to give them varying degrees of emphasis. Details which occupy musically strategic positions in the framework – the beginning of the chorus or its re-entrance after the bridge – have a better chance for recognition and favourable reception than details not so situated, for instance, middle bars of the bridge. But this situational nexus never interferes with the scheme itself. To this limited situational extent the detail depends upon the whole. But no stress is ever placed upon the whole as a musical event, nor does the structure of the whole ever depend upon the details.

Serious music, for comparative purposes, may be thus characterized:

Every detail derives its musical sense from the concrete totality of the piece which, in turn, consists of the life relationship of the details and never of a mere enforcement of a musical scheme. For example, in the introduction of the first movement of Beethoven's Seventh Symphony the second theme (in C-major) gets its true meaning only from the context. Only through the whole does it acquire its particular lyrical and expressive quality – that is, a whole built up of its very contrast with the *cantus firmus*-like character of the first theme. Taken in isolation the second theme would be disrobed to insignific-ance. Another example may be found in the beginning of the recapitulation over the pedal point of the first movement of Beethoven's 'Appassionata'. By following the preceding outburst it achieves the utmost dramatic momentum. By omitting the exposition and development and starting with this repetition, all is lost.

Nothing corresponding to this can happen in popular music. It would not affect the musical sense if any detail were taken out of the context; the listener can supply the 'framework' automatically, since it is a mere musical automatism itself. The beginning of the chorus is replaceable by the beginning of innumerable other choruses. The interrelationship among the elements or the relationship of the elements to the whole would be unaffected. In Beethoven, position is important only in a living relation between a concrete totality and its concrete parts. In popular music, position is absolute. Every detail is substitutable; it serves its function only as a cog in a machine.

The mere establishment of this difference is not yet sufficient. It is possible to object that the far-reaching standard schemes and types of popular music are bound up with dance, and therefore are also applicable to dance-derivatives in serious music, for example, the minuetto and scherzo of the classical Viennese School. It may be maintained either that this part of serious music is also to be comprehended in terms of detail rather than of whole, or that if the whole still is perceivable in the dance types in serious music despite recurrence of the types, there is no reason why it should not be perceivable in modern popular music.

The following consideration provides an answer to both objections by showing the radical differences even where serious music employs dance-types. According to current formalistic views the scherzo of Beethoven's Fifth Symphony can be regarded as a highly stylized minuetto. What Beethoven takes from the traditional minuetto scheme in this scherzo is the idea of outspoken contrast between a minor minuetto, a major trio, and repetition of the minor minuetto; and also certain other characteristics such as the emphatic three-fourths rhythm often accentuated on the first fourth and, by and large, dance-like symmetry in the sequence of bars and periods. But the specific form-idea of this movement as a concrete totality transvaluates the devices borrowed from the minuetto scheme. The whole movement is conceived as an introduction to the finale in order to create tremendous tension, not only by its threatening, foreboding expression but even more by the very way in which its formal development is handled.

The classical minuetto scheme required first the appearance of the main theme, then the introduction of a second part which may lead to more distant tonal regions – formalistically similar, to be sure, to the 'bridge' of today's popular music – and finally the recurrence of the original part. All this occurs in Beethoven. He takes up the idea of thematic dualism within the scherzo part. But he forces what was, in the conventional minuetto, a mute and meaningless game-rule to speak with meaning. He achieves complete consistency between the formal structure and its specific content, that is to say, the elaboration of its themes. The whole scherzo part of this scherzo (that is to say, what occurs before the entrance of the deep strings in C-major that marks the beginning of the trio), consists of the dualism of two themes, the creeping figure in the strings and the 'objective', stone-like answer of the wind instruments. This dualism is not developed in a schematic way so that first the phrase of the strings is elaborated, then the answer of the winds, and then the string theme is mechanically repeated. After the first occurrence of the second theme in the horns, the two essential elements are alternately interconnected in the manner of a dialogue, and the end of the scherzo part is actually marked, not by the first, but by the second theme which has overwhelmed the first musical phrase.

Furthermore, the repetition of the scherzo after the trio is scored so differently that it sounds like a mere shadow of the scherzo and assumes that haunting character which vanishes only with the affirmative entry of the Finale theme. The whole device has been made dynamic. Not only the themes, but the musical form itself have been subjected to tension: the same tension which is already manifest within the two-fold structure of the first theme that consists, as it were, of question and reply, and then even more manifest within the context between the two main themes. The whole scheme has become subject to the inherent demands of this particular movement.

To sum up the difference: in Beethoven and in good serious music in general – we are not concerned here with bad serious music which may be as rigid and mechanical as popular music – the detail virtually contains the whole and leads to the exposition of the whole, while, at the same time, it is produced out of the conception of the whole. In popular music the relationship is fortuitous. The detail has no bearing on a whole, which appears as an extraneous framework. Thus, the whole is never altered by the individual event and therefore remains, as it were, aloof, imperturbable, and unnoticed throughout the piece. At the same time, the detail is mutilated by a device which it can never influence and alter, so that the detail remains inconsequential. A musical detail which is not permitted to develop becomes a caricature of its own potentialities.

Standardization

The previous discussion shows that the difference between popular and serious music can be grasped in more precise terms than those referring to musical levels such as 'lowbrow and highbrow', 'simple and complex', 'naive and sophisticated'. For example, the difference between the spheres cannot be adequately expressed in terms of complexity and simplicity. All works of the earlier Viennese classicism are, without exception, rhythmically simpler than stock arrangements of jazz. Melodically, the wide intervals of a good many hits such as 'Deep Purple' or 'Sunrise Serenade' are more difficult to follow *per se* than most melodies of, for example, Haydn, which consist mainly of circumscriptions of tonic triads, and second steps. Harmonically, the supply of chords of the so-called classics is invariably more limited than that of any current Tin Pan Alley composer who draws from Debussy, Ravel, and even later sources. Standardization and non-standardization are the key contrasting terms for the difference.

Structural standardization aims at standard reactions. Listening to popular music is manipulated not only by its promoters, but as it were, by the inherent nature of this music itself, into a system of response-mechanisms wholly antagonistic to the ideal of individuality in a free, liberal society. This has nothing to do with simplicity and complexity. In serious music, each musical element, even the simplest one, is 'itself', and the more highly organized the work is, the less possibility there is of substitution among the details. In hit music, however, the structure underlying the piece is abstract, existing independent of the specific course of the music. This is basic to the illusion that certain complex harmonies are more easily understandable in popular music than the same harmonies in serious music. For the complicated in popular music never functions as 'itself' but only as a disguise or embellishment behind which the scheme can always be perceived. In jazz the amateur listener is capable of replacing complicated rhythmical or harmonic formulas by the schematic ones which they represent and which they still suggest, however adventurous they appear. The ear deals with the difficulties of hit music by achieving slight substitutions derived from the knowledge of the patterns. The listener, when faced with the complicated, actually hears only the simple which it represents and perceives the complicated only as a parodistic distortion of the simple.

No such mechanical substitution by stereotyped patterns is possible in serious music. Here even the simplest event necessitates an effort to grasp it immediately instead of summarizing it vaguely according to institutionalized prescriptions capable of producing only institutionalized effects. Otherwise the music is not 'understood'. Popular music, however, is composed in such a way that the process of translation of the unique into the norm is already planned and, to a certain extent, achieved within the composition itself.

The composition hears for the listener. This is how popular music divests the listener of his spontaneity and promotes conditioned reflexes. Not only does it not require his effort to follow its concrete stream; it actually gives him models under which anything concrete still remaining may be subsumed. The schematic build-up dictates the way in which he must listen while, at the same time, it makes any effort in listening unnecessary. Popular music is 'pre-digested' in a way strongly resembling the fad of 'digests' of printed material. It is this structure of contemporary popular music, which in the last analysis, accounts for those changes of listening habits which we shall later discuss.

So far standardization of popular music has been considered in structural terms – that is, as an inherent quality without explicit reference to the process of production or to the underlying causes for standardization. Though all industrial mass production necessarily eventuates in standardization, the production of popular music can be called 'industrial' only in its promotion and distribution, whereas the act of producing a song-hit still remains in a handicraft stage. The production of popular music is highly centralized in its economic organization, but still 'individualistic' in its social mode of production. The division of labour among the composer, harmonizer, and arranger is not industrial but rather pretends industrialization, in order to look more up-to-date, whereas it has actually adapted industrial methods for the technique of its promotion. It would not increase the costs of production if the various composers of hit tunes did not follow certain standard patterns. Therefore, we must look for other reasons for structural standardization – very different reasons from those which account for the standardization of motor cars and breakfast foods.

Imitation offers a lead for coming to grips with the basic reasons for it. The musical standards of popular music were originally developed by a competitive process. As one particular song scored a great success, hundreds of others sprang up imitating the successful one. The most successful hits, types, and 'ratios' between elements were imitated, and the process culminated in the crystallization of standards. Under centralized conditions such as exist today these standards have become 'frozen'.[2] That is, they have been taken over by cartelized agencies, the final results of a competitive process, and rigidly enforced upon material to be promoted. Non-compliance with the rules of the game became the basis for exclusion. The original patterns that are now standardized evolved in a more or less competitive way. Large-scale economic concentration institutionalized the standardization, and made it imperative. As a result, innovations by rugged individualists have been outlawed. The standard patterns have become invested with the immunity of bigness – 'the King can do no wrong'. This also accounts for revivals in popular music. They do not have the outworn character of standardized products manufactured after a given pattern. The breath of free competition is still alive within them. On the other hand, the famous old hits which are revived set the patterns which have become standardized. They are the golden age of the game-rules.

This 'freezing' of standards is socially enforced upon the agencies themselves. Popular music must simultaneously meet two demands. One is for stimuli that provoke the listener's attention. The other is for the material to fall within the category of what the musically untrained listener would call 'natural' music: that is, the sum total of all the conventions and material formulas in music to which he is accustomed and which he regards as the inherent, simple language or music itself, no matter how late the development might be which produced this natural language. This natural language for the American listener stems from his earliest musical experiences, the nursery rhymes, the hymns he sings in Sunday school, the little tunes he whistles on his way home from school. All these are vastly more important in the formation of musical language than his ability to distinguish the beginning of Brahms' Third Symphony from that of his Second. Official musical culture is, to a large extent, a mere superstructure of this underlying musical language, namely the major and minor tonality and all the tonal relationships it implies. But these tonal relationships of the primitive musical language set barriers to whatever does not conform to them. Extravagances are tolerated only in so far as they can be recast into this so-called natural language.

In terms of consumer-demand, the standardization of popular music is only the expression of this dual desideratum imposed upon it by the musical frame of mind of the public – that it be 'stimulatory' by deviating in some way from the established 'natural', and that it maintain the supremacy of the natural against such deviations. The attitude of the audience toward the natural language is reinforced by standardized production, which institutionalizes desiderata which originally might have come from the public.

Pseudo-individualization

The paradox in the desiderata – stimulatory and natural – accounts for the dual character of standardization itself. Stylization of the ever identical framework is only one aspect of standardization. Concentration and control in our culture hide themselves in their very manifestation. Unhidden they would provoke resistance. Therefore the illusion and, to a certain extent, even the reality of individual achievement must be maintained. The maintenance of it is grounded in material reality itself, for while administrative control over life processes is concentrated, ownership is still diffuse.

In the sphere of luxury production, to which popular music belongs and in which no necessities of life are immediately involved, while, at the same time, the residues of individualism are most alive there in the form of ideological categories such as taste and free choice, it is imperative to hide standardization. The 'backwardness' of musical mass production, the fact that it is still on a handicraft level and not literally an industrial one, conforms perfectly to that necessity which is essential from the viewpoint of cultural big business. If the individual handicraft elements of popular music were abolished altogether, a synthetic means of hiding standardization would have to be evolved. Its elements are even now in existence.

The necessary correlate of musical standardization is *pseudo-individualization*. By pseudo-individualization we mean endowing cultural mass production with the halo of free choice or open market on the basis of standardization itself. Standardization of song hits keeps the customers in line by doing their listening for them, as it were. Pseudo-individualization, for its part, keeps them in line by making them forget that what they listen to is already listened to for them, or 'pre-digested'.

The most drastic example of standardization of presumably individualized features is to be found in so-called improvisations. Even though jazz musicians still improvise in practice, their improvisations have become so 'normalized' as to enable a whole terminology to be developed to express the standard devices of individualization: a terminology which in turn is ballyhooed by jazz publicity agents to foster the myth of pioneer artisanship and at the same time flatter the fans by apparently allowing them to peep behind the curtain and get the inside story. This pseudo-individualization is prescribed by the standardization of the framework. The latter is so rigid that the freedom it allows for any sort of improvisation is severely delimited. Improvisations – passages where spontaneous action of individuals is permitted ('Swing it boys') – are confined within the walls of the harmonic and metric scheme. In a great many cases, such as the 'break' or pre-swing jazz, the musical function of the improvised detail is determined completely by the scheme: the break can be nothing other than a disguised cadence. Here, very few possibilities for actual improvisation remain, due to the necessity of merely melodically circumscribing the same underlying harmonic functions. Since these possibilities were very quickly exhausted, stereotyping of improvisatory details speedily occurred. Thus, standardization of the norm enhances in a purely technical way standardization of its own deviation – pseudo-individualization.

This subservience of improvisation to standardization explains two main socio-psychological qualities of popular music. One is the fact that the detail remains openly connected with the underlying scheme so that the listener always feels on safe ground. The choice in individual alterations is so small that the perpetual recurrence of the same variations is a reassuring signpost of the identical behind them. The other is the function of 'substitution' – the improvisatory features forbid their being grasped as musical events in themselves. They can be received only as embellishments. It is a well-known fact that in daring jazz arrangements worried notes, dirty notes, in other words, false notes, play a conspicuous role. They are apperceived as exciting stimuli only because they are corrected by the ear to the right note. This, however, is only an extreme instance of what happens less conspicuously in all individualization in popular music. Any harmonic boldness, any chord which does not fall strictly within the simplest harmonic scheme demands being apperceived as 'false', that is, as a stimulus which carries with it the unambiguous prescription to substitute for it the right detail, or rather the naked scheme. Understanding popular music means obeying such commands for listening. Popular music commands its own listening-habits.

There is another type of individualization claimed in terms of kinds of popular music and differences in name-bands. The types of popular music are carefully differentiated in production. The listener is presumed to be able to choose between them. The most widely recognized differentiations are those between swing and sweet and such name-bands as Benny Goodman and Guy Lombardo. The listener is quickly able to distinguish the types of music and even the performing band, this in spite of the fundamental identity of the material and the great similarity of the presentations apart from their emphasized distinguishing trade-marks. This labelling technique, as regards type of music and band, is pseudo-individualization, but of a sociological kind outside the realm of strict musical technology. It provides trade-marks of identification for differentiating between the actually undifferentiated.

Popular music becomes a multiple-choice questionnaire. There are two main types and their derivatives from which to choose. The listener is encouraged by the inexorable presence of these types psychologically to cross-out what he dislikes and check what he likes. The limitation inherent in this choice and the clear-cut alternative it entails provoke like–dislike patterns of behaviour. This mechanical dichotomy breaks down indifference; it is imperative to favour sweet or swing if one wishes to continue to listen to popular music.

Theory about the listener

Popular music and 'leisure time'

In order to understand why this whole *type* of music [i.e. popular music in general] maintains its hold on the masses, some considerations of a general kind may be appropriate.

The frame of mind to which popular music originally appealed, on which it feeds, and which it perpetually reinforces, is simultaneously one of distraction and inattention. Listeners are distracted from the demands of reality by entertainment which does not demand attention either.

The notion of distraction can be properly understood only within its social setting and not in self-subsistent terms of individual psychology. Distraction is bound to the present mode of production, to the rationalized and mechanized process of labour to which, directly or indirectly, masses are subject. This mode of production, which engenders fears and anxiety about unemployment, loss of income, war, has its 'non-productive' correlate in entertainment; that is, relaxation which does not involve the effort of concentration at all. People want to have fun. A fully concentrated and conscious experience of art is possible only to those whose lives do not put such a strain on them that in their spare time they want relief from both boredom and effort simultaneously. The whole sphere of cheap commercial entertainment reflects this dual desire. It induces relaxation because it is patterned and pre-digested. Its being patterned and pre-digested serves within the psychological household of the masses to spare them the effort of that participation (even in listening or observation) without which there can be no receptivity to art. On the other hand, the stimuli they provide permit an escape from the boredom of mechanized labour.

The promoters of commercialized entertainment exonerate themselves by referring to the fact that they are giving the masses what they want. This is an ideology appropriate to commercial purposes: the less the mass discriminates, the greater the possibility of selling cultural commodities indiscriminately. Yet this ideology of vested interest cannot be dismissed so easily. It is not possible completely to deny that mass-consciousness can be moulded by the operative agencies only because the masses 'want this stuff'.

But why do they want this stuff? In our present society the masses themselves are kneaded by the same mode of production as the arti-craft material foisted upon them. The customers of musical entertainment are themselves objects or, indeed, products of the same mechanisms which determine the production of popular music. Their spare time serves only to reproduce their working capacity. It is a means instead of an end. The power of the process of production extends over the time intervals which on the surface appear to be 'free'. They want standardized goods and pseudo-individualization, because their leisure is an escape from work and at the same time is moulded after those psychological attitudes to which their workaday world exclusively habituates them. Popular music is for the masses a perpetual busman's holiday. Thus, there is justification for speaking of a pre-established harmony today between production and consumption of popular music. The people clamour for what they are going to get anyhow.

To escape boredom and avoid effort are incompatible – hence the reproduction of the very attitude from which escape is sought. To be sure, the way in which they must work on the assembly line, in the factory, or at office machines denies people any novelty. They seek novelty, but the strain and boredom associated with actual work leads to avoidance of effort in that leisure-time which offers the only chance for really new experience. As a substitute, they crave a stimulant. Popular music comes to offer it. Its stimulations are met with the inability to vest effort in the ever-identical.

This means boredom again. It is a circle which makes escape impossible. The impossibility of escape causes the wide-spread attitude of inattention toward popular music. The moment of recognition is that of effortless sensation. The sudden attention attached to this moment burns itself out *instanter* and relegates the listener to a realm of inattention and distraction. On the one hand, the domain of production and plugging presupposes distraction and, on the other, produces it.

In this situation the industry faces an insoluble problem. It must arouse attention by means of ever-new products, but this attention spells their doom. If no attention is given to the song, it cannot be sold; it attention is paid to it, there is always the possibility that people will no longer accept it, because they know it too well. This partly accounts for the constantly renewed effort to sweep the market with new products, to hound them to their graves; then to repeat the infanticidal maneuver again and again.

On the other hand, distraction is not only a presupposition but also a product of popular music. The tunes themselves lull the listener to inattention. They tell him not to worry for he will not miss anything.[3]

The social cement

It is safe to assume that music listened to with a general inattention which is only interrupted by sudden flashes of recognition is not followed as a sequence of experiences that have a clear-cut meaning of their own, grasped in each instant and related to all the precedent and subsequent moments. One may go so far as to suggest that most listeners of popular music do not understand music as a language in itself. If they did it would be vastly difficult to explain how they could tolerate the incessant supply of largely undifferentiated material. What, then, does music mean to them? The answer is that the language that is music is transformed by objective processes into a language which they think is their own – into a language which serves as a receptacle for their institutionalized wants. The less music is a language *sui generis* to them, the more does it become established as such a receptacle. The autonomy of music is replaced by a mere socio-psychological function. Music today is largely a social cement. And the meaning listeners attribute to a material, the inherent logic of which is inaccessible to them, is above all a means by which they achieve some psychical adjustment to the mechanisms of present-day life. This 'adjustment' materializes in two different ways, corresponding to two major socio-psychological types of mass behaviour toward music in general and popular music in particular, the 'rhythmically obedient' type and the 'emotional' type.

Individuals of the rhythmically obedient type are mainly found among the youth – the so-called radio generation. They are most susceptible to a process of masochistic adjustment to authoritarian collectivism. The type is not restricted to any one political attitude. The adjustment to anthropophagous collectivism is found as often among left-wing political groups as among right-wing groups. Indeed, both overlap: repression and crowd-mindedness overtake the followers of both trends. The psychologies tend to meet despite the surface distinctions in political attitudes.

This comes to the fore in popular music which appears to be aloof from political partisanship. It may be noted that a moderate leftist theatre production such as 'Pins and Needles' uses ordinary jazz as its musical medium, and that a communist youth organization adapted the melody of 'Alexander's Ragtime Band' to its own lyrics. Those who ask for a song of social significance ask for it through a medium which deprives it of social significance. The uses of inexorable popular musical media is repressive *per se*. Such inconsistencies indicate that political conviction and socio-psychological structure by no means coincide.

This obedient type is the rhythmical type, the word rhythmical being used in its everyday sense. Any musical experience of this type is based upon the underlying, unabating time unit of the music – its 'beat'. To play rhythmically means, to these people, to play in such a way that even if pseudo-individualizations – counter-accents and other 'differentiations' – occur, the relation to the ground metre is preserved. To be musical means to them to be capable of following given rhythmical patterns without being disturbed by 'individualizing' aberrations, and to fit even the syncopations into the basic time units. This is the way in which their response to music immediately expresses their desire to obey. However, as the standardized metre of dance music and of marching suggests the coordinated battalions of a mechanical collectivity, obedience to this rhythm by overcoming the responding individuals leads them to conceive of themselves as agglutinized with the untold millions of the meek who must be similarly overcome. Thus do the obedient inherit the earth.

Yet, if one looks at the serious compositions which correspond to this category of mass listening, one finds one very characteristic feature: that of disillusion. All these composers, among them Stravinsky and Hindemith, have expressed an 'anti-romantic' feeling. They aimed at musical adaptation to reality – a reality understood by them in terms of the 'machine age'. The renunciation of dreaming by these composers is an index that listeners are ready to replace dreaming by adjustment to raw reality, that they reap new pleasure from their acceptance of the unpleasant. They are disillusioned about any possibility of realizing their own dreams in the world in which they live, and consequently adapt themselves to this world. They take what is called a realistic attitude and attempt to harvest consolation by identifying themselves with the external social forces which they think constitute the 'machine-age'. Yet the very disillusion upon which their coordination is based is there to mar their pleasure. The cult of the machine which is represented by unabating jazz beats involves a self-renunciation that cannot but take root in the form of a fluctuating uneasiness somewhere in the personality of the obedient. For the machine is an end in itself only under given social conditions – where men are appendages of the machines on which they work. The adaptation to machine music necessarily implies a renunciation of one's own human feelings and at the same time a fetishism of the machine such that its instrumental character becomes obscured thereby.

As to the other, the 'emotional' type, there is some justification for linking it with a type of movie spectator. The kinship is with the poor shop girl who derives gratification by identification with Ginger Rogers, who, with her beautiful legs and unsullied character, marries the boss. Wish-fulfillment is considered the guiding principle in the social psychology of moving pictures and similarly in the pleasure obtained from emotional, erotic music. This explanation, however, is only superficially appropriate.

Hollywood and Tin Pan Alley may be dream factories. But they do not merely supply categorical wish-fulfillment for the girl behind the counter. She does not immediately identify herself with Ginger Rogers marrying. What does occur may be expressed as follows: when the audience at a sentimental film or sentimental music become aware of the overwhelming possibility of happiness, they dare to confess to themselves what the whole order of contemporary life ordinarily forbids them to admit, namely, that they actually have no part in happiness. What is supposed to be wish-fulfillment is only the scant liberation that occurs with the realization that at last one need not deny oneself the happiness of knowing that one is unhappy and that one could be happy. The experience of the shop girl is related to that of the old woman who weeps at the wedding services of others, blissfully becoming aware of the wretchedness of her own life. Not even the most gullible individuals believe that eventually everyone will win the sweepstakes. The actual function of sentimental music lies rather in the temporary release given to the awareness that one has missed fulfillment.

The emotional listener listens to everything in terms of late romanticism and of the musical commodities derived from it which are already fashioned to fit the needs of emotional listening. They consume music in order to be allowed to weep. They are taken in by the musical expression of frustration rather than by that of happiness. The influence of the standard Slavic melancholy typified by Tchaikovsky and Dvorak is by far greater than that of the most 'fulfilled' moments of Mozart or of the young Beethoven. The so-called releasing element of music is simply the opportunity to feel something. But the actual content of this emotion can only be frustration. Emotional music has become the image of the mother who says, 'Come and weep, my child.' It is catharsis for the masses, but catharsis which keeps them all the more firmly in line. One who weeps does not resist any more than one who marches. Music that permits its listeners the confession of their unhappiness reconciles them, by means of this 'release', to their social dependence.

Notes

1 The basic importance of standardization has not altogether escaped the attention of current literature on popular music. 'The chief difference between a popular song and a standard, or serious, song like 'Mandalay', 'Sylvia', or 'Trees', is that the melody and the lyric of a popular number are constructed within a definite pattern or structural form, whereas the poem, or lyric, of a standard number has no structural confinements, and the music is free to interpret the meaning and feeling of the words without following a set pattern or form. Putting it another way, the popular song is "custom built", while the standard song allows the composer freer play of imagination and interpretation.' (Abner Silver and Robert Bruce, *How to Write and Sell a Song Hit*, New York, 1939, p. 2.) The authors fail, however,

to realize the externally superimposed, commercial character of those patterns which aims at canalized reactions or, in the language of the regular announcement of one particular radio programme, at 'easy-listening'. They confuse the mechanical patterns with highly organized, strict art forms: 'Certainly there are few more stringent verse forms in poetry than the sonnet, and yet the greatest poets of all time have woven undying beauty within its small and limited frame. A composer has just as much opportunity for exhibiting his talent and genius in popular songs as in more serious music' (pp. 2–3). Thus the standard pattern of popular music appears to them virtually on the same level as the law of a fugue. It is this contamination which makes the insight into the basic standardization of popular music sterile. It ought to be added that what Silver and Bruce call a 'standard song' is just the opposite of what we mean by a standardized popular song.

2 See Max Horkheimer, *Zeitschrift für Sozialforschung*, Vol. VIII, 1939, p. 115.

3 The attitude of distraction is not a completely universal one. Particularly youngsters who invest popular music with their own feelings are not yet completely blunted to all its effects. The whole problem of age levels with regard to popular music, however, is beyond the scope of the present study. Demographic problems, too, must remain out of consideration.

7.3

Raymond Williams
from *Culture and Society*
1780–1950 (1958)

Culture and which way of life?

We live in a transitional society, and the idea of culture, too often, has been identified with one or other of the forces which the transition contains. Culture is the product of the old leisured classes who seek now to defend it against new and destructive forces. Culture is the inheritance of the new rising class, which contains the humanity of the future; this class seeks, now, to free it from its restrictions. We say things like this to each other, and glower. The one good thing, it seems, is that all the contending parties are keen enough on culture to want to be identified with it. But then, we are none of us referees in this; we are all in the game, and playing in one or other direction.

I want to say something about the idea of 'working-class culture', because this seems to me to be a key issue in our own time, and one in which there is a considerable element of misunderstanding. I have indicated already that we cannot fairly or usefully describe the bulk of the material produced by the new means of communication as 'working-class culture'. For neither is it by any means produced exclusively for this class, nor, in any important degree, is it produced by them. To this negative definition we must add another: that 'working-class culture', in our society, is not to be understood as the small amount of 'proletarian' writing and art which exists. The appearance of such work has been useful, not only in its more self-conscious forms, but also in such material as the post-Industrial ballads, which were worth collecting. We need to be aware of this work, but it is to be seen as a valuable dissident element rather than as a culture. The traditional popular culture of England was, if not annihilated, at least fragmented and weakened by the dislocations of the Industrial Revolution.

What is left, with what in the new conditions has been newly made, is small in quantity and narrow in range. It exacts respect, but it is in no sense an alternative culture.

This very point of an alternative is extremely difficult, in terms of theory. If the major part of our culture, in the sense of intellectual and imaginative work, is to be called, as the Marxists call it, bourgeois, it is natural to look for an alternative culture, and to call it proletarian. Yet it is very doubtful whether 'bourgeois culture' is a useful term. The body of intellectual and imaginative work which each generation receives as its traditional culture is always, and necessarily, something more than the product of a single class. It is not only that a considerable part of it will have survived from much earlier periods than the immediatcly pre-existing form of society; so that, for instance, literature, philosophy and other work surviving from before, say, 1600, cannot be taken as 'bourgeois'. It is also that, even within a society in which a particular class is dominant, it is evidently possible both for members of other classes to contribute to the common stock, and for such contributions to be unaffected by or in opposition to the ideas and values of the dominant class. The area of a culture, it would seem, is usually proportionate to the area of a language rather than to the area of a class. It is true that a dominant class can to a large extent control the transmission and distribution of the whole common inheritance; such control, where it exists, needs to be noted as a fact about that class. It is true also that a tradition is always selective, and that there will always be a tendency for this process of selection to be related to and even governed by the interests of the class that is dominant. These factors make it likely that there will be qualitative changes in the traditional culture when there is a shift of class power, even before a newly ascendant class makes its own contributions. Points of this kind need to be stressed, but the particular stress given by describing our existent culture as bourgeois culture is in several ways misleading. It can, for example, seriously mislead those who would now consider themselves as belonging to the dominant class. If they are encouraged, even by their opponents, to think of the existing culture (in the narrow sense) as their particular product and legacy, they will deceive themselves and others. For they will be encouraged to argue that, if their class position goes, the culture goes too; that standards depend on the restriction of a culture to the class which, since it has produced it, alone understands it. On the other hand, those who believe themselves to be representatives of a new rising class will, if they accept the proposition of 'bourgeois culture', either be tempted to neglect a common human inheritance, or, more intelligently, be perplexed as to how, and how much of, this bourgeois culture is to be taken over. The categories are crude and mechanical in either position. Men who share a common language share the inheritance of an intellectual and literary tradition which is necessarily and constantly revalued with every shift in experience. The manufacture of an artificial 'working-class culture', in opposition to this common tradition, is merely foolish. A society in which the working class had become dominant would, of course, produce new valuations and new contributions. But the process would be extremely complex, because of the complexity of the inheritance, and nothing is now to be gained by diminishing this complexity to a crude diagram.

The contrast between a minority and a popular culture cannot be absolute. It is not even a matter of levels, for such a term implies distinct and discontinuous stages, and this is by no means always the case. In Russian society in the nineteenth century one finds perhaps the clearest example of a discontinuous culture within recent history; this is marked, it should be noted, by a substantial degree of rejection of even the common language by the ruling minority. But in English society there has never been this degree of separation, since English emerged as the common language. There has been marked unevenness of distribution, amounting at times to virtual exclusion of the majority, and there has been some unevenness of contribution, although in no period has this approached the restriction of contribution to members of any one class. Further, since the beginning of the nineteenth century it has been difficult for any observer to feel that the care of intellectual and imaginative work could be safely entrusted to, or identified with, any existing social or economic class. It was in relation to this situation that the very idea of culture was, as we have seen, developed.

The most difficult task confronting us, in any period where there is a marked shift of social power, is the complicated process of revaluation of the inherited tradition. The common language, because in itself it is so crucial to this matter, provides an excellent instance. It is clearly of vital importance to a culture that its common language should not decline in strength, richness and flexibility; that it should, further, be adequate to express new experience, and to clarify change. But a language like English is still evolving, and great harm can be done to it by the imposition of crude categories of class. It is obvious that since the development, in the nineteenth century, of the new definition of 'standard English', particular uses of the common language have been taken and abused for the purposes of class distinction. Yet the dialect which is normally equated with standard English has no necessary superiority over other dialects. Certain of the grammatical clarifications have a common importance, but not all even of these. On the other hand, certain selected sounds have been given a cardinal authority which derives from no known law of language, but simply from the fact that they are habitually made by persons who, for other reasons, possess social and economic influence. The conversion of this kind of arbitrary selection into a criterion of 'good' or 'correct' or 'pure' English is merely a subterfuge. Modern communications make for the growth of uniformity, but the necessary selection and clarification have been conducted, on the whole, on grounds quite irrelevant to language. It is still thought, for instance, that a double negative ('I don't want none') is *incorrect* English, although millions of English-speaking persons use it regularly: not, indeed, as a misunderstanding of the rule, which they might be thought too ignorant to apprehend; but as the continuation of a habit which has been in the language continuously since Chaucer. The broad 'a', in such words as 'class', is now taken as the mark of an 'educated person', although till the eighteenth century it was mainly a rustic habit, and as such despised. Or 'ain't', which in the eighteenth century was often a mark of breeding, is now supposed to be a mark of vulgarity: in both cases, the valuation is the merest chance. The extraordinary smugness about aspirates, vowel-sounds, the choice of this or that synonym ('couch' 'sofa'), which has for so long been a normal element of middle-class humour, is, after all, not a concern for good English, but parochialism. (The current controversy about what are called 'U' and 'non-U' speech habits clearly illustrates this; it is an aspect, not of major social differences, but of the long difficulty of drawing the lines between the upper and lower sections of the *middle* class.) Yet, while this is true, the matter is complicated by the fact that in a society where a particular class and hence a particular use of the common language is dominant a large part of the literature, carrying as it does a body of vital common experience, will be attracted to the dominant language mode. At the same time, a national literature, as English has never ceased to be, will, while containing this relation, contain also elements of the whole culture and language. If we are to understand the process of a selective tradition, we shall not think of exclusive areas of culture but of degrees of shifting attachment and interaction, which a crude theory either of class or of standards is incompetent to interpret.

A culture can never be reduced to its artifacts while it is being lived. Yet the temptation to attend only to external evidence is always strong. It is argued, for instance, that the working class is becoming 'bourgeois', because it is dressing like the middle class, living in semi-detached houses, acquiring cars and washing-machines and television sets. But it is not 'bourgeois' to possess objects of utility, nor to enjoy a high material standard of living. The working class does not become bourgeois by owning the new products, any more than the bourgeois ceases to be bourgeois as the objects he owns change in kind. Those who regret such a development among members of the working class are the victims of a prejudice. An admiration of the 'simple poor' is no new thing, but it has rarely been found, except as a desperate rationalization, among the poor themselves. It is the product either of satiety or of a judgement that the material advantages are purchased at too high a human cost. The first ground must be left to those who are sated; the second, which is more important, is capable of a false transference. If the advantages were 'bourgeois' because they rested on economic exploitation, they do not continue to be 'bourgeois' if they can be assured without such exploitation or by its diminution. The worker's envy of the middle-class man is not a desire to be that man, but to have the same kind of possessions. We all like to think of ourselves as a standard, and I can see that it is genuinely difficult for the English middle class to suppose that the working class is not desperately anxious to become just like itself. I am afraid this must be unlearned. The great majority of English working people want only the middle-class material standard and for the rest want to go on being themselves. One should not be too quick to call this vulgar materialism. It is wholly reasonable to want the means of life in such abundance as is possible. This is the materialism of material provision, to which we are all, quite rightly, attentive. The working people, who have felt themselves long deprived of such means in any adequacy, intend to get them and to keep them if they can. It would need more evidence than this to show that they are becoming vulgar materialists, or that they are becoming 'bourgeois'.

The question then, perhaps, is whether there is any meaning left in 'bourgeois'? Is there any point, indeed, in continuing to think in class terms at all? Is not industrialism, by its own momentum, producing a culture that is best described as classless? Such questions, today, command a significant measure of assent, but again, while drawing support from the crudities of certain kinds of class interpretation, they rest, essentially, on an external attitude alike to culture and to class. If we think of culture, as it is important to do, in terms of a body of intellectual and imaginative work, we can see that with the extension of education the distribution of this culture is becoming more even, and, at the same time, new work is being addressed to a public wider than a single class. Yet a culture is not only a body of intellectual and imaginative work; it is also and essentially a whole way of life. The basis of a distinction between bourgeois and working-class culture is only secondarily in the field of intellectual and imaginative work, and even here it is complicated, as we have seen, by the common elements resting on a common language. The primary distinction is to be sought in the whole way of life, and here, again, we must not confine ourselves to such evidence as housing, dress and modes of leisure. Industrial production tends to produce uniformity in such matters, but the vital distinction lies at a different level. The crucial distinguishing element in English life since the Industrial Revolution is not language, not dress, not leisure – for these indeed will tend to uniformity. The crucial distinction is between alternative ideas of the nature of social relationship.

'Bourgeois' is a significant term because it marks that version of social relationship which we usually call individualism: that is to say, an idea of society as a neutral area within which each individual is free to pursue his own development and his own advantage as a natural right. The course of recent history is marked by a long fighting retreat from this idea in its purest form, and the latest defenders would seem to the earliest to have lost almost the entire field. Yet the interpretation is still dominant: the exertion of social power is thought necessary only in so far as it will protect individuals in this basic right to set their own course. The classical formula of the retreat is that, in certain defined ways, no individual has a right to harm others. But, characteristically, this harm has been primarily interpreted in relation to the individual pursuit – no individual has a right to prevent others from doing *this kind of thing.*

The reforming bourgeois modification of this version of society is the idea of service, to which I shall return. But both this idea and the individualist idea can be sharply contrasted with the idea that we properly associate with the working class: an idea which, whether it is called communism, socialism or cooperation, regards society neither as neutral nor as protective, but as the positive means for all kinds of development, including individual development. Development and advantage are not individually but commonly interpreted. The provision of the means of life will, alike in production and distribution, be collective and mutual. Improvement is sought, not in the opportunity to escape from one's class, or to make a career, but in the general and controlled advance of all. The human fund is regarded as in all respects common, and freedom of access to it as a right constituted by one's humanity; yet such access, in whatever kind, is common or it is nothing. Not the individual, but the whole society, will move.

The distinction between these versions of society has been blurred by two factors: the idea of service, which is the great achievement of the Victorian middle class, and is deeply inherited by its successors; and the complication of the working-class idea by the fact that England's position as an imperial power has tended to limit the sense of community to national (and, in the context, imperialist) lines. Further, the versions are blurred by a misunderstanding of the nature of class. The contending ideas, and the actions which follow from them, are the property of that part of a group of people, similarly circumstanced, which has become conscious of its position and of its own attitude to this position. Class feeling is a mode, rather than a uniform possession of all the individuals who might, objectively, be assigned to that class. When we speak, for instance, of a working-class idea, we do not mean that all working people possess it, or even approve of it. We mean, rather, that this is the essential idea embodied in the organizations and institutions which that class creates: the working-class movement as a tendency, rather than all working-class people as individuals. It is foolish to interpret individuals in rigid class terms, because class is a collective mode and not a person. At the same time, in the interpretation of ideas and institutions, we can speak properly in class terms. It depends, at any time, on which kind of fact we are considering. To dismiss an individual because of his class, or to judge a relationship with him solely in class terms, is to reduce humanity to an abstraction. But, also, to pretend that there are no collective modes is to deny the plain facts.

We may now see what is properly meant by 'working-class culture'. It is not proletarian art, or council houses, or a particular use of languages; it is, rather, the basic collective idea, and the institutions, manners, habits of thought and intentions which proceed from this. Bourgeois culture, similarly, is the basic individualist idea and the institutions, manners, habits of thought and intentions which proceed from that. In our culture as a whole, there is both a constant interaction between these ways of life and an area which can properly be described as common to or underlying both. The working class, because of its position, has not, since the Industrial Revolution, produced a culture in the narrower sense. The culture which it has produced, and which it is important to recognize, is the collective democratic institution, whether in the trade unions, the cooperative movement or a political party. Working-class culture, in the stage through which it has been passing, is primarily social (in that it has created institutions) rather than individual (in particular intellectual or imaginative work). When it is considered in context, it can be seen as a very remarkable creative achievement.

To those whose meaning of culture is intellectual or imaginative work, such an achievement may be meaningless. The values which are properly attached to such work can, at times, seem overriding. On this, I would only point out that while it may have seemed reasonable to Burke to anticipate the trampling down of learning by the irruption of the 'swinish multitude', this has not in fact happened, and the swinish multitude itself has done much to prevent it happening. The record of the working-class movement in its attitudes to education, to learning and to art is on the whole a good record. It has sometimes wrongly interpreted, often neglected where it did not know. But it has never sought to destroy the institutions of this kind of culture; it has, on the contrary, pressed for their extension, for their wider social recognition, and, in our own time, for the application of a larger part of our material resources to their maintenance and development. Such a record will do more than stand comparison with that of the class by which the working class has been most actively and explicitly opposed. This, indeed, is the curious incident of the swine in the night. As the light came, and we could look around, it appeared that the trampling, which we had all heard, did not after all come from them.

7.4

Raymond Williams
'Popular' (1976)

Popular

Popular was originally a legal and political term, from *popularis*, L – belonging to the people. An **action popular**, from C15, was a legal suit which it was open to anyone to begin. **Popular estate** and **popular government**, from C16, referred to a political system constituted or carried on by the whole people, but there was also the sense (cf. COMMON) of 'low' or 'base'. The transition to the predominant modern meaning of 'widely-favoured' or 'well-liked' is interesting in that it contains a strong element of setting out to gain favour, with a sense of calculation that has not quite disappeared but that is evident in a reinforced phrase like **deliberately popular.** Most of the men who have left records of the use of the word saw the matter from this point of view, downwards. There were neutral uses, such as North's 'more popular, and desirous of the common peoples good will and favour' (1580) (where **popular** was still a term of policy rather than of condition), and evidently derogatory uses, such as Bacon's 'a Noble-man of an ancient Family, but unquiet and popular' (1622). **Popularity** was defined in 1697, by Collier, as 'a courting the favour of the people by undue practices'. This use was probably reinforced by unfavourable applications: a neutral reference to 'popular . . . theams' (1573) is less characteristic than 'popular error' (1616) and 'popular sickenesse' (1603) or 'popular disease' (C17–C19), in which an unwelcome thing was merely widespread. A primary sense of 'widely favoured' was clear by lC18; the sense of 'well liked' is probably C19. A lC19 American magazine observed: 'they have come . . . to take popular quite gravely and sincerely as a synonym for good'. The shift in perspective is then evident. **Popular** was being seen from the point of view of the people rather than from those seeking favour or power from

them. Yet the earlier sense has not died. **Popular culture** was not identified by *the people* but by others, and it still carries two older senses: inferior
kinds of work (cf. **popular literature, popular press** as distinguished from
quality press); and work deliberately setting out to win favour (**popular
journalism** as distinguished from *democratic journalism*, or **popular entertainment**); as well as the more modern sense of well-liked by many
people, with which of course, in many cases, the earlier senses overlap. The
recent sense of **popular culture** as the culture actually made by people for
themselves is different from all these; it is often displaced to the past as *folk
culture* but it is also an important modern emphasis. The range of senses can
be seen again in **popularize**, which until C19 was a political term, in the
old sense, and then took on its special meaning of presenting knowledge in
generally accessible ways. Its C19 uses were mainly favourable, and in C20
the favourable sense is still available, but there is also a strong sense of
'simplification', which in some circles is predominant.

In mC20 **popular song** and **popular art** were characteristically shortened
to **pop**, and the familiar range of senses, from unfavourable to favourable,
gathered again around this. The shortening gave the word a lively informality
but opened it, more easily, to a sense of the trivial. It is hard to say whether
older senses of **pop** have become fused with this use: the common sense of
a sudden lively movement, in many familiar and generally pleasing contexts,
is certainly appropriate.

Abbreviations

cf: compare
L: Latin
C: Century
lC: late Century
mC: mid Century

7.5

Tristan Tzara from 'Memoirs of Dadaism' (1920)

At the beginning of the year 1920, I arrived back in Paris, extremely glad to see my friends again. I took part in the demonstrations which aroused the rage of the Parisian public, in company with Aragon, Breton, Dermée, Eluard, Ribemont-Dessaignes, Picabia, Péret, Soupault, Rigaut, Marguerite Buffet and others. The début of Dadaism in Paris took place on the twenty-third of January, at the matinée organised by the Dadaist review *Littérature*. Louis Aragon, a slender young man with feminine features, A. Breton, whose behaviour displays the stigmata of the religious sectarians, G. Ribemont-Dessaignes, a man whose simple appearance conceals the fiery temper of the great accusers of humanity, and Philippe Soupault, whose facility of expression flows forth in bizarre images, gave readings from their works. Picabia, who has undergone so many influences, particularly those of the clear and powerful mind of Marcel Duchamp, exhibited a number of pictures, one of which was a drawing done in chalk on a blackboard and erased on the stage; that is to say, the picture was valid for only two hours. As for me, announced as 'Dada,' I read aloud a newspaper article while an electric bell kept ringing so that no one could hear what I said. This was very badly received by the public, who became exasperated and shouted: 'Enough! Enough!' An attempt was made to give a futuristic interpretation to this act, but all that I wanted to convey was simply that my presence on the stage, the sight of my face and my movements, ought to satisfy people's curiosity and that anything I might have said really had no importance.

At the Grand Palais des Champs Elysées, thousands of persons of all classes manifested very uproariously it is impossible to say exactly what – their joy or their disapproval, by unexpected cries and general laughter, which constituted a very pretty accompaniment to the manifestoes read by six people at once. The newspapers said that an old man in the audience gave himself up to behaviour of a character more or less intimate, that somebody set off some flashlight powder and that a pregnant woman had to be taken out. It is true that the papers had also announced that Charlie Chaplin was going to deliver a lecture on Dada. Although we denied the rumour, there was one reporter who followed me everywhere. He thought that the celebrated actor was up to some new stunt and was planning a surprise entrance. I remember with tenderness that Picabia, who was to have taken part in the demonstration, disappeared as soon as it began. For five hours it was impossible to find him. The séance ended with a speech by 'The King of the Fakirs,' M. Buisson, who has a curious occupation: he predicts the future every day to those who wish to listen to him, on the Boulevard de la Madeleine. In the evening he sells papers at the Metro exits.

Several days afterwards, there took place in a church which had been transformed into a cinema – premises of the Club du Faubourg – at the invitation of that association, which includes more than three thousand workers and intellectuals, an explanation of the Dadaist Movement. There were four of us on the stage: Ribemont-Dessaignes, Aragon and Breton; and I. M. Léo Poldès presided. On this occasion, the audience were more serious: they listened to us. Their disapproval was expressed in shrill cries. Raymond Duncan, the philosopher who walks about Paris in the costume of Socrates, was there with all his school. He came to our defence and quieted the audience. A debate followed. The very best Socialist orators took sides and spoke for or against us. We replied to the attacks and the audience boiled in unison. Aragon wrote a moving article on that memorable matinée in *Les Ecrits Nouveaux*.

A week later, a public debate on Dada took place at the Université Populaire. Eluard, Fraenkel, Dermée, Breton, Ribemont-Dessaignes, Soupault and I participated with all the force of our temperaments in a séance torn by political passions. All the manifestoes of the presidents appeared in the Dadaist review, *Littérature* – it is well known that the Dadaist Movement has three hundred and ninety-one presidents and that anyone can become a president without the slightest trouble.

391 was also the name of a review which several of us started; it expanded and became a periodical of world-wide reputation. People finally became afraid of it, because it described things as they really were without any attempt to soften them. How many critics came to regret having uttered so many imbecilities!

A scandal provoked by the hypocrisy of certain Cubists in the bosom of a modern art society brought on the complete schism between the Cubists and the Dadas – an event which gave great force or cohesion to the nineteen dissenting Dadaists.

Paul Eluard, whom we call the inventor of a new metal of darkness, began to publish his review *Proverbe* in which all the Dadaists collaborated and which contributed a vein of its own. It was chiefly a matter of contradicting logic and language. This is how Soupault characterises the collaborators of *Proverbe*:

Louis Aragon, the Glass Syringe.
Arp, Clean Wrinkles.
André Breton, the Glass of Water in a Storm.
Paul Eluard, the Nurse of the Stars.
Th. Fraenkel, the Great Earth Serpent.
Benjamin Péret, the Lemon Mandarin.
G. Ribemont-Dessaignes, the Steam Man.
Jacques Rigaut, the Hollow Plate.
Philippe Soupault, the Musical Urinal.
Tristan Tzara, the Man with the Pearl Head.

Dadaist hand-bills and books were spreading the agitation through Paris and the whole world.

In the month of May, the demonstration at the Théâtre de l'Œuvre, that courageous enterprise directed by Lugné-Poe, showed the vitality of Dada at its height. Twelve hundred people were turned away. There were three spectators for every seat; it was suffocating. Enthusiastic members of the audience had brought musical instruments to interrupt us. The enemies of Dada threw down from the balconies copies of an anti-Dada paper called *Non* in which we were described as lunatics. The scandal reached proportions absolutely unimaginable. Soupault proclaimed: 'You are all idiots! You deserve to be presidents of the Dadaist Movement!' Breton, with the house completely dark, read in his thunderous voice a manifesto far from gentle toward the audience. Then Ribemont-Dessaignes read a soothing and complimentary manifesto. Paul Eluard presented some 'examples.' I will give one: the curtain goes up; two people, one of them with a letter in his hand, appear from opposite sides of the stage and meet in the centre; the following dialogue takes place:

> *'Le bureau de poste est en face.'*
> *' – Que voulez vous que ça me fasse?'*
> *'Pardon, je vous voyais une lettre à la main. Je croyais . . .'*
> *' – Il ne s'agit pas de croire, mais de savoir.'*

After which, each goes his way, and the curtain falls. There were six of these examples, very widely varied, in which the mixture of humanity, idiocy and unexpectedness contrasted curiously with the brutality of the other numbers. I invented on the occasion of this performance a diabolical machine composed of a klaxon and three successive invisible echoes, for the purpose of impressing on the minds of the audience certain phrases describing the aims of Dada. The ones which created the most sensation were: 'Dada is against the high cost of living.' and 'Dada is a virgin microbe.' We also produced three short plays by Soupault, Breton and Ribemont-Dessaignes and 'La Première Aventure Céleste de M. Antipyrine,' which I had written in 1916. This play is a boxing match with words. The characters, confined in sacks and trunks, recite their parts without moving, and one can easily imagine the effect this produced – performed in a greenish light – on the already excited public. It was impossible to hear a single word of the play. Mlle. Hania Routchine was to have sung at the end of the play a sentimental song by Duparc. The audience either took this for a sacrilege or considered that a thing so simple – it was intended to produce a contrast – was out of place on this occasion; in any case, they did not restrain their language. Mlle. Routchine, who was accustomed to the great successes of the Vaudeville, did not understand the situation and, after exchanging some amenities with the public, refused to finish the song. For two hours we could hardly calm her, for she wept wildly.

At the Salle Gaveau, at the Dada Festival, the scandal was also great. For the first time in the history of the world, people threw at us, not only eggs, salads and pennies, but beef-steaks as well. It was a very great success. The audience were extremely Dadaist. We had already said that the true Dadaists were against Dada. Philippe Soupault appeared as a magician. As he called the names of the Pope, Clemenceau and Foch, children's balloons came out of a large box and floated up to the ceiling. Paul Souday in his notice in *Le Temps* said that really, at a certain distance, the faces of the persons summoned actually appeared on the surfaces of the balloons. The audience was so excited and the atmosphere so overcharged that a number of other ideas merely suggested took on the appearance of reality. Ribemont-Dessaignes did a motionless dance and Mlle. Buffet interpreted some Dadaist music. A flashlight taken by the newspaper *Comœdia* during a performance of a play by me shows everybody in the house waving their arms and with their mouths open shouting.

All the Paris celebrities were present. Mme. Rachilde had written an article in a newspaper inviting some *poilu* to shoot us with a revolver. This did not prevent her a year later from appearing on the stage and defending us. She no longer regarded us as a danger to the *esprit français*. They did not kill us in the Salle Gaveau, but all the journalists tried to do so in their notices. Columns were written declaring that Dada wasn't to be talked about any more – which suggested this observation to Jean Paulhan [the following is in English in the original]:

'If you must speak of Dada you must speak of Dada.
If you must not speak of Dada you must still speak of Dada.'

Among the other Dadaist reviews, *Cannibale* had a great success: it developed the absolutely anti-literary point of view which will be the relativist point of view of future generations. The superabundance of life of these future generations will find its place in the movement, and they will forget the rigid conventions, the paralysed ideas, of a tradition which is nothing but laziness.

SUMMARIES

1.1 Ferdinand de Saussure from *Course in General Linguistics* [trans. Wade Baskin (London: Fontana, 1974), pp. 111–19, 120–1; first published 1916].

While common sense seems to tell us that words reflect a reality outside language and are basically names for *things*, Saussureian linguistics diverges completely from this view to show that language is an internally self-sufficient system, consisting of values. Prior to Saussure the study of language had been mainly *diachronic*, that is, an analysis of its changing forms across history; Saussure distinguishes his area of concern as *synchronic*, considering how a language works at a given moment as a rule-governed system. In order to do this, he makes two further crucial distinctions: between *langue* and *parole*, between *signifier* and *signified*. What anyone actually says, their writing or utterance, is termed *parole* but the system of a particular language allowing someone to generate a meaningful utterance, according to rules for word-formation and sentence structure, constitutes its *langue*. On this basis Saussure argues that the common-sense notion of 'words' needs to be broken down and divided into signifier and signified (a distinction as old as classical rhetoric).

While the signifier consists of the sounds used by a particular language, arranged one after another in a temporal order, the signifieds are the concepts or meanings assigned to any conventional unit of sound. If we hear two people speaking in a language we don't know, we can pick up some of its signifiers but don't have access to the signified meanings that go with them. When signifier and signified are joined together they make up a sign. Out of the whole range of noises possible for the human voice a particular language draws on certain selected sounds to make up signifiers, the smallest unit used being a *phoneme*. But phonemes, as subsequent work has confirmed, are in themselves wholly arbitrary, defined only by their opposition or difference from one another, as /c/ in Modern English is contrasted with /b/. Signified meanings, similarly, are specified not by their relation to the real but in their relation to each other, their internal differences.

For these reasons Saussure claims that the relation between signifier and signified is by nature arbitrary (since no two languages use exactly the same sounds to act as phonemes) and that it is only because of the social convention operating for a particular language that a given string of phonemes (such as /c/a/t/) are agreed to mean a certain small furry mammal, while /b/a/t/ in contrast can work to mean a small flying rodent (and something you hit something with). It is crucial to his influence that in all of this Saussure steps aside from the question of the relation between the verbal sign ('word') and the referent (or real object). And it provides support for his account to note that signs work perfectly well although their referent may be very hard to define (such as the word 'if') or doesn't exist in reality at all (for example, 'dragon').

1.2 Roland Barthes from *Mythologies* [trans. Annette Lavers, (London: Jonathan Cape, 1972), pp. 109–17; first published 1957].

Between 1954 and 1956 Roland Barthes set himself the task of writing a short piece each month on a current aspect of French popular culture, attacking with all the satiric zest of a Parisian intellectual (and man of the left) the sacred objects of the French petit-bourgeoisie – Persil soap-powder advertising, the design of the latest Citroën, publicity for Garbo's face. He recognizes that the enormous growth and dissemination of the media – especially television – since 1950 pose new problems for critical analysis, particularly of the visual media. To this he brings two theoretical weapons, Saussure's account of the sign (see Section 1.1) and the Marxist conception of ideology (see Sections 2.1 and 2.2). To the concepts of signifier and signified Barthes adds the insights of the Danish linguist, Louis Hjelmslev, who had argued that a discursive mode – a style, use of a national or regional language, even a physiognomy – operated with a 'connotative semiotic' yielding a meaning over and above the signs of which it consisted (see 1961: 114–18). Taking the cover of a popular French weekly magazine Barthes argues that if the dots and colours of the photograph constitute the signifier and the image of the young Black saluting the national flag make up the signified, this completed sign acts as a *new* signifier for another, hidden signified ('that France is a great Empire', etc.).

Just as Freud had proposed there was a latent meaning to the dream denied by its manifest content and the philosopher of science, Gaston Bachelard, had sketched out the possible meanings of substances (blood, water), so Barthes shows how the overt denotation of the sign conceals and disavows a connoted meaning, and this Barthes calls 'myth' (so avoiding knee-jerk reactions to the word ideology). Myth is ideology nevertheless, for it comprehends the way bourgeois thought reassures itself by integrating novelty and difference into what seems to be always already safely familiar and the same, universal and eternal. Barthes is also keen that his ideological critique should step aside from the tradition represented by A. A. Zhdanov, whose speeches at the Congress of Soviet Writers in 1934 established the Stalinist line that texts must be seen primarily as true or false *reflections* of reality. For Barthes texts, including the largely visual texts of popular culture, are interventions which should be subject to ideological critique.

1.3 Pierre Macherey from *A Theory of Literary Production* [trans. Geoffrey Wall (London: Routledge and Kegan Paul, 1978), pp. 82–95; first published in Paris in 1966].

Tradition tells us that the object of criticism is to explain and interpret, to make explicit that which is implicit, to fill in the gaps and to expand upon the partial explanations provided by the text in order to make it whole and complete. What Macherey performs in *A Theory of Literary Production* is a critical analysis of this traditional assumption – a deconstruction of its terms – and in that process he advocates an alternative 'symptomatic' reading practice: a reading practice, that is, founded upon a search for the contradictions, discontinuities and omissions which are displayed within a literary work but of which it cannot speak. The project of such a practice is *not* to smooth over or to make up for the problems which the work embodies, but rather to expose them, to submit them to a process of questioning, and in so doing to produce a 'real' knowledge of the conditions of literary production, ideology and finally history.

For Macherey, the meaning of a literary work is not contained simply in what it says, but is rather produced in a relationship between that which it says and that which it *cannot* say. The work is divided – split between the spoken and the unspoken, both of which are necessary components of its conditions of existence. This split is formed as the result of a further division – between the ideological project of the work, and the constraints imposed upon that project by the conventions of its existence within specifically literary form. What is produced from this conflict is what Macherey calls (borrowing the concept from Freud) the unconscious of the work. This unconscious constitutes an absence at the works centre which, as Macherey argues, is what gives it 'life'. It constitutes the radical otherness of the work, containing that which is repressed – cast into the margins – in order that the conscious project may be fulfilled. As with the repressed which inhabits the unconscious of Freudian theory, however, the continual marginalization of the repressed of the text can never be guaranteed. The repressed can return, or at least within Macherey's terms, can be *made* to return by the efforts of a reading practice which privileges contradiction and omission. Through the practice of such a privileging the text can be made to turn upon itself, to perform a critique of its own terms and values, and ultimately to reveal within itself evidence not only of its own conditions of production but also of the limits of ideological representation, and of history as the history of struggle for the production and control of meaning.

1.4 Roland Barthes from *S/Z* [trans. Richard Miller (London: Jonathan Cape, 1975), pp. 16–21, first published in Paris in 1970].

That works of literature are matters not of individual (authorial) consciousness, but are rather produced from within the institution of the literary, is what Roland Barthes undertakes to demonstrate in *S/Z*. In this detailed analysis of Balzac's short story, *Sarrasine* (1836), Barthes unravels the recurring patterns of narrative convention, demonstrating as he does so the intertextual and cultural dependencies upon which the work is founded. While the close analysis which Barthes here performs might be seen as somewhat akin to Leavisian traditions of practical criticism (see Section 7.1), his reading is marked, none the less, by a conscientious refusal to locate within the analysis any semblance of a unifying structure. Contrar-ily, what in effect *S/Z* demonstrates is the *plurality* of the work. Its conventions are expounded, but its differences are also explored and the moments at which the work eludes or transgresses the conventions upon which it would seem to be based are duly celebrated.

S/Z is indeed many (often paradoxical) things: a science of narrative structure, and a homage to anarchy; a detailed series of classifications, and a representation of 'the very confusion of representation, the unbridled . . . circulation of signs' (*S/Z*, 1975: 222).

The analysis itself is predicated upon a distinction expounded elsewhere in the canon of Barthes writing (Section 3.5). The distinction, that is, between the 'readerly' text – that which, roughly speaking, offers the reassurance of realizable conventions; and the 'writerly' text – that which disturbs the reading relationship by transgressing or negating those conventions. *Sarrasine* is, it would seem, a readerly text – a nineteenth-century realist tale. Dividing the text into fragments (lexias) *S/Z* identifies the codes of narrative upon which each of those fragments depends for its meaning. Each code itself is in turn shown to depend upon a body of shared cultural knowledge (connoted by key words and phrases) through which the reader is then capable of recognizing particular sequences of action and particular cultural meanings. Yet, in the process of identifying the codes upon which that narrative conventionally turns, *S/Z* effectively undermines the distinction upon which it seemed, initially at least, to rely. In activating the tools by which the conventional structuring of *Sarrasine* can be examined, *S/Z* also begins to suggest that the meaning, as well as the functioning of the text, depends to a large extent upon the way in which it is produced by the practice of reading. *Sarrasine*, after all (by virtue of the work performed upon it by *S/Z*) can now be read as self-reflexive. A text, that is, which not only examines and undermines its own structures and conventions, but also those of the culture from which it is produced.

The point of the critical practice which Barthes performs is, like that of Macherey (see preceding extract), not simply that of interpretation or explanation, but rather of analysis of the means of production and the cultural implications they carry. Far from constituting a reductive methodology, the five codes of narrative provide a series of ways into the work. Ways of dividing and identifying the conventions from which texts are formed and from which they can, and do, escape. Ways of doing so, that is, without necessarily reducing the disruptive potentials of the play of meaning which is, ultimately, left in flux.

1.5   Colin MacCabe   'Realism and the Cinema: Notes on some Brechtian Theses' [from *Theoretical Essays* (Manchester: Manchester University Press, 1985), pp. 34–9; first published in *Screen* in 1974].

MacCabe's essay appeared first in a special number of the English film journal, *Screen*, concerned with Brecht and the possibility of radical cinema. Earlier this century the logician, Alfred Tarski, had distinguished between what is said in a sentence of a language – how a language is *used* – and a higher order or metalanguage in which that object language is mentioned or discussed. Drawing both on Roland Barthes's account of the five codes of a text (see preceding extract) and on Althusser's analysis of ideology (see Section 3.2) MacCabe argues that realism in novels, films and other texts should be understood not in terms of a *reflection* of reality but rather as an effect by which discourse positions its reader. Gathered together, the different discourses of a realist text are categorized into a hierarchy between object language and metalanguage. Corresponding to the empiricist view that knowledge can be obtained directly through experience, realism invites its reader to 'look through' the metalanguage and so 'see' as if directly what it represented in the object language (speech, character, narrated event). Thus the signifiers of the text become effaced as the reader accedes 'transparently' to the signified.

[The term 'classic realism' is used to isolate a type by distinguishing it from more controversial versions (Dickens, Dostoevsky); and the illustration by the contrast between direct and indirect speech is just that, an illustration. 'Dominant specularity', a concept borrowed from Lacan's analysis of the mirror stage (see Section Three, no. 1), refers to a position in which the subject is secured the apparent coherence and plenitude of the Imaginary, as it were outside and looking in.]

2.1 Karl Marx 'Preface' to *A Contribution to the Critique of Political Economy* [from Karl Marx and Frederick Engels, *Selected Works* (London: Lawrence and Wishart, 1950, 2 vols., vol 1, pp. 328–9)].

A passage of writing contested by commentary as much as anything in the Bible, Marx's account of how the economic base determines the social and ideological superstructure of society may perhaps best be read with the opening disclaimer firmly in mind ('the general result at which I arrived', etc.).

Across history one form of political economy has been transformed into another: from primitive communism (hunter-gatherers) to the Asiatic mode of production (slavery), the economies of ancient Greece and Rome, to feudalism. Characterizing an epoch, a mode of production consists of both *forces* (technology together with forms of organizing labour, such as the factory system) and *relations* (forms of property ownership). Transition occurs when development of the productive forces comes into conflict with the relations of production enabling a new, previously subordinate class to emerge as the dominant class for the next epoch. A classical example would be the emergence of the merchant class of feudalism as the bourgeois class with the development of market forces in the capitalist mode of production; and this will happen again when the proletariat, whose interests are not class-bound but universal, take over ownership of the forces of production so inaugurating communism and bringing to an end what Marx calls 'prehistory'. Intimately related to the 'shape' of society, the mode of production or economic base can also be seen to determine the legal and political superstructure of each epoch, as well as its ideology. Thus, against the conventional view that individuals think up ideas out of thin air, Marx argues that people's ideas are determined according to who they are and where they are in society. It may be noted, however, that, as well as a deterministic account of ideology, Marx also envisages it as having its own force and autonomy as the 'ideological forms' in which people become conscious of social conflict and fight it out.

2.2 Karl Marx and Frederick Engels from *The German Ideology* [from Karl Marx and Frederick Engels, *Collected Works* (London: Lawrence and Wishart, 1975, vol. 4, pp. 59–61)].

In the years after Hegel died (from cholera) in 1832 a group of 'Young' or 'Left' Hegelians began to turn Hegel's demand for a better world against itself, particularly by arguing that in religious belief people alienate themselves by imagining their own energies as belonging to God. Marx and Engels reply to Ludwig Feuerbach and the others in great detail at the level of content but also by treating these contemporary German ideas as a symptom and reading them as ideology; that is, as the interests of a class expressed in the form of ideas. As such, ideology works by re-presenting local and sectarian interests as universal and necessary, so exercising power not merely when a subordinate class is dominated but because the class holding such ideas is confirmed in its sense of itself.

2.3   Louis Althusser   from 'Ideology and Ideological State
Apparatuses (Notes towards an investigation)' [*Lenin and
Philosophy*, trans. Ben Brewster (London: New Left Books, 1971),
pp. 136–8, 152–3, 153–6, 159–64, 168–70; first published 1970].

Why, when political freedom is there to be taken, do people not grab it? That is the
question Althusser confronts in the year after the failure of the French revolution of
1968. His answer is twofold: that the state has penetrated more deeply into everyday
life than ever before; that ideology operates in us not simply as a set of conscious
opinions but at an unconscious level by making us who we are, constructing us to
think we are free (and so don't need to change anything). From Marx, Althusser
derives the principle that an economic system must not only produce material but
also reproduce the means of production (machines, factory buildings, etc.), especially
by reproducing labour power. By this he means people willing to accept their assigned
position in the productive process. From Gramsci, he borrows the concept of hegemony,
which recognizes that a ruling bloc wins obedience not only through force (and
Repressive State Apparatuses) but also by seeking consent (through the Ideological
State Apparatuses (ISAs)).

What the ISAs work on is the subject, taking babies (the merely physical human
being, which Althusser terms 'concrete individuals') and transforming them into
thinking beings, able to go off on their own five or six years later and answer 'Here'
when the teacher calls out their names in school. For this Althusser turns to psychoanalysis, to Freud's account of how the I, not innate, has to be developed in the
process of a split between conscious and unconscious, and to Lacan's analysis of the
mirror stage (see Section 3.1). When Althusser writes of subjects as living out an
'imaginary' relationship to their real conditions of existence, he is using Lacan's
account of how the ego is set up within the order of the Imaginary as distinct from
the Real. And in borrowing from French legal discourse the term *interpellation* to
describe the way ideology transforms individuals into subjects he is referring to at
least three things: (1) parents hailing their children ('Who's a good little boy, then?');
(2) the way any society imposes rules on its members through the functioning of
what Freud called the superego; (3) the model of religious vocation as when Samuel
hears God calling his name and is instructed to answer, 'Speak, for thy servant
heareth' (I Samuel 3: 1–14). In each of these kinds of relation the individual subject
recognizes/misrecognizes itself reflected in an Absolute Subject and accepts the situation as natural.

2.4   Edward Said   from *Orientalism* [(London: Random House,
1985), pp. 201–4, 226–31].

What Edward Said explores in *Orientalism* is the set of representations – categories,
images and classifications – which have produced the Orient as an object of (largely)
Western understanding, the Orient supposedly being all that is not Europe. The
Orient, he argues, is less a force of nature than a fact of cultural production. It is not
a given reality which exists simply to be described or distorted, but is rather *produced*
within the domain of Orientalism. A domain, that is, which has 'Orientalized' the
Orient by producing a variety of knowledges of it, and, as a result, has come to
exercise power over it in the process by which an active Western subject *knows* and
masters a passive Eastern object. *Orientalism* is in effect, then, a demonstration of the
inseparable relationship between representation and reality. It documents the ways
in which the former governs and dominates the latter; and it exposes the relations

of power inherent in systems of representation which, to a large extent, protest their innocence under the guise of scholarship.

In order to do this, Said draws specifically upon Foucault's notion of discourse as a system of regulation (see Section 3.3). Understood as a discourse, Orientalism becomes a way of structuring, regulating and placing the Orient through the production of a series of minutely detailed knowledges of it. These knowledges are drawn from fields as diverse as geography, science, culture, travel and war, and are so carefully detailed that they have come to invest almost every possible layer of life. What occurs in the process of the production of these knowledges is the whole fictioning of a culture, or cultural meanings, which is regulated in such minute ways that it comes, eventually, to be regarded as 'natural'. Indeed, over the long period of time in which the Orient has been the object of Western interest, such knowledges have become authoritative versions of it. The originally explicit political forces and activities which motivated the production of these knowledges have been relegated to the margins of history, and the discourse of Orientalism itself has been elided with a simple cultural 'truth' so that what the Orient 'really' is becomes forgotten.

The interests served by the discourse of Orientalism are clear. The relationship between the West and its object of knowledge is fundamentally a relationship of power and domination. Yet the implications of the Orientalization of the Orient extend also to the West. If we can say that the Orient exists (largely) as a fiction, then it is possible also to assert that it is a fiction necessary to the construction of an opposing fiction – that of the West. Just as Lacan had proposed that the identity of the human individual is produced in a dialectic between the subject and the Other (see Section 3.1), so Said suggests that the identity of the West is produced in its own dialectical relationship to the Orient. For Said, the meaning of both the Orient and the West is not inherent in either, but is rather constructed in a relationship of difference between the two. The Orientalization of the Orient, then, is useful to the West in as much as it defines that which the West is *not* – what Said calls its 'deepest and most recurring [image] of the Other'. Within these terms, the category of the 'White Man' (Said uses the masculine form throughout) is, like that of the 'Oriental', a product of discursive construction. Deeply felt and experienced as natural, it is, none the less, an existence which is, to a very large and very political extent, a fiction of culture.

3.1 Jacques Lacan 'The mirror stage as formative of the function of the I as revealed in psychoanalytic experience' [from *Écrits: A Selection*, trans. Alan Sheridan (London: Tavistock, 1977, pp. 1–7); originally a lecture delivered at the 16th International Congress of Psychoanalysis in Zürich on 17 July 1949].

'Who am I?' This seemingly reasonable question hides what it presupposes – that I am an identifiable speaking subject knowing language and so able to ask questions like this. How did I get to *be able* to do that in the first place? In 'The mirror stage' Lacan outlines an answer which has had revolutionary implications. For against Descartes's account of the I as a *Cogito* ('I think therefore I am') in which my identity and my being are at one, Lacan argues that the I depends on what is other than itself; the I is therefore an effect socially – discursively – constructed.

For Lacan 'I am a hole surrounded by something': the human subject originates not in presence and identity but rather in a lack or absence which Lacan terms *manque à être*; we define ourselves as human in the impossible task of phantasizing ourselves as complete, desiring (and thinking we find) a plenitude which will make good that originary lack. Of this wider process of attempted self-identification the mirror stage, affecting babies between six and eighteen months, is both a matrix and a compelling example.

During the 1920s and 1930s work in biology and psychology had drawn attention to the importance of sight and mimicry among animals: what Lacan stresses is the radically different effect that a mirror has on a human baby – unlike a dog or a pigeon he (Lacan treats the subject throughout as masculine) greets the reflected (or specular) image with jubiliation as his likeness. Why? The act of looking in a mirror encompasses two possibilities: (1) it is an optical effect producing an image of the face the wrong way round and much smaller; (2) I can say 'It's me'. The identity in the mirror is an external effect which I assume is me. For Lacan my identity is a likeness reflected back from everyone else (the other) (beginning, as it were with the parent who 'hails' the baby into language – 'Who's a good little girl, then?', etc.). My identity is not something I recognize because that would suppose I was *already there* able to do the recognizing (contrast Althusser's view, Section 2.3): my identity comes about in a dialectic between the subject and the other [a subject's ego is 'that which is reflected of his [*sic*] form in his objects', Lacan 1977a: 194]. Unreal, fictional, having an 'alienating destination' (like the asymptotic curve of a graph which will never actually coincide with an axis), this kind of I, achieved in exchange with the other, is the only one I can ever have.

Since my identity is not a recognition but a *misrecognition* (*méconnaissance*) why am I driven to seek it? Although in fact when I am born I am only a tiny part of reality, I don't know that (and 'I' am not yet there to know it anyway). At a point when the experience of the infant (Latin: *infans*, not speaking) consists largely of forms of *imago* (unconscious prototypical figures as theorized by Jung), but when the baby can move around, perhaps with a baby-walker, bumping into things, then the inner world (*Innenwelt*) and the world around (*Umwelt*) begin to become separated for it. Now lack expresses itself when the toddler experiences reality through a phantasy of 'the body in pieces' (*le corps morcelé*), and so it is captivated by the coherent form (*Gestalt*) promised to it by the mirror and the ideal of the body as an imaginary unity. (And why lack? Lacan follows biological thinking in referring to the human species as being born too soon.)

In the I, as in the specular image, the subject seems perfectly to master its own lack. But the apparent solidity and permanence of the ego must be constantly maintained against all that risks making it come to pieces. As Freud noted that in dreams a building may mean the dreamer, so Lacan suggests that the I is like a fortress which must constantly defend itself through denial (*Verneinung*) of everything that threatens to undo it. But then everything does. The I, then, is a paranoiac structure, likely to release aggression against whatever reminds it of its own unreality. [Here Lacan also draws on the work of Freud's daughter, Anna, especially *The Ego and the Mechanisms of Defence* (1937); he also refer to Roger Caillois, the French literary critic and sociologist of religion.]

3.2 Julia Kristeva from 'The System and the Speaking Subject' [(London: *Times Literary Supplement*, 12 October 1973), pp. 1249–50].

'The system and the speaking subject' posits a psycho-linguistic theory of the production of the subject in and through language. Focusing upon language as a signifying *process*, including transgressions as well as confirmations of the law of the symbolic, the essay moves away from the notion of the stable subject as master of the system.

It posits, instead, a notion of an unstable subject precariously produced upon the site of a tension between elements of language which at once confirm the rules of the system and at the same time threaten to undermine its existence as such. As a theory of the subject, then, the essay depends also upon a theory of language which makes several departures from those which precede it.

Kristeva begins by offering an overview of what she calls the field of semiology from her own critical perspective of the revolutionary potentials it offers or denies. The problem with semiology from this perspective is its reliance upon the notion of language as a system or structure. In order for signification to take place, the continuum of possible sounds (semiotic chora) must, like the subject of psychoanalysis, be divided, ordered and arranged. This splitting of sounds enables their arrangement into 'significant' and 'insignificant' sounds – those which have meaning, and those which do not. Sounds which have meaning are subject to the law which governs language – they obey a specific set of rules and structures of grammar, and as such are homogenous. Those which do not are repressed and exist only as a kind of rhythmical (yet also threatening) presence within symbolic language. The splitting of the continuum is what Kristeva calls the 'thetic' (or static) stage of language. Since it is the semiotic which offers the potential to disrupt the symbolic, any analysis which focuses exclusively upon this thetic, or structuring, stage of language is, within Kristeva's terms, inadequate. It excludes the disruptive dimension of language in favour of the structure of the system, and so excludes also the implication of language as a process centred upon the speaking subject.

Since the linguistic theory she outlines cannot encompass the disruptive elements of language Kristeva seeks to privilege, she advances in place of it her own critical framework – that of 'semanalysis.' Semanalysis focuses upon language as process which involves the acceptance of the symbolic law for the purposes of 'renovating' it. In order to do this, Kristeva draws upon the work of Freud, which theorizes the splitting of the subject (between conscious and unconscious) and that of Hegel and Marx, which theorizes the government of the subject in and through a series of social codes. In this way, Kristeva conceives of language as something which is much more than simply a system. Linguistic practice – language spoken by people – becomes both a drive-governed phenomenon and a social space. As such, it concerns the individual but is implicated at the same time in the constitution of the individual within the social order. Concerned with the possibilities of disrupting that order, Kristeva turns also to the work of Lacan (see Section 3.1).

She displaces Lacan's distinction between the Imaginary and the Symbolic into a distinction between the semiotic and the symbolic. While the symbolic stands for the law under which language operates, the semiotic refers to all of the disruptive elements present within the signifying process: non-linguistic sounds, moments of meaninglessness and even silences. The symbolic and the semiotic exist inevitably together. What Kristeva calls the 'phenotext' (language which obeys the rules of communication and presupposes a subject of speech as well as a subject which is addressed) exists in opposition to what she calls the 'genotext' (deviations which form a relative and shifting trajectory not restricted to two poles of communication between two fully formed subjects). Within the phenotext the presence of the genotext can always be traced, and it is the interaction between the two which constitutes the signifying process – what makes signification and subjectivity possible. Produced through the interaction between these two terms, the subject is caught in a paradox – a position which is at once both subversive and confirming, and which subsequently produces the subject as unstable, unfixed and, ultimately, like language itself, very much in process.

[Melanie Klein (1882–1960), whom Kristeva refers to, was a British psychoanalyst concerned especially to understand the objects phantasized by the pre-Oedipal infant.]

3.3   Michel Foucault   from *Discipline and Punish:*
The Birth of the Prison [trans. Alan Sheridan (London: Penguin,
1977), pp. 195–203, 205, 215–17; first published in Paris in
1975].

Contemporary society is, as Foucault contends, a disciplinary society. It functions
most effectively, therefore, not through the exertion of force, but rather through an
incitement to regulation. It works by dividing and individualizing the communal
group – investing each and everybody within that group with a distinct sense of
place, function and attribution. It operates according to a double mode: that of binary
division and branding – between individuals who are mad/sane, abnormal/normal,
sick/healthy and so on. It is efficient precisely because it produces people who *subject*
themselves to its terms, who regulate their own individual 'self' and, therefore, regulate
the body of society as a whole. It is not, Foucault insists, that the 'beautiful totality
of the individual is amputated, repressed [or] altered' by the social order, but rather
that the individual is carefully fabricated within it. What this extract traces, then, is
a history of specific historical events and circumstances which gave rise to this 'careful
fabrication'.

In order to do this Foucault focuses upon two particular historical events: the
organization of the city brought about by the plague at the end of the seventeenth
century, and the design of Bentham's 'panopticon' which revolutionized the prison
system in the nineteenth century.

The environment produced by the coming of the plague represents a significant
event in the organization of the community along individual lines. Operating a
technique of strict spatial partitioning, it ensured that each individual was assigned
to a place and fixed within it. All the inhabitants of the plague-ridden city were
compelled to speak the 'truth' of their own condition and with it the 'truth' of their
own existence. Against the plague discipline brought into play a specific form of
power which involved the confinement of individuals, but also their training as
individuals. Through the process of continual regulation and constant divisions between
sickness and health, each individual was subjected to a whole series of techniques for
surveillance, assessment, supervision and correction, producing in effect the 'Utopia'
of the perfectly governed city.

Bentham's design of the panopticon in the nineteenth century represents the
consolidation of this technique of power and constitutes the architectural development of its effectiveness. Basically it consists of a central watchtower surrounded
by a series of individual cells – cut off from each other but constantly and wholly
visible from the central tower. The central tower can be seen from the cells, but the
presence of an observer within that tower can never be verified. The subsequent
effect of the panoptic arrangement is what Foucault calls the 'automatic functioning
of power'. It creates within the individual a sense of being continually watched –
regardless of whether or not they actually are – so that, after a period of time,
individuals come to regulate their own behaviour. They become caught in a power
situation of which they are themselves the bearers, and the actual exercise of discipline
itself becomes unnecessary. 'A real subjection is born mechanically from a fictitious
relation.'

While he focuses here upon two specific institutions, Foucault is quick also to insist
that each has more general implications for the functioning of society as a whole. The
panopticon is not just a building, but a 'mechanism of power reduced to its ideal
form'. A mechanism of power, that is, which can now be diffused. It is no longer
necessarily operated by a central repressive apparatus, but rather invested within
each individual who in turn assumes responsibility for his or her own subjection. At

work in every institution – from the family to the madhouse – it is a mechanism of power which invests every layer of the human mind and body, and through which a whole type of individual and of society emerges.

[Jeremy Bentham was a British utilitarian philosopher, 1748–1832.]

3.4 Michel Foucault from *The History of Sexuality, Volume One: An Introduction* [trans. Robert Hurley (London: Penguin, 1978), pp. 64–73; first published in Paris in 1976].

Is sexuality spontaneous and rational or is it socially constructed? Is sexuality best understood as the site upon which the subject is produced simply through the process of repression, or, more insidiously, through an incitement to the inscription of the individual within positive forms of pleasure? These are the questions posed by *The History of Sexuality*. In return, Foucault offers no concrete solutions but posits instead the hypothesis that the techniques of power which govern the individual function most effectively when they are concealed, or rather when they are disguised as friendly forces. He takes as the focus of his investigation the production of the subject through the discourses of sex which emerged in the nineteenth century, and which, he implies, continue to control the constitution of the subject in the present day.

The hypothesis, then, is that power operates with regard to sex not simply by forbidding desire or refusing to recognize it, but rather by putting into circulation a whole mechanism by which 'true' discourses of sex are continually produced. This mechanism, within the nineteenth century, is what Foucault calls 'scientia sexualis', or the production of a specific form of knowledge of the individual, and a will to self-knowledge by the individual, through the scientific discourse of sex. It is Foucault's hypothesis that sex has come to function as an important means of producing and regulating the subject not by virtue of anything inherent in sex itself, but rather by virtue of the tactics of power inherent in the discourse of science.

For Foucault, these tactics of power gravitate around the procedures of confession. Originally a Christian rite of penance for the attrition of sin, the confession has increasingly come to function as a means of producing the truth of the individual through the articulation of the deepest secrets of their most private pleasures. Though the confession came to speak of sex, however, it was, by itself, inadequate to the analysis of 'human nature'. The pleasures of which the subject spoke had also to be inscribed within an ordered system of knowledge – a way of attributing meaning to that which was spoken (but not necessarily understood) so that science became an effective means of producing and governing the human subject. It accorded to sex, and to a proliferation of sexual pleasures to which individuals were then referred by the discourse of science, the status of truth. Scientia sexualis demands of sex that it speak its truth, but also that it tells us our truth, or rather, 'the deeply buried truth of that truth about ourselves which we think we possess in our immediate consciousness'. Confession is no longer a test, but a 'sign' – revealing the very core of the meaning of our existence.

Operating in this way, the revelation of truth comes to function not simply as the effect of a power that constrains the individual, but rather as the ultimate act of individual liberation. Scientia sexualis, then, is seen to produce a truth which belongs not to power, but to freedom.

3.5   Roland Barthes   from *The Pleasure of the Text* [trans. Richard Miller (London: Jonathan Cape, 1975), pp. 9–17].

Although Barthes's distinction between text of pleasure and text of bliss seems descriptively plausible and has entered critical currency, it rests on a theoretical basis which he leaves largely implicit, a basis which is essentially Lacanian (see Section 3.1). Lacan works with an ontological distinction between the Real, the Symbolic and the Imaginary. The real remains outside discourse since Lacan denies that human subjects can experience the real except as it is constructed in and by symbolization; the symbolic consists of the intersubjective order of representation and the signifier; in the imaginary the subject wins a sense of identity, meaning and presence for itself from the signifier (so in the example of the mirror phase, the mirror and the subject's body are real, the reflection in the mirror is symbolic, while the identity misrecognized in the reflection is imaginary). Lacan reserves the term *jouissance* for the possibility that the subject may encounter the real without mediation. Far from being pleasant such an encounter is much more likely to be terrible, a trauma like shell shock (in his book of that name published in 1920 Freud starts off his attempt to understand what is beyond the pleasure principle by discussing First World War traumas – see Freud *SE*, v. 18). In French *jouissance*, as well as meaning legal possession (enjoying a right) suggests orgasm and is hardly translatable ('bliss' misses the violence of what's at stake). Lacan treats sexual climax as like trauma because more than anything else it can simulate the fulfilment of desire in the real.

Thus the text of bliss for Barthes works by tearing a hole in signification so that the real, the body, comes through; or rather the *effect* of that, since the real cannot be felt except as it is symbolized (hence Barthes writes not of the real body but 'the body of the text'). In contrast to this loss, pleasure derives from imaginary presence, all the ways in which the I knows, intends, and masters meaning in what is after all only the organization of the signifier. It is important to stress that bliss and pleasure, although generally corresponding to realist versus modernist texts, are states of subjectivity and relative to each other. Barthes supposes that the reader of the realist text typically skips bits and introduces gaps so as to deflect pleasure towards bliss. Finally, of course, Barthes picks up the ideas of Bertolt Brecht in finding a political contrast between the text which confirms and the text which undermines conventional meaning by introducing differing into what appears to be unified and the same as itself.

[Barthes also enjoys his own play with language: *tmesis* means separating parts of a word by introducing a word into it (e.g. 'what things soever') though is used loosely here for the process of missing bits of text; *asyndeton* means omitting conjunctions; *speleology* is the study of caves; and a *phalanstery* was a utopian community of no more than 1800 persons as envisaged by the French socialist, François Fourier; for pheno-text (versus geno-text) see Kristeva (above, 3.2).]

4.1   Jacques Derrida   'Différance' [from *Margins of Philosophy*, trans. Alan Bass (Brighton: Harvester Press, 1982)].

The essay was first given as a lecture before the Sociéte français de philosophie at the Amphithéâtre Michelet on 27 January 1968 and, under the title 'La Différance', published simultaneously in the *Bulletin de la société français de la philosophie*, v. 60, n. 3, July/September 1968, pp. 73–101, and in *Théorie d'ensemble* (Paris: du Seuil, 1968; collection Tel Quel), along with contributions by members of the Tel Quel group, including Barthes, Kristeva, and the writer, Philip Sollers; in *Marges de la philosophie*, published in 1972, it is also entitled 'La différance'.

5.1 Sigmund Freud 'On the universal tendency to debasement in the sphere of love (Contributions to the psychology of love II)' [trans. Alan Tyson, from *Standard Edition*, ed. James Strachey (London: Hogarth Press, 1957) v. 11, pp. 177–90; Freud wrote three 'Contributions to the psychology of love': 'A special type of object choice made by men' (1910); this second; and a third on 'The taboo of virginity' (1917)].

If, as Juliet Mitchell argues in *Psychoanalysis and Feminism*, 'psychoanalysis is not a recommendation *for* a patriarchal society, but an analysis *of* one' (1975, p. xv), then Freud's psychoanalysis might well be wrong about femininity, yet right about masculinity. That problem is immediately signalled by the title of this essay – for, although the tendency is said to be universal, the essay is almost exclusively concerned with men (a situation not much mitigated even if we blame the translator for turning the German *Allgemeinste* or 'general' into the English 'universal').

'All women are whores except my mother, who is a saint' says an old Italian proverb (quoted in Truffaut's film, *The Bride Wore Black*). It is precisely this contradictory masculine attitude expressing itself in a ferociously imposed double standard which Freud in this essay seeks to exhibit and understand, a feature that would have been strikingly apparent to him in a Vienna where so many middle-class men lived one life with their wives and another with one of the huge number of prostitutes making a living in the city. In one respect Freud's answer is disarmingly simple if his theory of the Oedipus complex makes sense. For Freud 'the finding of an object is in fact a refinding of it' (*SE*, v. 7, p. 222); and so a man's sexual drive originates with his first love, his mother, but in response to the prohibition on incest becomes transformed into desire for another adult woman. It is difficult but necessary for men to separate the feeling for the other adult woman from the feeling for the mother on which it is modelled, and this leads to a polarizing of ideas of women between the overvalued Madonna figure who is loved and the undervalued Whore figure who is desired.

As the essay suggests, women are also subject to the same problem of psychical impotence expressing itself in frigidity but much less so, for reasons Freud discusses elsewhere [notably in his two essays on 'Female sexuality' (1931, *SE*, v. 21) and 'Feminine sexuality' (1933, *SE*, v. 22)]. While both the little girl and little boy take the mother as their first object, the girl moves (if she does) to the father and then to the other adult man, but the boy moves (if he does) *directly* from the mother to the other woman. For him the proximity of the two (and so the problem) is much more acute.

Freud also begins to explore reasons why sexual desire cannot be satisfied, beginning by noting that the original object must be represented by 'an endless series of substitutive objects', suggesting that human culture may be incompatible with the satisfaction of sexual drive, and then turning to history to develop this theme. Not only does the polarization of masculine desire have a clear cultural and historical expression in the instituted forms of Eros versus Agape, love 'sacred' and 'profane', but further Freud speculates that Courtly Love, developed under the influence of Christianity, was needed to give a value to the sexual relation unknown in antiquity.

[Psychoanalysis works with a technical vocabulary. The word 'object' has a formal sense as a thing or person which is the object of a drive and so caught up in forms of phantasy (in this respect an object is mainly symbolic). 'Libido' is the reservoir of psychic energy which becomes divided between ego and sexual instincts (or drive) and channelled into various kinds of investment or 'cathexis'. Drive which remains stuck with an earlier object is said to be 'fixated'. An 'imago' is an unconscious prototypical figure (see also p. 72 above); in a 'reaction-formation' an attitude occurs diametrically opposed to a repressed wish; 'sublimation' is the process in which sexual drive is taken up in relation to the ego and so directed towards another aim. The view that 'we are born between the piss and the shit' (inter urinas and faeces nascimur) is not Freud but St Augustine.]

5.2 Hélène Cixous 'Sorties: Out and Out: Attacks/Ways Out/ Forays' [from The Newly Born Woman by Hélène Cixous and Catherine Clément, trans. Betsy Wing (Manchester: Manchester University Press and Minneapolis: University of Minnesota Press, 1986), pp. 63–4, 83–9, 91–7; first published in Paris in 1975].

Cixous's writing is, in and of itself, a call to action, revolution and transgression. Privileging contradiction, silence and the sliding of the signifier, she operates within theoretical structures only to subvert them. Her primary concern is to undermine the logocentrism (the idea that meaning is fully present in the word) and phallocentrism (the privileging of the phallus as the ultimate signifier) inherent in Western philosophical discourse. She posits instead a notion of the feminine as a positive source of energy, instability and diversity, capable of subverting that which has traditionally worked to oppress and to silence women. To do this, Cixous draws upon the work of established theorists (Derrida, Kristeva and Lacan) but always with the traces of escape from their terms carefully woven into the fabric of her own text.

For Cixous the subject 'woman' is the product of linguistic difference – the effect of a hierarchical structuring of thought (activity/passivity, Culture/Nature and so on) all of which comes down, she suspects, to the ultimate coupling of man/woman. As long as we remain stuck within these binary oppositions, victory always comes down to the same thing: the 'glorious phallic monosexuality' of male privilege. What Cixous seeks, then, are ways out (sorties) from the rigid structures which place woman in a gendered and heterosexually determined relationship of difference to man.

In order to do this she revives a notion of bisexuality – not as the fantasy of a complete being which replaces the fear of castration, but rather as the location within the 'self' of a split, an unstable division between contradictory elements which simply co-exist. The effect of this division is mobility – a constantly shifting self the meaning of which may at moments be fixed but which contains within it the possibility always of moving on – accepting rather than repressing the other of the 'I' within discourse. While psychoanalysis has traditionally denied the femininity of masculine sexuality – theorizing the construction of both upon the terms of loss and fear of loss – Cixous sees no reason why it must be so. 'Nothing compels us' she asserts 'to deposit our lives in these lack-banks' (see Lacan, Section 3.1). She argues, instead, for the celebration of difference and anomaly, the 'springing up of selves we didn't know', and the 'I/play of bisexuality' which circumvents the closure of meaning through différance (see Section 4).

It is, however, more likely to be women who are capable of maintaining the play of difference which Cixous's notion of bisexuality demands; and it is, for historical reasons, also women who are most likely to benefit from the transgressions of the patriarchal order which it performs. Paradoxically, if there is a self proper to woman it is her capacity to 'depropriate' herself without self interest, and it is this capacity for depropriation which holds possibilities for the future. This capacity is linked explicitly to the female body and female desire. While masculine sexuality is centred upon the penis, female sexuality is multiply diverse – not constrained to a single signifier but spread throughout the body and capable at any moment of performing an 'explosive return'. If the constitution of the masculine depends upon the rigid binaries which structure language and thought, and is wholly susceptible to the repression of that which transgresses those binaries, the feminine still reverberates with the instabilities of that which 'comes-before-language'. That is, precisely all of the libidinal drives and rhythmical flows of the pre-Oedipal stage (see Kristeva's notion of the disruptive presence of the semiotic within the symbolic, Section 3.2).

There is, then, a link between the economy of femininity which Cixous describes and the act of writing as transformation and creation. The call to action which she sounds is the call to feminine writing (*écriture féminine*) – a form of writing which works upon difference and plurality. Woman must, Cixous asserts, write her body. She must produce texts which destroy the closure of binary oppositions and celebrate instead the pleasures (*jouissance*) (see Section 3.5) of open-ended textuality. Texts which, like the female erotic, cannot be defined or theorized, enclosed or coded, texts which will 'blow up' the patriarchal law of language itself, challenging the law of the symbolic by ceaselessly displacing the system of couples and positions by which it fixes the subject 'woman'.

Though feminine writing is most obviously linked to the body it is not exclusively the property of woman. To claim it as such would indeed be to return us to the arena of binary oppositions Cixous seeks to destroy. Feminine writing is, rather, that which displays the libidinal femininity of transgression and diversity, and as such can theoretically be located in works produced by writers of either sex.

5.3 Laura Mulvey from 'Visual pleasure and narrative cinema' [*Screen* v. 16, n. 3 (Autumn 1975), pp. 6–14, 17–18].

Juliet Mitchell in *Psychoanalysis and Feminism* (1974) drew fresh attention to Freud's 1931 account of female sexuality (see *SE*, v. 21: 221–43). Since both little girls and little boys are equally active in seeking the mother during the pre-Oedipal phallic stage, what needs to be explained, Mitchell argues, is how women's activity and drive may be turned toward a passive aim, unconsciously internalising patriarchy. In a well-known footnote added to *Three Essays on the Theory of Sexuality* of 1915, Freud denied that sexuality was simply '*biological*' or '*sociological*', proposing that 'masculine' and 'feminine' were equally attributes of a single subject, equivalent to 'active' and 'passive' (*SE*, v. vii: 218–19). Mulvey analyses the reproduction of sexual imbalance by a visual regime which extends well beyond Hollywood (into magazine photography and advertising, for instance).

This works through the superimposition of a series of binaries, narcissism/desire, looking/being looked at, active/passive, masculine/feminine. Psychoanalysis distinguishes between self-love and love for the other (narcissism or 'ego libido' and desire or 'sexual instinct'). In Hollywood cinema men are invited to identify with a male protagonist in looking at and desiring women as objects, while women are to identify with the female figures passively looked at. Women's own desire – and identification with an active figure – become effaced. In the typical Hollywood narrative women's otherness is mastered either through sadistic aggression or by being fetishized (in his essay on 'Fetishism' Freud argues that this is an essentially male response to the threat imputed to women if they are seen to lack the phallus, the fetish being a phantasy object erected in place of the lack which is disavowed, see *SE*, v. 21; 147–57).

Mulvey's essay has provoked a small library of feminist scholarship (see her own subsequent essay on the female viewer, 1989; Cowie 1984; de Lauretis 1984; Doane 1987; Modleski 1988). [The 'Name of the Father' is the signifier in whose virtue, Lacan argues, patriarchy instates lack; 'scopophilia' (*Schaulust*) means simply 'visual pleasure'; for the 'mirror phase', see Lacan (Section 3.1); the *diegesis* of a film is all that is represented in its narrative.]

5.4   Gayatri Chakravorty Spivak   from 'Displacement and the discourse of woman' [from *Displacement: Derrida and After*, ed. Mark Krupnick (Bloomington: Indiana University Press, 1983), pp. 169–79, 184–6].

Is deconstruction just another example of the use of woman as an instrument of self-assertion within the discourse of man, or does it offer us the grounds of an analysis which *can* be developed in the interests of a feminist practice? In this extract, Gayatri Chakravorty Spivak suggests that deconstruction's critique of phallogo-centrism (see Section Four) is useful but also problematic to the project of the feminist critic. In a detailed critique of the work of Jacques Derrida, she takes deconstruction to task for its erection of a practice in which the power of the male is implicitly retained through the taking of the figure of the female as its model of uncertainty.

Arguably, women can simulate orgasm, men can't. According to Nietzsche (see 1974) the artistry of woman is her capacity for masquerade (see Riviere 1929) – for the organization of self-(re)presentation (fake orgasm) without an actual pre-sence (of sexual pleasure) to re-present (this is the *originary displacement* of woman). In this, woman is irreducibly different from man whose 'pen must write or prove impotent', and it is this difference which deconstruction seeks to master in its analysis of the uncertainty of presence in the textual operation of writing. Although Derrida criticizes the phallocentrism of Nietzsche's formulation, by taking this model of woman as an exemplar of deconstructivist analysis he none the less appropriates the displaced place of woman. By announcing in the introduction to *Eperons* that his subject will be woman, for example, Derrida takes for deconstruction the 'ownness' (see Hegel 1942) of its subject/object, and the figure of woman becomes *doubly displaced* within the analysis that follows (see also Freud's account of the double displacement of the girl from her object of desire through the Oedipus complex – 5.1, this section).

This double displacement is compounded in Derrida's 'La double séance' (see Derrida 1972) where Derrida offers the undecidable feminine figure of the hymen as a general textual effect of 'Mimique', a fiction by the French symbolist writer Mallarmé. The hymen is indeed a useful figure since, like the fake orgasm, it has the capacity to be both itself and not itself – metaphorically broken, yet literally intact, and located both inside and outside the body. But its undecidability is founded upon a dissymmetry – on one side of which is virginity, and on the other is marriage as a legal assurance of the passage of property. The figure itself conceals a hidden agenda – the formulation of virginity as the property of the sexually undisclosed phallus as master of the dialectics of desire ('virgin' being a sexist term if it applies to women and not men). Taken as a figure of the law of textual operation, the hymen becomes doubly displaced by the appearance of the phallus as the masquerading 'thing' which comes close to faking the orgasm because the phallus is symbolic, the penis is not. Not only is a language of women's desire occluded within this model, but the basis of a politics of feminist practice is also made impossible.

For deconstruction to be useful to feminist practice, then, woman must cease to be the object either of its analysis or its question. Caught on the other side of sexual difference, the female deconstructivist must turn the tables by asking the question of man: 'What is man that the itinerary of his desire creates such a text?' This gesture not only reinstates a historical differential in which the political economy of 'the property of man as holder of property' is made clear, but also 'restores us to the position of questioning subject'.

6.1 Jean-François Lyotard from *The Postmodern Condition: A Report on Knowledge* [trans. Geoff Bennington and Brian Massumi (Manchester: Manchester University Press and Minneapolis: Minnesota University Press, 1984), pp. 31–41; first published in Paris in 1979].

For Jean-François Lyotard the condition of postmodern culture is intimately related to the condition of knowledge within the post-industrial world. Within the analysis he offers here, the postmodern condition itself is characterized by the delegitimation of knowledge – the breakdown of the single and overriding narrative (meta – or, grand, narrative) which has served to guarantee the truth, or use-value of knowledge throughout history. He takes as the focus of his analysis the status of science, and traces the principles by which it has been legitimated.

There are, Lyotard argues, two major versions of narrative legitimation: the political and the philosophical. Within the political narrative legitimation depends upon the rhetoric of 'freedom' and emancipation of 'the people', and science assumes the status of a 'means to an end'. All people have the right to scientific knowledge, and if their liberation is to be achieved, that right to knowledge must be fulfilled. According to this version scientific knowledge finds its legitimation not in itself, but in the practical subject – humanity – and in recourse to the freedom of will of that subject. Science is legitimated, then, by its use-value, the belief in the grand narrative principle of justice, humanity and emancipation. (Lyotard draws on Wittgenstein's argument that all knowledge comes about on the basis of variable 'language games' (see Wittgenstein 1967: 5ff.).)

Within the philosophical narrative, on the other hand, the legitimation of science depends upon the principle, or what Lyotard calls the 'metaprinciple', of 'speculation'. Within these terms, scientific knowledge first finds its legitimation within itself, not as a means to an end, but rather more as an end in itself. It is never wholly an end in itself, however, since it depends also upon a notion of what Lyotard calls the 'Spirit of the Nation' and the 'Life of the Spirit'. For Lyotard, this mode of legitimation demands a different kind of language game – not the utilization of prescriptive statements of justice, but rather of declarative statements of authenticity, or truth.

Within contemporary post-industrial society and postmodern culture, however, the grounds upon which the question of the legitimation of knowledge is formulated have shifted. The grand narrative (of humanity or science) regardless of its legitimation through the narratives either of emancipation or speculation, has lost its credibility. While related to developments in technology and the technological control of information (the whole 'technoscience' of advanced capitalism), the delegitimation which Lyotard traces is the culmination of the 'problem of legitimation' inherent in the language games of the history of the legitimation of knowledge itself. As Lyotard asks succinctly in *The Postmodern condition*, 'What proof is there that my proof is true?' (p. 24).

Founded upon a notion that knowledge is really only knowledge when it is capable of reduplicating itself by citing its own statements in a second order of discourse which then functions to legitimate them, science can never, ultimately, guarantee itself as anything more than an act of faith. Science, in other words, plays only its own games. It can neither guarantee nor control the languages of other discourses or forms of knowledge. As a result, a variety of fields of knowledges and narratives proliferate, and the notion of a universal (unifying) metalanguage is lost.

For Jean-François Lyotard, then, the postmodern condition is the condition of a culture in which the grand narrative has collapsed, leaving culture itself as the site of a patchwork of smaller, diverse and fragmented narratives with no single unifying guarantee outside of themselves.

6.2 Fredric Jameson   from *Postmodernism or, The Cultural Logic of Late Capitalism* [(Durham, NC: Duke University Press, 1991), pp. 16–25; first published in 1984].

For Jameson the postmodern condition is not the effect of the internal erosion of the logic of narratives of legitimation, as Lyotard has suggested (see preceding extract) but rather the direct result of what he calls the 'cultural logic of late capitalism'. His analysis depends, then, upon a base and superstructure model (see Section 2.1) in which culture is determined by its relationship to the mode of production. Within these terms, the cultural mode of realism is understood to be the logical effect of the mode of market capitalism; modernism is seen as an effect of the shift from the market to monopoly capitalism; and postmodernism is produced as the effect of multi-national diversification. Tied to a concept of the mode of production in this way, Jameson's analysis does not embrace the collapse of the grand narrative. In the face of Lyotard's patchwork of multiple narratives, it reasserts the validity of claims to a single narrative which orders and places all others in the name of emancipation, namely Hegelian Marxism.

For Jameson the problem with the cultural condition produced by multi-national capitalism is its fragmentation of the collective subject and the subsequent isolation of that subject from the history of its collective and radical past. Within these terms, postmodernism can be seen to produce the death of the subject by forcing it free of its traditional grounding within the referent of the real in the form of 'real' history.

Jameson centres his discussion around what he calls the lost 'style' of cultural representation. The style of modernism, for example, with its grounding in a sense of shock and alienation related to real historical time, has given way to the 'codes' of pastiche which eclipse the sense both of time and of history. Characterized by what Jameson calls an 'irrational eclecticism', pastiche is no longer a coherent style grounded in the referent of historical reality, but rather the illogical and random borrowing of codes which *simulate* (see following extract) a variety of historical moments with no necessary connection to the 'original' moments themselves. Through the loss of a connection to the 'real' past in this way, the practices of postmodernism can also be seen to embody the broader inability of the contemporary subject to engage with the realities of, or to accurately represent the experiences of, the present. Representation of, and even critical commentary upon, the referent of the real are thus collapsed into the 'reification' of a kind of media speech. That is, a fragmented speech which, with no reference to any reality outside of its own, reduces the real material struggles of society to the status of spectacle.

Within the nostalgia film, for example, there is no 'representation' of the 'real' past, but rather the aesthetic simulation of 'pastness' through stylistic connotation –

signifiers with no referent in the real, only the filmic codes of the nostalgia mode (fashion, music, the use of black and white and so on). Similarly, though any historical novel undoubtedly involves some kind of mobilization of historical knowledge, this is only narratively possible through a codification of connotations of historicity. A narrative dialectic is set up between a distant memory of the real (historical figure/event) and the stylistic codes through which a sense *not* of 'real' history but of 'historicity' is connoted. From this dialectic 'real' history emerges only as a trace in the aesthetic effect of the lost historical referent.

That this is an occasion of mourning for Jameson is founded precisely upon a refusal to relinquish the grand Hegelian Marxist concept of the totality of history as a grand narrative legitimation of the class struggles of the present. Just as Baudrillard has argued (without a sense of regret, however) that the 'real' America is lost in simulations which no longer have any reference to a reality outside of their own, so Jameson sees the fate of 'real' history lost in the glossy media simulations of historicity, a historicity which, within the postmodern condition of late capitalism, places real history for ever out of reach.

6.3 Jean Baudrillard from *Simulations* [trans. Paul Foss, Paul Patton and Philip Beitchman (New York: Semiotext(e), 1983), pp. 1-4, 23-6; first published in Paris in 1975].

Disneyland *is* the real America: a frightening thought, or the confirmation of deep-seated Anglo/European suspicions? For Jean Baudrillard, perhaps, the answer would be both, although Europe itself could never be vindicated since within his terms America is by no means exclusive in its foundation of a society through the process of simulation. For Baudrillard the importance of the answer lies in its analysis of the condition of postmodernity.

This condition is generated by what Baudrillard calls 'the age of simulation' or, the 'third order' of simulation in a long history stretching from feudal times to the present day. Breaking with the belief in a fixed hierarchy of signs which were simply construed as the real – the belief that signs could *exchange* for meaning, and that something could guarantee that exchange (usually God in medieval times) – the first order of signification constructed reality through the process of representation (the production of signs which sought to imitate the real, to reflect it). In the second order – what the German Marxist Walter Benjamin has called 'the age of mechanical reproduction' (see 1973) – signification came to function through the process of reproduction of 'original' representations (signs which referred to signs which, in turn, referred to reality).

While the first and second orders maintain a notion of connection between representation and the real for the third order of what Baudrillard calls 'simulation', such a connection is no longer valid. We now participate in, and are constructed through, a system of signs which devour representation, signs which no longer refer to something outside themselves – a presence whose absence they mark – but rather serve to mask the absence of any exterior, or basic reality (see Lyotard, 6.1 of this section). When the real is no longer what it used to be, nostalgia proliferates in the form of myths of origin and signs of reality, simulation.

In the postmodern world of simulations, what Baudrillard calls the 'representational imaginary' (the imaginary relation between the real and its representation) is dissolved. In its place springs forth a world of 'hyperreality', a world of self-referential signs (see Derrida, Section 4) engendering a reality more real than any shreds of a memory of the real itself.

In this extract he takes as one illustrative example the American phenomenon of Disneyland. The Disneyland imaginary constitutes neither the real America nor an unreal version of it, but functions rather as imaginary in order to maintain the fiction that the America outside of Disneyland is real. Disneyland functions, then, in the same way that prisons function in a disciplinary society – to conceal the fact that society *as a whole* is carceral (see Foucault, Section 3.3). Disneyland functions as an imaginary simulation to conceal the fact that America *as a whole* is itself a series of simulations.

7.1   F. R. Leavis   from *Mass Civilisation and Minority Culture* [Minority Pamphlets number 1 (Cambridge: Gordon Fraser, 1930), pp. 3–5].

The split between high and popular culture, the culture of the gentry and that of the working class, has widened since the Renaissance but become a yawning divide with the development after 1880 of the mass media, first the popular press, then cinema, radio, and television. Writing the year after the Great Crash of 1929, conscious both of the threat of Soviet Marxism and the working-class movement in his own country, Leavis defines a binary opposition between high and popular culture and calls on the canon and an élite able to respond to it as the only means to defend an increasingly embattled culture.

7.2   Theodore Adorno   from 'On popular music' (with George Simpson) [*Studies in Philosophy and Social Science* (Zeitschrift für Sozialforschung), v. 9 (1941) pp. 17–48].

In addition to the effect of ideology (see Sections 2.1 and 2.2) Marx also wrote of how 'the dull compulsion of the economic', the simple necessity (for those with jobs) to get up and go to work each day, operates to maintain the prevailing social order. The Marxist concept of alienation claims that, if the institution in which you work is owned and controlled by someone else, then the harder you work the less your work is your own. Developing the Hegelian dialectic of subject and object in 'The fetishism of commodities and the secret thereof' (see *Capital* (1970), v. 1: 76–87), Marx argues that commodity production conceals people's actual labour from them by making the world of commodities appear magically self-sustaining, like a primitive totem or fetish. This account is further developed by the Hungarian Marxist, Georg Lukács (see *Biographies*), in *History and Class Consciousness* (1971). In the major essay of that volume ('Reification and the consciousness of the proletariat', see 1971: 83–222) Lukács describes how under capitalism rationalisation of the work-process and modern mass-production 'objectifies' labour so that subjective consciousness becomes correspondingly partial, specialized and fragmented, and a sense of totality becomes lost.

Following on from the work of Lukács, the Frankfurt School developed a sociological analysis of the split between high and popular culture: popular culture, produced and disseminated by the marketing institutions of capitalist society, appeals to the masses not so much through ideology but because it functions as entertainment defined in opposition to labour and necessity; high culture, especially since the Modernist revolution, promises at least some alternative to the passive consumerist commodification of the texts in mass culture.

Adorno's essay works out this account in a detailed study of that domain least susceptible to convincing formal analysis, music. In doing so, he discriminates the music of high and popular culture with a set of oppositions: complex/simple; expressive/conventional; spontaneous/conditioned; individual/structured; educated/ 'natural'. In *The Interpretation of Dreams* (*SE*, vs. 5–6) Freud argued that dreams expressed in disguised form the fulfilment of wishes, and Adorno draws on this to explain how popular music addresses its subjects, as well as the notions of stimulus/ response and conditioned reflex from more conventional cognitive psychology. Of course the popular music he knew was that of the 1930s, particularly jazz; Adorno proposes that the work of such Modernist high cultural composers as Igor Stravinsky and Paul Hindemith constitutes a challenge to the traditional tonal system of popular music, a view it would be interesting to test on some of the counter-cultural music of the 1960s.

7.3 Raymond Williams 'Culture and which way of life?'
[from *Culture and Society 1780–1850* (London: Chatto and Windus: 1958), pp. 319–28].

As Williams shows in *Culture and Society*, the tradition of British cultural studies originates with Romanticism and the endeavour of writers such as Blake and Wordsworth to define culture as a subjective and personal domain standing opposed to the rapidly expanding economic and social forces unleashed by the Industrial Revolution. He traces the concept of culture from Carlyle, Dickens, Ruskin and Arnold through turn-of-the-century writers such as Shaw and Oscar Wilde down to D. H. Lawrence, R. H. Tawney and F. R. Leavis. Traces but also contests, for in this tradition culture came to be identified specifically with *high* culture, art and literature. Such a usage is most obviously signalled by Matthew Arnold in 1867 when in *Culture and Anarchy* he discriminates between our 'ordinary' and our 'best' self so that in our ordinary selves 'we are separate, personal, at war', while in 'our *best self* we are united, impersonal, at harmony' (1960: 94, 95): culture is assumed to reside in this best self.

Williams challenges the double manoeuvre by which the English gentry has privileged itself: by separating culture from society and its institutions; by equating culture with art and literature, so denying the possibility of working-class culture. In this section from the conclusion to *Culture and Society* Williams begins with a qualified rejection of Marxist accounts of culture as simply class determined between bourgeois and proletarian culture, especially as this latter was given a prescriptive definition by some Marxist writers in the 1930s. Humanist both in regarding culture as a form of more or less spontaneous expression and in celebrating what is common to people (and a national culture) rather than what divides them, he goes on equally to reject views prevalent in the 1950s that increasing affluence had made the working class bourgeois, undermining collective identity. Such cultural identity still maintains a traditional expression in working-class institutions as part of a whole way of life – one which, Williams asserts, will 'stand comparison' with that of the gentry.

Writing in considerable isolation in a period which Daniel Bell famously characterized as witnessing 'the end of ideology' and so writing in a particularly cagey style, Williams nevertheless is able to breach the prevailing opposition between literature and popular culture, initiating a mode of cultural analysis which (among others things) has made this present Reader possible.

[Williams mentions 'U' and 'non-U', terms from a silly book of the time which discriminated between Upper and Non-Upper Class forms of social etiquette; he also refers to 'council houses', homes then provided for the poor by local government. 'The incident of the swine in the night' alludes both to the story of the Gadarene swine (Matthew 8: 28–34) and to Edmund Burke's notorious reference to contemporary organized mass demonstrations as 'the swinish multitude' in *Reflexions on the French Revolution* (1790).]

7.4 Raymond Williams 'Popular' [from *Keywords* (London: Harper Collins, 1976), pp. 198–9].

How often do we say, or have said to us, even within our own speech community 'We're just not speaking the same language here'? Often enough, it would seem, to suggest that language itself is a slippery and difficult phenomenon. Words have more than one meaning, and any one meaning may vary according to the context in which the word is used. Differences also open up between words that are written and those that are spoken. And, of course, meanings change over time.

In his study of the term 'popular' Raymond Williams traces the layers of meaning embedded in a word which currently has both a general and a variable usage. Going beyond simple dictionary definitions, Williams offers us a range of variable meanings. By looking at historical changes a complexity of meanings and values is revealed. But it is not just that meaning is historically variable for the force of the word also varies within different discourses. Within legal, political and literary terms, for example, 'popular' carries meanings which range from legal action to that which is familiar. Embedded within discursive difference, differences of value may also be revealed. 'Pop' within music terms can mean lively or base, but it can also mean both. Connected or related to other words, as in the terms 'popular literature' and 'the popular press', for example, the word 'popular' itself takes on different values and even carries different meanings.

Such variations and complexities are important for they show that meaning is embedded in actual relations as well as processes of social and historical change. Language does not simply reflect the processes of society and history – on the contrary, key social and historical processes occur *within* language, and language itself becomes the site upon which contemporary values and beliefs are contested.

7.5 Tristan Tzara 'Memoirs of Dadaism' [reprinted in Edmund Wilson, *Axel's Castle* (New York: Charles Scribner's Sons, 1931), pp. 304–9].

In many languages repeated dentals (da-da, ta-ta) make a baby word for daddy but Dada is also the French for a hobby horse as well as 'Yes! Yes!' in Rumanian. After what seems to have been its beginnings at the Cabaret Voltaire in Zurich in 1916, the Dada movement rapidly spread to Berlin, Hanover, Cologne and New York before coming to temporary rest in Paris around 1917. Up to 1923 it included a number of writers, musicians and painters (of whom Marcel Duchamp and Man Ray may be now the most well known – a full *dramatis personae* is given by Hans Richter, himself a participant, in *Dada: Art and Anti-Art* (1965)). From about 1923 in Paris, under the leadership of the poet, André Breton, it was transformed into something more coherent, the Surrealist movement, dedicated to opposing the existing social order by calling on the authority of the unconscious (and joined by new personnel, including the painters Max Ernst and Salvador Dali).

Dada perfectly represents the cultural intervention of an avant-garde, albeit through parody (naming itself by its principles, like Cubism and Futurism, publishing manifestos, holding exhibitions, etc.). Its effect can now be seen as an attempt to deconstruct a series of associated oppositions: high/popular culture; art/labour; passive/active; individual/social; conscious/unconscious; masculine/feminine; an élite/the masses; serious/silly. But its main enemy was the high-art tradition, staged around the Great Creative Individual whose works were to be contemplated in silence by a select, respectful and obedient public. To the extent that it acts out what Tzara terms an 'absolutely anti-literary point of view' it remains predicated on the very canon it would deny.

[Dada was profoundly affected by the much greater madness of its own time, the First World War, and Tzara mentions a *poilu* or 'hairy', the nick-name used of themselves by French soldiers. Eluard's 'example' cited translates:

'The post-box is opposite.'
' – What do you expect me to do about it?'
'Sorry, I saw you had a letter in your hand. I thought . . .'
' – It's not a matter of thinking but of knowing.']

BIOGRAPHIES

(Dates are for first publication; English translations are listed in *References*).

Theodore Adorno German social scientist (1903–69); with others (including Max Horkheimer, Walther Benjamin and Herbert Marcuse) worked in the Institute for Social Research founded at the University of Frankfurt, 1923; with the rise of Nazism fled to the USA in 1934; returned to Frankfurt, 1960; *Dialectic of Enlightenment* with Max Horkeimer, 1946; *Negative Dialectics*, 1966; *Philosophy of Modern Music*, 1966.

Louis Althusser French Marxist philosopher (born Algeria 1918; died 1989); *For Marx*, 1965; *Reading Capital* with Étienne Balibar, 1968; *Lenin and Philosophy*, 1971.

Roland Barthes French literary critic and semiotician (1915–80); Professor of Semiology at the Collège de France from 1976; *Mythologies*, 1957; *Elements of Semiology*, 1964; *S/Z*, 1970; *The Pleasure of the Text*, 1973; *A Lover's Discourse: Fragments*, 1977.

Jean Baudrillard French writer and critic (b. 1929); from 1966–87 taught Sociology at the University of Nanterre; *For a Critique of the Political Economy of the Sign*, 1972; *The Mirror of Production*, 1973; *Forget Foucault*, 1977.

Hélène Cixous French feminist writer, born in Algeria in 1937; Professor of English Literature at the University of Vincennes; *The Exile of James Joyce*, 1968; 'The laugh of the Medusa', 1975; *The Newly Born Woman* with Catherine Clément, 1975.

Jacques Derrida French philosopher, born in Algeria in 1930; teaches philosophy at the École Normale Supérieure in Paris; *'Speech and Phenomena' and Other Essays on Husserl's Theory of Signs*, 1967; *Of Grammatology*, 1967; *Writing and Difference*, 1967; *Dissemination*, 1972; *Margins of Philosophy*, 1972; *The Post Card from Socrates to Freud and Beyond*, 1980 (for full bibliography, see Norris 1987).

Frederick Engels German co-author with Karl Marx (1820–95); ran a business in

Manchester after exile; *The Condition of the Working Class in England in 1844* (1845) (see Marx and Engels, *Collected Works*).

Michel Foucault French philosopher and historian of ideas (1926–84); Professor of History and Systems of Thought at the Collège de France; *Madness and Civilisation*, 1961; *The Order of Things*, 1966; *The Archaeology of Knowledge*, 1969; *Discipline and Punish: The Birth of the Prison*, 1975; *History of Sexuality*, vs. 1, 2 and 3, 1976 and 1984.

Sigmund Freud German founder of psychoanalysis (1856–1939); fled from Nazism to London, 1938; *The Interpretation of Dreams* (1900) (see *Standard Edition*).

Antonio Gramsci born in Sardinia, 1891; died, 1937; worked for Italian Communist Party and was imprisoned by Mussolini in 1926; *Prison Notebooks*, 1971.

Martin Heidegger German philosopher (1889–1976); 1929, Chair of Philosophy at Freiburg in succession to Edmund Husserl (below); made Rector of the University under the Nazis, 1934 but resigned in 1935; removed from Chair in 1945 on charge that he had served the interests of the Nazi movement; *Being and Time*, 1927; *An Introduction to Metaphysics*, lecture 1935, published 1953 (see *Basic Writings*, 1978).

Edmund Husserl German philosopher (1859–1938); Professor at University of Freiburg, 1916; *Ideas*, 1913; *Logical Investigations*, 1922 (written, 1900–1); *Cartesian Meditations*, 1929; developed phenomenology, project for producing an analysis of the contents of consciousness while suspending (or 'bracketing') the question of the relation between consciousness and the real.

Fredric Jameson American Marxist literary critic, b. 1934; Professor of Literature at Duke University; *Marxism and Form*, 1971; *The Prison-House of Language*, 1972; *The Political Unconscious*, 1981; *Postmodernism or the Logic of Late Capitalism*, 1991.

Julia Kristeva French feminist writer, literary critic, and psychoanalyst; born Bulgaria, 1941; Professor at the University of Paris VII; *Revolution in Poetic Language*, 1974; *Desire in Language*, 1979; 'Women's time', 1981.

Jacques Lacan (1901–81) French psychoanalyst; his weekly seminars, which started in 1953, were attended, especially during the 1960s, by (among others) Althusser, Barthes, Derrida and Kristeva; *The Four Fundamental Concepts of Psychoanalysis*, seminar 1964–5, published 1953; *Écrits*, 1977; (see also *The Language of the Self*, 1953; *Feminine Sexuality*, 1982); his complete works, over 20 volumes of the 'Séminaires' (*The Four Fundamental Concepts* represents only v. 11) is being prepared by Jacques-Alain Miller and gradually published in English.

F. R. Leavis English literary critic (1895–1978); Fellow of Downing College, Cambridge, and finally Reader in English, 1960; with Denys Thompson published *Culture and Environment*, 1933; *New Bearings in English Poetry*, 1932; *The Great Tradition*, 1948; he was the husband of Q. D. Leavis, who published an innovatory study of popular culture, *Fiction and the Reading Public*, in 1932.

Emmanuel Levinas philosopher, born in Lithuania in 1906; attended lectures given by Husserl at Freiburg, 1928–9; 1945, director of the École Normale Israélite Orientale, Paris, 1946; Professor of Philosophy at the Sorbonne, 1973; *Time and the Other*, originally lectures, 1946–7, 1979; *Totality and Infinity*, 1961; Levinas rejects any philosophic rationalizing in favour of a sense of experience open to the Other (see Hand, 1989).

Claude Lévi-Strauss Belgian anthropologist, b. 1908; Chair of Social Anthropology at the Collège de France, 1958; his work tended to show that binary oppositions were basic to human thought; *Structural Anthropology*, 1958; *The Savage Mind*, 1962.

Georg Lukács Hungarian Marxist philosopher and literary critic (1885–1971); *History and Class Consciousness*, 1923; *The Historical Novel*, 1937; *The Meaning of Contemporary Realism*, 1958.

Jean-François Lyotard French philosopher, b. 1924; Professor at the University of Paris VIII, 1972–87; *Discours, figure*, 1971 not translated; *The Postmodern Condition*, 1979; *The Differend*, 1983; with Jean-Loup Thébaud, *Just Gaming*, 1979.

Colin MacCabe English literary critic, b. 1951; Professor at University of Strathclyde after non-renewal of lectureship at Cambridge University in 1980, now at British Film Institute; *James Joyce and the Revolution of the Word* (1978); *Theoretical Essays* (1985).

Pierre Macherey French literary critic, b. 1938; member of the French Communist Party and colleague of Louis Althusser; teaches philosophy at the University of Paris; *A Theory of Literary Production*, 1966; with Étienne Balibar, 'On literature as ideological form', 1974 (see Young 1981).

Karl Marx German political economist (1818–83); exiled to London in 1849; *Capital* (1867) (see *Collected Works*).

Laura Mulvey British film maker and feminist critic, b. 1941; 'Riddles of The Sphinx' (1977); 'Amy' (1980); *Visual and Other Pleasures* (1989).

Edward Said a Palestinian literary critic, born Jerusalem 1935; member of the Palestine National Council; went to the United States in the late 1950s; Parr Professor of English and Comparative Literature at Columbia University; *Orientalism*, 1978; *The Question of Palestine*, 1979; *The World, the Text, and the Critic*, 1983.

Ferdinand de Saussure Swiss linguist (1857–1913); professor at the University of Geneva, 1891; three series of lectures on general linguistics (1907, 1908–9, 1910–11) were collated by Charles Bally and Albert Sechahaye and published after his death as the *Course of General Linguistics*, 1916.

Gayatri Chakravorty Spivak Bengali feminist critic (b. 1941); Professor of Literature at the University of Pittsburgh; translator of Derrida's *Of Grammatology* (1976); *In Other Worlds* (1987); *The Post-Colonial Critic* (1990).

Tristan Tzara Rumanian poet and dramatist (1896–1963); born Samuel Rosenfeld, came to Zurich in 1915 and helped to start Dada; moved to Paris in 1919 (see Hans Richter, *Dada*, 1965).

Raymond Williams born in Wales in 1921, died 1988; taught in University of Oxford Extra-Mural Department; from 1961 lecturer in English and later Professor of Drama at University of Cambridge; *Culture and Society, 1780–1950*, 1958; *The Long Revolution*, 1961; *The Country and the City*, 1973; *Marxism and Literature*, 1977.

REFERENCES

Adorno, Theodore (1941). 'On Popular Music' (with George Simpson), *Studies in Philosophy and Social Science* [Zeitschrift für Sozialforschung], v. 9, pp. 17–48.

—— (1973a). *Negative Dialectics* (1966), trans. E. P. Ashton. London, Routledge & Kegan Paul.

—— (1973b). *Philosophy of Modern Music* (1966), trans. A. G. Mitchell and W. V. Bloomster. London: Sheed & Ward.

—— and Horkheimer, Max (1979). *Dialectic of Enlightenment* (1946), trans. J. Cumming. London: Verso.

Althusser, Louis (1969). *For Marx* (1965), trans. Ben Brewster. London: New Left Books.

—— (1971). *Lenin and Philosophy* (1971), trans. Ben Brewster. London: New Left Books.

—— (1976). *Essays in Self-Criticism*. London: New Left Books.

—— and Balibar, Étienne (1970). *Reading Capital* (1968), trans. Ben Brewster. London: New Left Books.

Arnold, Matthew (1960). *Culture and Anarchy* (1867) (Cambridge: Cambridge University Press).

Barthes, Roland (1967). *Elements of Semiology* (1964), trans. Annette Lavers and Colin Smith. London: Jonathan Cape.

—— (1972). *Mythologies*, trans. Annette Lavers. London: Jonathan Cape.

—— (1975). *S/Z* (1970), trans. Richard Miller. London: Jonathan Cape.

—— (1975). *The Pleasure of the Text*, trans. Richard Miller. London: Jonathan Cape.

—— (1978). *A Lover's Discourse: Fragments* (1977), trans. Richard Howard. New York: Farrar, Straus and Giroux.

Baudrillard, Jean (1975). *The Mirror of Production* (1973), trans. Mark Poster. St Louis: Telos Press.

—— (1981). *For a Critique of the Political Economy of the Sign* (1972), trans. Charles Levin. St Louis: Telos Press.

—— (1983). *Simulations* (1975), trans. Paul Foss *et al.* New York: Semiotext(e).

Baudrillard, Jean (1987). *Forget Foucault* (1977), trans. Sylvere Lautringer. New York: Semiotext(e).

Benjamin, Walter (1973). 'The work of art in the age of mechanical reproduction' in *Illuminations*, trans. Harry Zohn. London: Fontana/Collins.

Bennett, Tony (1979). *Formalism and Marxism*. London: Methuen.

Burgin, Victor (1986). *The End of Art Theory: Criticism and Postmodernity*. New Jersey: Humanities Press International.

Cixous, Hélène (1972). *The Exile of James Joyce* (1968), trans. Sally Purcell. New York: David Lewis.

—— (1976). 'The laugh of the Medusa' (1975), trans. Keith Cohen and Linda Cohen, in *Signs*, I, Summer: 875–99.

—— (1981). 'Castration or decapitation?' (1976), trans. Annette Kuhn in *Signs*, 7, 1: 41–55.

—— with Catherine Clément (1986). *The Newly Born Woman* (1975), trans. Betsy Wing. Manchester: Manchester University Press.

Cowie, Elizabeth (1984). 'Fantasia', *m/f*, n. **9**: 71–105.

Debord, Guy (1983). *Society of The Spectacle* (1976). Detroit, Michigan: Black & Red.

de Lauretis, Teresa (1984). *Alice Doesn't: Feminism, Semiotics, Cinema*. Bloomington: Indiana University Press.

Derrida, Jacques (1972). 'La double seance' in *La dissemination*. Paris: Seuil.

—— (1973a). *'Speech and Phenomena' and Other Essays on Husserl's Theory of Signs* (1967), trans. D. B. Allison. Evanston: Northwestern University Press.

—— (1973b). 'Avoir l'oreille de la philosophie' in L. Finas, S. Kofman, R. Laporte and J. M. Rey (eds.), *Écarts: Quatre essais à propos de Jacques Derrida*. Paris: Fayard.

—— (1976). *Of Grammatology* (1967), trans. Gayatri Spivak. London: Johns Hopkins Press.

—— (1978). *Writing and Difference* (1967), trans. Alan Bass. London: Routledge & Kegan Paul.

—— (1979). *Éperons: Les Styles de Nietzsche* (1972), trans. as *Spurs: Nietzsche's Styles*, by Barbara Harlow. Chicago: University of Chicago Press.

—— (1981). *Dissemination* (1972), trans. Barbara Johnson. London: Athlone Press.

—— (1982). *Margins of Philosophy*, trans. Alan Bass. Brighton: Harvester.

—— (1987). *The Post Card: From Socrates to Freud and Beyond* (1980), trans. Alan Bass. Chicago: Chicago University Press.

Doane, Mary Ann (1987). *The Desire to Desire: The Woman's Film of the 1940s*. London: Macmillan.

Eagleton, Terry (1983). *Literary Theory: An Introduction*. Oxford: Blackwell.

—— (1991). *Ideology: An Introduction*. London: Verso.

Foucault, Michel (1970). *The Order of Things* (1966), trans. A. M. Sheridan. London: Tavistock.

—— (1971). *Madness and Civilisation: A History of Insanity in the Age of Reason* (1961), trans. Richard Howard. London: Tavistock.

—— (1972). *The Archaeology of Knowledge* (1969), trans A. M. Sheridan Smith. New York: Pantheon.

—— (1977). *Discipline and Punish* (1975), trans. A. M. Sheridan. London: Allen Lane.

—— (1978a). *Introduction: The History of Sexuality*, vol. 1 (1976), trans. Robert Hurley. London: Penguin Books.

—— (1978b). *I, Pierre Rivière* (1973), trans. Frank Jellinek. London: Peregrine.

—— (1980). *Herculine Barbin* (1978), trans. Richard McDougall. Brighton: Harvester Press.

—— (1985). *The Use of Pleasure: The History of Sexuality*, vol. 2 (1984), trans. Robert Hurley. London: Penguin Books.

Foucault, Michel (1986). *The Care of The Self: The History of Sexuality, vol. 3* (1984), trans. Robert Hurley. London: Penguin Books.

Freud, Anna (1937). *The Ego and the Mechanisms of Defence*. London: Hogarth.

Freud, Sigmund (1953–76). *Standard Edition*, trans. James Strachey, 22 vols. London: Hogarth Press in association with the Institute of Psycho-Analysis (abbreviated in text as *SE*).

Gramsci, Antonio (1971). *Selections from the Prison Notebooks*, trans. Quintin Hoare and Geoffrey Nowell-Smith. London: Lawrence & Wishart.

Hall, Stuart (1980). 'Cultural studies: Two paradigms', *Media, Culture and Society*, vol. 2: 57–72.

Hand, Sean (ed.) (1989). *The Levinas Reader*. Oxford: Blackwell.

Hawkes, Terry (1977). *Structuralism and Semiotics*. London: Methuen.

Hegel, Georg Wilhelm Friedrich (1942). *Philosophy of Right*, trans. T. M. Knox. Oxford: Clarendon Press.

Heidegger, Martin (1959). *An Introduction to Metaphysics* (1953), trans. Ralph Manheim. New Haven: Yale University Press

—— (1962). *Being and Time* (1927), trans. John Macquarrie and Edward Robinson. Oxford: Blackwell.

—— (1978). *Basic Writings: from 'Being and Time', 1927, to 'The Task of Thinking', 1964*, ed. D. F. Krell. London: Routledge & Kegan Paul.

Hjelmslev, Louis (1961). *Prolegomena to a Theory of Language* (1843), trans. F. J. Whitfield. Madison: University of Wisconsin Press.

Husserl, Edmund (1960). *Cartesian Mediations: An Introduction to Phenomenology* (1929), trans. D. Cairns. The Hague: Nijhoff.

—— (1970). *Logical Investigations* (1922), trans. J. N. Findlay. London: Routledge & Kegan Paul.

—— (1983). *Ideas Pertaining to a Pure Phenomenology and to a Phenomenological Philosophy, First Book* (1913), trans. F. Kersten. The Hague: Nijhoff.

Hutcheon, Linda (1989). *The Politics of Postmodernism*. London and New York: Routledge.

Irigaray, Luce (1985a). *Speculum of the Other Woman* (1974), trans. Gillian Gill. Ithaca, NY: Cornell University Press.

—— (1985b). *This Sex Which is Not One* (1977), trans. Catherine Porter. Ithaca, NY: Cornell University Press.

Jameson, Fredric (1971). *Marxism and Form*. Princeton, NJ: Princeton University Press.

—— (1972). *The Prison-House of Language*. Princeton, NJ and London: Princeton University Press.

—— (1981). *The Political Unconscious*. London: Methuen.

—— (1991). *Postmodernism or, the Logic of Late Capitalism*. Durham, NC: Duke University Press.

Jencks, Charles (1977). *The Language of Postmodern Architecture*. London: Academy.

Kirby, Michael (1975). 'Post-modernism dance issue: An introduction' in *Drama Review*, **19**, 1: 3–4.

Kitzinger, Celia (1987). *The Social Construction of Lesbianism*. London: Sage.

Kristeva, Julia (1973). 'The system and the speaking subject', *Times Literary Supplement*, 12 October; 1249–50.

—— (1980). *Desire in Language* (1979), trans. Thomas Gora, Alice Jardine and Leon S. Roudiez. Oxford: Basil Blackwell.

—— (1981). 'Women's time', trans. Alice Jardine and Harry Blake in *Signs*, **7**, I: 13–35.

—— (1984). *Revolution in Poetic Language* (1974), trans. Margaret Waller. New York: Columbia University Press.

Lacan, Jacques (1976). *The Language of the Self* (1953), trans. Anthony Wilden. Baltimore: Johns Hopkins University Press.

Lacan, Jacques (1977a). *The Four Fundamental Concepts of Psychoanalysis* (1973), trans. Alan Sheridan. London: Hogarth.

—— (1977b). *Écrits: A Selection*, trans. Alan Sheridan. London: Tavistock.

—— (1982). *Feminine Sexuality*, trans. Jacqueline Rose. London: Macmillan.

Leavis, F. R. (1930). *Mass Civilisation and Minority Culture.* Cambridge: Gordon Fraser.

Leavis, F. R. (1962). *The Great Tradition* (1948). Harmondsworth: Penguin.

—— (1963). *New Bearings in English Poetry* (1932). Harmondsworth: Penguin.

—— and Thompson, Denys (1964). *Culture and Environment: The Training of Critical Awareness* (1933). New York: Barnes and Noble.

Leavis, Q. D. (1965). *Fiction and the Reading Public* (1932). London: Chatto & Windus.

Levinas, Emmanuel (1961). *Totalité et infini: essai sur l'exteriorité.* The Hague: Nijhoff. (English translation forthcoming.)

—— (1987). *Time and the Other* (1979), trans. Richard Cohen. Pittsburgh: Duquesne University Press.

Lévi-Strauss, Claude (1963). *Structural Anthropology* (1958), trans. C. Jacobson and B. G. Schoepf. New York: Basic Books.

—— (1966). *The Savage Mind* (1962), no translator given. London: Weidenfeld & Nicholson.

Lukács, Georg (1962). *The Historical Novel* (1937), trans. Hannah and Stanley Mitchell. London: Merlin.

—— (1963). *The Meaning of Contemporary Realism* (1958), trans. John and Necke Mander. London: Merlin.

—— (1971). *History and Class Consciousness* (1923), trans. Rodney Livingstone. London: Lawrence & Wishart.

Lyotard, Jean-François (1984). *The Postmodern Condition* (1979), trans. Geoff Bennington and Brian Massumi. Manchester: Manchester University Press.

—— (1989). *The Differend* (1983), trans. G. Van den Abbele. Minneapolis: University of Minnesota Press.

—— and Thébaud, Jean-Loup (1985). *Just Gaming* (1979), trans. Wlad Godzich. Minneapolis: University of Minnesota Press.

MacCabe, Colin (1978). *James Joyce and the Revolution of the Word.* London: Macmillan.

—— (1985). *Theoretical Essays.* Manchester: Manchester University Press.

McHale, Brian (1987). *Postmodernist Fiction.* London and New York: Methuen.

Macherey, Pierre (1978). *A Theory of Literary Production* (1966), trans. Geoffrey Wall. London: Routledge & Kegan Paul.

—— and Balibar, Étienne (1981). 'On literature as ideological form' in *Untying The Text*, ed. Robert Young. London: Routledge & Kegan Paul: 79–100.

Marx, Karl (1970). *Capital* (1867). London: Lawrence & Wishart.

—— and Engels, Frederick (1950). *Selected Work*s, 2 vols. London: Lawrence & Wishart.

—— and Engels, Frederick (1975). *Collected Works*, 44 vols. London: Lawrence & Wishart.

Mitchell, Juliet (1974). *Psychoanalysis and Feminism.* London: Allen Lane.

Modleski, Tania (1988). *The Women Who Knew Too Much: Hitchcock and Feminist Theory.* New York: Methuen.

Morgan, Robert P. (1977). 'On the analysis of recent music' in *Critical Inquiry*, 4, 1: 33–53.

Mulvey, Laura (1989). *Visual and Other Pleasures.* London: Macmillan.

Nietzsche, Friedrich Wilhelm (1974). *The Gay Science* (1882), trans. Walter Kaufmann. New York: Vintage Books.

Norris, Christopher (1987). *Derrida.* London: Fontana.

Quintana, Alvina (1990). 'Politics, representation and the emergence of a Chicana/o aesthetic' in *Cultural Studies*, vol. 4, 3, October 1990: pp. 257–63.

Richter, Hans (1965). *Dada: Art and Anti-Art.* London: Thames & Hudson.

Riviere, Joan (1929). 'Womanliness as a masquerade', in *International Journal of Psychoanalysis*, **10**; 303–13.

Rose, Jacqueline (1984). *The Case of Peter Pan*. London: Macmillan.

—— (1988). *Sexuality in the Field of Vision*. London: Verso.

Said, Edward (1979). *The Question of Palestine*. New York: Times Books.

—— (1983). *The World, the Text, and the Critic*. Cambridge, Mass.: Cambridge University Press.

—— (1985). *Orientalism* (1978). New York: Random House.

Sánchez, Rosaura (1990). 'Ethnicity, ideology and academia' in *Cultural Studies*, 4. 3, October 1990: 294–302.

Saussure, Ferdinand de (1974). *Course in General Linguistics*, trans. Wade Baskin. London: Fontana.

Spivak, Gayatri Chakravorty (1983). 'Displacement and the discourse of woman' in *Displacement: Derrida and After*, ed. Mark Krupnick. Bloomington: Indiana University Press: 169–90.

—— (1987). *In Other Worlds: Essays in Cultural Politics*. New York: Methuen.

—— (1990). *The Post-Colonial Critic*, ed. Sarah Harasym. London: Routledge.

Trachtenberg, Stanley (ed.) (1985). *The Postmodern Moment*. Connecticut: Greenwood Press.

Tzara, Tristan (1931). 'Memoirs of Dadaism' in Edmund Wilson, *Axel's Castle*. New York: Charles Scribner's Sons, pp. 304–9.

Voloshinov, V. N. (Mikhail Bakhtin) (1973). *Marxism and the Philosophy of Language* (1929), trans. Ladislav Matejka and I. R. Titunik. New York and London: Seminar Press.

Williams, Raymond (1958). *Culture and Society, 1780–1950*. London: Chatto & Windus.

—— (1961). *The Long Revolution*. London: Chatto & Windus.

—— (1973). *The Country and the City*. London: Chatto & Windus.

—— (1976). *Keywords*. London: Harper Collins.

—— (1977). *Marxism and Literature*. London: Oxford University Press.

Wittgenstein, L. J. J. (1967). *Philosophical Investigations* (1953), 3rd edn, trans. G. E. M. Anscombe. Oxford: Blackwell.

Young, Robert (ed.) (1981). *Untying the Text*. London: Routledge & Kegan Paul.

INDEX